Global Stage

Teacher's Book 5

Michelle Worgan

macmillan education

Macmillan Education
4 Crinan Street
London N1 9XW
A division of Springer Nature Limited.

Companies and representatives throughout the world

Teacher's Book ISBN 978-1-380-00259-4
Teacher's Blended Pack ISBN 978-1-380-00258-7

Written by Michelle Worgan

First published 2019

Designed by emc design ltd
Front cover design and concept by 3CD
Cover adaptation by Roberto Martinez

The author and publishers would like to thank the following for permission to reproduce their photographs: Matthew Hayes (p. 16), Lina Acosta Sandaal (p. 18)

The author and publishers are grateful for permission to reprint the following copyright material: p. 11 Extract from 'Framework for 21st Century Learning' © 2017 Partnership for 21st Century Skills. Reprinted with permission; p. 17 Extract from 'Collaborative for Academic, Social, and Emotional Learning' © 2017 CASEL. Reprinted with permission.

Full acknowledgements for illustrations and photographs in the facsimile pages can be found in
the **Language Book** ISBN: 978-1-380-00004-0 and
Literacy Book ISBN: 978-1-786-32594-5.

Printed and bound by CPI Group (UK) Ltd, Croydon CR0 4YY

2023 2022 2021 2020 2019
10 9 8 7 6 5 4

Contents

macmillan education

Unit	Vocabulary	Explore Language	Global Citizenship
Language Review	**Vocabulary** *Travel and Trade; Emotions; Art; Friendship; Early Civilizations; Actions and Survival* **Grammar** *Tag Questions; First Conditional; Modal Verbs of Obligation; Too and Enough; Present Perfect; Used to*		
1 Let's Get Moving page 10	**Sports and Equipment** *beginner, BMX racing, expert, harness, helmet, pads, rappelling, Rollerblading, rope, skiing, snowboarding, trampolining* **Fundraising Through Sports** *charity, fun run, get fit, give up, race, raise money, sponsor, take part in, team, train* (v) **Beatnik Rap** *Back to School Challenge*	Review of Verb Forms: Present, Past, and Future Indefinite Pronouns: *Everyone, Everything, Everywhere, etc.*	How do sports bring people together? **Listening Skills** Listening for gist and details
2 Circles of Life page 22	**Animals and Their Life Cycles** *be born, behavior, die, female, food chain, habitat, male, pouch, pregnant, trunk* **Controlling Nature** *encourage, endangered, extinct, get rid of, harm, native, pesticide, poison, predator, prey* **Poem** *Welcome to Our Habitat*	Present Perfect With *Already, Just,* and *Yet* Present Perfect With *For* and *Since*	How do humans affect nature? **Listening Skills** Listening for gist and details
Put It Together	Review Units 1 and 2 *I've Just …*		
3 Figure It Out page 36	**Investigating Crimes** *alibi, clue, commit a crime, criminal, detective, fingerprint, interview, investigate, suspect, suspicious, thief* **Committing and Preventing Crime** *guilty, opportunity, prevent, report* (v), *risk* (n), *solve, steal, track* (v), *victim, witness* (n) **Rap** *Ace Detective*	Reported Speech: Statements Reported Speech: Requests and Commands	Why is it important to be observant? **Listening Skills** Listening for gist and details
4 When I Grow Up page 48	**Jobs and Qualifications** *architect, challenging, comedian, creative, degree, party planner, pet psychologist, qualifications, rewarding, stressful, talented, underwater photographer* **Work and Skills** *ambition, boss, business, experience, independent, inspired, observant, reliable, resourceful, skills* **Poem** *That's the Job for Me*	Infinitive of Purpose Tag Questions	Why are all jobs important? **Listening Skills** Listening for gist and details
Put It Together	Review Units 3 and 4 *The Detectives Game*		
5 Express Yourself page 62	**Emotions 1** *confused, delighted, determined, disappointed, enthusiastic, furious, optimistic, pessimistic, upset, worried* **Emotions 2** *confident, fail, frustrating, improve, insecure, make mistakes, negative, positive, succeed* **Blues Poem** *Expedition Blues*	Modal Verbs of Deduction Adverbs of Probability	How do our emotions affect our learning? **Listening Skills** Listening for gist and details

Writing	Speaking	International English	Literacy Book
		Literacy: *Predicting; Making Inferences; Points of View; Visualizing Changes; Scanning; Identifying Main Idea and Details; and Identifying Cause and Effect* **Spelling:** *Soft g, Soft c and Final -ed*	
aragraph Building rganizing Information **Vord Study** Vord Families **roduct** n Instructional Flyer	**Conversation** Making and Responding to Suggestions **Pronunciation** Connected Speech: Consonant-Vowel Linking	**US** *rappelling; awesome, give it a try, Good job!; flyer, organize* **UK** *abseiling; brilliant, have a go, Well done!; leaflet, organise*	**Story** *You're Out!* **Instructional Text** *The Ultimate Game* **Reading Skill** Understanding Skimming and Scanning
aragraph Building iving Facts, Reasons, and Details **entence Building** onjunctions **roduct** n Infographic	**Presentation** Using Rhetorical Questions to Create Interest **Pronunciation** Sentence Stress: Weak Forms *and, of* (Schwa)	**US** *behavior; Did you see a baby owl yet?, I just read it.* **UK** *behaviour; Have you seen a baby owl yet?, I've just read it.*	**Fantasy** *Arthur's Adventures* **Persuasive Text** *Fire Ecology* **Reading Skill** Understanding Sequence of Events
aragraph Building rganizing Elements in a Story **Vord Study** sing Adjectives and Adverbs or Atmosphere **roduct** Crime Story	**Conversation** Showing Interest and Responding to What You Hear **Pronunciation** Word Stress: First and Second Syllable		**Informational Text** *Solving Crime With Science* **Story** *The Red-Headed League* **Reading Skill** Drawing Conclusions
aragraph Building upport Reasons with acts and Details **Vord Study** djective Collocations **roduct** Biography	**Conversation** Using Fillers to Buy Time to Think in an Interview **Pronunciation** Intonation in Incomplete *Yes/No* Questions	**US** *realized; in college* **UK** *realised; at university*	**Biography** *The Hero of Lime Rock* **Story** *Delivery Dan* **Reading Skill** Understanding Points of View
aragraph Building sing Expressive Language Poetry **Vord Study** miles and Metaphors **roduct** crostic Poems	**Presentation** Offering Encouragement and Dealing with Nerves **Pronunciation** Sentence Stress: Content Words	**US** *pretty sure; recognize* **UK** *quite sure; recognise*	**Instructional Text** *Using Your Emotional Toolbox* **Poems** *How I Feel* **Reading Skill** Identifying Sensory Details

Writing	Speaking	International English	Literacy Book
aragraph and Sentence Building rganizing and Presenting Information o Argue a Case **roduct** Persuasive Essay	**Presentation** Appealing for Help **Pronunciation** Word Stress: Third and Fourth Syllable	**US** *public transportation* **UK** *public transport*	**Persuasive Text** *Not-So-Fantastic Plastic* **Poem** *A Greener Life* **Reading Skill** Understanding Author's Purpose
aragraph Building esearching, Organizing, and resenting Information **roduct** n Informational Flyer	**Presentation** Adding Suspense to a Story **Pronunciation** Connected Speech: Consonant-Vowel Linking with /r/	**US** *Band Aid; First Aid Tent; waterwings, first aid kit; pharmacy; sound the alarm, first responder; fire marshal* **UK** *plaster; First-Aid Tent; armbands, first-aid kit; chemist; raise the alarm, emergency services; fire warden*	**Story** *The Chopper* **Instructional Text** *First Aid for Beginners* **Reading Skill** Understanding Main Idea and Details
enre Focus ecognizing Fact and Opinion **entence Building** hrases to Link Cause and Effect **roduct** n Informative Article	**Presentation** Structuring, Transitioning, and Concluding **Pronunciation** Connected Speech: Elision, Dropping the *t*	**US** *civilization; it's too bad* **UK** *civilisation; it's a pity*	**Fable** *The Great Race* **Informational Text** *Mysterious Malta* **Reading Skill** Recognizing Genres
enre Focus reating a Narrative Voice **Vord Study** uffixes and Prefixes **roduct** Story	**Conversation** Offering Opinions, Agreeing, and Disagreeing **Pronunciation** Sentence Stress: Weak Form *to* (Schwa)	**US** *empathize* **UK** *empathise*	**Informational Text** *Storytelling Around the World* **Folk Tale** *The Weaver* **Reading Skill** Understanding Characters
aragraph Building etter-Writing Conventions **entence Building** ormal and Informal Language **roduct** Letter of Complaint	**Conversation** Exploring Options and Reaching Agreement **Pronunciation** Connected Speech: Intrusive /w/	**US** *customize; Yours truly* **UK** *customise; Yours faithfully*	**Informational Text** *Designing Drones* **Science Fiction** *The Restore Key* **Reading Skill** Making Inferences

Unit	Reading 1	Reading 2	Reading Skill	Content Area	Social and Emotional Learning	Key Concept	Language Book
Literacy Review	Predicting; Making Inferences; Points of View; Visualize Changes; Soft *g* and Soft *c* Scanning; Identifying Main Idea and Details; Identifying Cause and Effect; Final *ed*						
1 Let's Get Moving page 8	**Fiction** *You're Out!* Play **Literary Term** idiom	**Nonfiction** *The Ultimate Game* Instructional Text	Understanding Skimming and Scanning	Social Studies: Sports and Recreation	Relationship Skills: Exhibit cooperative learning and working toward group goals	Why are rules important for sports?	**Vocabulary** sports and equipment, and fundraising through sports **Grammar** review of verb forms: present, past, and future indefinite pronouns
2 Circles of Life page 24	**Fiction** *Arthur's Adventures* Fantasy **Literary Term** antonym	**Nonfiction** *Fire Ecology* Persuasive Text	Understanding Sequence of Events	Science: Biology	Self-awareness: Possess self-efficacy and self-esteem	How do life cycles represent change?	**Vocabulary** animals and their life cycles, and controlling nature **Grammar** present perfect simple with *already*, *just*, and *yet*, and *for* and *since*
3 Figure It Out page 40	**Nonfiction** *Solving Crime With Science* Informational Text	**Fiction** *The Red-Headed League* Story **Literary Term** closed compound	Drawing Conclusions	Science: Forensics	Self-awareness: Accurately recognize own strengths and limitations	How do we use clues to solve problems?	**Vocabulary** investigating, committing, and preventing crimes **Grammar** reported speech: statements, requests, and commands
4 When I Grow Up page 56	**Nonfiction** *The Hero of Lime Rock* Biography **Literary Term** synonym	**Fiction** *Delivery Dan* Story	Understanding Points of View	Social Studies: Careers	Self-management: Set plans and work towards goals	Why do we work?	**Vocabulary** jobs, qualifications, work, and skills **Grammar** infinitive of purpose tag questions
5 Express Yourself page 72	**Nonfiction** *Using Your Emotional Toolbox* Instructional Text	**Fiction** *How I Feel* Poems **Literary Term** metaphor	Identifying Sensory Details	Science: Psychology	Self-awareness: Label and recognize own and others' emotions	How do we identify emotions?	**Vocabulary** emotions **Grammar** modal verbs of deduction adverbs of probability

Unit	Reading 1	Reading 2	Reading Skill	Content Area	Social and Emotional Learning	Key Concept	Language Book
6 **Go Green** page 88	**Nonfiction** *Not-So-Fantastic Plastic* Persuasive Text **Literary Term** word choice: variety	**Fiction** *A Greener Life* Poem	Understanding Author's Purpose	Science: Ecology	Self-awareness: Identify own needs and values	What can we do in our own lives to help the environment?	**Vocabulary** eco-tourism and sustainable living **Grammar** first conditional with modal verbs; *too* and *enough* with infinitives
7 **In Safe Hands** page 104	**Fiction** *The Chopper* Story **Literary Term** simile	**Nonfiction** *First Aid for Beginners* Instructional Text	Understanding Main Ideas and Details	Science: Medicine	Self-management: Manage personal and interpersonal stress	What can we do to help in an emergency?	**Vocabulary** injuries and first aid, and preparing for an emergency **Grammar** simple present passive; reflexive pronouns
8 **Way Back Then** page 120	**Fiction** *The Great Race* Fable **Literary Term** transition words	**Nonfiction** *Mysterious Malta* Informational Text	Recognizing Genres	History: Archaeology	Social Awareness: Appreciating diversity	How do we explain the mysteries from ancient civilizations?	**Vocabulary** discoveries and inventions and developing knowledge and ideas **Grammar** past modal verbs of obligation; simple past passive
9 **Tell Me a Story** page 136	**Nonfiction** *Storytelling Around the World* Informational Text	**Fiction** *The Weaver* Folk Tale **Literary Term** word choice: adverbs of intensity	Understanding Characters	Social Studies: Traditions	Self-management: Monitor progress toward personal and academic short- and long-term goals	Why do we tell stories?	**Vocabulary** storytelling and sharing stories **Grammar** second conditional positive statements, negative statements, and questions
10 **Why Was It Made?** page 152	**Nonfiction** *Designing Drones* Informational Text	**Fiction** *The Restore Key* Science Fiction **Literary Term** word choice: degrees of intensity	Making Inferences	Science: Engineering	Relationship Skills: Manage and express emotions in relationships, respecting diverse viewpoints	How can design solve problems?	**Vocabulary** design and design to solve problems **Grammar** reported speech: questions and agreeing with *too, so, either, neither*

Welcome to *Global Stage*

You have in your hands a complete language and literacy course that will support you and your students in developing their English skills, and their love of reading and the English language.

The **Language Book** contains the building blocks of language skills and systems. Students will focus on learning the language and how it works. Beautiful picture dictionary scenes, lively poetry, and contextualized grammar sections support them in figuring out and learning new language. Photos and texts about children around the world will inspire them to explore thought-provoking questions about what it means to be a Global Citizen. Live-action videos will expose learners to other children using the language they are learning before they take their turn.

The **Literacy Book** contains a variety of fictional and nonfictional texts, as well as activities for learners to explore literacy concepts, develop reading skills, and respond to the texts they have read. As they work through the course, students will further develop their thinking skills, and they will build self-reflection skills, which will allow them to become increasingly more effective and independent learners.

Together, the **Language** and **Literacy Books** explore topics across the curriculum while exposing students to differences in American and British English through the International English feature.

How to Use the Books Together

The **Language Book** and **Literacy Book** units are designed to provide a complete English language learning experience. There is no prescribed order for teaching the books: You may start with either book. You can choose to work through a whole unit and then move to the other book. Alternatively, you can start with the first **Literacy Book** reading, then move to the **Language Book**, then back to the second **Literacy Book** reading.

Used together, the two books cover the four skills, provide a solid foundation in vocabulary and grammar, and help train your learners to become competent users of English and independent thinkers.

Pedagogical Philosophy

The goal of ***Global Stage*** is to support children in becoming competent and confident English speakers while also developing as self-directed, inquisitive learners and responsible global citizens.

Global Stage starts with the child and looks out towards the world.

Global Stage assumes that every learner comes to school with a wealth of knowledge, thoughts, and opinions about their lives and the world, and that this is the starting point for their continued learning. All units include moments for students to consider and share their experiences, as well as consider others' points of view. This not only validates their thoughts, priming them to be open to learning, but is also the basis for learning empathy, which is one of the goals of our Global Citizenship lesson.

We know that children learn best when they feel safe to express their emotions. This is why we have carefully interwoven a social and emotional learning strand into the course. When you read the texts with your class, you will find opportunities to pause and reflect on how the characters feel and why, as well as opportunities for the students to think about how they feel in their lives when they encounter similar situations. Building and strengthening the ability to reflect will support students in becoming considerate, thoughtful citizens of the world.

Global Stage encourages self-reflection and a growth mindset to support children in increasing their academic achievement.

Every child has strengths they can build on, as well as areas they should develop and strengthen. We also know that what students and their teachers believe about intelligence influences academic achievement. A growth mindset is the belief that intelligence is not fixed, but rather can grow and continue to develop. Carol Dweck, who coined this term, and her colleagues demonstrated that a growth mindset empowers children to increase their academic achievement.

Global Stage supports students by helping them learn to reflect on their learning. Teachers can further support their students by focusing their praise on children's effort and improvement from where they start on their learning journey. This kind of feedback that focuses on growth reinforces the notion that children have the power to make progress by working toward it, encouraging students to view their progress and skills as something they can improve, rather than purely the result of their static abilities.

Global Stage includes various forms of review to support children in improving self-reflection skills: Our **Language Book** reviews, the Think It Over pages, are always open-ended, prompting students to think about what they have learned, how they have learned it, how they think they might learn better, and what they think they should continue to work on. When you do these lessons in class, you can take advantage of this social moment for students to hear from each other. One child may mention that they learned the most with the unit poem, while another might recall a game or a story. Children will benefit from considering what has worked for them and for others, while also planning for how to continue to learn. These are also moments for you to praise the class for their effort, pointing out where they've made progress.

Our **Literacy Book** includes Think Together pages, a space for students to get used to reflecting on how they respond to texts, and how working with those texts might have enriched what they think about the Key Concept questions at the top of the page.

Finally, our **Student's App** on **Navio** allows learners to review the language and skills they have studied and receive instant feedback, as well as increasing challenges as they progress. Students will be supported in learning and improving their English, while having fun and working at their own pace.

Helping children notice where they are making progress will help them build their self-reflection skills and also encourage them to seek further challenge.

Global Stage helps you teach beyond the test.

In ***Global Stage*** you will find a robust and engaging course. With its dual-book approach to language and literacy, and its focus on engaging the students and allowing them to develop their thinking and self-management skills, ***Global Stage*** supports children in learning beyond the language needed for doing well on tests.

Students are challenged to learn at a stimulating pace. They encounter a variety of topics and language points, as well as texts and ideas. But you and they have strong support every step of the way. Whether it is the way the **Language Book** sets up a speaking or writing task in incremental steps so the learner knows what to work on and the teacher can see where they need help, or the way thinking opportunities are woven into the two books, encouraging children not only to learn information but also get better at analyzing it, ***Global Stage*** supports students' long-term development. For example, throughout the six levels of ***Global Stage***, learners will be developing the ability to figure out the meaning of Words in Context. They will learn that words have many layers of meaning, and they will learn to develop strategies to figure out aspects of the meaning themselves, from the context in each text. Their goal won't be to learn the word, but rather to understand the overall meaning of the text, and to make an educated guess about what the word may mean in that context. This skill will help them become better readers, learners, and test takers throughout their academic lives in English and in whatever other language they happen to be studying.

Global Stage supports children in developing 21st Century Skills.

In their widely accepted *Framework for 21st Century Learning*, which outlines their vision for student success in the new global economy, the Partnership for 21st Century Skills says that:

> *Learning and innovation skills increasingly are being recognized as the skills that separate students who are prepared for increasingly complex life and work environments in the 21st century, and those who are not. A focus on creativity, critical thinking, communication, and collaboration is essential to prepare students for the future.*

Global Stage infuses these important skills into every unit in a way that challenges the children and enhances the learning objective in each lesson. Students are consistently given opportunities to think and discuss everything from readings and skills to grammar points and writing mechanics. This ensures they are actively communicating to form a solid and personalized understanding of English. Our Think Together lesson, in the **Literacy Book**, includes a cooperative learning activity where learners can practice collaborating in a structured way, building the skills to listen to others, participating responsibly, and contributing equally to the activity outcome. Finally, lessons like Take the Stage and Write About It encourage creativity as students plan and produce individual presentations, conversation role-plays, and texts and critical thinking as they are supported to organize their thoughts.

Course Components

Language Book

The **Language Book** contains seven lessons per unit:

- Two Vocabulary lessons. One includes spoken word poetry and work on pronunciation and features of connected speech. The other lesson is linked to Global Citizenship themes and includes listening activities.
- Two Explore Language lessons with grammar presentation and practice.
- A writing lesson (Write About It) that explores different genres of writing linked to one of the texts in the **Literacy Book** unit. Carefully staged activities take students through the steps of Process Writing, helping them develop good habits and strategies to use with any writing task now and in the future. Four additional Process Writing lessons at the back of the book explore different techniques which students can try out in the different units.
- A speaking lesson (Take the Stage / Talk About It) that presents either a presentation or conversational skill and functional language for different situations.
- A Think It Over lesson that encourages self-reflection: getting students to think about what they've learned, how they learn, and setting goals.

Inductive Approach

Throughout ***Global Stage***, students are exposed to a simplified inductive approach to grammar, vocabulary, and skills. They are guided to look at language in context so that they can discover concrete patterns. When students are given an opportunity to figure out a concept for themselves, they are much more likely to develop a deeper understanding, appreciation, and retention of knowledge.

Recycling

Opportunities to review and recycle what they have learned are built into the course as language is reused in new contexts in later units within the **Language Book**, as well as in the **Literacy Book**. In addition, a Put It Together review after every two units allows students to revisit and practice the target language in a communicative game. These fun games can be played again and again, thereby maximizing the opportunities for recycling and practice.

Literacy Book

There are two texts in each unit of the **Literacy Book**, which are fully explored in a series of lessons:

- A Get Ready to Read lesson introduces the unit topic and creates interest. It also includes the reading skill focus.
- A Reading lesson presents a fictional or nonfictional text.
- An Explore the Reading lesson includes post-reading comprehension and analysis activities. A focus on Literary Terms explores how different techniques and writers' choices enhance the reader experience.
- Each unit ends with a Think Together lesson that draws the two readings together and explores the Key Concept for each unit.

In each unit, students encounter a reading skill and learn the use of the skill through practice in context. Learning these skills helps students read more quickly and effectively, and gives them greater confidence, which in turn means they get more enjoyment from reading.

Each text includes a Words in Context feature in which students are encouraged to figure out the meaning of words from their context, rather than learn the words as vocabulary.

The **Literacy Book** develops Social and Emotional Learning (SEL) and Content and Language Integrated Learning (CLIL), while also including Visible Thinking Routines (VTR) and opportunities for Critical Literacy. Students are encouraged to work collaboratively by discussing and exploring ideas through Cooperative Learning Routines.

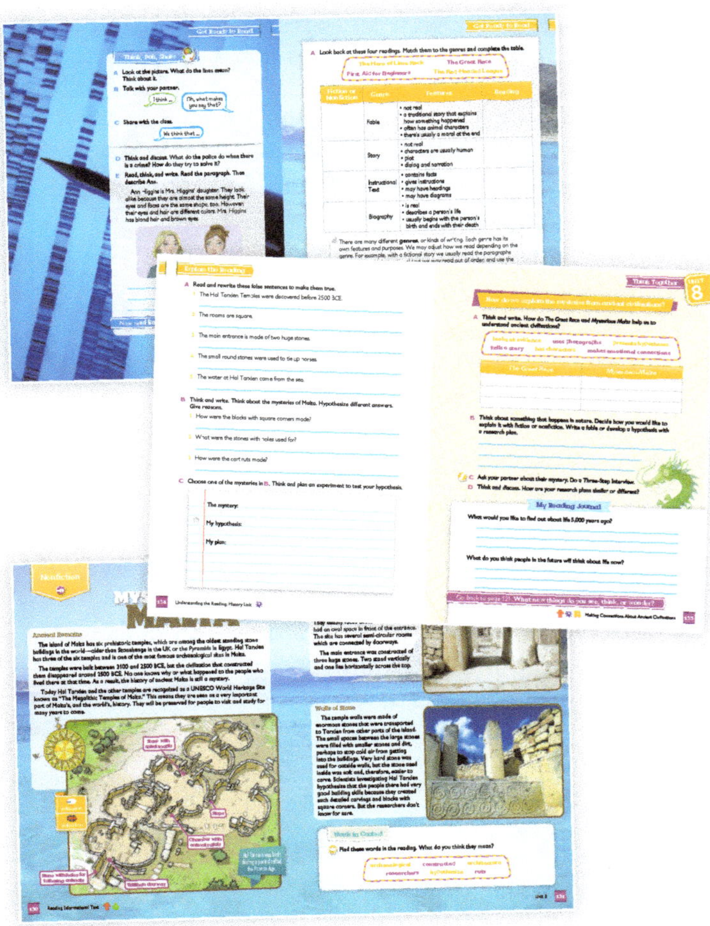

Three-Stage Reading Approach

The goal of the reading lessons is to get students reading for pleasure and to absorb information, rather than focusing on the mechanics of language in the text. The teaching notes suggest a three-stage approach to achieve this:

- Stage 1 **Engage with the Text.** This stage should be purely about reading for enjoyment and might include a prediction question to keep students motivated to find the answer.
- Stage 2 **Analyze the Text and Features.** In this stage, students read the text once again, while you help them analyze the text through the embedded callout questions. These questions will strengthen students' ability to make sense of the text and encourage them to begin thinking critically about what they are reading.
- Stage 3 **Interact with the Text.** This stage is about encouraging students to become actively involved in the learning process. They may be asked to act out a part of the reading or do reconstruction or analysis activities. When students interact more deeply with the text, their reading comprehension and writing skills improve, as they develop a greater understanding of how texts are constructed.

Literary Terms

Becoming a competent reader means understanding not only the words in a text, but also being able to analyze, interpret, and appreciate why the writer chose specific words and phrases. Learning to recognize literary terms and how they are used in different genres of text helps students understand more about the details and emotions in a text and develop a deeper connection with the author's intent, which helps them build more tools to tackle and create all kinds of texts now and in the future.

The **Literacy Book** helps students learn about the techniques, styles, and formatting used by authors. Each term has been selected from curricula used in US and UK schools. Each Literary Term section is linked to one reading in each unit as part of an Explore the Reading lesson, with further practice in the **Student's App** on **Navio**.

Literary Term Transition Words

Transition words provide a connection between ideas, sentences, and paragraphs. They are usually at the beginning of a sentence.

Read. Then underline the transition words.

In the living room, we watched a movie in the dark. Suddenly, there was a loud noise behind us. Then, the front door smashed opened. Now, everybody was quiet. Dad appeared behind the couch. Of course, there was nothing to be afraid of.

Now find all the transition words in the reading.

Together, the two books lay the foundation for an inductive approach to learning, encouraging students to recognize patterns and think critically through ordering, analysis, and categorization tasks.

The Unit 1 Walkthrough notes give more in-depth information about the purpose and learning outcomes for each activity, as well as further guidance on addressing core features such as visualization, inductive grammar, international English, reading skills, Words in Context, and learning reflections.

Student's App on Navio

The **Student's App** on **Navio** is where students find their practice activities for the course. It expands on the topic and objectives found in the **Language Book** and **Literacy Book**. It includes automatically graded interactive exercises for each unit, which can be done in class or for homework, so that children receive immediate feedback. These exercises cover reading and listening skills, spelling and literary terms, speaking skill and pronunciation practice, extended writing practice, as well as grammar and vocabulary.

Learning powered by NAVIO

The **Student's App** on **Navio** world also provides support and guidance for more introspective objectives such as reading comprehension, SEL, and CLIL activities. It transforms the classroom-based lessons found in the **Language Book** and **Literacy Book** into an immersive, self-directed, game-like experience that students can do alone.

Using the **Student's App** on **Navio** with your students can take different forms:

Classroom study with **Language and Literacy Books** and Tap & Teach lessons.

- Study and practice alone in a computer lab with **Student's App**.
- Study and practice alone at home with **Student's App**.
- Study and practice with parents with **Student's App**.

Each gameplay produces data which is then sent to the teacher's gradebook, providing deeper insight into each student's strengths and weaknesses, and concrete data that can be quickly accessed to create more insightful feedback.

The activities on the **Student's App** on **Navio** are benchmarked to Cambridge English online practice, ranging from *Starters* for the lower levels to *Preliminary for Schools* for Level 6. This benchmarking covers both content and web app functionality, preparing students academically and equipping them for the practical experience of online testing.

Teacher's Book

This Teacher's Book provides all the steps you need to bring each lesson of the **Language** and **Literacy Books** to life, including lesson objectives, warm up and cool down activities, and full answer keys. Audio and video scripts are at the back of the book, and Unit 1 contains a comprehensive walkthough, with clear explanations of the purpose of each activity and tips on how to make the most of them in class. The notes also remind the teacher of the additional support available through the Tap & Teach Lessons (TTL) for heads-up learning, the supplementary printouts in the Resource Bank, and extra practice students can do in class or at home.

Teacher's App on Navio

The **Teacher's App** on **Navio** is your primary source for classroom resources and supplements, and is designed to work on both laptops and tablets. It includes Tap & Teach Lessons (projectable classroom lessons), the Resource Bank, the Test Generator, Student's Progress Tracker, the **Enhanced Teacher's eBook**, as well as access to the **Student's App**.

Tap & Teach Lessons (TTL)

Tap & Teach Lessons (TTL) are the course projectables. They contain tools for delivering dynamic and stimulating lessons, including class audio, videos, and interactive activities.

Every reading in the **Literacy Book** can be accessed through the Story Player in the TTL, which allows you to project the reading in *Read* (text only), *Listen* (audio only), or *Listen and Read* (audio and text) modes. If you use the TTL with an interactive whiteboard, you will be able to use all the standard features, such as highlighting and hiding content.

There are two types of video in ***Global Stage***:

- **Spoken Word Poetry Videos** (optional). These appear in Lesson 1 of the **Language Book** and feature a child or children performing the poem. Watching the performances on video offers another way to practice some of the vocabulary from the first lesson, and also to work on features of rhythm and stress patterns in English.
- **Speaking Videos** (essential). These appear in Lesson 6 of the **Language Book** and feature a child or children modeling a presentation or conversation, which includes functional language. Students will analyze the language and use the video as a model when planning and preparing for their own presentation or conversation.

Videos at Home: The Flipped Classroom Approach

If you are unable to watch the videos in class or you want to provide students with additional support, consider asking them to watch the videos at home before the lesson. This allows students to engage with the content in a way that suits them, pausing and rewatching it as many times as they want. It also offers parents the opportunity to watch the video with their child and support their learning.

Give students a question or task to think about while they are watching: they will come to class feeling relaxed, confident, and prepared with ideas and observations to share. If students watch the speaking video at home, you could also have them do activities A and B from Take the Stage / Talk About It before the lesson. Watching the videos at home also frees up class time for collaborative and communicative activities.

Resource Bank

The Resource Bank is where you can find:

- **Literary Terms Printouts.** Extra practice of the literary terms covered in each unit of the **Literacy Book**.
- **Writing Support and Extension.** Attractive "Support" writing templates for the Write About It lessons in the **Language Book** for students who need them, as well as Writing Games printouts which add some fun and give students more opportunities to experiment and work with the language learned.
- **Review Unit Support.** Extra practice for the review units at the start of each student book. These cover grammar, vocabulary, reading skills, and literacy activities.
- **Grammar Printouts.** Extra practice for each grammar lesson in the **Language Book**.
- **Tests.** Unit, mid-year, and end-of-year tests.
- **Cambridge English Exam Materials.** Practice for students preparing for *Starters*, *Movers*, or *Flyers*, as well as *Key for Schools*, and *Preliminary for Schools*.
- **Letters to Parents.**
- **Other Printouts.** Graphic organizers to aid Visible Thinking Routines and reading skills in the **Literacy Book**, as well as extra materials for some of the Put It Together games and extension activities in the **Language Book**.
- **Videos and audio tracks** to support the course.
- **Curricula and Framework mapping documents.**

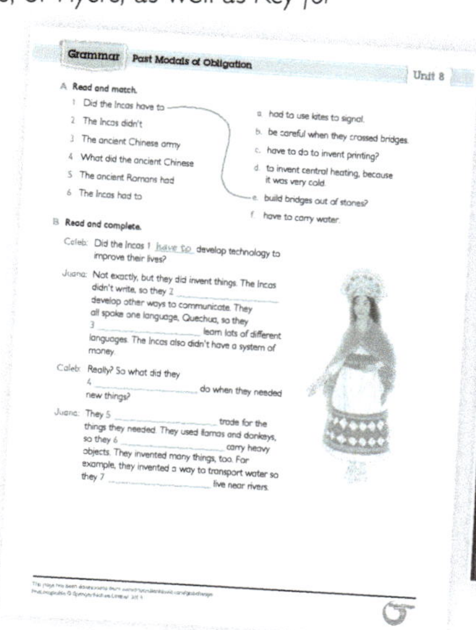

Grammar Past Modals of Obligation Unit 8

A Read and match.

1 Did the Incas have to
2 The Incas didn't
3 The ancient Chinese army
4 What did the ancient Chinese
5 The ancient Romans had
6 The Incas had to

a had to use kites to signal.
b be careful when they crossed bridges.
c have to do to invent printing?
d to invent central heating, because it was very cold.
e build bridges out of stones?
f have to carry water.

B Read and complete.

Caleb: Did the Incas 1 have to develop technology to improve their lives?
Juana: Not exactly, but they did invent things. The Incas didn't write, so they 2 ______ develop other ways to communicate. They all spoke one language, Quechua, so they 3 ______ learn lots of different languages. The Incas also didn't have a system of money.
Caleb: Really? So what did they 4 ______ do when they needed new things?
Juana: They 5 ______ trade for the things they needed. They used llamas and donkeys, so they 6 ______ carry heavy objects. They invented many things, too. For example, they invented a way to transport water so they 7 ______ live near rivers.

Test Generator

The Test Generator contains the pre-written unit, mid-year, and end-of-year test activities, as well as extra activities that allow teachers to generate and edit new tests.

Student's Progress Tracker

The Progress Tracker is an interactive gradebook that allows you to track your students' progress within ***Global Stage*** and the **Student's App** on **Navio**.

Student's App on Navio

As the teacher, you have full access to the **Student's App** on **Navio** so you can assign homework and activities for your students, and explore the digital world yourself.

Enhanced Teacher's eBook (ETB)

The digital **ETB** is an extended version of this **Teacher's Book**. In addition to teaching notes, it provides classroom management tips; ideas for differentiating activities; projects to support the Global Citizenship lessons; plus a range of activity and lesson extension ideas to develop, among others, Social and Emotional Learning (SEL), Discussion, Genre, Video Focus, Critical Thinking, Creative Thinking, and Collaboration. The **ETB** also highlights key links between the **Language Book** and the **Literacy Book**.

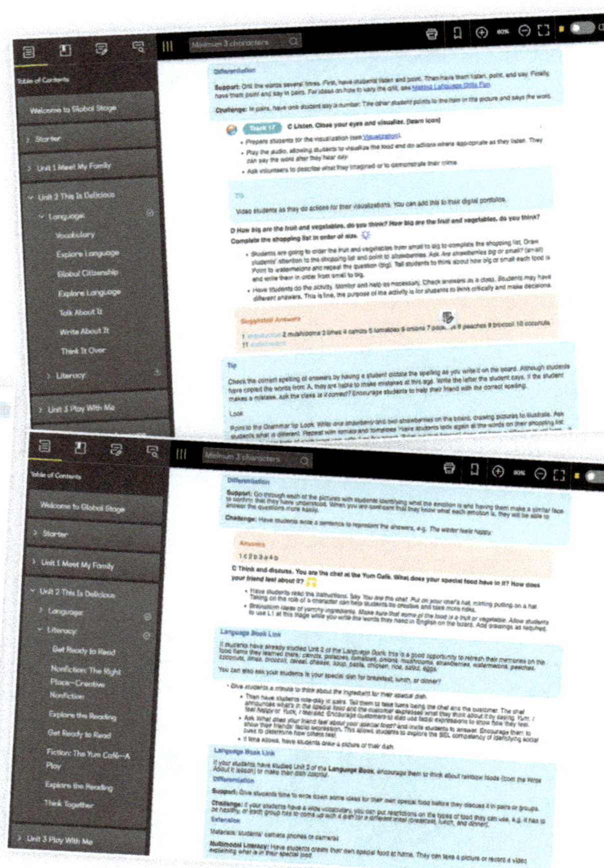

Holistic Learning

While the success of students and schools may be measured in terms of tests and grades, ***Global Stage*** believes in taking a holistic approach by developing the whole child and preparing him/her to take on the challenges of global living. Through its subject matter and in its activity types, the course encourages students to develop thinking skills, engage in cooperative learning activities, develop social and emotional learning (SEL) skills, and gain an awareness of global citizenship.

Global Citizenship Education

> *Global Citizenship Education (GCE) aims to empower learners to assume active roles, to face and resolve global challenges, and to become proactive contributors to a more peaceful, tolerant, inclusive and secure world.*

—United Nations Educational, Scientific and Cultural Organization The **Language Book** includes a Global Citizenship lesson in each unit, which has been designed to teach students about the lives of other children through the context of a listening activity. Discussion questions help them explore ideas and make connections to their own lives. The long-term objective is to prepare students for experiences outside of their everyday world and to fulfil aspirations to travel and study abroad.

In Level 5, lessons raise awareness about global issues through interesting and engaging topics designed to get students thinking about the things they can do as global citizens. Key questions raised include: How do sports bring people together?; How do humans affect nature?; Why are all jobs important? and Why do we need design? The Unit 1 Walkthrough notes for the **Language Book** provide guidance for teaching Global Citizenship lessons.

Matthew Hayes is a doctoral researcher at the Institute of Education in London under Douglas Bourn, Professor of Development Education. His research concerns Global Citizenship Education in English language textbooks.

What is GCE?

What does the future hold for your students, many of whom will graduate well into the 2030s? From the environment to the economy, poverty to jobs, challenges abound. But whatever the future holds, there is one thing we can be certain of: the biggest challenges facing humanity are not constrained by national borders or language but are truly global in scale and character. These are global problems requiring global solutions, and those of us working in education have a unique responsibility and opportunity to prepare the next generation for these challenges. GCE offers a solution to these challenges and has emerged in recent years as a high-profile policy agenda in education systems all over the world.

With this in mind, GCE can be an effective toolkit for teachers wishing to prepare their students for the challenges and opportunities of the 21st century. The skills and values it espouses are essential if our students are to successfully navigate all the future holds. GCE is too important to languish on the fringes of the curriculum, competing for space as an arbitrary additional subject in an already overcrowded timetable or sandwiched into one-off school events. Just as Digital Literacy is moving beyond ICT (information and communication technology) and into every corner of the curriculum, GCE thrives best where it is embedded in mainstream curriculum subjects. Few subjects better provide the context and aspiration called for by GCE than the teaching of English as a second language.

There is much scope for creativity too. Although GCE is a declared target of the United Nations' Sustainable Development Goals, one of its virtues is that it is not owned or prescribed by any supranational organization. There is no mandated curriculum and no accreditation body. The core concepts underpinning GCE have been traced back to some of our earliest history and are not only to be found in Western culture and philosophy. Arab scholars, for example, have written of the influence of medieval Muslim thinkers on GCE theory.

This democratic quality to GCE enables a wide variety of policy and practice, as GCE can be adapted to local contexts and cultures, and to your classroom. There are three broad themes in current GCE thinking and practice and as you work through this textbook, you will see these throughout the exercises and subject matter.

Global orientation: Often referred to as cosmopolitanism, this area of GCE cultivates a student's awareness of the world—its structures, cultures and politics—with a positive "orientation." Its focus is on tolerance and understanding, developing citizens that can comfortably and successfully navigate the world in all its variety.

Global skills: This area is about the competencies aspired to by global citizens. You may recognize it as closely related to "21st Century Skills" and "Life Skills," and it cultivates skills such as collaboration, creativity, critical literacy, and communication. This not only prepares students for success in a competitive global knowledge economy, but for lives as contributing global citizens able to identify and solve problems that are both local and global.

Global conscientiousness: This third theme runs through all aspects of GCE and is its most distinguishing feature. It is signalled through the word "citizenship," denoting an individual's legal status as a member of a given community, with this status granting them certain rights and responsibilities. While historically this community has been restricted to the nation-state, *global* citizenship looks beyond the national to the global community of which we are all a part. Its rights and responsibilities are global in nature, calling each of us to action. This can take many forms and there should be no universal prescription of actions to be taken. It is being an *active* global citizen which is required of us. This means listening to our conscience and, when it identifies global injustice, being motivated by this to act.

Your selection of this high-level English language textbook means English is a leading subject in your curriculum and timetable. No doubt you acknowledge the English language as the *lingua franca* of the modern era, enabling your students to participate on a global scale—whether in work or life. As educators, then, what better context in which to use GCE to encourage your students to think beyond their immediate community, and be globally oriented, competent and conscientious. The English language may have an historical affinity to the West, but GCE recognises that it should not be a pedestal to promote one culture and education above any other. On the contrary, through embedding GCE in English language teaching we can encourage our students to question an unjust world and its imbalanced perspectives.

By using this textbook to teach English in a creative, forward-thinking and global way you will be providing your students with the skills and values to go out into the world and be truly active global citizens.

Social and Emotional Learning (SEL)

> *Social and emotional learning (SEL) is the process through which children and adults acquire and effectively apply the knowledge, attitudes, and skills necessary to understand and manage emotions, set and achieve positive goals, feel and show empathy for others, establish and maintain positive relationships, and make responsible decisions.*
>
> —Collaborative for Academic, Social, and Emotional Learning

Research shows that SEL can positively affect students' connection to school, promote positive behavior, and lead to academic achievement. Helping students develop social and emotional skills lays the foundation for behaviors that will lead to positive personal development and professional success.

The five SEL areas are shown below.

Self-Awareness

The ability to recognize emotions, thoughts, strengths, and weaknesses. This includes having confidence and optimism.

Self-Management

The ability to regulate emotions, thoughts, and behaviors in different situations. This includes managing stress and working toward goals.

Social Awareness

The ability to empathize with others, to understand social norms, and to recognize resources and support in family, schools, and community.

Relationship Skills

The ability to establish and maintain healthy relationships. This includes active listening, cooperating, and handling conflict well.

Responsible Decision-Making

The ability to make good choices based on ethics, safety, and social norms. This includes considering the well-being of oneself and others.

SEL is integrated into the **Literacy Book** and a key concept area is addressed throughout the fictional text in each unit. As part of the reading strategy, students are guided to make connections between the SEL concept and the people and events in the text and, ultimately, to their own lives.

Lina Acosta Sandaal, MA, LMFT is the founder of Stop Parenting Alone, a parenting and therapy center in Miami in the USA. She is the parenting expert of a national morning show, and consults for MomsRising, a lobbying organization for family rights.

What is SEL?

Your mouth is dry, and your heart is in your ears. Some of your students look frozen, while others wriggle in their chairs. No one is truly into the day's well-planned discussion. What is happening? Why is the lesson failing? The lesson is suffering the effect of emotions, social awareness, and self-judgment in the classroom. In every moment of a teacher's day, the mind, brain, and body flow through the interactions between the external information and the internal understanding and reflecting of the environment. So when I am asked what is SEL and why do we need it, my response is whether you intentionally teach it or not, you have been a model for SEL from the first day you stepped into a classroom.

The goal of integrating and implementing social and emotional learning into the curriculum is to build students' ability for self-awareness, self-management, social awareness, relationship skills, and decision making. Students attain these competencies by practicing ways to understand and manage emotions, build and manage relationships, and show care and concern for others. The Fetzer Group coined the term, and the word "learning" was intentional. Social emotional skills and development are not stagnant; they continue to grow and expand with each experience students have with caregivers, teachers, friends, and the culture/community at large. If you hold this in mind, that your students are learning through repetition how to be self-aware, how to manage emotions and focus, how to continue to build and manage relationships and practice decision making, then the task of social and emotional learning in your curriculum will not feel so difficult.

Why SEL Is Important to Your Classroom

It is an absurd task to attempt to separate what happens socially and emotionally to a student from what they are cognitively learning from your lesson. When you ignore how SEL and academic achievement work together you are only teaching a percentage of your student, and not the whole child. A majority of teachers understand that their students walk into the classroom full of emotions, thoughts, and experiences that hinder their academic achievement. Deficits in social and emotional development hamper students' ability to learn, which leads to them disrupting the classroom. A student who cannot manage their emotional state will become overwhelmed with fear and embarrassment if you ask them to speak to you in a language in which they are not fluent. Focus, cognitive flexibility, and decision-making are impacted when we have low self-awareness and management of our emotional states.

Recall the difficulty of writing emails at work when you have just had a fight with a loved one on the phone. When we have a strong emotional and social response, it is hard to focus on the task at hand. If it is difficult for an adult, imagine a young student. If your curriculum includes social and emotional learning, your students will be practicing skills to make those daily stressors less intrusive to their learning. Research supports this. Children in the HighScope Perry Preschool Study showed how social and emotional skills attained in preschool continued to bring positive outcomes to those students through age 40. HighScope moved "non-cognitive" skills to the forefront of their curriculum. Conversely, the Adverse Childhood Experiences Study (ACEs) showed that children who suffer adverse experiences and do not process those emotions fare poorly both in their mental and physical health. Social and emotional learning helps students thrive throughout their entire lives.

What Well-Accomplished SEL Looks Like

Now, stop and imagine your classroom in a group discussion: one of the students is playing with his lip while rocking slightly, another student is raising her hand as high as possible, hoping you will see that she wants to speak next, and another student is mumbling in response to the story you just read together. In a classroom that prioritizes SEL, all of these examples of self-management and relationship skills are accepted. Why? Because you understand that the student who is playing with his lips and rocking regulates his emotional and physical states this way, instead of standing up and disrupting the class. The student who knows to raise her hand and contain her emotions is making a responsible, self-aware decision in managing her excitement as to not interrupt her friend who is speaking.

Finally the student who is speaking slowly, quietly and under his breath is at last risking to discuss in a group because you have spoken to your students about what it means to feel scared, how to tolerate that fear, and how to work through it. Today you reap the benefit of that continued social-emotional message. How amazing that your quiet, observant student has made the decision to speak, experiences the safety to manage his fear and the opportunity to strengthen his relationships with his friends and you, his teacher.

Content and Language Integrated Learning (CLIL)

Research has shown that content-based learning increases motivation as students see language being used in real-life contexts. The nonfictional texts in the **Literacy Book** include content from a range of different subject areas. They feature engaging topics and provide opportunities for thinking and discussion.

In Level 5, students will learn through social studies, science, and history.

Competencies

Global Stage incorporates five competencies that have been identified and linked to outcomes such as better academic performance and positive peer relationships. Relevant icons appear in the footers of each lesson, and the teaching notes in this Teacher's Book and **ETB** highlight which activities are connected to each competency to allow for further exploration in the classroom.

Me	Activities that develop social and creative skills and consider lifestyle choices.
Act	Activities that help develop a sense of social responsibility, mutual understanding, tolerance, and ethical behavior.
Think	Activities that develop thinking skills to explain, infer, classify, discuss, notice, and discover.
Learn	Activities that foster learning autonomy and help develop learning strategies.
Communicate	Activities that promote interpersonal and collaborative skills to develop teamwork, leadership, empathy, and responsibility.

Self-Reflection

Self-reflection is an important part of any learning process. Research shows that without regular review and reflection time, much of a lesson can be forgotten. Self-reflection increases students' understanding of how they learn best, making future learning more effective and leading to improvements in achievement.

Self-reflection is a critical feature of *Global Stage*. Students are asked to reflect on their performances and written work in the Writing and Speaking lessons in the **Language Book** and to reflect more deeply about their learning in the end-of-unit lessons in both the **Language Book** and **Literacy Book**.

The Think It Over lessons in the **Language Book** provide a series of graphic organizers guiding students to focus on different aspects of their learning journey: what went well, what they enjoyed, and what goals they have for the next units or weeks. The purpose of these questions is to get students into the habit of self-reflection from an early age, helping them begin to learn how to learn and to take responsibility for their learning.

In the My Reading Journal section of the Think Together lesson in the **Literacy Book**, students are asked to give a personalized response to the readings and reflect on the unit as a whole. They are encouraged to think critically about what they enjoyed and why, what they would like to learn more about, and to identify strengths and weaknesses.

In Level 5, the **Language** and **Literacy Book** encourage students to start making connections between what they enjoyed and what they learned, which will help them understand how successes were achieved, how less successful experiences can be turned into learning experiences, and how to find strategies for working through activities they find less enjoyable.

The Unit 1 Walkthrough notes for both books provide more information on making these lessons a valuable and successful experience.

Learning Techniques

Visible Thinking

Visible Thinking is a flexible research-based framework developed out of Harvard University for enriching classroom learning and fostering students' intellectual development. Some of its key goals are:

- To develop deeper understanding of content.
- To encourage greater motivation for learning.
- To develop learners' thinking and learning abilities.
- To develop learners' attitudes toward thinking and learning and their alertness to opportunities for thinking and learning.
- To create a shift in classroom culture toward a community of enthusiastically engaged thinkers and learners.

Visible Thinking employs thinking routines—short, easy-to-learn strategies that help extend and deepen students' thinking. These routines make it easier for you to see how the students are thinking and interpreting content: *Are students explaining things to one another? Are they offering creative ideas? Are they brainstorming and debating plans?* Visible Thinking encourages students to develop discussion skills and to find personal meaning in the content. This stimulates their continued interest and commitment to their own learning in the classroom.

In Level 5, each opening lesson in the **Literacy Book** features one of five Visible Thinking Routines (VTR): See, Think, Wonder; Question Starts; Think, Pair, Share; Step Inside; or Explanation Game. These routines stimulate students' curiosity and encourage them to make predictions, observations, and interpretations about the picture. They provide an opportunity for students to think about the overarching theme/topic of each **Literacy Book** unit and tie into a pre-reading activity to prepare students cognitively for what they are about to read.

See, Think, Wonder

Students are asked what they see in the picture, then what they think about it, and finally what they wonder about it. This routine works best when students have to think of ideas individually before sharing them with the class. In this way, students begin to use English meaningfully, although it is acceptable to use L1 to express more complex ideas.

Question Starts

This routine encourages students to get into the habit of questioning things beyond what they see on the page. Students look at the picture and think of some questions they would like to ask about it, using the prompts Who? What? Where? When? Why? How? They then practice negotiation skills by working in groups to decide on the three they think are the most interesting or that they would most like to know the answer to, before discussing the answers as a class. Finally, students work in pairs again to discuss any new questions or ideas they have based on the class discussion. At this point, they should move beyond what they see and think of ideas connected to some of the themes suggested by the picture.

Think, Pair, Share

This routine encourages individual participation and can be used with all abilities and class sizes. It is also used as a cooperative learning routine.

Think. Students first think independently about the question, forming ideas and questions of their own.

Pair. Students are grouped in pairs to discuss their thoughts. This step allows students to articulate their ideas and to consider those of others. They are encouraged to listen to each other and use phrases like *I agree/disagree* and *Me, too.*

Share. Student pairs share their ideas with the whole class and give their reasons. The benefit of using this routine for discussion questions is that students get to try out their ideas in a safe setting (a pair), refining their thoughts and learning from others before presenting to a bigger group.

Step Inside

Students are asked to explore different perspectives and viewpoints as they try to imagine what a person, animal, or object in the picture can see, what they believe, and what they care about. As well as developing social and emotional skills, this routine encourages creative thinking.

Explanation Game

This routine focuses students on individual aspects of a picture and encourages them to explore all manner of explanation. First, students are asked to choose something in the picture. Then, working in pairs they say everything they notice about it, before suggesting reasons why it's like it is. Finally, they expand on these reasons as a class, explaining further their thought processes, ideas, and explanations. The routine can be repeated with different things/ideas, and different pairs.

For all five routines, it is important to scaffold student responses by asking follow-up questions, e.g. *What makes you say that?* and to encourage students to do the same, so that they begin to lead the discussion. Make sure you keep students' thinking visible by noting down and displaying their ideas to return to in the Think Together lesson.

VTRs provide a great way to engage learners at the start of a topic, but they can also be used at different points in the unit to keep students connected to the topic or as a way to reflect on what they have learned in a meaningful way.

Cooperative Learning Routines

Using Cooperative Learning Routines provides opportunities for multiple students to participate in class. Along with higher academic achievement, you will see a reduction in the gap between high- and low-achieving students, improved social skills, higher self-esteem, more enthusiasm for learning, and the emergence of leadership and conflict-resolution skills.

The following routines are used in Level 5 in both the **Literacy Book** and **Language Book**:

Round Robin. In groups of four, students take turns brainstorming orally as many different answers to a discussion question as they can within a limited time frame (e.g. one minute). A **Rally Robin** is the same but with pairs.

Roundtable. Similar to a **Round Robin**, but students take turns within their groups writing or drawing their ideas on paper.

Three-Step Interview. Students work with a student from a different group to interview each other about a topic (steps 1 and 2). Then, they return to their original groups to share what they learned from their partners (step 3). This way, everyone is responsible for producing, receiving, and sharing information.

Chalk Talk. Write different words on large sheets of paper and have groups of students brainstorm everything they can think about that word. This is a chance to generate new ideas, review language, and bring a topic into focus.

Numbered Heads Together. Students get in groups and each person is given a number (from one to the maximum number in each group). The teacher asks a question and groups "put their heads together" to figure out the answer. The teacher calls out a specific number to respond for the group. This strategy encourages each member of a group to participate and listen: everyone must be prepared in case their number is called.

Options Explosion. Students discuss and share to generate new ideas or solutions to a problem. Use questions to guide them, e.g. What happens next? What if that solution doesn't work? In groups, they can appoint a scribe to write down all the problems/solutions suggested. Then split the groups into pairs to think again, going beyond the obvious and really using their imaginations: all ideas are valid; nothing is too crazy!

Inside–Outside Circle. You will need to make some space in the classroom for this routine. Students stand in concentric circles facing each other. Students in the outside circle ask questions, and those who are inside answer the question. On a signal, students rotate to create new partnerships. On another signal, students trade inside/outside roles. Talking one-on-one with a variety of partners gives extensive practice in speaking and active listening skills. Interactions can be structured to focus on specific skills and/or target language.

Tips for Setting Up Class Discussions

- Display the question(s) on the board, and give students a minute to reflect in silence.
- If there is more than one discussion question, deal with each in turn, giving students time to think and discuss in pairs or small groups. Allow the use of L1 for more complex ideas.
- Help students structure their discussions by using graphic organizers, such as mind maps, or providing slips of paper to help build up a graphic organizer.
- You will not always be able to ask everyone for their ideas. Be sure you choose different students each time, so no one feels left out.
- Have students share their ideas in teams. Have each team choose a name or color. During each lesson or activity, one person will give the team's answers and responses. Record who the speaker is for each activity so everyone gets a turn.
- Use the Cooperative Learning Routines to structure the discussions and share information discussed.
- When sharing ideas as a class, Group Time can provide a relaxed atmosphere, which may encourage students to contribute more. See the **Group Time** box for more suggestions.

Group Time

Designate a particular area of the classroom for Group Time, free from distractions. Set out a circle of chairs, with no desks, so students can see each other clearly. You should also sit on a chair as part of this circle, so that it is clear your role is to encourage and facilitate discussion, rather than to lead it. At the beginning of the year have students discuss and agree on some rules for Group Time, e.g. one person speaks at a time; everyone listens to each other; students can disagree with each other, but must do so respectfully; Group Time is fun! Nominate a student to be the scribe and write up the rules the class decides on.

During Group Time, ask open-ended questions and encourage students to give reasons for their answers. Pass an object, such as a cardboard microphone, around so it is clear who is speaking. Encourage everyone to join in the discussion, but give students a safe word to use, such as "pass," if they need more thinking time. Let them know it's OK to need time to think and that you will come back to them. At the end of the Group Time discussion, praise students for their ideas.

Visualization

Visualizations are used in the vocabulary lessons of each unit to encourage students to create mental images of the new words, using their senses, previous experiences, and imaginations. Visualizations provide a different way for students to engage personally with the language and help them learn new words.

Set up a visualization activity as follows:

- Take several deep breaths with students, slowly saying *breathe in, breathe out.*
- Count down slowly from ten to one using a calm voice.
- Say *Close your eyes and visualize*, pointing to your temples with both hands to demonstrate *imagining*. If students prefer to keep their eyes open, that's fine, too. The key is for them to feel calm and relaxed, so avoid using phrases like *You must keep your eyes closed* or *Don't look!* which will restrict students.
- Play the audio track and encourage students to imagine or act out as prompted. Pauses have been included in the audio to give students time for reflection. They then repeat the word.
- At the end of the audio, give students time to reflect and share their ideas in pairs. At this level, they should be able to discuss the ideas, but they could use drawings if it helps.
- Emphasize that everyone's visualizations will be different and that all ideas are valuable.

The first few times you do a Visualization activity, you may want to play each prompt twice to give students time to understand the prompt and then think.

The more regularly you do this, the more comfortable students will feel, and the more they will get out of the activity. A visualization track for the vocabulary in the Global Citizenship lesson is available in the TTL, though it is not highlighted on the **Language Book** page.

Words in Context

Successful readers of English need to have a bank of strategies for dealing with words they don't yet know, just as they do in their L1. Understanding a word fully builds up over time so ***Global Stage*** is designed to give extensive exposure to words in different contexts, thereby encouraging students to revisit and revise assumptions as they read.

In Levels 5 and 6, the approach to Words in Context in the **Literacy Book** builds on previous levels as now, students actively choose and try out different strategies. In this way, they will come to recognize that different words will need different strategies depending on the contextual clues provided. Having students experiment and take responsibility for their learning prepares them for dealing with unknown words in all manner of texts they come across in the future.

In Level 5 this feature is developed in three ways:

- Students are given a selection of strategies to use and they figure out which strategies work best for each of the words/phrases. In all cases, more than one strategy may be used, and you can encourage students to explain their choices.

- Students are given a selection of strategies to use, but one of them can't be used effectively (a red herring). This way, students have to analyze how the strategies work, which will highlight why some don't and encourage them to use a variety of strategies, and not to rely on just one or two.
- Students themselves brainstorm different strategies to use. This helps students begin to take responsibility for their choices and sets them up to be more independent in the reading and learning.

The strategies can be roughly categorized as using the text, knowledge of English, and general knowledge. Students should be encouraged to notice what kind of word it is (noun, adjective, verb, etc.) and to look for all instances within the text as key words will appear more than once and each entry gives more clues. The following strategies are suggested for the texts in this level, but others could also be used:

Using the text

- **Pictures:** use any visuals (illustrations, photos, graphics) which may provide a context or actually show the word.
- **Surrounding words/phrases/sentences/paragraphs:** the words and sentences before and after the key word will give clues about what kind of word it is (noun, adjective, plural, singular), and what would make sense in the context. Sometimes there will be an explanation, definition, or even the same idea repeated in a different way.
- **Positive/negative:** noticing the tone can help narrow down the options of meaning. Looking at the grammar of a word as well as the surrounding words/phrases will help with this.
- **Contrasting ideas:** in some texts a writer will compare different ideas to make their point stronger. Contrasting ideas can help us figure out what a word *isn't*, which helps figure out what it is.

Knowledge of English

- **Word building/families:** recognizing what kind of word it is can help narrow down ideas, e.g. plural/singular, compound nouns. Also, key words may appear several times in a text in different forms, providing more clues in different sentences.
- **Prefixes/Suffixes:** looking at the beginning and ends of words not only helps us identify what kind of word it is, but may also provide contrasting information, positive/negative, opposite ideas, etc.
- **Sentence structure / grammar:** recognizing grammar, sentence features such as quotation marks, and how sentences are constructed in English can give more context.
- **Word sounds:** occasionally thinking about how a word sounds and noticing the style of the writing can also help.
- **Making connections (cause & effect):** using textual clues such as conjunctions (e.g. *so*) show what relation an idea has to the previous/next one.

General knowledge

- **World knowledge:** thinking logically and drawing on the knowledge they already have about the world is a really important strategy to use. Students should always be encouraged to guess based on what they already know.
- **Personal experience:** drawing on their own experiences is another invaluable strategy to use. However, they should be sure to read the text carefully to check if the writer's experience is the same or different.

Multimodal Literacy

To become fully literate in today's world, students must become as proficient with the new literacies of search engines, web pages, email, instant messages, blogs, podcasts, e-books, wiki pages, digital photos, videos, and apps as they are with the traditional literacies of paper, pencil, and books. To do this, students need to develop skills to use each of these technologies effectively, e.g. searching for key words, navigating a nonlinear reading pathway via hyperlinks, and utilize critical-thinking skills for online reading. In an age when anyone can publish anything on the internet, it is more important than ever to equip students with the tools to evaluate source material.

Both the **Language Book** and the **Literacy Book** provide opportunities for developing higher-order thinking skills through activities that teach students to analyze, question, and to foster thoughtful discussion. In addition, the digital **ETB** includes Multimodal Literacy ideas for taking lessons beyond the book and integrating them with the students' own technologies, e.g. for a research project, students can find more information about a topic by using both print and digital resources. Projects can be researched at home with parental support, or teachers can set up small groups to collaborate together, culminating in a class presentation.

Students can also be encouraged to create using different technologies (including digital cameras, videos, apps) and to choose work to upload to a digital portfolio, which can be shared with parents.

Ideas for Introducing Multimodal Literacy Skills and Concepts

- **Encourage students to use *Global Stage's* digital resources.** The **Student's App** provides important early experiences of navigating an online interface in a controlled and safe environment.
- **Show how putting precise keywords into search engines can help you find better information.** If you have access to computers and the internet in school, give students a question to answer in pairs, but tell them they can only use one keyword. Discuss how successful they were, then have them repeat the activity with two and then multiple keywords. Elicit that using more keywords helps you be more specific and gives you better information to answer the question.

- **Highlight the importance of scanning for key information.** Before having students research online, elicit what they need to look out for to scan effectively. Scanning is a core reading skill in the **Literacy Book**, so you can make the connection with online research.
- **Have less-confident readers teach more-confident readers.** When you introduce a new technology or skill in class, differentiate by teaching it to less-confident readers first so that they become the experts, and then empower them to teach others. That way, everyone is given the chance to be good at something and no one gets left behind.
- **Use digital portfolios.** Digital portfolios replace traditional folders as a way to capture and store students' work. You can put students in charge of what gets included in their portfolio as a way to encourage independence, responsibility, and reflection. They enable you to:
  - Demonstrate oral skills through videos and audio recordings, alongside on-paper tasks.
  - Empower students struggling with writing and reading by giving them alternative ways to express themselves and demonstrate learning.
  - Share students' learning easily and frequently with parents.

Digital portfolios also allow students to view their learning journey and become a valuable tool for self-reflection. The digital **ETB** provides suggestions for digital portfolios.

Classroom Management

Making Language Drills Fun

The **Language Book** audio contains language drills to practice the new language presented in each Vocabulary and Explore Language lesson. Drilling helps familiarize students with the language and encourages them to notice the correct pronunciation and rhythm, which gives them confidence when they speak in freer activities.

Drilling works by being repetitive, but you can add some variations to make it fun and keep students engaged:

- **Volume**. Have students whisper and then get progressively louder and then quieter again.
- **Emotion**. Have students use a happy voice and then repeat with sad, angry, tired, and excited voices.
- **Speed**. Have students speak very slowly, then get progressively faster, and then slower again.
- **Voices**. Have students imagine they are different people or animals, e.g. a lion, a mouse, a robot, a famous character/actor. Even when speaking in these different styles, students must use the correct pronunciation and intonation.

Play the audio several times so students can focus first on copying the pronunciation of the individual words and sounds accurately, and then intonation for phrases/sentences. For grammar drills, focus on rhythm and chunks of language, not just individual words. After practicing the recorded sentences, have the students build a substitution drill on the board from prompts you give, e.g. *I've already* ____________ *(bus/lunch).* Students could suggest *seen three buses, eaten my lunch*, etc. Then have them practice saying the new sentences in pairs.

Role-play in the Classroom

Performing role-plays in class is a great way for students to interact with the new language or stories and gain confidence using the language in a more informal way. Both the **Language** and **Literacy Books** offer many opportunities for role-play, such as the presentation dialogues in the Explore Language lessons and the stories in the **Literacy Book**.

Five Stepping Stones to Performance

- **Step 1** Put students into groups according to how many parts there are in the dialogue or story. Vary the groups so students work with classmates they don't normally work with. Pair confident students with less-confident classmates. Allow students to assign themselves roles within their groups, as this will allow them to practice negotiating skills.
- **Step 2** Play any audio or video tracks first for students to follow along. Encourage students to think about how the characters are feeling at key moments in the story. Have students notice sound effects and ask them what these add to the overall effect. Play the audio/video again for students to say their lines out loud along with their character, copying intonation and rhythm.
- **Step 3** Give students time to practice their role-play on their own, focusing not only on delivering the correct lines, but also on what's being said, their character's personality, and how he/she feels. At this point they can start to include some suitable facial expressions and actions. You can challenge stronger students to continue the conversation or add embellishments to their character.
- **Step 4** Have pairs or groups come to the front and perform their role-play for the class. Make sure everyone gets a chance to perform at some point during the course. Encourage students to video record each other's performances and to add them to their digital portfolios.
- **Step 5** Organize an open event for parents or other classes in the school. Students can prepare and act out different stories from the **Literacy Book** or the situations from the **Language Book**. Give students extra practice time to give them confidence to perform in front of an audience. Encourage them to think about suitable props, costumes, and sound effects to use in their performance (e.g. rustling paper for rain), or to source these through sound-effect apps.

Tip At an open event, you can bring together a variety of performance pieces, including spoken word poems/chants (with or without choreography), presentations from Take the Stage lessons, oral storytelling using part of a story, or a role-play.

Differentiated Learning

Even across one class, students differ in many ways; from age, energy, interests, adaptability, experience, and familiarity with the world outside the home, to emotional maturity, linguistic aptitude, and physical development. As a way of targeting learning to meet individual students' needs, the **ETB** lesson notes include below-level *Support* differentiation ideas to help students achieve the activity goal and above-level *Challenge* ideas to extend activities. For print users, the following are ways you can differentiate activity types:

Vocabulary

Support: Ask questions to guide and help confirm understanding.

Challenge: Have students think of synonyms and antonyms. Establish if the synonyms are "true" or have specific uses and contexts.

Language Drills

Support: Play the audio several times before having students repeat. Break down the phrases into smaller chunks and build them up until students have the full sentence.

Challenge: Have students substitute words in the drill to make new questions and statements. Ask them to come up with wild and funny ideas!

Conversations

Support: At this level, conversations should be spontaneous, but students can make notes about what they want to say. Have them select a few functional phrases, writing each one on a different piece of paper. They turn it over when they've used it.

Challenge: Encourage students to take the lead in ensuring the conversation is balanced, encouraging all speakers to participate.

Writing

Support: Have students discuss their ideas with a partner before completing their plan. This will help them organize their thoughts into writing.

Challenge: Students should challenge themselves to use complex sentence structure and longer sentences including conjunctions, and show a rich range of vocabulary.

Question Starts Visible Thinking Routine

Support: Suggest example questions using each question word and write them on the board. Also ask students what they think they know about the picture, which will lead into an interesting discussion and should generate more questions.

Challenge: For every question generated, encourage students to provide a secondary question that links to the previous one; e.g. *Who's the girl? And where's she from?*

Step Inside Visible Thinking Routine

Support: Write prompts on the board to help students phrase their answers, e.g. *I think he/she/it can see … / I think he/she/it believes that … / He/she/it probably cares about ….*

Challenge: Encourage students to link their ideas for what they care about to what they are looking at and what they believe, e.g. *I think he cares about (x) because he's looking at (y), and I think he believes that (z).* or *He's looking at (y), and I think he believes (z), so I think he cares about (x).*

Reading Comprehension

Support: Have students work in pairs to answer questions. Both students should look back at the reading to find the answer. They can then compare their answers before writing them in their books.

Challenge: Encourage students to answer the questions in their own words and with full sentences when appropriate, rather than just copying from the text.

Discussion

Support: Give students a list of questions to think about and answer before they talk. Writing notes or answers first can help shy students or those lacking confidence to join in.

Challenge: Encourage students to respond to a point made by someone else, summarizing it before giving their opinion.

Role-plays (in the **Literacy Book**)

Support: Play the audio while students perform the story. This way, students don't have to worry about their lines and can focus on interpreting each scene.

Challenge: Have students improvise the story, making their own changes to the dialogue.

Games Bank

3–2–1 Challenge

Give students one minute to think of and write down three, two, and one words or ideas related to the topic, e.g. 3 water sports, 2 racquet sports, and 1 mountain sport. Students can work in pairs or in teams. Students get one point for each answer but two points if their answer is original, i.e. no one else has the same word. The team with the most points wins.

Alphabet Race

Have students look back through the unit to find words related to the topic beginning with the letters of the alphabet from A to Z.

Backs to the Board

Place a chair in front of the board and choose a student to sit with his/her back to the board. Write a word or phrase on the board. Divide the class into two teams. Each team takes turns trying to explain the word or phrase on the board. You could also have students play in pairs or small groups.

Bingo!

Have students draw a 3x2 grid in their notebooks and write a phrase/word in each cell from a given set. Call out phrases for students to cross out. The first person to cross out all the words, says *Bingo!* and wins. You can also play by having students listen out for phrases/words in a dialogue or text.

Board Race

Divide the class into two teams and divide the board vertically in two halves. Give a board pen to one of the students on each team. Tell students the theme and give teams two minutes to write as many words connected to that theme as they can. Each word must be written by a different student on the team, and only one student from each team is allowed to be standing at any time. When finished, have the teams check each other's spelling and count how many correct words each team had.

Chain Game

Use chain memory games to practice the target language or lesson concepts. Have students sit in a circle. One student says a sentence using the target language, e.g. with *going to: I'm going to try snowboarding next winter* (sentences don't have to be true). Model an example first. The next student repeats that sentence and then adds a new one, e.g. Student B: *I'm going to try snowboarding next winter and I'm going to fall over!* This continues until someone gets mixed up or can't remember what the last person said. That student says a new sentence and starts the chain again. To increase the challenge, have students change the sentences they repeat into third person. This can also be played in teams. The team that continues one chain for the longest time wins!

Correct the Teacher

Call out lines from songs, stories, or dialogues but make mistakes. When students hear a mistake, they raise their hands and call out *No!* Then let a student correct the mistake.

Cross the Circle

Have students sit in a circle. Call out a statement that describes some of the students in the class and tell them to cross the circle in a certain way, e.g. *If you have brown hair, cross the circle like an elephant.* Students then cross the circle in this way (e.g. stomping their feet and waving their arm as a trunk) and sit down in a different chair on the other side.

Detectives

Tell students that a crime has been committed. Choose one student to be the detective, who goes outside the classroom. Choose one student to be the criminal. Make sure that everyone knows who this is. Have them look at what that student is wearing and notice any details about their appearance. The detective comes back in and asks questions to the class, e.g. *Is the suspect a girl? Is she wearing earrings? Does she have brown eyes?* When the detective is sure who the criminal is, he/she guesses.

Different Uses

Show students an everyday object or a picture of one and give them two minutes to think of as many different ways to use it as possible. Encourage students to use their imaginations and be creative.

Draw It!

Have a volunteer come to the front and show him/her a word from the vocabulary set you wish to practice, or whisper it into his/her ear. The student draws the word on the board. Have students raise their hands and guess the word.

Disappearing Sentences

Ask students what they consider to be the most important words in a text and write them on the board (up to about 15 words). You could also elicit key vocabulary words from a unit. Have them turn away and then erase one word from the board. Have students turn back and identify which word is missing. Elicit how the word was used in the text or why it was important in the unit. Continue until the board is empty.

Flashbacks

Have students choose a picture, scene, or activity they have done earlier in the unit from either the **Language Book** or the **Literacy Book**. Students act it out and the other students try to find the page in their books. The first person to call out the page number wins.

Freeze

Call out actions or vocabulary. Students perform the action or mime the word. When you say *Freeze!*, they should stop and stay in that position like a statue. Go around the class, inspecting students to make sure they are completely still. If a student moves, he/she is out.

Funniest Sentence

Give students a set of words or a grammar point and have them work in pairs to write the funniest sentence they can, using that grammar structure or those words. Then have students read their sentences to another pair of students and try to make them laugh.

I'm the Expert

Divide the class into teams and have each team choose an "expert." Give the expert students a topic and tell them that they have to talk about their topic for one minute. If they can speak for the full minute, they win a point. This can also be played in pairs or small groups.

I Spy …

Play *I Spy …* with objects around the classroom or within the pages of the **Language Book** and **Literacy Book** (ideally projected on the board). Say *I spy with my little eye something beginning with (A)*, and have students guess what you are looking at, then have them continue the game. Alternatively, play with adjectives: *I spy with my little eye something (rough).* Point out they may find something that matches your description, but if it isn't the object you're thinking of, they have to continue guessing!

Just a Minute

This is a variation of *I'm the Expert*. Divide the class into teams. Write a list of topics on the board and have each team choose a topic. Each team decides who is going to start talking. The team has to talk about the topic for one minute without stopping, but each team member must say one sentence each. When everyone in the team has spoken, they start again from the first students until the time is up.

Last Letter, First Letter

Have students play in teams. Give one team a word and tell them they have to think of a word that begins with the last letter of that word. They pass that word on to the other team, and the game continues until one of the teams can't think of another word.

Mime It!

The same as *Draw It!* (TB p. 25) but students act out the word you give them.

Odd One Out

Play in pairs. Write three or more words on the board. All the words except one should be connected to one another in some way. Students must look at the words and decide in their pairs which word is the "odd one out" and why, e.g. write *pineapple, strawberry, chocolate, lemon* on the board. *Chocolate* is the "odd one out" because it is not a fruit. Repeat with other words. At the end, invite pairs to say which words they have circled and why. Did everyone choose the same words? Sometimes there may be more than one possible answer, so reward students who can give reasons for their choices.

Pass the Whisper!

Have students stand in a line. Whisper a sentence or question using the target language to one student and have him/her pass it on until it reaches the student nearest the door. That student must say the sentence or question aloud. Repeat as required.

Running Spelling

Divide the class into two teams. Give one student in each team a board pen. Divide the board in two. Say a word twice. The students with the pens run to the board and write the first letter of the word. Then they hand the pen to the next student on their team, who writes the next letter. Both teams stop writing when one team finishes the word. Check the spelling. Then play again with a different word. The team with the most correctly spelled words at the end of the game wins.

Shark

Before the game starts, draw on the board a simple series of ten steps leading down to water. On the top step, draw a stick figure. In the water, draw a shark waiting with an open mouth. Use words from the lesson or unit and draw a series of lines on the board, one for each letter. Have students raise their hands to guess the letters. For each correct guess, write the letter on the line. For each incorrect guess, erase the stick figure and draw it again one step nearer the shark. Write the wrong letters on the board so they are not repeated.

Simon Says

This game practices actions and imperatives. Give an instruction. Tell students that if you say *Simon says* before the instruction, students should do it. If you don't say *Simon says*, students should stay still. You can vary this game to practice grammar structures, e.g. if you say an action using the modals *You have to* or *You must (look through a telescope)*, students do the action. If you don't use the modals, students should stay still.

Stand Up, Sit Down

Call out statements that use the target language, e.g. *I've lived in this city for 5 years.* If the statement is true for students, they stand up. If it is not true, they stay sitting down. Alternatively, you can have students put their hands on their heads for true statements and keep their hands by their sides for false ones. You can play this game for any true/false statements.

Ten Words

Tell students that they are going to write down ten words that they think are necessary in a conversation or text about the topic. This activity can also be used to review readings in the **Literacy Book**. They should try to choose words that they think are essential. Students can write down verbs, nouns, and adjectives (but not conjunctions or articles). Give students one minute to write their lists. Then have students compare their lists with another group. They get one point for each word that is in both lists.

Tic-Tac-Toe

Draw a 3x3 grid on the board and write a word you want students to use in each square. Students have to make sentences with the words in the squares. Teams can choose their own squares to play, or they can choose for the other team. Each team uses the symbol O or X. Teams take turns playing. If the sentence is correct, write their symbol (O or X) in the grid. The first team to make a line of their symbol (vertical, horizontal, or diagonal) wins. This can be used to practice grammar structures with prompts in the squares.

Twenty Questions

One student chooses an object, person, or animal. The other students take turns asking yes/no questions to try to guess what it is. They must try to guess before 20 questions are asked, so have one student keep track of how many questions are asked. The student who guesses correctly then thinks of a new object. If no one can guess, the same student chooses a new object. Students can play this game in groups.

Unscramble

Write the target vocabulary on the board with all the letters scrambled. Tell students what vocabulary set they belong to, e.g. toys, food, or family. Have students work in pairs to unscramble them. This could be turned into a race or you could provide a time limit. If students find it difficult, give them the first letter of each word. You could then have each pair or group demonstrate the meaning of one of the words in any way they like, e.g. through mime, drawing, definition, or an example sentence.

What's the Next Word?

Divide the class into small groups. Read sentences from a story, dialogue, or presentation and stop before key words. Have students decide in their groups what the next word is and raise their hands to answer.

What's the Scene?

Divide students into groups and have them mime one scene from the story. The other students must guess which scene they are miming.

What Was the Last Word?

Divide the class into two teams and give each team a board pen. Play the audio or video and stop after key vocabulary. One member of each team runs to the board and writes the last word heard.

Who Said It?

Review dialogue and characters from readings. Make handwritten cards with a quotation from the reading. First, check that students remember the names of the characters. Then hold up one of the cards, saying *What does it say?* and have students read it aloud all together. Say *Who said it?* When they have answered for each sign, play the reading audio or use the Story Player in the TTL to check answers. Alternatively, say the quotations aloud without writing them down.

Word Sneak

Students play in pairs. Divide the board into two sections. You will write five different words on each side. Students have a conversation about any topic they like, but they have to try to sneak their word into the conversation and it must sound natural. When they have included the first word, they move on to the next. The winners are the students who successfully sneak all five words into their conversation.

Word Tennis

In this game, pairs of students will pass words or sentences between them. Students take turns saying words connected to a particular topic, e.g. *sports equipment*: Student A: *pads*, Student B: *helmet*, Student A: *racquet*, Student B: *ball*.

Would You Rather?

Prepare questions with two answer options to find out about students' preferences on the topic of the lesson, e.g. *Would you rather do judo or go snowboarding?* Students can respond with a physical response (see *Yes/No Game*) or tell a friend.

Yes/No Game

Write a big *Yes* on the left of the board and a big *No* on the right. Tell students you will say sentences. If they agree with the sentence or think it is true, they point left and say *Yes!* If they disagree or think it is false, they point right and say *No!* Alternatively, make the game into a TPR (Total Physical Response) game by assigning *Yes* to one side of the room and *No* to the other and having students move from one side to the other as you say each item.

Language Review

Vocabulary

Lesson Objectives

- to review and practice vocabulary for talking about travel and trade, emotions, art, friendship, early civilizations, and actions and survival

Materials
Audio Track 1

Warm Up

Tell students to imagine traveling in a time machine to when the Vikings lived. In pairs, have them discuss the different things they might see, including what people looked like, what they were doing, and what objects they used.

A TRACK 1 TB p. 215 **Look and write what Miguel and his friends saw at the Viking Museum. Then listen to Miguel talking to his mom about the trip. Match the names to the people.**

- Have students look at the picture on p. 6. Encourage them to describe the picture in as much detail as possible. Ask students if they can see anything in the picture that they imagined in the Warm Up.
- Have students look at the words in the box. Tell them to match the words to the items in the picture. Point out the example (1) and have students find *wood* in the picture. Then have them write the other words in pairs.
- Tell students they are going to listen to Miguel describing the picture. Have students find Miguel (he's the boy looking at the Viking ship with his name on his T-shirt).
- Refer students to the children's names. Elicit whether each one is a boy's or girl's name. Tell students to listen to find out who each person in the picture is. Then play the audio. Display the answers on the board for students to check.

Answers
1 *wood* 2 honey 3 wheat 4 pottery 5 fur
6 jewelry 7 coins 8 leather
a *Anna* b Rob c Katie d Daisy e George

B Unscramble the words used to describe pictures and complete the opposites.

- Tell students that when we are describing a picture, we can use certain words to talk about where things are or what things look like.
- Refer students to the scrambled words on the page. Point out the example *simple*. Elicit the opposite of *simple* and point to the incomplete word (detailed). Give students a few minutes to unscramble the other words in pairs and complete the opposites. Check answers as a class.

Answers
1 *simple*; detailed 2 foreground; background
3 dark; light 4 bright; pale

C Match. Then answer for you and tell a friend.

- Look at the example together. Elicit the meaning of *falling out* (an argument or fight). Point out that students should look at the last words of the numbered part of the sentence and the beginning words of the sentence endings with letters.
- Have students do the matching activity individually. Then have students think about their answers to the questions and then ask and answer with a friend. Do an example with the first question by asking the class and having a student answer.

Answers
1 c 2 e 3 b 4 a 5 h 6 g 7 f 8 d

D Think and write.

- Refer students to the example answer and read the clue. Have students read the clues and complete the crossword.
- Display the crossword using the Tap & Teach Lessons (TTL) or write numbers 1–8. Ask students to spell out their answers. Write them on the board.

Answers
Across: 2 *fight* 3 shield 4 hunt 6 weave 7 crops
8 sword
Down: 1 village 3 stew 4 helmet 5 warrior

E Read and complete. Write the missing vowels.

- Have students skim the text to find out what it is about. Ask students what adventure the children had and elicit answers from the class.
- Tell students that they have to complete the blanks by looking at the incomplete words in the box. Elicit that the vowels are missing in each word. Tell students to think about what words they can form only by adding vowels. Copy the example onto the board and have students say which vowels are missing.
- Have students read the text and try to complete the blanks in pairs. Point out that some words may have more than one vowel, and sometimes these might be together. Check answers as a class.
- Have students pretend to be Gus and his friend and act out the text in pairs.

Answers
1 *survive* 2 crawl 3 build 4 rope 5 shelter
6 hammocks

Cool Down

Play *Running Spelling* (see TB p. 26) with vocabulary from this lesson.

Practice
Resource Bank: Language Review Vocabulary Printouts
Student's App: Vocabulary Review

Explore Language

Lesson Objectives

- to review grammar from previous levels, including tag questions; first conditional; modal verbs of obligation: *must, should, don't have to*; *too* and *enough*; present perfect; and *used to*

Materials
Audio Track 2

Warm Up

Ask students if they have ever taken part in a school play or other performance. Ask *What did you do? Did you enjoy it? Did anything go wrong? What part did you play?* Have them discuss their answers in pairs and then share their experiences with the class.

A TRACK 2 TB p. 215 **Read and complete the tag questions. Listen and check.**

- Have students look at the picture and find Miguel (Miguel is the boy with the paintbrush and can of paint). Ask students what they think he and his friends are doing. Elicit that they are putting on a play. (Students may recognize that the play is *Alice in Wonderland*—students read *The Beginning of Alice's Adventures* in Level 3.)
- Look at the example together and elicit how we form tag questions. Remind students that we use auxiliary verbs or modal verbs in tag questions. Tell students to identify the auxiliary or modal verb in the sentence and use the same one. If there isn't one (like in the example), they will need to use the correct form of *do*.
- Have students complete the tag questions individually. Then play the audio for them to check their answers.

Answers
1 You painted the background, *didn't you?* 2 I don't have to sing, do I? 3 He should finish that later, shouldn't he? 4 She won't do that tonight, will she? 5 We're all ready, aren't we?

B Read and complete. Use the correct first conditional verb forms.

- Students are going to review first conditional statements. Have students read the sentences about the show. Look at the example and ask students if it's possible the audience will leave (yes) and why (because the children might sing badly). Elicit that in the first conditional, the first verb is in a future form and the second verb is in the simple present. Have students notice that all the sentences contain *if* and that this is a clue to help them choose the correct verb forms.
- Have students complete the sentences individually and then compare answers with a partner.
- Check answers as a class.

Answers
1 *will leave; sing* 2 falls; will laugh 3 will/'ll tell; forget 4 learn; won't be 5 don't work; won't feel 6 won't recognize; wear

C Read the dialogue and choose.

- Students are going to review modal verbs of obligation and *too* and *enough*. Have students read the dialogue quickly and say who they think Annabel is in the picture. Review the use of modal verbs *should* (to give advice), *have to / must / mustn't* (obligation), *don't have to* (not necessary). Encourage students to give an example sentence using each verb. Then review *too* and *enough* with an example: *The students aren't quiet enough / The students are too loud.* Elicit that both sentences have the same meaning and highlight the forms by having students notice that *not loud* is the same as *quiet*.
- Refer students to the example and ask why it is *should* (because she thinks it's a good idea).
- Have students choose words to complete the dialogue. Invite two students to read the completed dialogue and check answers.

Answers
1 *should* 2 don't have to 3 loud enough 4 too late 5 have to 6 calm enough

D Put the words in order to make questions. Then answer the questions for you.

- Students are going to review the present perfect and *Used to*. Look at the example together. Have students notice the order of the words in the question. Point out that the question word is *How many times* and the verb is in the present perfect. Tell students that some questions are in the present perfect and others are with *used to*. Elicit the uses of both verb forms.
- Have students do the ordering activity individually, then compare answers with a friend. Check answers as a class.
- Have students read the questions again and answer them in their notebooks. Then have them ask and answer the questions in pairs.
- For additional practice of the grammar from previous levels, use the Review printouts.

Answers
1 *How many times have you sung on stage?*
2 Have you ever been in a play?
3 Have you ever cleaned the windows?
4 Did you use to write in pencil?
5 Who did you use to sit next to last year?
6 What time did you use to go to bed when you were five?
Students' own answers

Cool Down

Play *Pass the Whisper!* (see TB p. 26) with sentences from this lesson.

Practice **Resource Bank:** Language Review Grammar Printouts
Student's App: Grammar Review

Fiction

Lesson Objectives

- **to preview predicting, making inferences, points of view, and visualize changes**
- **to review soft *g* and soft *c***

Materials
Audio Track 1

Warm Up

Ask students what adventure stories they have read. Have them share what it was about and who the characters were. Ask *Were the characters people or animals?*

A TRACK 1 TB p. 229 **Look at the pictures and the title. What do you think the story is about? Write your prediction. Then listen, read, and check.**

- Students are going to preview the reading skill of predicting by looking at the title and pictures of a story. Using the TTL, display the pictures. Ask students to guess what the story is about and have them discuss in pairs.
- Have students write down their ideas before reading the text to check their predictions.

Suggested Answer
An egg falls out of a bird's nest on the side of a volcano because the volcano starts shaking. One of the birds flies down to try to save the egg when it falls into the sea below.

B Think and write. What do you think happened to Barry and Bella next? Make an inference.

- Students are going to preview the reading skill of making inferences by making connections. Ask *What do you know about Barry and Bella? What does the text tell us about eggs?* (they can't survive in cold water).
- Tell students to think about what could happen next, using what they know to help them. Have students write their ideas then compare their answers with a friend.

Answer
Students' own answers

C Answer the questions. Then discuss.

- Check understanding of key words in the questions. Then have students scan the text to find the answers. Check answers together.

Answers
1 Their nest was on the side of a volcano. 2 Barry panicked because the volcano was erupting. 3 The egg fell because the volcano erupted. 4 The seawater was dangerous for the egg because it was too cold. The text says that Barry thought, "The egg won't survive in the cold water." 5 He dived into the water because he wanted to save the egg. The text says Bella asked him to save it, and also he is a good father.

D Draw and discuss. Visualize the past and the future. How did the nest look in the past? How will it look in the future?

- Elicit that the picture is from the beginning of the story.
- Ask students to imagine what happened before and after. Ask *What were the birds doing? What did the nest look like?*
- Have students draw and write about their ideas, then discuss in pairs. Ask *Do you think that Barry rescued the egg?*

Suggested Answers
Past: (drawing) an empty nest or Barry and Bella together as young birds / (written) There aren't any eggs yet.
Future: (drawing) two hatched chicks in the nest if they think the egg was returned to the nest, or they may only draw one / (written) There is only one baby bird.

E Imagine you are Barry. Rewrite the story from a first-person point of view. How do you feel?

- This activity previews the reading skill of understanding points of view by thinking about how Barry feels. Ask students to imagine themselves as Barry and complete the sentence with their feelings. Ask one or two students to share their ideas with the class.

Answer
Students' own answers

Spelling Patterns: Soft c and Soft g

Find the words in the puzzle. Then check words with the soft g.

- Remind students of the pronunciation of soft *c* and soft *g*. Write two examples on the board: *bicycle* and *energy* on the board and highlight the sounds /s/ and /ʤ/.
- Have students complete the word search. Then have them check the words that contain the soft *g* sound. Check answers
- Have students look back at the story in A and find more examples of words for each sound.

Answers

P	H	P	L	Q	F	E	O	K	Q	S	N	C
L	E	Y	X	P	A	S	S	E	N	G	E	R
H	E	N	E	R	G	Y	T	X	X	N	L	M
T	I	V	C	Q	H	R	T	L	X	N	D	Z
R	Z	K	Q	I	E	S	B	L	G	M	W	E
W	E	G	M	H	L	I	P	C	H	S	C	L
O	D	C	B	U	Q	J	S	K	M	N	E	N
B	E	T	B	I	I	M	A	G	I	N	E	U
I	X	E	O	J	C	G	V	R	E	P	W	U
W	H	I	C	T	G	Y	P	X	H	V	E	S
D	N	H	X	F	V	M	C	C	W	G	P	W
R	Q	R	R	V	Y	J	Z	L	S	Q	Z	I
N	F	A	E	N	G	I	N	E	E	R	Q	V
G	P	A	L	A	C	E	X	A	T	P	L	V

Words from the reading: dangerous, place

Cool Down

Play *Draw It!* (see p. 25) using words from the reading and the spelling activity.

Practice
Resource Bank: Literacy Review Reading Skills Printout
Student's App: Reading Skills Practice; Spelling Patterns Practice

Nonfiction

Lesson Objectives

- to preview scanning; identifying the main idea and details; and identifying cause and effect
- to review final *ed*

Materials

Audio Tracks 2 and 3; a map of the world (Warm Up, WU)

Warm Up

Show students a map of the world and have them choose an island. Give students two minutes to make a list in pairs of animals they think they would find there.

A TRACK 2 TB p. 229 **Scan *Welcome to the Galápagos Islands* and answer the questions. Then listen and read.**

- Students are going to preview the reading skill of scanning by looking quickly at the text to see if it includes an animal they mentioned in the Warm Up. Then have students find the Galápagos Islands on the map.
- Have students read the questions. Give them one or two minutes to find the answers and write them in their books. Then check answers.

Answers

1 It's about the Galápagos Islands. 2 an iguana, a penguin, and a blue-footed booby 3 an encyclopedia / animal atlas / travel guide

B Write *True* or *False*. Then rewrite the false sentences to make them true.

- Read the first sentence together. Ask *Is it true or false?* Have them scan the text. Elicit the answer (it is false). Have students provide evidence from the text. Ask *How can we change the sentence to make it true?*
- Now have students do the rest of the activity. Remind them to scan the reading to find the right part of the text, then read that part more carefully to find the answers.
- Have students compare answers with a friend before checking answers as a class. Note that we need to infer the answer to question 4, (it tells us that they can dive from 100 meters in the air). If students are struggle with the inference, ask *How can a bird can get 100 meters in the air?* Elicit that the only way is by flying.

Answers

1 False. Marine iguanas are the only sea lizards in the world.
2 False. They eat seaweed from the salty water, not fish.
3 False. Most penguins live in Antarctica. 4 True

C Choose an animal from the reading. Write the details about it.

- Students are going to preview the skill of understanding the main idea and details in a text by looking at the text about marine iguanas. Elicit that we know what kind of animal it is, when it came to the island, what it eats, and what it can do. Copy the diagram on the board.
- Check answers by eliciting answers about each animal.

Suggested Answers

Marine iguana: lizard, eats seaweed, can swim; Galápagos penguin: eats fish, hunts in the day, survives because cold water flows past the islands; Blue-footed booby: has blue feet, eats fish, can dive

D Match the cause and effect.

- Students are going to preview the skill of understanding cause and effect by matching the sentence halves. Remind them to look back at the text to help them match the ideas. Check answers together.

Answers

1 b 2 d 3 a 4 c

My Reading Journal

One thing I learned from the reading is …

This question focuses on self-evaluation and encourages students to think about what they have learned. Give students time to look back at the reading, think and write their answer, then discuss in pairs or small groups.

Example Answers

… there are lots of wonderful animals on the Galápagos Islands, like penguins and iguanas.

Spelling Pattern: Final ed

TRACK 3 TB p. 229 **Listen and write. Complete the table.**

- Display the table using the TTL. Point out that the simple past regular ending –*ed* sometimes requires changes. Do an example for each column. Elicit that we only add –*d* if the word already ends in –e and that we need to double the consonant before adding the ending in one-syllable verbs that end in a vowel + consonant.
- Play the audio, have students repeat the words and complete the table.
- Have students look for more words in the text with –*ed* endings. Then check answers.

Answers

–***d***: recognized, decided, moved
–***ed***: waited, pointed, learned
Double Letter –***ed***: slipped, grabbed, hugged

Cool Down

Play *Cross the Circle* (see TB p. 25) by calling out actions that the animals in the reading might do, e.g. *dive like a blue-footed booby* or *hunt for fish.*

Practice **Resource Bank:** Literacy Review Reading Skills Printouts
Student's App: Reading Skills Practice; Spelling Patterns Practice

UNIT 1 Let's Get Moving

Unit Overview

Themes

How sports can help people

The importance of rules and teamwork

Synopsis

In this unit, students will explore why sports are important. They will learn about unusual sports and their rules. They will discuss the benefits of sports and how sports scan help bring people together. Students will plan and prepare a conversation suggesting different sports and write an instructional flyer.

Language Book

Vocabulary

beginner, BMX racing, expert, harness, helmet, pads, rappelling, Rollerblading, rope, skiing, snowboarding, trampolining

Pronunciation: connected speech: consonant-vowel linking

p. 35

Explore Language

Review of Verb Forms: Present, Past, and Future

p. 37

Global Citizenship

How do sports bring people together?

charity, fun run, get fit, give up, race, raise money, sponsor, take part in, team, train

p. 39

Explore Language

Indefinite Pronouns: *Everyone, Everything, Everywhere,* etc.

p. 41

Write About It

An Instructional Flyer

Paragraph Building: organizing information

Word Study: word families

p. 43

Talk About It

Conversation: making and responding to suggestions

p. 45

Think It Over

Review and Reflection: 3.2.1

p. 47

Literacy Book

Think Together
Why are rules important for sports?
p. 61

Visible Thinking
See, Think, Wonder
p. 49

Nonfiction
Instructional Text: *The Ultimate Game*

Words in Context: *defends, flip a coin, on offense, substituted, referee, foul*
p. 57

Fiction
Play: *You're Out!*

Words in Context: *hosts, tougher, strikes, shaking, sportsmanship*
p. 51

Reading Skill
Understanding skimming and scanning
p. 55

Literary Term
Idiom
p. 59

Language and Literacy Connections

The connecting theme for Unit 1 is sports and good sportsmanship.

	Language	Literacy
Vocabulary	**Set 1:** sports and equipment **Set 2:** fundraising through sports	**Fiction:** you're out, hotshot, step up to the plate, out of bounds, it's neck and neck, sportsmanship **Nonfiction:** organize, take part in, team
Grammar	**Review of Verb Forms: Present, Past, and Future** I'm looking for a new sport. I was watching you. I haven't tried snowboarding before. I'll find it easy. Are you going to go back to skiing? **Indefinite Pronouns: Everyone, Everything, Everywhere, etc.** Everyone's so colorful. No one has trained harder than me! I'm glad I had something to eat. I can't see him anywhere!	**Fiction:** A group of students and teachers are stretching. It's going to be a much tougher game today. There hasn't been a game this close since first grade. You're out of bounds.
Skills	**Pronunciation:** connected speech: consonant-vowel linking **Process Writing:** generating ideas	**Reading:** understanding skimming and scanning **Literary Term:** idiom
International English	rappelling/abseiling; awesome/brilliant; give it a try/have a go; Good job!/Well done!; flyer/leaflet; organize/organise	soccer field/football pitch; flip a coin/toss a coin; on offense/attacking; on defense/defending

Lesson 1 Walkthrough Vocabulary

This lesson introduces the theme of the unit, and presents and practices the first vocabulary set.

The teaching notes provide Warm Up and Cool Down ideas to help set the tone for the lessons, often in the form of games or discussion points.

In the **Enhanced Teacher's eBook**, there is also a Two-Minute Review which looks back at language from previous lessons.

A Contextualized Presentation: Picture Dictionary Scene

The unit starts with a dynamic dialogue set in the context of a picture dictionary scene which helps students activate their world knowledge and ignites their interest in the topic. Several of the new words for the unit are contextualized in this audio.

Unit Topic

The unit title is the same in the **Language Book** and the **Literacy Book**, with the topic explored in different ways across the two books.

D Controlled Practice & Critical Thinking

A critical thinking activity provides controlled written practice of the new words. By having to think and at times discuss and justify their choices, students engage actively with the words. Practice of the written forms will also help cement them in the mind.

Characters

One character in each unit "travels" to the next, helping to reinforce the idea of Global Citizens and how we're connected.

A character or element from the same unit in the **Literacy Book** is part of the picture dictionary scene in the **Language Book**.

B Drill & Controlled Vocabulary Practice

The vocabulary presentation and drill of up to 13 words/phrases has the students look at the picture (which may include definitions) and number the words in the list, before checking with the audio. This can also be used as a pronunciation drill.

Encouraging students to make educated guesses and engage with the image helps them to start thinking actively about the words and meanings.

C Visualization

A visualization activity supports the students to assimilate the new words by making them their own. They are guided to build images, memories, or word-associations via an audio track.

E Spoken Word

A spoken word rap, chant, or poem provides a new context for the vocabulary by exploring SEL competencies or other aspects of the topic. It also gives students the chance to practice saying the words in connected speech. There is audio and video to support this activity.

F Pronunciation

Features of connected speech are pulled from the spoken word activity to analyze and practice. This builds on the individual sounds work from previous levels.

Language

Vocabulary

Lesson Objectives

- to learn sports and equipment vocabulary: *beginner, BMX racing, expert, harness, helmet, pads, rappelling, Rollerblading, rope, skiing, snowboarding, trampolining*
- to say a rap about embracing a new challenge
- to practice features of connected speech: consonant-vowel linking

Materials
Audio Tracks 3 to 7; Video

Warm Up

Have students talk in pairs about the different sports they play and if they have ever tried a new sport. Encourage students to remember sports and activities from previous levels.

A TRACK 3 TB p. 215 **Listen. Which sports do Nishi and Miguel try?**

- Have students look at the picture and discuss in pairs what activities they do or would like to try. Ask students to find Miguel from the Language Review (Miguel is Rollerblading).
- Tell students that they are going to listen to two children, Nishi and Miguel, talk about some of the activities. Play the audio and have students look at the picture.
- Remind students of the gist question *Which sports do Nishi and Miguel try?* Play the audio again. Check answers as a class and ask students which sport they would like to try.

Answer
Nishi and Miguel try Rollerblading and rappelling.

B TRACK 4 TB p. 215 **Find and number the words in A. Then listen and check.**

- Have students look at the list of words. Point out the example (1) and have students find *rappelling* in the picture. Tell students that they need to match the numbers for each activity with the words.
- Have students find the other words in the picture and write the numbers in their books.
- Have students compare their answers with a friend. Then play the audio to check answers and drill the words.

Answers
1 *rappelling* 2 BMX racing 3 trampolining
4 snowboarding 5 beginner 6 harness 7 rope
8 skiing 9 expert 10 pads 11 Rollerblading
12 helmet

International English

Ask students if they can find the flags. Ask *Which word is American English? Which word is British English?* Drill the pronunciation of both.

C TRACK 5 TB p. 215 **Close your eyes. Listen, visualize, and say.**

- Prepare students for the visualization activity (see Visualization).
- Play the audio, allowing students to visualize the actions as they listen. Pause the audio where necessary to give students time to think.
- Have students share what they imagined in pairs.

D **Look and write. Complete the missing heading.**

- Display the table using the TTL. Check understanding of the headings and elicit examples.
- Have students complete the activity in their books, using the picture to help them. Then check answers as a class.

Answers
Sports: *BMX racing*, rappelling, Rollerblading, skiing, snowboarding, trampolining
Sports equipment: harness, helmet, pads, rope
Ability: beginner, expert

E TRACK 6 TB p. 215 **Listen and write. Then watch and say.**

- Play the video or audio for *Back to School Challenge* Use just the audio if you want to focus on pronunciation.
- Give students time to read the lyrics and try to complete the blanks. Remind students that all the words can be found in A. Play the rap video or audio and have students check their answers.
- Play the video or audio again and have students join in with the rap.

Answers
1 *Rollerblading* 2 snowboarding 3 pads 4 helmet
5 beginner 6 skiing 7 expert

F TRACK 7 TB p. 215 **Pronunciation. Listen and say. Copy the linking. Find other examples of linking in the rap.**

- Display the three examples from the rap on the board. Have students notice the last and first letter sounds and the linking lines. These lines connect the sounds of final consonants and beginning vowels. Have students repeat the phrases. Then play the audio for them to listen and repeat, noticing how the sounds are linked.
- Have students look for more examples of consonant-vowel linking in the rap.

Answers
like_a monkey; pick_up some pads; Just_a beginner?; you're_into; you're_an expert

Cool Down

Play a version of *Mime It!* (see TB p. 26). Students choose one of the sports from the lesson and mime getting ready to do it instead of miming the actual sport, e.g. *rappelling* – putting on a helmet, connecting the harness, checking the rope.

Practice **Resource Bank:** Writing Game, *Ready, Get Set, Go!*

Lesson 2 Walkthrough Explore Language

This grammar lesson presents and practices the first target structure using a simplified inductive approach.

A Contextualized Presentation

The target grammar structures are presented in context through a comic strip cartoon story, dialogue, or monologue and have an accompanying audio recording.

B Grammar Analysis Table

Students fill in the grammar table by finding the examples in the story in activity A, focusing on form. The key language is highlighted to help students spot patterns in how the structure is constructed. In this level, a "noticing question" draws students' attention to a particular aspect, encouraging students to start to question and think about grammar for themselves.

C Inductive Analysis

Concept questions help focus students on the meaning and when to use the target grammar. This simplified inductive approach encourages students to make assumptions, discuss, and verify ideas using the examples in activity A. By taking an active role in their learning, they will gain a better understanding of language, and will be better equipped for new ideas in the future.

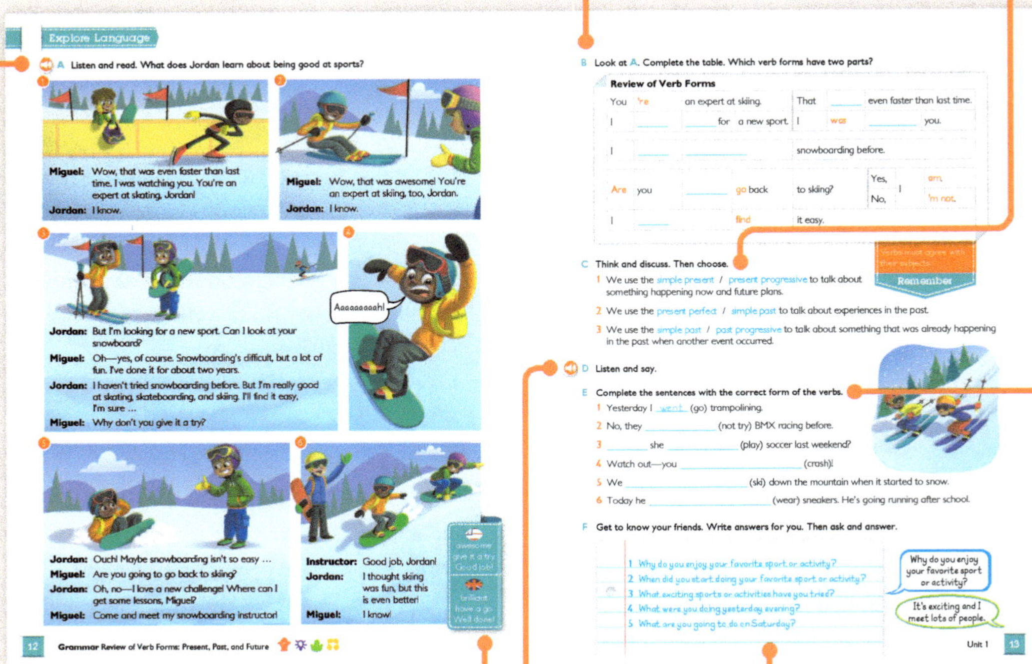

International English

Regular *International English* features highlight differences between American and British English, helping raise awareness of different Englishes around the world. Audio for these words is available on the **TTL**.

D Drill: Sentence Level

An audio recording provides example sentences and questions for pronunciation practice. Drilling new grammar structures helps students become comfortable with how they sound before using them in a freer context. (See also TB p. 23)

E Controlled Practice: Written

Controlled written practice helps consolidate the grammar.

F Freer Practice: Communication

The lesson ends with an activity which allows students to use the grammar in a freer context. There is always a speaking task, and it may also include some writing.

Explore Language

Lesson Objectives

- to review verb forms: present, past, and future
- to practice sports and equipment vocabulary

Materials
Audio Tracks 8 and 9

Warm Up

Ask students which sports they enjoy playing. Ask *Which sports are you good at? Were you always good at (soccer)? How did you get better?*

A TRACK 8 TB p. 215 **Listen and read. What does Jordan learn about being good at sports?**

- Tell students they are going to listen to Miguel talking to his friend Jordan about the sports they do. Play the audio and have students follow the dialogue in their books.
- Ask the gist question *What does Jordan learn about being good at sports?* and elicit the answer. Play the audio again to check. Ask further comprehension questions. See the **Enhanced Teacher's eBook** (ETB).

Answers
He learns that practice makes perfect. Just because someone is good at one sport, doesn't mean they're automatically good at another sport.

B **Look at A. Complete the table. Which verb forms have two parts?**

- Display the table using the TTL. Explain that the sentences students need are all in the dialogue in A. The focus for this activity is on the form, and how each tense is made, rather than meaning or usage. Have students complete the table individually and then compare answers in pairs.
- Check answers, having students complete the blanks on the board. Ask if each sentence refers to the present, past, or future. Elicit the name of the verb form and how each one is made. Ask the question *Which verb forms have two parts?* Elicit and discuss answers, e.g. present progressive is the verb *be* plus the main verb ending in *–ing*.

International English

Draw students' attention to the different words and expressions. Elicit which are American English and which are British English. Ask if they have heard any of these expressions before.

- Remind students' of the Grammar tip *Remember.* Write the subject pronouns on the board. Elicit the forms of the verbs *be* (simple present), *be* (simple past), and *have* (simple present) for each subject. Call out a sentence or question from the table, point to a different subject and have students change the sentence, e.g. *I'm looking for a new sport.* (THEY) *They're looking for a new sport.*

Practice **Resource Bank:** Grammar Printout
Student's App: Grammar Practice

Answers
was; 'm looking; watching; haven't tried; going to; 'll
The present progressive, past progressive, present perfect, future with *going to*, and future with *will* all have two parts.

C **Think and discuss. Then choose.**

- Have students read the sentences. This activity focuses on meaning and usage so that students understand how and when each structure is used.
- Elicit what an *experience* is. Have students work in pairs. Refer them to the table in B for examples of verbs in each tense. Check answers. Make sure that students understand when to use each verb tense and how to form it correctly.

Answers
1 present progressive 2 simple past 3 past progressive

D TRACK 9 TB p. 216 **Listen and say.**

- Play the audio, having students repeat each sentence chorally. Encourage them to copy the linking and intonation.
- For ideas on how to vary the drill, see TB p. 23.

E **Complete the sentences with the correct forms of the verbs.**

- This activity provides controlled practice of the verb forms. Look at the example together. Have students notice that *yesterday* tells us to use the simple past and identify time phrases in the other sentences that can help them decide which verb form to use.
- Have students complete the sentences individually. Remind them to look at the table in B for help. Check answers.

Answers
1 *went* 2 haven't tried 3 Did; play
4 're going to crash 5 were skiing 6 's wearing

F **Get to know your friends. Write answers for you. Then ask and answer.**

- This activity provides freer practice of the verb forms. Have students read the questions and underline the verbs to ensure that they use the correct forms in their sentences. Give students a few minutes to think about and write their answers.
- Have students work in small groups to ask and answer their questions. Encourage students to respond to each other as in a conversation.

Answers
Students' own answers

Cool Down

Play a Chain Game to practice the different tenses (see TB p. 25). Encourage students to choose a different tense each time. Students will need to listen carefully in order to remember the sentence and repeat it using the same tense.

Lesson 3 Walkthrough Global Citizenship

This lesson presents and practices the second vocabulary set, and explores the Global Citizenship topic through listening and discussion.

A Contextualized Vocabulary

A dialogue, discussion, or monologue provides initial input on the Global Citizenship theme and contextualizes some of the new vocabulary for the lesson.

Comprehension questions are provided in the **ETB**.

Opening Question

The lesson starts with an Opening Question to get students thinking about the lives of other children around the world and issues which affect us globally. There are no right or wrong answers for this as the focus is on raising awareness and provoking thought and discussion.

B Drill & Controlled Vocabulary Practice

The second vocabulary set of up to 12 words/phrases is presented and practiced through a matching activity, which is then checked with an audio recording. The vocabulary items are represented in photos or as definitions.

A Visualization recording is available on the **TTL** for this vocabulary set.

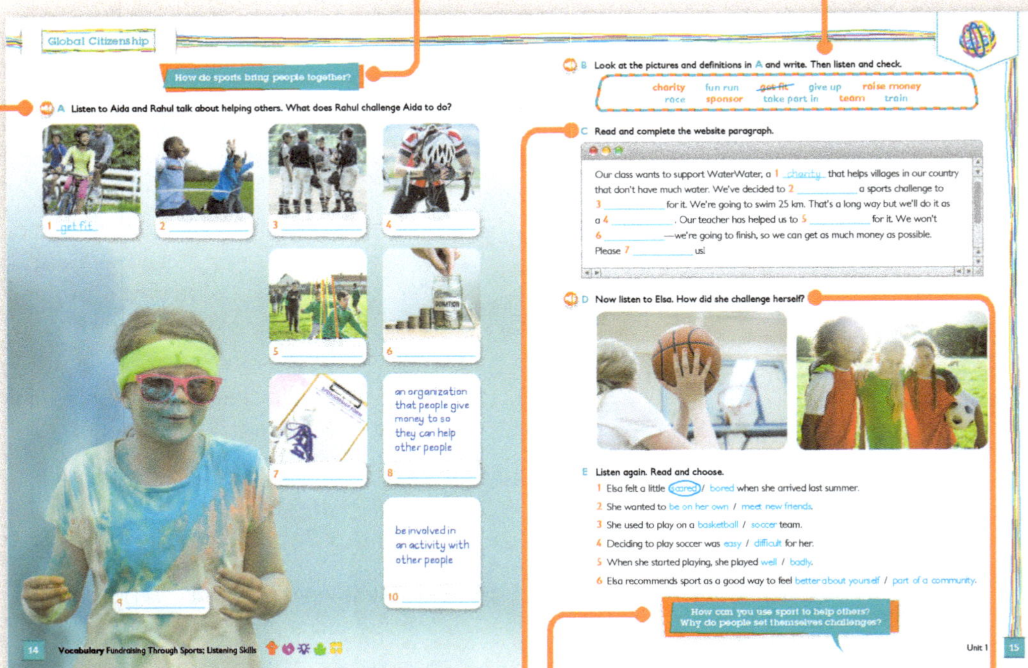

Global Citizenship

How do sports bring people together?

A Listen to Aida and Rahul talk about helping others. What does Rahul challenge Aida to do?

1 get fit
2 ______
3 ______
4 ______
5 ______
6 ______
7 ______
an organization that people give money to so they can help other people
8 ______
9 ______
be involved in an activity with other people
10 ______

14 **Vocabulary** Fundraising Through Sports; Listening Skills

B Look at the pictures and definitions in A and write. Then listen and check.

charity fun run ~~get fit~~ give up raise money race sponsor take part in team train

C Read and complete the website paragraph.

Our class wants to support WaterWater, a 1 charity that helps villages in our country that don't have much water. We've decided to 2 ______ a sports challenge to 3 ______ for it. We're going to swim 25 km. That's a long way but we'll do it as a 4 ______. Our teacher has helped us to 5 ______ for it. We won't 6 ______—we're going to finish, so we can get as much money as possible. Please 7 ______ us!

D Now listen to Elsa. How did she challenge herself?

E Listen again. Read and choose.

1 Elsa felt a little scared / bored when she arrived last summer.
2 She wanted to be on her own / meet new friends.
3 She used to play on a basketball / soccer team.
4 Deciding to play soccer was easy / difficult for her.
5 When she started playing, she played well / badly.
6 Elsa recommends sport as a good way to feel better about yourself / part of a community.

How can you use sport to help others?
Why do people set themselves challenges?

Unit 1 15

C Controlled Vocabulary Practice: Written

Students practice at least six of the new vocabulary in a written context related to the lesson topic.

D & E Listening for Gist and Details

A second audio recording delves further into the Global Citizenship topic, as a monologue or interview. The speakers may be from different countries, or have a particular interest or expert knowledge to share.

The first listening focuses on understanding the gist, while the second looks at the details, using a variety of activity types often seen in exams.

Discussion Questions

The lesson ends with Discussion Questions to stimulate thought and conversation about what students have learned from the lesson. One question focuses on their personal experience, while the other encourages them to think more globally. Further notes on developing this discussion and ideas for project work are given in the **ETB**.

Global Citizenship

Lesson Objectives

- to learn fundraising vocabulary: *charity, fun run, get fit, give up, race, raise money, sponsor, take part in, team, train* (v)
- to explore how sports help bring people together
- to practice listening for gist and detail

Materials

Audio Tracks 10 to 12; Audio Track A; a map of the world (Activity D); pieces of paper (Cool Down, CD)

Opening Question

Ask the opening question: *How do sports bring people together?* Elicit ideas and encourage students to think about the different ways people can be involved in sports. Record students' ideas in some way, e.g. in a mind map, and come back to these at the end of the lesson.

A TRACK 10 TB p. 216 **Listen to Aida and Rahul talk about helping others. What does Rahul challenge Aida to do?**

- Tell students they are going to listen to two children talking about helping others through sports.
- Ask the gist question *What does Rahul challenge Aida to do?* Have students predict the answer in pairs, then play the audio and the check answer.
- Play the audio again and ask students how Aida feels about running five kilometers. Ask students if they would like to challenge themselves by taking part in a fun run. Then ask further comprehension questions (see **ETB**).

Answer

He challenges her to do a five-kilometer fun run.

B TRACK 11 TB p. 216 **Look at the pictures and definitions in A and write. Then listen and check.**

- Point out the example for number 1, *get fit*. Refer students to the vocabulary box in B and have them write the words for each picture and definition in A in pairs or individually.
- Play the audio for students to check their answers. Use the audio to drill the pronunciation of the words.

Answers

1 *get fit* 2 race 3 team 4 give up 5 train
6 raise money 7 sponsor 8 charity 9 fun run
10 take part in

TRACK A TB p. 216 **Visualization**

- The TTL has a visualization for this vocabulary set. (See TB p. 21.)

C **Read and complete the website paragraph.**

- Have students quickly skim the paragraph. Ask *What is the purpose of the text?* (to encourage people to sponsor the students in their charity swimming race)
- Look at the example together. Then have students complete the sentences individually. Check answers as a class. Point out that the answer for number 5 can be *train* or *get fit*.

Answers

1 *charity* 2 take part in 3 raise money 4 team
5 train / get fit 6 give up 7 sponsor

D TRACK 12 TB p. 216 **Now listen to Elsa. How did she challenge herself?**

- Tell students they are going to listen to a girl, Elsa, talking about a new challenge. Have students look at the two pictures and elicit the sports. Ask students where they think Elsa is from (Sweden). Challenge students to find Sweden on a map of the world and elicit anything students know about Sweden.
- Ask the gist question *How did she challenge herself?* and play the audio. Check the answer with the class. Ask *How did she feel when she moved to the USA?* (lonely) *What sport did she use to play in Sweden?* (basketball) Ask students if they can think of a time when they challenged themselves.

Answer

She joined a soccer team and made new friends.

E **Listen again. Read and choose.**

- Listening for detail: have students read the sentences before they listen again. Then play the audio and have students circle the correct option in each sentence.
- Check answers as a class. Ask students why sports have been so important for Elsa. (She was lonely, and joining the team helped her make new friends). Elicit other ways of making friends in a new city or country.

Answers

1 *scared* 2 meet new friends 3 basketball 4 difficult
5 badly 6 part of a community

Discussion Questions

- Draw students' attention to the discussion questions. Have students discuss each question in pairs or small groups (see **ETB**). Elicit responses from someone in each group and write the suggestions on the board. Guide students to conclude that we can all use sports to help others in many different situations. Encourage them to see the importance of setting achievable goals and working hard to reach them.
- Return to the opening question to ask again: *How do sports bring people together?* Revisit any ideas discussed at the beginning of the lesson and encourage students to share any new ideas.

Cool Down

Give each student a slip of paper. Tell them to write one thing they learned or enjoyed in the lesson. Then do an Inside-Outside Circle routine (see p. 21).

Practice **Student's App:** Vocabulary Practice; Listening Practice

Lesson 4 Walkthrough Explore Language

This grammar lesson presents and practices the second target structure using a simplified inductive approach. Differentiation ideas to support or challenge students are given in the **ETB** wherever it would be useful. See also TB p. 24 for some general ideas for differentiated learning. Further written practice is also available through Grammar Printouts in the Resource Bank.

A Contextualized Presentation

A gist question focuses students on the story and further comprehension questions are provided in the **ETB**.

B Grammar Analysis Table

The grammar table is reproduced in the **TTL**, allowing for this to be completed as a heads-up class activity.

Grammar Tip

After every grammar analysis table, there is a tip with additional information. These are divided into three categories:

Watch Out: highlights common errors

Remember: aspects of language students have seen before, e.g. contractions

Look: additional features students should be aware of, e.g. spelling patterns

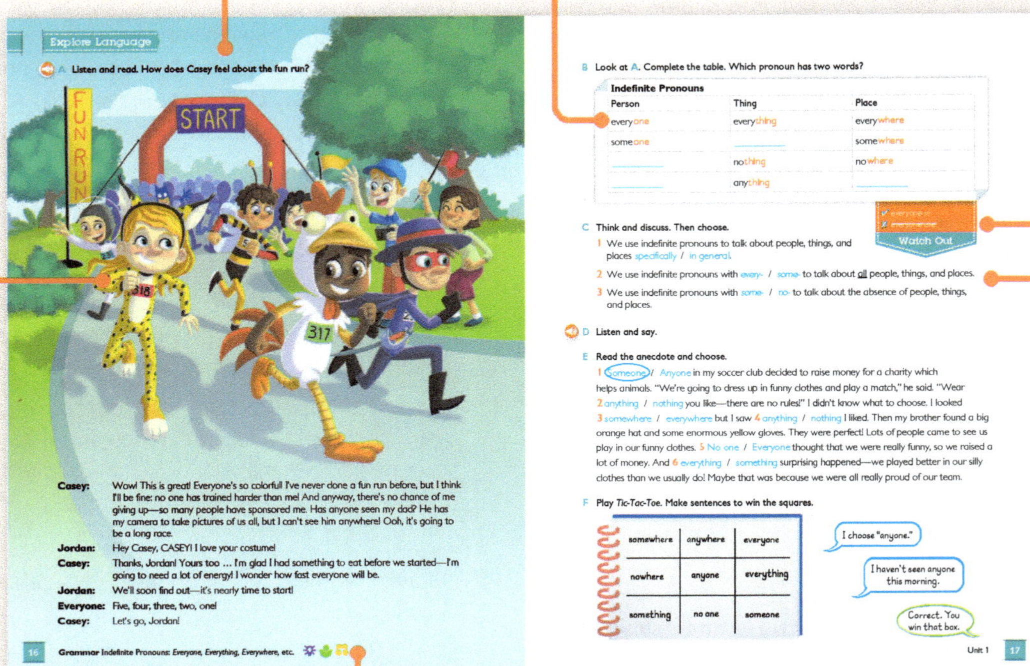

Explore Language

A Listen and read. How does Casey feel about the fun run?

Casey: Wow! This is great! Everyone's so colorful! I've never done a fun run before, but I think I'll be fine: no one has trained harder than me! And anyway, there's no chance of me giving up—so many people have sponsored me. Has anyone seen my dad? He has my camera to take pictures of us all, but I can't see him anywhere! Ooh, it's going to be a long race.

Jordan: Hey Casey, CASEY! I love your costume!

Casey: Thanks, Jordan! Yours too ... I'm glad I had something to eat before we started—I'm going to need a lot of energy! I wonder how fast everyone will be.

Jordan: We'll soon find out—it's nearly time to start!

Everyone: Five, four, three, two, one!

Casey: Let's go, Jordan!

16 **Grammar** Indefinite Pronouns: *Everyone, Everything, Everywhere, etc.*

B Look at A. Complete the table. Which pronoun has two words?

Indefinite Pronouns

Person	Thing	Place
everyone	everything	everywhere
someone	______	somewhere
______	nothing	nowhere
______	anything	______

Watch Out

C Think and discuss. Then choose.

1 We use indefinite pronouns to talk about people, things, and places specifically / in general.

2 We use indefinite pronouns with every- / some- to talk about all people, things, and places.

3 We use indefinite pronouns with some- / no- to talk about the absence of people, things, and places.

D Listen and say.

E Read the anecdote and choose.

1 Someone / Anyone in my soccer club decided to raise money for a charity which helps animals. "We're going to dress up in funny clothes and play a match," he said. "Wear 2 anything / nothing you like—there are no rules!" I didn't know what to choose. I looked 3 somewhere / everywhere but I saw 4 anything / nothing I liked. Then my brother found a big orange hat and some enormous yellow gloves. They were perfect! Lots of people came to see us play in our funny clothes. 5 No one / Everyone thought that we were really funny, so we raised a lot of money. And 6 everything / something surprising happened—we played better in our silly clothes than we usually do! Maybe that was because we were all really proud of our team.

F Play *Tic-Tac-Toe*. Make sentences to win the squares.

somewhere	anywhere	everyone
nowhere	anyone	everything
something	no one	someone

I choose "anyone."

I haven't seen anyone this morning.

Correct. You win that box.

Unit 1 17

Characters

One of the characters in this scene will appear in the next unit, in a new setting with a new group of friends.

Competency Icons

Competency icons indicate the areas covered in each lesson (see TB p. 19). The teaching notes tell you which activities address which competencies.

Differentiation ideas to support or challenge students are given in the **ETB** wherever it would be useful.

See also TB p. 24 for some general ideas for differentiated learning.

Further written practice is also available through Grammar Printouts in the **Resource Bank**.

Explore Language

Lesson Objectives

- to learn how to use indefinite pronouns
- to practice fundraising vocabulary

Materials
Audio Tracks 13 and 14

Warm Up

Ask students if they have ever taken part in a fun run. If possible, show an image of people participating in a fun run in fancy dress costumes. Say *Imagine you are choosing a costume for a fun run. What costume would you wear?*

A TRACK 13 TB p. 216 **Listen and read. How does Casey feel about the fun run?**

- Tell students that they are going to listen to Jordan doing a different sport with his new friend, Casey. Ask students if they remember the sport Jordan tried last time (snowboarding). Play the audio and have students follow the dialogue in their books.
- Ask the gist question *How does Casey feel about the fun run?* and elicit the answer. Ask students if they think she will finish the race.

Answer
Casey feels excited about starting the race.

B Look at A. Complete the table. Which pronoun has two words?

- Display the table using the TTL. Draw students' attention to the three headings in the table and the examples. Have students find the missing words in A and complete the table individually or in pairs.
- Check answers as a class. What do students notice about the words? Elicit that all the words in each column have the same endings. Elicit that, as the second part of the pronoun, *thing* refers to things, *where* refers to places, and *one* refers to people. Have students find an example sentence with an indefinite pronoun from the dialogue. Ask students where the indefinite pronoun is placed in the sentence. Elicit that indefinite pronouns go in the same place as a noun would go in the sentence.
- Then ask the question *Which pronoun has two words?* (no one)
- Draw students' attention to the Grammar tip *Watch Out*. Ask *Is "one" singular or plural?* Point out that although *everyone* refers to a group of people, it is a singular noun and we must use the third-person singular form of the verb. Tell students to remember that pronouns ending in *one* are always singular, like the number *one*.

Answers
Person: no one, anyone
Thing: something
Place: anywhere
The pronoun *no one* has two words.

Practice **Resource Bank:** Grammar Printout
Student's App: Grammar Practice

C Think and discuss. Then choose.

- Have students work in pairs to discuss the sentences and choose their answers. If necessary, check understanding of *absence*. Refer students to the dialogue in A for examples of the indefinite pronouns in context. Then check answers. Clarify any misunderstandings. Review the meaning of *some* and *any* when used in affirmative sentences (Level 1, Unit 10).
- Point out that *no–* and *any–* can both have a negative meaning but that we need a negative verb before *any*.
- For further practice, have students work in teams to use indefinite pronouns to make statements about things or people in the classroom. Call out an indefinite pronoun and have teams think of a sentence, e.g. *Everyone is working hard.* The first team to make a correct sentence gets a point.

Answers
1 in general 2 every– 3 no–

D TRACK 14 TB p. 216 **Listen and say.**

- Play the audio, having students repeat each sentence chorally. Encourage them to copy the linking and intonation.
- For ideas on how to vary the drill, see TB p. 23.

E Read the anecdote and choose.

- This activity provides controlled practice of indefinite pronouns. Read the example including both options. Ask *Why is "someone" the correct answer?* Elicit that the sentence is talking about one specific person (*anyone* is used to talk about a nonspecified person in affirmative sentences).
- Have students read the anecdote and circle the correct options in their books. Then check answers as a class.

Answers
1 *Someone* 2 anything 3 everywhere 4 nothing
5 Everyone 6 something

F Play *Tic-Tac-Toe*. Make sentences to win the squares.

- This activity provides freer practice of indefinite pronouns. Tell students they are going to play a game of *Tic-Tac-Toe* in small groups. See TB p. 27 for how to play.
- Have one group demonstrate the game using the examples on the page.
- Have students play in their groups until one team wins. Students can then play again if time allows.

Answers
Students' own answers

Cool Down

Play *Stand Up, Sit Down* (see TB p. 26). Call out statements using indefinite pronouns, e.g. *Everyone in the class had cereal for breakfast.* Students decide whether they think the statement is true or false.

Lesson 5 Walkthrough Writing

This first productive skills lesson is dedicated to writing, which now occupies a double page. In Levels 5 and 6, the lessons explore different genres of text, linked to those in the **Literacy Book**, and take students through the different stages of Process Writing.

The left-hand page presents the genre and highlights the structure, key features, and aspects of language. The right-hand page scaffolds students to produce their own writing, through carefully staged activities focusing on each step of Process Writing cumulatively: Units 1 and 2 look at brainstorming; Units 3–5 work on brainstorming and planning; Units 6–8 explore brainstorming, planning, and drafting & revising; Units 9 and 10 bring it all together to finish with editing and publishing.

A Contextualized Writing Mechanics

A model text continues the topic of the unit and a gist question ensures students are engaged with the text as "readers", before becoming writers.

Further comprehension questions are provided in the **ETB**.

D Brainstorming

In every unit, students are encouraged to brainstorm ideas as the first step to writing. A variety of examples are given on the page to encourage students to be flexible and choose the right technique for the final product.

Process Writing

The pencils icon in Units 1, 3, 6 and 9, refer students to a page at the back of the book exploring a Process Writing stage. These can be done before the activities in the unit to give them a better understanding of why each stage is important and useful.

B Text Analysis

Students are guided to analyze the structure and textual features for the text type.

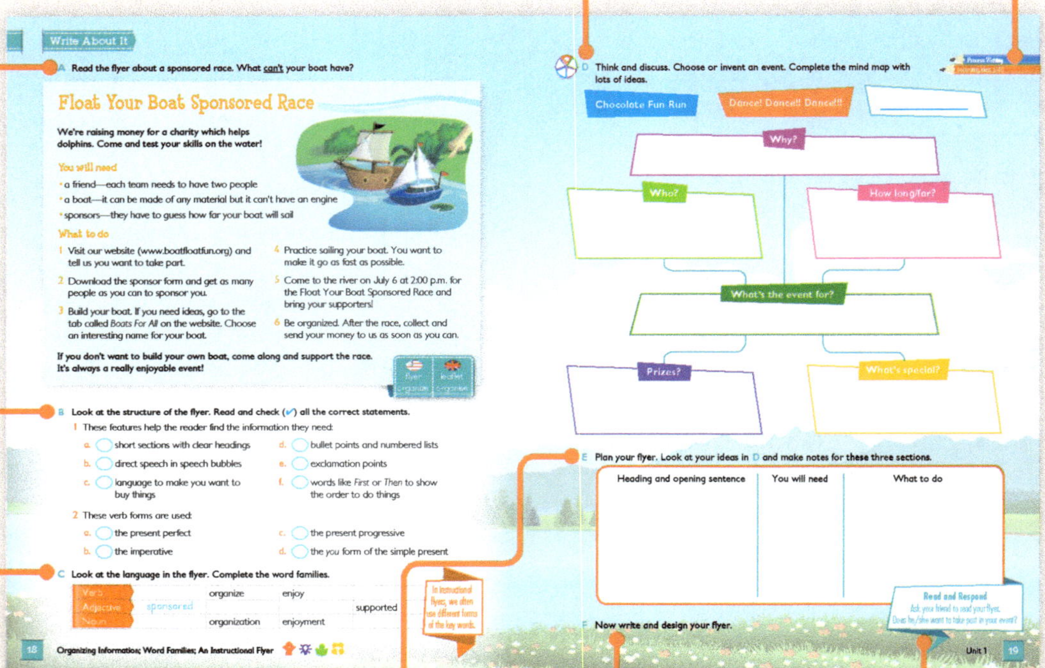
Write About It

A Read the flyer about a sponsored race. What can't your boat have?

Float Your Boat Sponsored Race

We're raising money for a charity which helps dolphins. Come and test your skills on the water!

You will need

- a friend—each team needs to have two people
- a boat—it can be made of any material but it can't have an engine
- sponsors—they have to guess how far your boat will sail

What to do

1 Visit our website (www.boatfloatfun.org) and tell us you want to take part.
2 Download the sponsor form and get as many people as you can to sponsor you.
3 Build your boat. If you need ideas, go to the tab called Boats For All on the website. Choose an interesting name for your boat.
4 Practice sailing your boat. You want to make it go as fast as possible.
5 Come to the river on July 6 at 2:00 p.m. for the Float Your Boat Sponsored Race and bring your supporters!
6 Be organized. After the race, collect and send your money to us as soon as you can.

If you don't want to build your own boat, come along and support the race. It's always a really enjoyable event!

B Look at the structure of the flyer. Read and check (✓) all the correct statements.

1 These features help the reader find the information they need:
a. short sections with clear headings
b. direct speech in speech bubbles
c. language to make you want to buy things
d. bullet points and numbered lists
e. exclamation points
f. words like First or Then to show the order to do things

2 These verb forms are used:
a. the present perfect
b. the imperative
c. the present progressive
d. the you form of the simple present

C Look at the language in the flyer. Complete the word families.

Verb		organize	enjoy	
Adjective	sponsored			supported
Noun		organization	enjoyment	

18 Organizing Information; Word Families; An Instructional Flyer

D Think and discuss. Choose or invent an event. Complete the mind map with lots of ideas.

Chocolate Fun Run
Dance! Dance!! Dance!!!
Why?
Who?
How long/far?
What's the event for?
Prizes?
What's special?

E Plan your flyer. Look at your ideas in D and make notes for these three sections.

Heading and opening sentence	You will need	What to do

F Now write and design your flyer.

Read and Respond

Unit 1 19

C Language Analysis

This activity focuses students on language used in the model text that they may find useful in their own writing.

Where relevant, a *callout* provides additional insights into the features or language in the model text.

E Planning

Every unit includes a planning stage, which is more scaffolded in the earlier units, drawing on the ideas gathered in Activity D.

F (& G) Production: Writing Task

The final writing task can be done in notebooks. *Support* printouts are available from the **Resource Bank** for those students who need it.

For some more light-hearted writing practice, there is a Writing Game for each unit in the **Resource Bank**.

Read and Respond

Students are invited to share their work with a friend, who will offer an opinion or some advice. This encourages students to write with a reader in mind, and to get into the habit of editing and making improvements to their work.

Write About It

Lesson Objectives

- to learn how to generate ideas (Process Writing: Step 1)
- to plan and write an instructional flyer
- to learn how to organize information
- to learn about word families

Materials

Support writing printout from the Resource Bank, one per student (F)

Warm Up

Ask students if they have ever made a paper or model boat and invited volunteers to demonstrate for the class.

A Read the flyer about a sponsored race. What can't your boat have?

This text is also modeled in the Literacy Book for this unit, The Ultimate Game.

- Draw students' attention to the flyer and look at the title, pictures, and headings. Review the meaning of *sponsored*.
- Have students read the flyer. Ask the comprehension question *What can't your boat have?* and elicit the answer.
- Ask students if they'd like to take part in the event. Ask further comprehension questions (see **ETB**).

Answer

Your boat can't have an engine.

International English

Draw students' attention to the two words and elicit which are American English and which are British English. Ask students which words are similar and which words are different.

B Look at the structure of the flyer. Read and check (✔) all the correct statements.

- Draw students' attention to the instructions. Explain that some texts have features that help us find information.
- Have students look at the text in A to try to find examples of each feature. Show one example, then have students complete. Check answers and elicit examples for each.
- Refer students to question 2. Review the forms of the different tenses, writing an example of each on the board. Have students complete and check the answers.

Answers

1 a; d; e 2 b; c; d

C Look at the language in the flyer. Complete the word families.

- Explain that we can group words together that have a common base form that we can use to make other words, e.g. verbs, nouns, adjectives. These groups of words are called word families. Give an example using a familiar word, e.g. *create, creativity, creative*.
- Have students complete the table individually and check answers as a class.
- Draw students' attention to the callout. Remind students that they can use all these words in their own writing.

Answers

sponsor, sponsor; organized; enjoyable; support, supporters

Now ask students to turn to p. 140 to learn about Process Writing Step 1: Generating Ideas (see TB p. 211 for teaching notes). Students will need to do this lesson before they do D.

D Think and discuss. Choose or invent an event. Complete the mind map with lots of ideas.

- Tell students they are going to generate ideas for a flyer using a mind map. Prompt them to use their answers from the previous activities to brainstorm for this activity.
- Look at the two examples and ask students if they think these events sound like fun. Give students one or two minutes to think of more ideas. Then elicit suggestions.
- Have students complete their mind maps in pairs.

E Plan your flyer. Look at your ideas in D and make notes for these three sections.

- Refer students to the flyer in A and highlight the different sections in the table. Tell them to look at their ideas in D and decide where each piece of information should go.
- Have students complete the table individually.

F Now write and design your flyer.

- Have students write a rough draft of their flyer in their notebooks. Encourage them to think about layout and design and how to organize their information. Then have them write up their flyer on paper or the Support printouts from the Resource Bank.
- Have students read each other's flyers. Remind students to make positive comments about the writing.

Cool Down

Have students display their flyers around the room for others to read. Then have students vote on the event they would most like to take part in. Remind students not to vote for their own event.

Practice **Student's App:** Writing Practice
Resource Bank: Writing Game, *Ready, Get Set, Go!*

Lesson 6 Walkthrough Speaking

The second productive skills lesson is dedicated to speaking and functional language, and at this level is set on a single page. There are five *Take the Stage* lessons focusing on presentation skills, and five *Talk About It* lessons focusing on conversation skills. Each lesson starts with a video showing a child/children presenting or having a conversation, which helps to bring the language alive. If it isn't possible to watch the video during class time, encourage students to watch it at home beforehand (see The Flipped Approach TB p. 15).

A Video Showcase

The video sets the context for the lesson, showing students what they are working towards. It provides a natural context for the functional language as well as an opportunity to recycle some of the vocabulary and structures from the unit. A gist question gives them an initial reason to watch, and further comprehension questions are in the **ETB**.

Watch

The *Watch* callout encourages students to use all the clues available in the video to help figure out what makes the presentation/ conversation successful.

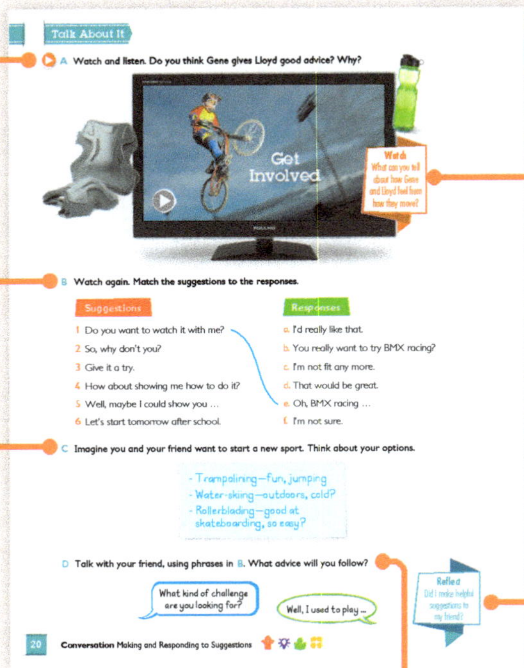
Talk About It

A Watch and listen. Do you think Gene gives Lloyd good advice? Why?

B Watch again. Match the suggestions to the responses.

Suggestions	Responses
1 Do you want to watch it with me?	a. I'd really like that.
2 So, why don't you?	b. You really want to try BMX racing?
3 Give it a try.	c. I'm not fit any more.
4 How about showing me how to do it?	d. That would be great.
5 Well, maybe I could show you …	e. Oh, BMX racing …
6 Let's start tomorrow after school.	f. I'm not sure.

C Imagine you and your friend want to start a new sport. Think about your options.

- Trampolining—fun, jumping
- Water-skiing—outdoors, cold?
- Rollerblading—good at skateboarding, so easy?

D Talk with your friend, using phrases in B. What advice will you follow?

20 Conversation Making and Responding to Suggestions

B Functional Language

Students work with the functional language from the video, which they can use in their own presentations/ conversations.

Reflect

As with the writing lessons, students are invited to give constructive feedback to their peers with the *Reflect* question. This analysis also helps them reflect on their own contributions and performance.

C Planning

Students are encouraged to brainstorm ideas and plan what they want to keep for the presentations.

For the conversations, students are encouraged to be spontaneous in Levels 5 and 6, so while some brainstorming and preparation activities are given, students are not expected to write a full dialogue.

D Production

Students have their conversations in pairs/ groups, or give their presentations to a group or the class using the language from Activity B. They should build on their notes and use the opportunity to pull together everything they have learned.

Talk About It

Lesson Objectives

- to prepare and have a conversation about sports
- to learn how to make and respond to suggestions

Materials
Video

Warm Up

Ask students what new sports they would like to try. Elicit answers from the class, encouraging students to use vocabulary from the unit where relevant. Then play *Would You Rather?* (see TB p. 27). Choose pairs of sports or activities, e.g. *Would you rather do judo or go snowboarding?*

A TB p. 239 **Watch and listen. Do you think Gene gives Lloyd good advice? Why?**

- Tell students they are going to watch a video of two boys having a conversation about a sport.
- Have students look at the picture on the TV screen and say what sport the boy in the picture is doing. Ask students if they think this sport looks fun.
- Tell students that one boy is giving advice to the other boy. Ask the gist question *Do you think Gene gives Lloyd good advice? Why?* Tell them to listen for the answer and watch the body language in the video.
- Play the video and then check the answer. Ask further comprehension questions, e.g. *What sport did Lloyd use to do?* (BMX racing) *Why did he give it up?* (He fell off his bike and hurt his arm.)

Answers
Yes, he does. He encourages Lloyd to start racing again by asking Lloyd to help him learn to do BMX racing.

B Watch again. Match the suggestions to the responses.

- This activity looks at functional language and useful phrases from the conversation. Have students read the suggestions and responses and check comprehension of key words and phrases.
- Play the beginning of the video and look at the example together. Then play the rest of the video and have students do the matching activity. Play the video again for students to check. Then check answers.
- Have students practice saying the suggestions and responses in a drill, encouraging them to use intonation to convey meaning.

Answers
1 e 2 c 3 f 4 b 5 a 6 d

C Imagine you and your friend want to start a new sport. Think about your options.

- Tell students they are going to plan a conversation where they give and respond to advice about trying a new sport.
- Look at the example notes together. Have students work in pairs to think of ideas they can use in their conversation. They need to include two or more sports, and they should think of reasons why they would or wouldn't like to try each sport.
- Give students time to plan their conversations in their notebooks individually. Remind students that they only need to write notes as prompts during the conversation and not full sentences.
- Encourage students to think about the sequence of their conversation. How will it start? How will it end? If they wish to, they can include some of the suggestions and responses in their plans. Planning will help students structure their conversations, but they will need to be able to respond to what their friend says spontaneously. At this level, conversations should be more spontaneous and natural than at lower levels; they need to be active listeners and respond to what is being said.

D Talk with your friend, using phrases in B. What advice will you follow?

- Demonstrate the start of a conversation with a confident student by asking the example question on the page and then making a suggestion based on the student's answer.
- Have students have their conversations in pairs. Remind them to take turns and listen when their partner is speaking. Encourage them to use gestures and appropriate body language to show enthusiasm and encourage their partner.
- Have students analyze their own performances in pairs.

Cool Down

Students individually choose a sport or activity that they would like to try and write it down, without telling anyone. Then they stand up and walk around the classroom suggesting their activity, e.g. *How about going trampolining?* When they find somebody with the same activity, they form a group. Allow two minutes for this, and then see how many groups have been formed.

Practice **Student's App:** Speaking Skills Practice; Speaking Video

Lesson 7 Walkthrough Think It Over

The final lesson in the **Language Book** encourages students to reflect on what they have learned and what they need to work on. In Levels 5 and 6, students see different graphic organizers based on key strategies of Assessment for Learning: students reflect on their starting point, what they have learned, and what they need to learn or the next steps they can take to continue learning. By taking an active role in their learning, students can discover what works for them and their responses can help you, the teacher, to adapt future lessons to suit their needs or recommend targeted practice.

Graphic Organizers

There are six different graphic organizers: *3-2-1; Looking Back; Two Stars and a Wish; My Planning Sheet; My Favorite Mistakes*; and *Monthly Goal Reflection.*

For each one, it's important that the students take time to reflect and respond for themselves on their progress or what they struggled with, rather than doing this as a class or group activity. Full sentences aren't necessary; the focus should be on the reflection and planning for ongoing learning.

Looking Forward

At the end of every unit is a teaser question linking one of the characters with the next unit.

Put It Together

After Units 2, 4, 6, 8 and 10 there is a game that brings together the language and vocabulary of the two previous units. By setting the language in new contexts and adding in a fun and sometimes competitive element, students will want to play them again and again.

Think It Over

Lesson Objectives

- to review what has been learned in the unit
- to reflect on the unit and their own progress

Warm Up

Do a quick quiz with the class about Unit 1. Ask questions about pictures, words, or information and have students find the answers in their books. Have students play in teams. Possible questions: *How many children are trampolining in the Sports Experience Center?* (2) *Who is walking down the stairs in the Sports Center? What color is Jordan's ski helmet? What is the Grammar tip Watch Out on p. 17? What's the word for picture 9 on p. 14?*

How well did you meet the challeng of Unit 1? Read and respond.

3–2–1

- Tell students they are going to review what they learned in the unit and also think about their own learning. Let them know that it's important that they think about themselves and not worry about what other people think or say, as different students will remember or enjoy different things. Tell them that it's ok if they found something difficult that their friend found easy, as their friend may have struggled with something they found easy. Explain that reflecting on what they've learned and what they enjoyed or found difficult can help them think about what to focus on next time or what they need to practice more or do again. It can help them learn about themselves.
- Draw a spidergram on the board with the following categories: *words; grammar; conversation phrases; things I learned about an instructional text; things I learned about another country; facts; interesting ideas; things that made me think*. Brainstorm things students remember from the unit as a class, but don't prompt them too much. It is important that students lead this brainstorming session and that the ideas generated are things they remember rather than the things you want them to remember.
- When you have a variety of suggestions in the spidergram, refer students to the graphic organizer in their book and the prompt sentences: *3 things I learned in this unit, 2 questions I have, 1 thing I struggled with*. Have students talk in pairs about the different sections. Encourage them to focus particularly on the second section and to discuss what outstanding questions they have about things they learned. Write some prompts on the board to support their conversation, e.g. *I liked … / I didn't like …; I thought … was interesting / boring / fun; I remember we … / I don't remember doing …; I'd like to know / learn more about …; Next time, I'm going to …*
- When you feel they have enough ideas, have students work individually to fill in the graphic organizer. Remind them that they should write their own responses about themselves. Monitor and help as necessary. Look at what students are writing so you can tailor your classes and any additional practice to their needs.
- If you feel it is appropriate for your class, have students share their ideas with a friend. Encourage them to think together of how they can improve or practice the thing they struggled with. They can use phrases from the speaking lesson to give each other advice.

Looking Forward

Draw students' attention to the character at the bottom of the page. Elicit who it is and what they remember about her. (Casey appeared in Lesson 4, p. 16.) Ask *What costume was Casey wearing in the fun run?* (lynx) Have students read the speech bubble and make predictions about what Casey is interested in. Tell them they will find out in the first lesson of Unit 2.

Practice **Resource Bank:** Unit Test
Student's App: Vocabulary and Grammar Review

Lesson 1 Walkthrough Get Ready to Read

There are two sections to this lesson: Section 1 is a Visible Thinking Routine (VTR) and Section 2 has pre-reading activities, which also preview the reading skill that will be explored in more detail in Lesson 4. The sections can be done in one lesson or spread over two lessons, e.g. allowing you to devote more time to the VTR and to do the pre-reading activities immediately before the reading text. In this lesson, there is no Cool Down activity suggested, but the **ETB** has plenty of additional extension ideas if you choose to end the lesson after the pre-reading activities.

Warm Up activities are designed to generate interest in the topic and activate schema, thereby helping students make connections between their own experiences and the unit topic and readings. These activities are purposely not focused on vocabulary to give the **Literacy Book** a distinct first language (L1) feel.

In the **ETB**, there is also a Two-Minute Review that helps students make connections between the units.

A, B, C & D Visible Thinking Routine

The first three activities take students through the Visible Thinking Routine using the striking opening image to foster thoughtful and constructive discussion. Five different routines are used in Levels 5 and 6, building on those seen in lower levels. The teaching notes give clear instructions for how to set them up and encourage participation without leading students to specific answers, including example conversations and prompts. See TB p. 19 for details on each VTR.

Unit Topic

The unit title is the same in the **Language Book** and the **Literacy Book**, with the topic explored in different ways across the two books.

Competency icons indicate the areas covered in each lesson (see TB p. 19). The teaching notes tell you which activities address which competency.

Transition

A question linking the VTR discussion with the pre-reading activities is provided in the teaching notes. This could also be used as a Warm Up activity if you decide to do the pre-reading and reading on different days.

D, E (& F) The pre-reading activities aim to prepare and motivate students for the reading text: fiction or nonfiction. The first activity focuses on critical thinking and discussion, and the second gives a preview of the reading skill that will be fully explored with the second text.

Get Ready to Read

Lesson Objectives

- to activate prior knowledge about team sports and their rules
- to guide inquiry and deepen understanding through a See, Think, Wonder VTR
- to preview the reading skills of skimming and scanning

Materials

VTR printout from the Resource Bank (Activities A, B, C)

Warm Up

Ask students if they have ever tried a new or unusual sport. Have students raise their hands if they think they have played a sport that no one else in the class has played, then have them explain the sport.

See, Think, Wonder

A Look at the picture. What do you see?

- This See, Think, Wonder VTR encourages students to make predictions, observations, and interpretations about the image of people playing bubble soccer. Start by asking *What do you see?* and give them up to a minute to look and think silently.
- Guide students to focus on what is visible, not their interpretation. Have students share more answers in small groups or pairs before bringing the groups together. The main focus here is helping students articulate their ideas.
- Record the students' ideas from each stage of the VTR to revisit in the Think Together lesson.

B What do you think?

- Ask students *What do you think about the picture?* Give them one minute to think silently about the picture and then share their ideas in pairs before sharing as a class. Encourage students to discuss with each other.

Here's an example of this part of the routine.

Teacher: What do you think about the game?
Student A: I think it's difficult.
Student B: Why do you think that?
Student A: Because I don't think the players can see.
Student C: I think they will fall over because they can't move their arms.
Teacher: Interesting. Does anyone have any more ideas?
Student B: I think the game is funny (to watch)!

C What do you wonder?

- Say *I wonder what happens if someone falls.* Then ask *What do you wonder? What questions do you have?* Give students one minute to look at the picture and think.
- Have students discuss their ideas in groups or as a class.

Here's an example of this part of the routine.

Teacher: What do you wonder?
Student A: Is it hot in the bubble?
Teacher: Good question—what do you think? Is it hot?
Student B: Yes, when you play soccer you get hot.
Teacher: Do you think it's hotter playing soccer in the bubble or out of the bubble?
Student A: In the bubble.
Student B: Why do you think that?
Student A: It's plastic. Wearing plastic is hot.
Teacher: Great. What else do you wonder?

Transition

Ask students what they think the sport in the picture is called. Have students call out suggestions and write them on the board. Then have the class vote on the best name.

D Think and write. How many different sports do you know? Make a list.

- Tell students they are going to make a list of sports. Have students write their lists in their notebooks in pairs. The pair with the most sports on their list wins. Check answers by having the winning pair read their list to the class.

Answers

Students' own answers

E Read and write. Skim *You're Out!* and write the answer.

- This activity previews the skill of skimming text for gist.
- Give students up to one minute to skim the reading on pp. 10–15. Remind them that they shouldn't read the text, just have a quick look at the title, pictures, and captions to get a general sense. Have students discuss their ideas in pairs or small groups.

Suggested Answer

I think the story is about a sport/game.

F Read and write. Read the question. Then scan *You're Out!* and write the answer.

- This activity previews the reading skill of scanning a text for specific information.
- Draw the students' attention to the question. Ask *What information do you need to find?* (the name of a teacher) Remind students not to read the story. They only need to look and find one teacher's name.
- Give students one minute to scan the text. Elicit answers from the class.

Answer

Any one of the following: Mr. King, Ms. Ruiz, Mr. Martin, Ms. Sanchez, Mr. Nuñez, Ms. Era

Now read *You're Out!*

Lesson 2 Walkthrough Reading 1

The reading lessons develop literacy in English and aim to foster a love of reading, encouraging students to become lifelong readers and learners. Specific language is sometimes slightly above level because research shows that with the right support, this sort of challenge significantly improves overall reading skills.

Text Type

Every unit has one fictional and one nonfictional text, spread over 10 pages. Texts are laid out to emulate first language (L1) / ESL materials, allowing students to draw on all the relevant contextual clues to support their understanding. Nonfictional texts provide an opportunity for students to learn new concepts and broaden their view of the world. With a realistic look and feel based on websites, articles and nonfiction books, these types of texts often appeal to reluctant readers.

Fiction

YOU'RE OUT!

Luis | Victoria | Principal | Mr. King (Team Captain) | Sara (Team Captain) | Camilo | Ms. Ruiz

Additional Characters: Max, Ryan, Josh, Erica, Mr. Martin, Ms. Sanchez, Mr. Nuñez, Ms. Era

(*On the court. A group of students and teachers are stretching.*)

Luis: (*as a sports announcer*) Hello, and welcome to the students-versus-teachers dodgeball game. I'm Luis.

Victoria: (*as a sports announcer*) And I'm Victoria. We're your hosts for this exciting game today. The referee is our principal and the whole school is here, waiting for the game to begin.

(*Mr. King and Sara are each whispering to their team to make a plan.*)

Victoria: Last year, the teachers won easily, but it's going to be a much tougher game today. The students trained a lot!

Luis: These are not beginners, Victoria, and there's a big reward for the students if they win: a pizza and movie party.

Victoria: The students' team has a new captain, Sara Lopez. (*Sara waves at the crowd.*) Sara is a dodgeball hotshot. Bay Elementary has never seen a player catch so well, or throw so fast.

Luis: Sara's the player to watch today.

10 Reading a Play

(*Both teams move to their lines and get ready to run.*)

Victoria: Everyone looks ready to step up to the plate!

(*The principal blows the whistle. Both teams run to center court.*)

Luis: Everyone dashes towards the balls.

(*Ms. Ruiz throws a ball at Max.*)

Victoria: Oh! The librarian, Ms. Ruiz, gets the first out.

Max: (*walks off court sadly*) Aw, man.

Luis: Max did NOT see that coming.

(*Sara shoots the ball like a cannon. It hits Mr. Martin.*)

Victoria: Out! Mr. Martin, the math teacher, is gone.

Words in Context

Find these words in the reading. What do you think they mean?

hosts tougher strikes shakes sportsmanship

Unit 1 11

Genre

The footer tells you the genre of text, highlighting the wide variety of text types.

Words in Context

See the Walkthrough notes for lesson 5, TB p. 21.

Three-Stage Reading Approach

The teaching notes are broken into three stages, allowing students to read and work with the text on different levels and with different criteria (see TB p. 13). The main comprehension activities are in the next lesson.

First Reading: focuses on engagement and understanding the main idea. You can use prediction questions to stimulate curiosity and play the audio, with sound effects and character voices, to help set the scene and motivate students to want to understand the details.

Second Reading: encourages students to read more critically, using the embedded comments/questions as a guide. *Text Focus* comments embedded in blue in the texts highlight features of the genre so that students can recognise these traits in other similar texts.

Third Reading: takes students beyond the text to respond in different ways, e.g. perform a role-play, summarize it or think about the characters' feelings.

Fiction: *You're Out!—Play*

Lesson Objectives

- to read a play about a student vs. teacher dodgeball match
- to explore the SEL competency of relationship skills by exhibiting cooperative learning and working toward group goals
- to make a personal connection to the reading

Materials

Audio Tracks 4 and 5

Warm Up

Ask students if they have ever played dodgeball. If this sport is new to students, have them predict the rules of the game by looking at the pictures in their books. Elicit how players become *out*.

TRACK 4 TB p. 229 Reading Approach

Engage with the Text

- Using the TTL, project the opening spread of the reading or use the Story Player. Ask students to notice the title and characters on the page and predict what the story will be about. Elicit that a play always has a character list at the top of the script.
- Play the audio and have students follow along. Pause after the second page for students to make predictions about who will win the game.
- Have students read the whole play before looking at the Words in Context.

TRACK 5 TB p. 229 Words in Context

- Draw students' attention to the Words in Context box. Give students a few minutes to find and highlight each instance of each word (they may appear more than once).
- Have them identify if the words are nouns, adjectives, verbs, or adverbs, and elicit how they know (by looking at the structure of the sentences and at the form of the words themselves).
- Write these strategies on the board for students to use to find the meaning of the words: *pictures*; *surrounding words and sentences*; *positive/negative*; *contrasting ideas*; *world knowledge*; *word building, prefixes/suffixes*. (See TB p. 21.)
- Have students work in pairs to discuss the words. Remind them that different words will require different combinations of strategies.

hosts (p. 10, noun) The people who look after an event or a party. In this event, Luis and Victoria are commentators; students can find them in the picture and listen to the audio to confirm what their role is. Strategies to use: pictures

tougher (p. 10, comparative adjective) This is the comparative form of the adjective *tough*. An antonym, *easily*, is in the first clause of the sentence. Strategies to use: contrasting ideas, prefixes/suffixes

strikes (p. 12, verb) The surrounding words show this is an action, and the pictures above also show players getting hit. The synonym *hits* is in the section above. Strategies to use: surrounding words and sentences, pictures

shakes (his head) (p. 14, verb) Reading to the end of the sentence and the following lines tells us Camilo's disagreeing. Strategy to use: surrounding words and sentences

sportsmanship (p. 15, noun) The students can break this word down to understand its meaning. The suffix –*ship* tells us it's a noun.

- Go through each word to elicit the meaning Play the audio to practice pronunciation.

Analyze the Text and Features

- Have students read the text individually. Ask students to find three (or more) things that make Camilo a good player. (Possible answers: he can throw, jump, and catch; he is fast; he shows great sportsmanship)
- Now discuss the yellow callouts with the class.
  - **Personalization** (p. 10): *Do you like competitions?* Encourage students to talk about competitions they have competed in and how they felt.
  - **SEL** (p. 13): *Why is playing fair important? Ask How does Camilo play fairly?* (He always tells the truth.) Is it more important to win or to have fun? This links to the unit SEL focus of working toward group goals.
  - **Personalization** (p. 15): *What sports do you enjoy?* Have students discuss in small groups, giving reasons why.
  - **Genre Focus** Review the features of plays (a list of characters at the beginning, character names followed by a colon, direct speech, stage directions for the actors) and have students identify these in their books.

Interact with the Text

- Now that students are very familiar with the story and characters, have them work in pairs to choose a section of the play and role-play the commentators, Luis and Victoria.
- Choose a scene or double-page spread and play that part of the audio again, having students repeat the lines. Have students focus on how the characters sound, e.g. excited or enthusiastic, and encourage them to project those emotions into their voices.

Cool Down

Have students write a one-line summary for *You're Out!* The sentence should contain the most important details of the story, e.g. *Star student Camilo helps make students champions!* or *Everyone's a winner in the student vs. teacher dodgeball match.*

Lesson 3 Walkthrough Explore the Reading

This lesson is dedicated to detailed comprehension, analysis, and discussion of the text on the previous pages.

A Reading Comprehension

The first activity provides heads-down comprehension questions and students are often directed to write full sentences or provide evidence from the text.

Students should be encouraged to use strategies they have learned, such as scanning for key words or using pictures or headings, rather than re-reading the whole text.

B/C Post-Reading Discussion & SEL Competency

Fictional texts contain a social and emotional message which is explored in this lesson, often through discussion and reflection. The teaching notes provide ideas and further questions to help develop this discussion. (See TB p. 17)

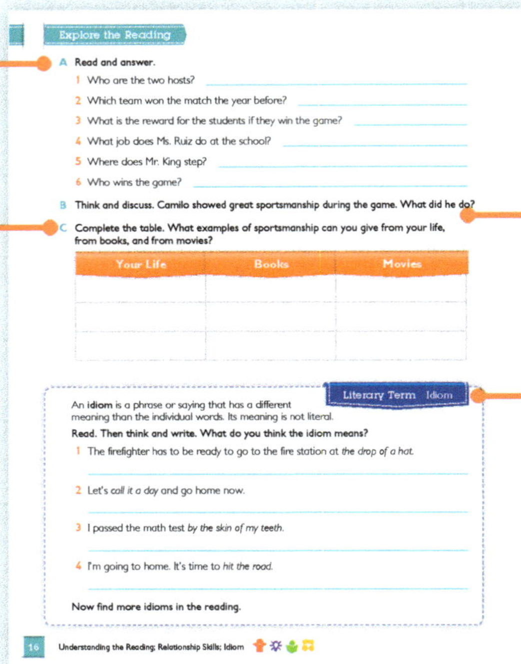
Explore the Reading

A Read and answer.

1 Who are the two hosts?

2 Which team won the match the year before?

3 What is the reward for the students if they win the game?

4 What job does Ms. Ruiz do at the school?

5 Where does Mr. King step?

6 Who wins the game?

B Think and discuss. Camilo showed great sportsmanship during the game. What did he do?

C Complete the table. What examples of sportsmanship can you give from your life, from books, and from movies?

Your Life	Books	Movies

Literary Term Idiom

An **idiom** is a phrase or saying that has a different meaning than the individual words. Its meaning is not literal.

Read. Then think and write. What do you think the idiom means?

1 The firefighter has to be ready to go to the fire station at *the drop of a hat.*

2 Let's *call it a day* and go home now.

3 I passed the math test *by the skin of my teeth.*

4 I'm going to home. It's time to *hit the road.*

Now find more idioms in the reading.

16 Understanding the Reading; Relationship Skills; Idiom

B/C Text Analysis

Further analysis of the text encourages critical thinking, critical literacy, and often includes opportunities for personalization.

Literary Terms

Building on the work on phonics and spelling in earlier levels, literacy is further developed through the section on Literary Terms, looking at devices and structures writers use to convey their ideas. Having an awareness of these terms can help students analyze and understand a text. This section appears in one of the readings only. (See TB p. 13)

A **Cool Down** activity in the teaching notes helps bring the lesson to a close, often with a game, summarizing activity, or collaborative task.

Explore the Reading

Lesson Objectives

- to understand and analyze *You're Out!* through reading comprehension activities
- to explore the SEL competency of relationship skills by exhibiting cooperative learning and working toward group goals
- to understand some common idioms
- to make a personal connection to the reading

Warm Up

Ask *What equipment do you need to play dodgeball?* Name different items of equipment, e.g. a soft ball, a net, sneakers. If students have already done Lesson 1 in the **Language Book** on pp. 10–11, take the opportunity to recycle the vocabulary words.

A Read and answer.

- Refer back to *You're Out!* in the **Literacy Book**. Have a Group Time discussion (see p. 21) to help students to remember more details about the story. Ask questions to prompt students to retell the story in their own words, e.g. *Who are the characters? Tell me about Camilo. What happens at the beginning?* Students can look back at the reading in their books if they need to.
- Have students look at the activity and do the first question together as an example, encouraging students to look back at the reading. Then have students find the rest of the answers individually. Check answers as a class.

Answers

1 The two hosts are Luis and Victoria. 2 The teachers won the match the year before. 3 The reward for the students if they win the match is a pizza and movie party. 4 Ms. Ruiz is the school librarian. 5 Mr. King steps out of bounds. 6 The students win the game.

B Think and discuss. Camilo showed great sportsmanship during the game. What did he do?

Students are going to explore different ways of showing good sportsmanship. This draws on the SEL relationship skills competency of exhibiting cooperative learning and working toward group goals.

- Review the meaning of *sportsmanship*. Have students find the word in the reading and look at the picture on p. 14 to recall what happened. Have students explain why Camilo's actions were good sportsmanship. Elicit an example of a way in which we can show good sportsmanship and write it on the board.
- Have students do a Think, Pair, Share routine (see TB p. 20) to answer the question with a friend. (Suggested answers: playing by the rules, being friendly to opponents, not cheating, respecting other players and referees)

C Complete the table. What examples of sportsmanship can you give from your life, from books, and from movies?

- Students are going to make connections between the reading and their own lives. This activity builds on the SEL relationship skills competency of exhibiting cooperative learning and working toward group goals.
- If you are using the TTL, display the table. Elicit one example for each column in the table and write it on the board. Give students a few minutes to think and write their ideas in the table individually.
- Do a Three-Step Interview (see TB p. 20) to have students share their ideas.
- End the discussion by asking the following questions: *Why is it important to play by the rules? Why is it important to treat your opponents with respect? What other ways can you show good sportsmanship?* (Suggested answers: be a good loser, share your equipment with others, try not to hurt others, encourage your teammates, make positive comments about the losing team)

Answers

Students' own answers

Literary Term: Idioms

Read. Then think and write. What do you think the idiom means?

- Draw students' attention to the explanation of *idiom*. Point out that *figurative* and *literal* are opposites. Explain that *literal* means that the words have their usual meaning. *Figurative* means that the words suggest a different meaning by painting a picture in their minds.
- Do the first sentence as a class. Ask *Do you think the firefighter drops his hat?* Elicit from the class that this is an idiom and that the meaning is not literal. Ask *What do you think it means?* Cover the idiom and brainstorm different ways of ending the sentence.
- Have students do the activity in pairs. Give them a few minutes and then check answers as a class. Clarify any problems by providing visual examples, e.g. 51% for the math test.
- Then have students work in pairs to find more idioms in the reading and elicit examples.

Suggested Answers

1 right away 2 end it now 3 just barely 4 leave
In the reading: hotshot, step up to the plate, neck and neck, go the distance

Cool Down

Play *Mime It!* (see TB p. 26) using the idioms from the lesson.

Practice
Resource Bank: Literary Term Printout
Student's App: Reading Practice; Literary Term Practice

Lesson 4 Walkthrough Get Ready to Read

This lesson sets up the second reading, with focus on a reading skill and pre-reading activities to activate schema and create interest in the text.

A Reading Skill Focus

Using an inductive approach and building on skills they have learned in earlier levels, the first activity provides an opportunity for students to work with the reading skill in a short context. Sometimes drawing on texts read previously, students will actively notice what they have done, before reading the description in the *Skills Box*. Having students use the skill without thinking too much will encourage them to draw on reading skills from L1. At this level, reading skills include: skimming and scanning; sequence of events; drawing conclusions; understanding points of view; identifying sensory details; understanding author's purpose; main ideas and details; recognizing genres; understanding characters; and making inferences.

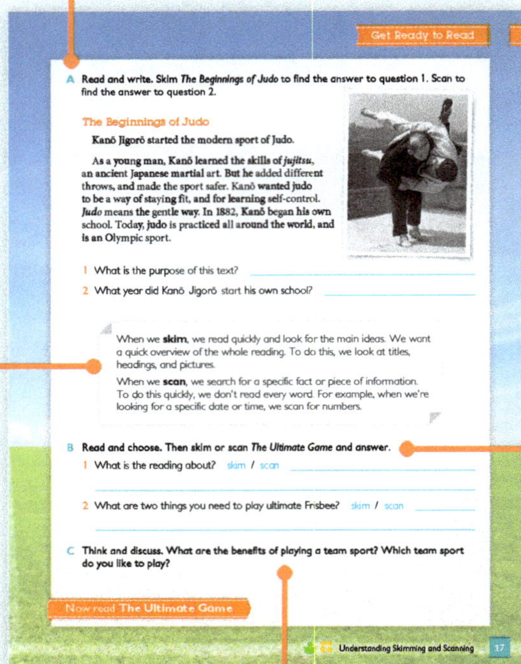

Get Ready to Read

A Read and write. Skim *The Beginnings of Judo* to find the answer to question 1. Scan to find the answer to question 2.

The Beginnings of Judo

Kanō Jigorō started the modern sport of Judo.

As a young man, Kanō learned the skills of *jujitsu*, an ancient Japanese martial art. But he added different throws, and made the sport safer. Kanō wanted judo to be a way of staying fit, and for learning self-control. *Judo* means the gentle way. In 1882, Kanō began his own school. Today, judo is practiced all around the world, and is an Olympic sport.

1 What is the purpose of this text? ________

2 What year did Kanō Jigorō start his own school? ________

When we **skim**, we read quickly and look for the main ideas. We want a quick overview of the whole reading. To do this, we look at titles, headings, and pictures.

When we **scan**, we search for a specific fact or piece of information. To do this quickly, we don't read every word. For example, when we're looking for a specific date or time, we scan for numbers.

B Read and choose. Then skim or scan *The Ultimate Game* and answer.

1 What is the reading about? skim / scan ________

2 What are two things you need to play ultimate Frisbee? skim / scan ________

C Think and discuss. What are the benefits of playing a team sport? Which team sport do you like to play?

Now read **The Ultimate Game**

Understanding Skimming and Scanning 17

B Reading Skill Practice

In this activity students put into practice the reading skill from Activity A. This is often related to the next reading. In this way, they work with the skill more consciously and their interested is piqued about what the text to come.

C Pre-Reading Discussion

A discussion question activates schema for the next reading, often encouraging personal reflection, or for students to express an opinion before having it challenged by the text.

Get Ready to Read

Lesson Objectives

- to activate prior knowledge about ultimate Frisbee
- to practice the reading skills of skimming and scanning

Warm Up

To practice the skills of skimming and scanning, show students a website advertising a fun sport such as bubble soccer. Tell them to look at the website to find out what it is about. Then have them find out one specific detail that can be clearly seen on the page, e.g. a price or the location of the company.

A Read and write. Skim *The Beginnings of Judo* to find the answer to question 1. Scan to find the answer to question 2.

Students are going to review and practice the reading skills of skimming and scanning.

- With books closed, ask students if they have ever played or seen judo. Ask *What does judo involve? Is it similar to any other sports?* Elicit answers, then have students open their books.
- Draw students' attention to the first question *What is the purpose of this text?* Elicit that the *purpose* of a text is the reason the author wrote it. Then have them read the second question *What year did Kanō Jigorō open his own school?* and underline the key information they need to look for.
- Tell students to quickly read the text to find the answers. Give a short time limit to encourage them to skim and scan, not read for detail. Check answers as a class.
- Have students look at the reading skills box. Ask *What do you look at when you skim? What do you look for when you scan? What were you looking for in question 2?* (a number)

Answers

1 The author wants to tell us about how judo started.
2 in 1882

B Read and choose. Then skim or scan *The Ultimate Game* and answer.

- Draw students' attention to the questions. Ask *Which skill do you need to do to find out what the reading is about?* (skimming) *Which skill do you use to find two things you need to play ultimate Frisbee?* (scanning)
- Then have students skim and scan the text to find the answers. Give students a time limit, e.g. one minute. Check answers as a class, having students say where in the text they found their answers.

Suggested Answers

1 Skim. The reading is about how to play ultimate Frisbee.
2 Scan. You need a flying disc and a field about the same size as a soccer field. (Other options: two teams of at least seven players, two end zones)

C Think and discuss. What are the benefits of playing a team sport? Which team sport do you like to play?

Students are going to make connections between their own lives and the SEL competency of teamwork.

- Do a Round Robin cooperative learning routine (see TB p. 20). Before you start, brainstorm ideas about the first question with the class and write them on the board.
- Give students two to three minutes to do the Round Robin for both questions. Then have groups share their ideas with the class.

Answers

Students' own answers

Now read **The Ultimate Game**

Lesson 5 Walkthrough Reading 2

The second reading lesson follows the same structure as the first, and will be a fictional or nonfictional text depending on the first text. As before, multiple exposure and work with the text, including audio and visual support, helps develop strong literacy skills leading towards autonomy in reading.

Both the fictional and nonfictional texts can also be accessed through the Story Player in the TTL and the **Student's App** on **Navio** (see TB p. 14).

Photos and Illustrations

Nonfictional texts make use of photos wherever appropriate and are graphically dynamic, providing opportunities to develop skills in identifying hierarchy and reading paths.

International English

Regular *International English* features highlight differences between American and British English, helping raise awareness of different Englishes around the world. Audio for these words is available on the TTL.

Text and Feature Analysis

Every text, both fictional and nonfictional, has several comments/questions in colored boxes to help guide students to take a critical approach to reading. These are dealt with in turn in the Second Reading stage of the lesson, and the teaching notes provide further ideas to prompt discussion on the different themes such as a Language Focus, Personalization, Making Connections (e.g. CLIL/SEL).

Words in Context

This activity focuses on building strategies to deal with unknown words in a text, which is an important skill for a competent reader. These are not words to be learned or pre-taught. In Levels 5 and 6, the teaching notes encourage students to experiment actively with different strategies and to recognize that different texts/words will need different strategies. Each word is recorded in isolation on the audio.

Nonfiction: *The Ultimate Game—* Instructional Text

Lesson Objectives

- to read an instructional text about the game ultimate Frisbee
- to make a personal connection to the reading

Materials
Audio Tracks 6 and 7; a Frisbee or ball (Cool Down, CD)

Warm Up

Play *Different Uses* (see TB p. 25). Bring in objects that could be used for sports, games, or other activities, e.g. a shuttlecock, bottle tops, a skipping rope.

TRACK 6 TB p. 230 Reading Approach

Engage with the Text

- Using the TTL, project the opening spread of the reading. Ask students what they notice first. Elicit the different text features, e.g. title, text, and images, and have students find these. Have them predict one or two ideas about the game.
- Have students read the text individually. While they read, give them questions to answer, e.g. *Would you like to play ultimate Frisbee? Do you think you would be good at it?*

TRACK 7 TB p. 230 Words in Context

- Draw students' attention to the Words in Context box. Give students a few minutes to find and highlight each instance of each word in the reading.
- Have them identify the type of word by looking at the form and the sentence.
- Write these strategies on the board for students to use *using pictures; surrounding words and sentences; contrasting ideas; world knowledge.* (See TB p. 21.)
- Have students work in pairs to discuss the words.

defends / on offense (p. 19, verb / p. 19, adjective) These words refer to how sports teams play against each other. *Defends* is explained in the second part of the sentence in point 1. Students can find *on defense* in point 4 to contrast with *on offense.* Strategies to use: surrounding words and sentences, world knowledge of sports

flip a coin (p. 19, verb) Knowledge of the word *coin* and what generally happens with a coin at the start of sporting matches explains the meaning. Strategies to use: surrounding words and sentences, world knowledge

substituted (p. 20, verb) This word is explained in the clause that follows, *or replaced.* Strategy to use: surrounding words and sentences

referee (p. 21, noun) The second part of the sentence explains this word, and a synonym is also given, *umpire.* Strategies to use: surrounding words and sentences, world knowledge of sports

foul (p. 21, noun) A similar word, *problem,* is used as an alternative here. Students can use their knowledge of sports to understand what kinds of problems there may be. Strategy to use: surrounding words and sentences

Second Reading: Analyze the Text and Features

- Play the audio for the second reading and have students follow along in their books. If you are using the TTL, the reading is also available on the Story Player.
- Now discuss the green callouts with the class. You could use Group Time for this stage (see TB p. 21).
  - **Personalization** (p. 18): Have you ever played Frisbee? Ask if students like it and how often they play.
  - **Fun Fact** (p. 18): More than 300 million Frisbees have been sold in the last 40 years. Ask Is that a lot? Do you have a Frisbee?
  - **Fun Fact** (p. 20): Ultimate is played in more than 80 countries by about 7 million people. Ask In which continents/countries do you think people play Frisbee? Ask students if they know any other sports that are popular in so many different countries.
  - **Personalization** (p. 21): *Will you and your friends try ultimate?* Why or why not? Have students discuss in pairs and justify their choice.
  - **Text Focus** (p. 19): Subheadings help organize related information so it is easier for us to read and understand. Have students identify the subheadings in the reading.

International English

Point to the flags and elicit which words are American English and which words are British English. Tell students that *attacking* and *defending* can be used as adjectives and must go before the noun, e.g. *the attacking team.* Have them compare this with *the team on offense.*

Interact with the Text

- Now that students are more familiar with the text, have them work in pairs to choose famous people for their "dream ultimate Frisbee" team. They should discuss who would be good at offence or defense, and who would make a good captain and why.

Cool Down

Play ultimate. You will need space for this game. Ask questions about the reading. The student who catches the Frisbee or ball answers. Students can continue by asking their own questions.

Practice **Student's App:** Story Player

Lesson 6 Walkthrough Explore the Reading

This lesson follows the same structure as Lesson 3, with comprehension, analysis, and discussion activities related to the second reading.

A Reading Comprehension

The heavds-down comprehension questions include many activities similar to tasks students might see in an exam. The variety of tasks ensures students are engaged and challenged throughout the course.

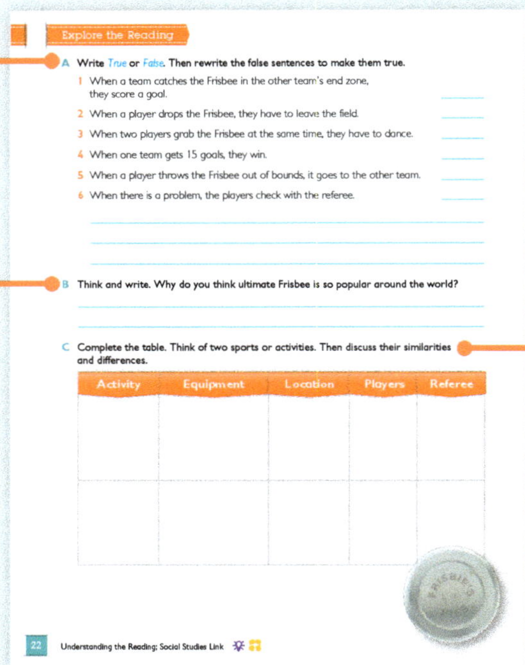

Explore the Reading

A Write *True* or *False*. Then rewrite the false sentences to make them true.

1 When a team catches the Frisbee in the other team's end zone, they score a goal. _____
2 When a player drops the Frisbee, they have to leave the field. _____
3 When two players grab the Frisbee at the same time, they have to dance. _____
4 When one team gets 15 goals, they win. _____
5 When a player throws the Frisbee out of bounds, it goes to the other team. _____
6 When there is a problem, the players check with the referee. _____

B Think and write. Why do you think ultimate Frisbee is so popular around the world?

C Complete the table. Think of two sports or activities. Then discuss their similarities and differences.

Activity	Equipment	Location	Players	Referee

22 Understanding the Reading: Social Studies Link

B/C Text Analysis & Practice

Further practice of the reading skill is provided, where appropriate, and often students are asked for their opinion or a personal response, which encourages them to engage more deeply with the text, whether fictional or nonfictional.

B/C Post-Reading Discussion & CLIL Focus

The nonfictional texts are used as a springboard for a cross-curricular link, giving students the opportunity to pull together knowledge from across their learning journey. This helps to bring the language alive in a real-world context. The **ETB** has more ideas for exploiting this link. (See TB p. 18)

Explore the Reading

Lesson Objectives

- to understand and analyze *The Ultimate Game* through reading comprehension activities
- to make a personal connection to the reading
- to learn about social studies through CLIL: sports and recreation

Warm Up

Play *What's the Next Word?* (see TB p. 27) using sentences from the reading.

A Write *True* or *False*. Then rewrite the false sentences to make them true.

- Have a Group Time discussion (see TB p. 21) to help students remember the details of how to play ultimate Frisbee. Ask questions to prompt students where necessary, e.g. *What is the objective of the game? How do you score points? What actions are not allowed?* Students can look back at the reading in their books if they need to.
- Have students look at the activity. Do the first question as an example with the class, encouraging them to look back at the reading.
- Have students do the rest of the activity individually. Check answers as a class.

Answers

1 True 2 False. The other team gets the Frisbee. 3 False. The Frisbee goes to the player whose team is trying to score a goal. 4 True 5 True 6 False. When there is a problem, the players work it out together.

B Think and write. Why do you think ultimate Frisbee is so popular around the world?

- Remind students of the callout on p. 20: *Ultimate is played in more than 80 countries by about 7 million people.* Ask students why they think the game is so popular and brainstorm one or two ideas with the class.
- Have students write their ideas in their books and then discuss their ideas in pairs. (Possible ideas: it's cheap to buy a Frisbee, it's fun, you don't need any special equipment, any number of players can play, you don't need to be strong or fast)

Answers

Students' own answers

C Complete the table. Think of two sports or activities. Then discuss their similarities and differences.

- This activity allows students to further explore the CLIL social studies focus of sports and recreation by thinking about the similarities and differences between different sports and activities. Have students read aloud the list of sports they brainstormed in the opening lesson on p. 9 or brainstorm a new list.
- Choose a sport with the class and do an example on the board, eliciting examples for each column.
- Have students choose two different sports and complete the table in their books individually. Then have them discuss the similarities and differences between the sports in groups.

Answers

Students' own answers

Cool Down As an exit pass, students have to recall one rule of ultimate Frisbee. They have to explain the rule to a friend before they can leave the classroom.

Practice **Student's App:** Reading Practice

Lesson 7 Walkthrough Think Together

This last lesson in the **Literacy Book** brings the unit full circle, uniting the two readings and the overarching theme to further develop critical literacy.

Key Concept Question

The lesson stems from the key concept question that brings together the concepts explored in the reading texts. As students work through the activities, they will be considering the question; it is not necessary to answer it at the start.

A Text Comparison

The first activity is a text-to-text comparison, reviewing and comparing what they read in each.

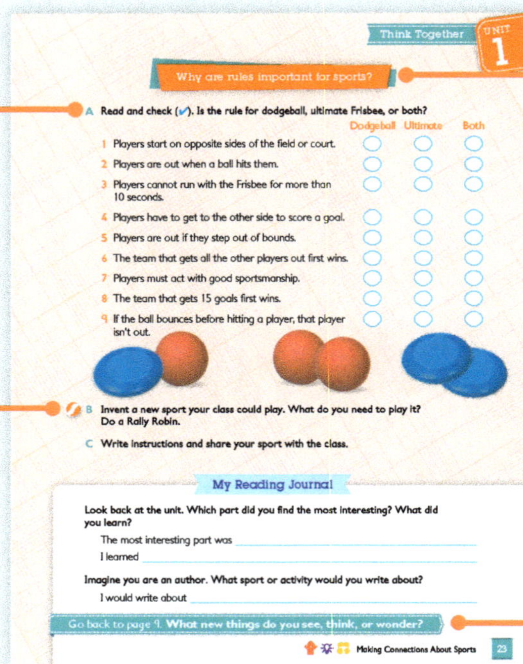

Think Together UNIT 1

Why are rules important for sports?

A Read and check (✓). Is the rule for dodgeball, ultimate Frisbee, or both?

	Dodgeball	Ultimate	Both
1 Players start on opposite sides of the field or court.	◯	◯	◯
2 Players are out when a ball hits them.	◯	◯	◯
3 Players cannot run with the Frisbee for more than 10 seconds.	◯	◯	◯
4 Players have to get to the other side to score a goal.	◯	◯	◯
5 Players are out if they step out of bounds.	◯	◯	◯
6 The team that gets all the other players out first wins.	◯	◯	◯
7 Players must act with good sportsmanship.	◯	◯	◯
8 The team that gets 15 goals first wins.	◯	◯	◯
9 If the ball bounces before hitting a player, that player isn't out.	◯	◯	◯

B Invent a new sport your class could play. What do you need to play it? Do a Rally Robin.

C Write instructions and share your sport with the class.

My Reading Journal

Look back at the unit. Which part did you find the most interesting? What did you learn?

The most interesting part was ______

I learned ______

Imagine you are an author. What sport or activity would you write about?

I would write about ______

Go back to page 9. What new things do you see, think, or wonder?

Making Connections About Sports 23

B/C Speaking Routine

These activities are designed to promote discussion with a text-to-world outlook, helping students compare, contrast, and draw conclusions for the key concept question. A cooperative learning routine helps ensure all students participate and creates an opportunity for purposeful communication and collaboration. (See TB p. 20)

My Reading Journal

In the Reading Journal students give a personalized response to the readings and reflect on the unit as a whole. Through this self-reflection, students are empowered to guide their learning and motivated to participate actively in the process.

Finally, students are directed to return to the image at the start of the unit and revisit the VTR with new ideas and ways of thinking. This allows students to revise opinions and ideas and also serves to show students how much they have learned.

Think Together

Lesson Objectives

- to make connections between the readings
- to explore the key concept: Why are rules important for sports?
- to reflect on the unit and provide personal thoughts and opinions

Warm Up

Play *Correct the Teacher* (see TB p. 25). Call out false statements about either of the two readings, e.g. *In ultimate Frisbee, any number of players can play.* (at least seven on each team) *In "You're Out!" Camilo didn't play by the rules.* (Camilo showed good sportsmanship) *In "The Ultimate Game," it says that a group of teachers invented the game.* (A group of students invented it.)

A Read and check (✔). Is the rule for dodgeball, ultimate Frisbee, or both?

- Students will make connections between the readings and the key concept *Why are rules important for sport?*
- Quickly review some of the rules of dodgeball and ultimate Frisbee.
- Give students a few minutes to read the sentences and check the boxes individually. Remind students that they can look back at the two readings if they need to—this is not a memory test. Then check answers as a class.
- Ask *What happens if players don't play by the rules?* and have a Group Time discussion (see TB p. 21). Encourage students to give personal responses about their own experiences. Ask questions to prompt them where necessary, e.g. *How did you feel when that happened?*

Answers
1 Both 2 Dodgeball 3 Ultimate 4 Ultimate
5 Dodgeball 6 Dodgeball 7 Both 8 Ultimate
9 Dodgeball

B Invent a new sport your class could play. What do you need to play it? Do a Rally Robin.

- Tell students they're going to invent a new sport. Ask *What do you need to think about?* Elicit that students need to think about equipment, location, number of players, how to score and win, and so on. Write these ideas on the board. Ask *What things are not allowed? Who will control the game?*
- Give students a couple of minutes to do the Rally Robin (see TB p. 20) to generate ideas. Have them share their sport with a new partner.

C Write instructions and share your sport with the class.

- Tell students that they are now going to write the rules of the game. Give them plenty of time to write the instructions and rules of their new game individually. Fast finishers can draw pictures illustrating different aspects of their sport, e.g. equipment, where to play, uniform, actions required.
- Then have students come to the front and explain (and if they wish, demonstrate) their sport. With large classes, you may need to do the activity in groups or pairs.
- When everyone has shared their ideas, have students vote on the sport they would most like to play.

My Reading Journal

Look back at the unit. Which part did you find the most interesting? What did you learn?

This question focuses on personalization. Ask a student which reading or pages they thought were the most interesting. Then elicit ideas from the class about what they learned during the unit.

Have students complete the sentences. Then encourage students to compare their ideas with a friend.

Example Answer
The most interesting part was the reading about ultimate Frisbee.
I learned how to play the game and I learned the rules.

Imagine you are an author. What sport or activity would you write about?

This question focuses on personalization. Ask a student which sports they would write about and why. Tell students to choose a sport they know about and write it in their books.

Example Answer
I would write about basketball, because I play basketball.

Go back to page 9. What new things do you see, think, or wonder?

Have students look back at the VTR picture on pp. 8–9. If you are using the TTL, project the image onto the board. Ask students how they think the picture connects to the two readings in the unit. Then repeat the See, Think, Wonder routine, asking *What new things do you see, think, or wonder now?* If you recorded students' ideas in Lesson 1, display these. Encourage students to think of new questions and ideas they have now, e.g. *What are the rules of bubble soccer? Is there a referee?*

Cool Down

Have students work in groups of three to write three quiz questions about the unit. The questions can be about the two readings, the VTR picture, or the Literacy Term section. Students can choose to write true or false questions, multiple-choice questions, or challenge questions (e.g. name five rules in dodgeball). Then they get together with another group and quiz the students.

Practice **Resource Bank:** Unit Test
Student's App: Key Concept Practice

UNIT 2

Circles of Life

Unit Overview

Themes

Animals, life cycles, and protecting nature

Life cycles and change

Synopsis

In this unit, students will explore the importance of protecting nature. They will learn about animals and their life cycles. They will discuss how we can help protect animals and plants and how life cycles represent change. Students will plan and prepare a presentation about a problem and solution and write an infographic.

Language Book

Vocabulary

be born, behavior, die, female, food chain, habitat, male, pouch, pregnant, trunk

Pronunciation: sentence stress (weak forms)

p. 64

Explore Language

Present Perfect With *Already, Just*, and *Yet*

p. 65

Global Citizenship

How do humans affect nature?

encourage, endangered, extinct, get rid of, harm, native, pesticide, poison, predator, prey

p. 66

Explore Language

Present Perfect With *For* and *Since*

p. 67

Take the Stage

Presentation: using rhetorical questions to create interest

p. 68

Write About It

An Infographic

Paragraph Building: organizing information

p. 69

Think It Over

Review and Reflection: Looking Back

p. 70

Literacy Book

Think Together
How do life cycles represent change?
p. 77

Visible Thinking
Question Starts
p. 71

Nonfiction
Persuasive text: *Fire Ecology*
Words in Context: *accident, natural disasters, canopy, benefit, deliberately, scavengers, species*
p. 75

Fiction
Fantasy: *Arthur's Adventures*
Words in Context: *shell, protect, shiny, ordinary, sea anemone*
p. 72

Reading Skill
Understanding sequence of events
p. 74

Literary Term
Antonym
p. 73

Language and Literacy Connections

The connecting theme for Unit 2 is the natural world and animal life cycles.

	Language	Literacy
Vocabulary	**Set 1:** animals and their life cycles; **Set 2:** controlling nature	**Fiction:** be born **Nonfiction:** die, prey
Grammar	**Present Perfect With Already, Just, and Yet** Have you seen a baby owl yet? Jon's already seen three! And I haven't seen a hawk catch a mouse yet. That hawk's just stolen my hat! **Present Perfect With For and Since** How long have cane toads lived in Australia? Surprisingly, they've only been there since 1935. It's lived in the forest for a long time.	**Fiction:** You've lived in this tide pool since you were born. You've both grown a lot since we last saw you. **Nonfiction:** It hasn't rained for a long time. These plants have already completed their life cycles.
Skills	**Pronunciation:** sentence stress (weak forms) **Process Writing:** generating ideas	**Reading:** understanding sequence of events **Literary Term:** antonym
International English	behavior/behaviour; Did you see a baby owl yet?/Have you seen a baby owl yet?; I just read it./I've just read it.	

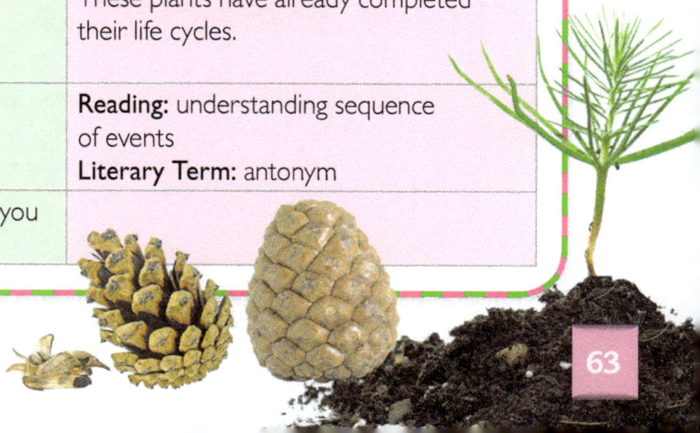

Vocabulary

Lesson Objectives

- to learn vocabulary about animals and their life cycles: *be born, behavior, die, female, food chain, habitat, male, pouch, pregnant, trunk*
- to say a poem about animals and their habitat
- to practice sentence stress: weak forms

Materials

Audio Tracks 15 to 19; Video; pictures of baby animals (WU)

Warm Up

Do a Chalk Talk routine (see TB p. 20) using pictures of animals as prompts. Tell students to write what they know about each animal, including its physical characteristics.

A TRACK 15 TB p. 216 **Listen. Which animal looks after its young longer?**

- Have students explore the picture and say what they see. Encourage students to notice different parts of the picture, including the food chain poster and the door.
- Tell students that they are going to listen to Casey and her friend Faris tell their classmates about some of the animals in the picture. Remind students of the challenge from the end of Unit 1. Ask *What do you think Casey is interested in?*
- Play the audio and have students point to the picture as they listen.
- Ask the gist question *Which animal looks after its young longer?* Explain that we use the word *young* to talk about baby animals in general. Listen again to check answers.

Answer

The elephant looks after its young longer.

B TRACK 16 TB p. 216 **Find and number the words in A. Then listen and check.**

- Have students look at the words. Point out the example (1) Ask *Where is the food chain?* Have students complete the activity in pairs. Listen again to check answers.

Answers

1 *food chain* 2 pouch 3 pregnant 4 be born
5 habitat 6 die 7 trunk 8 behavior 9 female
10 male

International English

Draw students' attention to the two words and elicit which is American English and which is British English. Ask students how the two words differ (spelling).

C TRACK 17 TB p. 216 **Close your eyes. Listen, visualize, and say.**

- Prepare students for the visualization (see Visualization).
- Play the audio, allowing students to visualize the ideas as they listen.
- Have students compare their ideas in groups.

D **Look and write.**

- Use the TTL to look at the example in the table together. Have students find more words in A that we use to talk about animals and their life cycles.
- Have students discuss their ideas in pairs and complete the table in their books, using the pictures. This activity is a categorizing activity. Then check answers as a class.

Answers

Some discussion might be had about *habitat*.
About animals: female, male, pouch, trunk
Life cycle: *be born*, behavior, die, food chain, habitat, pregnant

E TRACK 18 TB p. 217 **Listen and write. Then watch and say.**

- Play the video or audio of the poem. To focus on the pronunciation, use just the audio initially. Ask students to guess which animal they think the poem is about.
- Have students read the poem and complete the blanks. Play the poem video or audio to check answers.
- Ask *Which animal is the poem is about? (kangaroos) Why?* Play the video or audio again and have students join in.

Answers

1 *habitat* 2 born 3 die 4 behavior 5 pouch
6 food chain

F TRACK 19 TB p. 217 **Pronunciation. Listen and say. Copy the weak forms. Find other examples in the poem.**

- Point out that some words in the poem have a stronger stress than others. Have students try saying the phrases. Play the audio and have them listen and repeat, noticing the stressed and weak words.
- Point out the pronunciation of the schwa in the weak form of *of*. Explain that this is because the word isn't stressed.
- Remind students that although these words may have different vowels, the weak form is always pronounced with the schwa. Play the video or audio again for students to listen for more forms and check answers.

Answers

we're born and /ən/ die; our feet are /ə/ big and /ən/ funny; got a /ə/ dingo

Cool Down

Play the *Yes/No Game* (see TB p. 27). Students use words from the lesson to make statements, e.g. *Lions have a pouch.*

Practice **Student's App:** Vocabulary Practice; Spoken Word Video

Explore Language

Lesson Objectives

- to learn how to use the present perfect with *already*, *just*, and *yet*
- to practice vocabulary related to animals and their life cycles

Materials

Audio Tracks 20 and 21

Warm Up

Have a quick discussion about the types of food students eat to personalize the concept of food chains. Have students draw their own simple food chains for their diet. Then have students share their food chains in small groups and notice if anyone's food chain is different and why.

A TRACK 20 TB p. 217 **Listen and read. How many parts are there in the food chain Faris describes?**

- Have students look back at the picture on pp. 22–23 and ask if they can see a door. Then have them look at the picture on p. 24 and notice where the children are. Tell students they are going to listen to Faris from Lesson 1 talking to his friend Carmen about what animals eat. Play the audio while students follow the dialogue in their books.
- Ask the gist question *How many parts are there in the food chain Faris describes?* and elicit the answer. Listen again and check. Ask further comprehension questions (see **ETB**).

Answers

Four parts: the grass grows; an insect like a grasshopper eats the grass; a mouse eats the grasshopper; a hawk eats the mouse

International English

Draw students' attention to the International English feature. Have them look at the sentences and elicit the differences. Remind students that the past perfect is generally used in British English, but in American English, the simple past is usually used instead.

B Look at A. Complete the table. Which word comes at the end of the question?

- Display the table using the TTL. Look at the first sentence together. Tell students that the sentences are all in dialogue in A and ask them to complete the table . Students can work individually or in pairs.
- Check answers together. Review how to form the present perfect by conjugating the verb *have* on the board and eliciting the past participles from the table. Have students notice the position of the adverbs. Then ask *Which word comes at the end of the question?* and elicit the answer.
- Draw students' attention to the Grammar tip *Remember.* Ask *Why can't we use "already" here?* Elicit that the sentence is negative. In C, students will think more about the meaning of each adverb and when we use them.

Answers

seen; 's just; haven't, yet; Have, yet; haven't
The word *yet* comes at the end of the question.

C Think and discuss. Then choose.

- Look at the first sentence together. Ask *When did Jon see three baby owls?* Elicit that we don't know exactly when. Refer students to the statement and elicit the correct option.
- Have students work in pairs to discuss the remaining sentences. Refer them to the table in B for examples of sentences with the adverbs. Then check answers.

Answers

1 any time 2 already; just 3 negative

D TRACK 21 TB p. 217 **Listen and say.**

- Play the audio, having students repeat each sentence chorally.
- For ideas on how to vary the drill, see TB p. 23.

E Put the words in order.

- This activity provides controlled practice of the verb forms and adverbs. Look at the example together. Have students identify the adverb (*yet*) and say where in the sentence it goes (*yet* usually goes at the end of a sentence or clause).
- Have students complete the sentences individually. Remind them to look at the table in B to help them. Check answers as a class.

Answers

1 *Have the babies been born yet?* 2 We've just come back from the bird sanctuary. 3 My dad's already fed the fish. 4 I haven't read this book about owls yet.
5 The female lion's just caught the giraffe!
6 Why haven't you finished your homework yet?

F Play a chain game. Ask and answer with your friends about things you have and haven't done.

- This activity provides freer practice of the grammar. Ask *What things do you usually do?* Elicit verbs from the class and write them on the board. Then elicit the question form in present perfect using one of the verbs and ask a student, e.g. *Have you done your homework yet?* Elicit an answer and write it on the board.
- Have everyone sit in a circle. Have three students demonstrate using the examples on the page. Then play as a class or in smaller groups.

Answers

Students' own answers

Cool Down

Play *Pass the Whisper* (see TB p. 26). Have one student choose a sentence or question in the present perfect.

Practice **Resource Bank:** Grammar Printout
Student's App: Grammar Practice

Global Citizenship

Lesson Objectives

- to learn vocabulary related to controlling nature: *encourage, endangered, extinct, get rid of, harm, native, pesticide, poison, predator, prey*
- to explore how humans affect nature and how humans can protect nature
- to practice listening for gist and detail

Materials
Audio Tracks 22 and 24; Audio Track B

Opening Question

Ask the opening question: *How do humans affect nature?* Elicit ideas and encourage students to think about different aspects of nature (wildlife, plants, trees, the ocean, etc.) and how people might affect it. Record students' ideas in some way, e.g. in a spidergram, to come back to at the end of the lesson.

A TRACK 22 TB p. 217 **Listen to Iván and his dad talk about a problem in their garden. What solution do they decide on?**

- Tell students they are going to listen to a boy and his dad talking about mosquitoes. Ask students *Have you been bitten by a mosquito?* Ask *What kinds of places do mosquitoes live in? Would you be happy if there were no mosquitoes?* Encourage a class discussion.
- Ask the gist question *What solution do they decide on?* and play the audio. Check the answer with the class. Ask students what is the problem with pesticides, and if they agreed with Dad and Iván's final decision.

Answer
They decide to use natural predators to control the mosquitoes in their garden.

B TRACK 23 TB p. 217 **Look at the pictures and definition in A and write. Then listen and check.**

- Point out the example answer for number 1, *pesticide*. Refer students to the vocabulary box in B and have them write the words for each picture and definition in A.
- Play the audio to check answers and drill pronunciation.

Answers
1 *pesticide* 2 encourage 3 extinct 4 poison
5 harm 6 native 7 endangered 8 get rid of
9 prey 10 predator

TRACK B TB p. 217 **Visualization**

- The TTL has a visualization audio track for this vocabulary set. (See TB p. 21.)

C **Read and complete the paragraph.**

- Have students read the paragraph. Ask *What is the purpose of the text?* (to make us think about how we can protect nature).
- Look at the example together. Ask *What do pesticides do?* (kill insects and plants) Remind students to look at the words before and after each blank to help them decide what kind of word is missing.
- Have students complete the sentences, then check answers together.

Answers
1 *pesticides* 2 get rid of 3 harm 4 endangered
5 extinct 6 encourage

D TRACK 24 TB p. 217 **Now listen to a science program. What do humans do that affects animal habitats?**

- Have students look at the two pictures and say what they see.
- Ask the gist question *What do humans do that affects animal habitats?* Play the audio, then check the answer with the class.
- Ask students if they can think of any other ways that humans affect animal habitats that weren't mentioned in the audio and brainstorm ideas.

Answer
Humans cut down forests; use fossil fuels that cause temperatures to rise; put trash in rivers and poison the plants.

E **Listen again. Write *True*, *False*, or *Doesn't Say*.**

- Have students read the sentences before they listen again to see what they remember. Point out that there is a third option, *Doesn't Say*, for information that doesn't appear in the listening.
- Play the audio and have students complete the activity. Check answers as a class, encouraging students to explain their answers. Have students discuss the different ways humans affect nature that appear in the science program.

Answers
1 *False* 2 False 3 True 4 Doesn't Say 5 True
6 Doesn't Say

Discussion Questions

- Have students discuss each question in pairs or small groups (see **ETB**). Guide students to conclude that even small actions can help. Elicit ideas of what students can do themselves. Focus on the concept of conservation for both plants and animals, encouraging students to recognize the lasting effects of their actions.
- Return to the opening question: *How do humans affect nature?* Revisit any ideas from the beginning of the lesson and encourage students to share any new ideas.

Cool Down

Play the *Yes/No Game* (TB p. 27) by calling out statements using the vocabulary, e.g. *We should encourage people to stop using plastic.*

Practice **Student's App:** Vocabulary Practice; Listening Practice

Explore Language

Lesson Objectives

- to learn how to use the present perfect with *for* and *since*
- to practice using vocabulary related to controlling nature

Materials

Audio Tracks 25 and 26

Warm Up

Write *Toads are …* on the board. Put students in pairs and give them one minute to finish the sentence in as many different ways as they can.

A TRACK 25 TB p. 217 **Listen to Susie and Carmen and read. What effect have people had on these toads and frogs?**

- Tell students that they are going to listen to Susie and Carmen reading an online article. Ask *What do you think they will learn?* Play the audio and have students follow the text. (Note: The beginning and end of the conversation are not on the page.)
- Ask the gist question *What effect have people had on these toads and frogs?* and elicit the answer. Play the audio again for students to check. Ask students *Why are the toads a problem?*

Answers

People introduced the cane toad to Australia; the toads are dangerous to humans and other animals; the government can't control them.
The yellow-black rain frog is endangered because humans are cutting down the forests where they live.

B **Look at A. Complete the table. Which question words do we use?**

- Display the table using the TTL. Have students find the missing words in A and complete the table individually or in pairs.
- Check answers. Have students notice the position of *for* and *since*. Ask *What comes after "for" and "since"?* Elicit that both *1935* and *many years* refer to time. Then ask the question *Which question word do we use?* and elicit the answer. Point out that we use *for* and *since* to answer a question with *How long?*

Answers

have, lived; been, since; has, for
We use *How long …?*

- Draw students' attention to the Grammar tip *Watch Out*. Have students notice the use of the simple past in the second part of the sentence and elicit its uses.

C **Think and discuss. Then choose.**

- Ask students how long different activities are, e.g. a soccer game (90 minutes) or their journey to school. Then ask them *How long have you lived in your house?* Give your own response, e.g. *I've lived there for five years / since 2014.*
- Have students work in pairs to discuss the sentences. Refer them to the article in A for examples. Then check answers.

Answers

1 for 2 since

D TRACK 26 TB p. 218 **Listen and say.**

- Play the audio, having students repeat each sentence chorally. Encourage them to copy the linking and intonation.
- For ideas on how to vary the drill, see TB p. 23.

E **Write full sentences and questions with *for* or *since*.**

- This activity provides controlled practice of the verb forms with *for* or *since*. Elicit that the verbs in the prompts are infinitives and that students need to use the present perfect with *for* or *since* for each question. Ask *Is "a long time" the duration or when it started?* Then ask *How do you know if you should use "for" or "since"?* Remind students that if the time phrase is a date or year, we usually use *since* because it tells us when the action started.
- Have students do the activity individually and then check answers.

Answers

1 *Native predators have hunted here for a long time.*
2 Dinosaurs have been extinct for millions of years.
3 How long have you lived here? Since last year.
4 These pesticides have harmed animals since 2014.
5 How long has she played the guitar? For six months.
6 I haven't visited the USA since 2015.

F **Play *True or False*. Write a list of activities. Then trade lists and ask and answer.**

- Tell students to write ten activities they do in their notebooks and then trade lists with a friend.
- For this freer oral practice, students ask and answer questions about the activities on their lists. Have two students read the examples on the page. Then have students play in groups. Have students count the number of times they guess true or false correctly, to see who knows their friend best.

Answers

Students' own answers

Cool Down

Play *Stand Up, Sit Down* (see TB p. 26). Call out statements using the present perfect with *for* or *since*, e.g. *You've studied English for five years.*

Practice **Resource Bank:** Grammar Printout
Student's App: Grammar Practice

Write About It

Lesson Objectives

- to plan and make an infographic
- to learn how give facts, reasons and details
- to learn about conjunctions
- to learn to generate ideas to help your writing

Materials
Support printout from the Resource Bank (F)

Warm Up

Ask students what they remember about food chains. Do a Think, Pair, Share routine (see TB p. 20) to give students time to think. Elicit some examples of food chains from the class.

A Read the infographic about an imaginary food chain. Which animal is the prey of two predators?

This text type is also modeled in the Literacy Book for this unit, Fire Ecology.

- With books closed, display the infographic using the TTL. Then have students tell a friend what they noticed.
- Have students open their books and read the infographic. Make sure students realize that the place and animals are not real but invented. Ask the comprehension question *Which animal is the prey of two predators?* and elicit the answer. Ask students how they found this information.

Answer
The bliefan is the prey of two predators.

B Look at the structure of the infographic. Read and answer.

- Using the TTL, display pp. 30–31. Go through the questions and quickly have students point out the features in the infographic.
- Then have students answer the questions individually. Check answers as a class, encouraging students to justify their answers.

Answers
1 The arrows show which plants and animals are prey or which are predators. 2 It gives information about the animals' habitats and how some of them hunt their prey. 3 To make it easy and enjoyable for readers to find information 4 Two 5 It makes it easier for the reader to understand.

C Look at the language in the infographic. Read and respond.

- Review conjunctions and elicit that we use conjunctions to link or connect ideas. Explain that different conjunctions are used to add more information, to give reasons, or to show the difference between two opposite ideas.
- Have students scan the infographic for the conjunctions and circle them as they find them and answer question 1.
- Have students work in pairs to discuss and answer question 2.

Answers
1 The writer doesn't use the conjunctions *when, that,* and *where.*
2 **a** although **b** so **c** because

- Draw students' attention to the callout. Tell students that we can understand information better if we have an explanation or more details about it.

D Think and discuss. Research or invent some plants and animals for a food chain. Use a Generating Ideas technique.

- Tell students they are going to create their own infographic. Review ways to generate ideas in **Process Writing Step 1: Generating Ideas** on p. 140.
- Tell students to choose a way of generating ideas to think of at least four new plants or animals of their own, using their imaginations, and their knowledge of plants and animals. Ask *Are your new animals are herbivores, carnivores, or omnivores? What is your new species called?.*

Answers
Students' own answers

E Plan your food chain. Use your notes in D, decide on the order, and what information you want to highlight.

- Tell students to think about how the plants and animals they have invented fit together to make a food chain. Have them notice that other food chains they've studied start with a plant and end with a carnivore, and that the animals usually increase in size.
- Have students organize their ideas from D to make a food chain and write the sequence in their books.

Answers
Students' own answers

F Now write and illustrate your infographic.

- Discuss what makes an infographic attractive and easy to follow, such as the title, font size and color, text boxes, and images. Remind students to think about how to fit all their content on the page. They will need up to six main sections, the introduction and space for arrows.
- Students may complete their infographics in their notebooks or using the Support printouts from the Resource Bank.
- Have students give each other feedback.

Answers
Students' own answers

Cool Down

Have some students write the name of one of their new plants or animals on the board and draw a simple picture. Then have students vote on the most imaginative species. They can't choose their own!

Practice **Student's App:** Writing Practice
Resource Bank: Writing Game, *Truth or Lie?*

Take the Stage

Lesson Objectives

- to prepare and give a presentation explaining a problem and solution
- to learn how to use rhetorical questions to create interest

Materials
Video

Warm Up

Ask students what they know about bees. Elicit ideas from the class and write them on the board. Then do a Question Starts routine to help students come up with some questions on the topic (see TB p. 20).

A TB p. 239 **Watch and listen. What could you do to help bees?**

- Tell students they are going to watch a video of two girls giving a presentation about bees.
- Ask students what problems bees might have and elicit ideas. Then ask the question *What could you do to help bees?* Elicit a few suggestions from the class and write them on the board. Tell students not to worry if they don't know, as they will find out in the video.
- Play the video once and have students listen to see if their ideas are mentioned.
- Play the video again and have students listen for the different things that people can do to help bees. Check answers as a class.

Suggested Answers
Write to food producers to ask them to stop using pesticides; make yards more bee-friendly; become a beekeeper; plant flowers that bees like.

B **Watch again. Check (✔) the questions Linda and Maria use in their presentation. Who answers these questions?**

- Have students read the questions before they rewatch the video and see how much they remember. They should check the boxes of the questions that they think are included in the video.
- Play the video once and have students check their answers. Then play the video again and tell students to pay attention to who *answers* the questions (the same person who asks the question).
- Ask *Do Linda and Maria know the answers to the questions?* (yes) Explain that these are called rhetorical questions and sometimes we include them to help us organize our ideas in a presentation or in some types of writing, e.g. articles. Questions are similar to headings. They also make the listener curious and want to know more.

Answers
1 Maria 3 Linda 6 Maria

C **Prepare a presentation with a friend called *The Empty Sea*. Think and plan.**

- Tell students they are going to plan a presentation about problems and solutions. Have students look at the title for their presentation and guess what the topic might be. Have them look at the newspaper, book, and notepad to help them.
- Give students time to read the information. Ask *What's the problem?* (There aren't enough fish.) *Why?* (because the seas are getting warmer, so fish and birds are moving to other places) *Where can we find out what we can do?* (in the notepad)
- Tell students to work in pairs to plan their presentations, choosing three questions from B and adapting them to suit their topic, e.g. *Why do we need fish? What can we do to stop fish from disappearing?* Students should make sure they answer their questions in their plan.

Answers
Students' own answers

D **Practice with your friends using phrases in B. Then share with the class. Make notes.**

- Remind students that it is very important to listen carefully when someone is giving a presentation. Taking notes while you listen can help you focus on the information and how the speaker presents it. Tell students that they are going to listen to their classmates and think about their presentations.
- Discuss with the class what makes a good presentation. Write the following two headings on the board: *Content* and *Delivery*. Then write the following questions in each section:

  Content: e.g. *Are questions used to structure the presentation? Is the information clear and interesting?*

  Delivery: e.g. *Is the presentation split clearly between the two speakers? Do both speakers maintain eye contact / speak clearly?*
- Have students practice their presentations in small groups first. Then have a few pairs perform their presentations for the class. The rest of the class listens and makes notes using the questions on the board to help.
- Have students analyze their own performances and encourage students to make positive comments about each other's presentations.

Answers
Students' own answers

Cool Down

Play *Just a Minute* (see TB p. 26). For this unit, topics could be bees, fish, rain frogs, polar bears, rainforests, and mosquitoes.

Practice **Student's App:** Speaking Skills Practice; Speaking Video

Think It Over

Lesson Objectives

- to review what has been learned in the unit
- to reflect on the unit and their own progress
- to think about learning strategies and how to continue learning at home

Warm Up

Do a quick quiz with the class about Unit 2. Ask questions about pictures, words, or information and have students find the answers in their books. Have students play in teams. Possible questions: *How many children are there in the museum on p. 22? What animal is in the rap? What did the hawk steal? What's the word for picture 6 on p. 26? What's the Grammar tip on p. 29? Name one invented plant or animal from the infographic.*

How well did you meet the challenge of Unit 2? Read and respond.

Students are going to review what they did in the unit. Allowing students to make a personal response and to reflect on their own learning will help them retain knowledge and engage with the learning points.

Looking Back

- Give students time to think about and discuss activities in the unit before they complete each section of the graphic organizer. *Looking Back* encourages students to remember enjoyable moments in the unit. By sharing ideas with friends, they will remember more activities and things they learned, and they may also be encouraged to go back and review things they had forgotten.
- Tell students they are going to review what they learned in the unit and also think about their own learning. Let them know that it's important that they think about themselves and not worry about what other people think or say, as different students will remember or enjoy different things. Remind students that reflecting on what they've learned and what they enjoyed or found difficult can help them think about what to focus on next time.
- Have students do a Chalk Talk routine (TB p. 20) to recap as many things that they have done during the unit as possible. Elicit categories from the class, e.g. words; grammar; presentation phrases; things I learned about infographics; things I learned about the natural world; facts; interesting ideas. Write each one in the middle of a large sheet of paper. Give students a couple of minutes to do each stage of the Chalk Talk routine.
- When students have finished adding ideas to the Chalk Talk posters, have them stick the posters on the wall for reference. Then refer students to the graphic organizer in the book and the prompt sentences: *My favorite activity was …, One thing I learned is …, I'll never forget when …, The funniest moment this month was when …* Have students talk in pairs about the different sections. Remind students to give reasons for their answers by explaining why they have chosen these things. Ask students what they particularly remember from the unit. Making connections between the material, activities, and personal emotions can help students remember what they have learned.
- If students find it difficult to think of anything funny, suggest one or two moments that you think students may have found amusing, e.g. the kangaroo in the poem video on p. 23; the part of the story on p. 24, where the hawk steals Faris' hat; or the invented plants and animals from the writing lesson. You could also encourage students to remember any funny moments that happened in class that are not related to the activities on the page. There may have been a game where students had fun and laughed, e.g. during a miming game.
- When you feel they have enough ideas, have students work individually to fill in the organizer. Remind them that they should write their own responses about themselves. Monitor to help as necessary. Look at what the students are writing so you can tailor your classes and any additional practice to their needs.
- If you feel it is appropriate for your class, have students share their ideas with a friend.

Looking Forward

Draw students' attention to the character at the bottom of the page. Elicit who it is and what they remember about her. (Susie appeared in Lesson 4, p. 28.) Ask *What was Susie reading about?* (rain frogs) Have students read the speech bubble and make predictions about what Susie is good at. Tell them that they will find out in the first lesson of Unit 3.

Put It Together

To further review and recycle the language in Units 1 and 2, play the game *I've just …* on pp. 34–35. See TB p. 206 for teaching notes.

Practice **Resource Bank:** Unit Test
Student's App: Vocabulary and Grammar Review

Get Ready to Read

Lesson Objectives

- to activate prior knowledge about animal life cycles
- to guide inquiry and deepen understanding through a Question Starts VTR
- to preview the reading skill of understanding the sequence of events

Materials

VTR printout from the Resource Bank (A, B, C)

Warm Up

Ask students if they know any animals that change as they grow older. Elicit examples and have students say how they change, e.g. snakes shed their skin, young lions grow manes, tadpoles turn into frogs.

Question Starts

A Look at the picture. Then brainstorm questions. Write a list.

- This VTR encourages students to look at the picture of the different stages of the life of a caterpillar and think of questions they would like to ask about it. Start by having students look at the picture for one minute and say what they see.
- Draw students' attention to the question words. Ask *What questions do you have about the picture?* Give students a few minutes to think of and write questions in their notebooks. Students can do this individually or in pairs. The objective of the activity is to practice developing good questions and to provoke thinking and deep inquiry.
- Elicit questions from the class and write them on the board. Record the students' ideas from the VTR to revisit in the Think Together lesson.

Here's an example of this part of the routine.

Teacher: What questions do you have about the picture?
Student A: How many days old is each chrysalis?
Teacher: What an interesting question! Do you have any other questions?
Student B: What will it look like after?
Student C: Why is this (one) yellow and that (one) green?

B Look at your list from A. Which questions seem most interesting? Discuss them with the class.

- Ask students to look at their list of questions and to choose those they most want to know the answers to.
- Tell students that they are going to practice negotiation skills by working as a group to decide which three questions they want to ask. Have students work in groups of three to review the questions and discuss possible answers. This will help them decide which questions they think are the most interesting. Have students write the questions in their books.

C What new ideas or questions do you have now? Talk about your ideas with your partner.

- Encourage students to use the picture to ask questions about life cycles in general. They shouldn't limit their ideas to what they see in the picture. Give students one to three minutes to talk about their ideas in groups. Then elicit some ideas.
- Allow students to ask as many questions as they want to and express their ideas. Students can be as imaginative and creative as they like. Encourage students to discuss together, not just with you.

Transition

Have students think about the different stages of the caterpillar before it pupates and after it emerges from its chrysalis. Elicit that a caterpillar starts as an egg and ask students *What other animals lay eggs?* Write the students' suggestions in two groups: terrestrial and aquatic.

D Think and discuss. Choose a living thing. What are the different stages in its life cycle?

- Have students work in pairs to choose an animal or living thing. They should then think about the life cycle of that animal or living thing, from its birth to its death. Remind students to think about any physical changes that may occur during the life of their living thing and to think about how it reproduces (e.g. by laying eggs, giving birth, pollination). Don't require too many details, as they will learn more about life cycles during the unit.
- Have students share their ideas with the class.

Answers

Students' own answers

E *Arthur's Adventures* is about a young hermit crab named Arthur. Put the events in order.

- This activity previews the skill of understanding the sequence of events.
- Ask *What's the title of the story?* (*Arthur's Adventures*) Who's the main character? (Arthur) *What do we know about Arthur?* (He is a hermit crab; he is young.)
- Have students read the four sentences about the story. Have students find the first sentence. Elicit how they know it is the first sentence (because it starts with *First*). Remind students that time expressions like *first* help us understand the order of events. Have students number the four sentences. Then check answers as a class.

Answers

3, 1, 4, 2

Now read **Arthur's Adventures**

Fiction: *Arthur's Adventures—Fantasy*

Lesson Objectives

- to read a fantasy story about the adventures of a young hermit crab
- to make a personal connection to the reading

Materials

Audio Tracks 8 and 9; pictures of animals that have shells, e.g. a snail or turtle (WU)

Warm Up

Show students pictures of a snail or a turtle. Point to the shell and ask *Why do some animals have shells?* and elicit answers.

TRACK 8 Reading Approach

Engage with the Text

- Using the Story Player TTL, show the opening spread of the story. Ask students who they think this story is about, where it is set, and what type of story it is.
- Play the audio while students follow along in their books. Pause after the second page and ask students to predict what will happen to Arthur.
- Have students read the whole story before looking at the Words in Context.

TRACK 9 TB p. 230 Words in Context

- Draw students' attention to the Words in Context box. Give students a few minutes to find and highlight each instance of each word in the reading.
- Have them identify the type of word by looking at the form and the sentence.
- Write these strategies on the board for students: *using pictures; using prefixes; surrounding words and sentences; positive/negative; world knowledge.*
- Have students work in pairs to discuss the words.

shell / sea anemone (p. 26 / p. 30, nouns) Both words are used in sentences with *are* (verb) following, and both are used with adjectives, which describe nouns (*strong, beautiful, cool*). Strategies to use: pictures, surrounding words (especially the adjectives), world knowledge of creatures in the sea

protect (p. 26, verb) The following sentences include the contrasting adjectives *safe* and *dangerous*. Strategies to use: surrounding words and sentences, world knowledge of things that guard against danger in their own lives (e.g. a bike helmet)

shiny (p. 26 / p. 28, adjective) The sentences show that *shiny* is a positive adjective describing how something looks. Strategies to use: positive/negative, surrounding sentences

ordinary (p. 29, adjective) This is contrasted with *shiny* and has a slightly negative meaning. A synonym from an earlier sentence (p. 28) is *plain*, and the following sentence says *but I also want to look good*. Strategies to use: positive/negative, contrasting ideas, surrounding sentences

- Go through each word to elicit the meaning and how they know. Play the audio to practice pronunciation.

Analyze the Text and Features

- Have students read the text individually. While they read, give them questions to answer: *What decisions does Arthur make? Are they good decisions?*
- Tell students to find the yellow callouts and discuss the questions with a partner.
  - **Critical Thinking** (p. 26): *How should Arthur decide which shell to buy?* Have students think about why hermit crabs need shells and the qualities a shell should have.
  - **Making Connections** (p. 27): *Why do you think the fisherman threw Arthur back into the water?* Ask *What's the fisherman looking for?* (fish, seafood) *What does Arthur look like?* (a shell) Elicit that Arthur's new shell protected him from the fisherman.
  - **Making Connections** (p. 28): *Why is the open sea scary?* Ask students what dangers might there might be and elicit what kinds of predators there are for small animals in the ocean.
  - **Personalization** (p. 31): *Have you ever added things to your clothes to make them more interesting?* Have students discuss the question in pairs.
  - **Text Focus** (p. 30): *The most exciting part of the plot is called the climax.* Read the paragraph at the top of p. 30 again up until the text focus question and ask *Why is this part exciting?* Elicit that Arthur is scared and we don't know what is behind him.

International English

Guide students to notice that the second noun is the same. Tell students that *tide* is the movement of the water. When the tide goes out, it leaves behind smaller pools of water. Ask *Why do you think it is called a "rock pool" in British English?*

Interact with the Text

- Now that students are familiar with the story and characters, have them choose one of the characters, to think about their point of view and feelings in each scene. In pairs, students tell each other what their character is thinking or saying in the scenes in which they appear.

Cool Down

Have students do *30-Second Speeches* about the reading in pairs. They each have 30 seconds to tell their partner as much as they can about one of the readings.

Practice **Student's App:** Story Player

Explore the Reading

Lesson Objectives

- to understand and analyze *Arthur's Adventures* through reading comprehension activities
- to explore the SEL competency of self-awareness by possessing self-efficacy and self-esteem
- to make a personal connection to the reading

Warm Up

Using the TTL or your book, show students a page from the story and tell them to write down the first three words that come to their minds. Repeat with other pages from the story. Then have students compare their words with a friend. Which words are the same?

A Read and answer.

- Refer back to *Arthur's Adventures*. Ask questions to help students remember the story, characters, and main events. Students can look back at the reading in their books if they need to.
- Draw the students' attention to the questions and do the first one together. Encourage students to refer to the reading for support. They should write their answers as full sentences.
- Have students do the rest of the activity individually and then compare with a friend. Check answers as a class.

Answers

1 Arthur was born in a tide pool. 2 No, Arthur's dad didn't like the shiny shell because it was weak. 3 Arthur broke his first shell on a rock. 4 Conrad gave his old shell to Arthur. 5 Deka was watching Arthur. 6 They both put sea anemones on their shells.

B Think and write. At the end of the story, how is Arthur different than he was at the beginning? Write three examples.

This activity practices the critical thinking skills of analysis and evaluation by having students think about how Arthur changes through the story.

- Ask *What was Arthur like at the beginning of the story?* Elicit a few ideas from the class. Then ask *What was Arthur like at the end?* Put students in pairs and have them make two lists in their notebooks: *Beginning* and *End*. Encourage them to think not only about Arthur's physical appearance but also about his mental state and how his experiences shape those changes. They can look back through the reading to help them.
- Then have students write three ideas in their books, in full sentences.
- Elicit answers from a few students and write them on the board.

Suggested Answers

Arthur is bigger than he was at the beginning.
At the beginning, Arthur chooses a shell that looks good but isn't very strong. At the end, he finds a shell that protects him and looks good.
Arthur understands that protection is more important than looking good.

C Think and discuss. How does Arthur feel in his different shells? Why? How do different clothes and hairstyles make you feel?

- This activity explores the SEL competency of self-esteem by helping students make connections between Arthur's struggles for self-identity and their own feelings about their appearance.
- Write the questions on large sheets of paper and do a version of a Chalk Talk routine (see TB p. 20). In this version, there are only two questions, so it is not necessary to rotate the papers. Give them one question to answer first. After a few minutes, give them the second.
- Have students compare and discuss their ideas in their groups. Finally, ask some students to share their ideas with the class, encouraging them to give personal examples of what makes them feel good.

Answers

Students' own answers

Literary Term: Antonym

Write the antonyms. Now find three pairs of antonyms in the reading.

- Draw students' attention to the explanation of *antonym*. Elicit some opposites from the class and write on the board. Common examples are *hot/cold*, *big/small*, and *good/bad*.
- Look at the words in the colored lozenges together with the class and check understanding of the adjectives.
- Have students do the activity individually. Then check answers as a class. Have two students demonstrate each opposite by acting out a situation, e.g. *strong/weak*—one student mimes carrying a very heavy box, and the other pretends he/she can't pick it up.
- Have students find more examples of antonym pairs in the reading. Check answers as a class.

Answers

1 short 2 difficult 3 strong 4 young
5 dangerous 6 bored
Words and their antonyms in the reading: strong/weak, bigger/smaller, ordinary/fancy

Cool Down

As an exit pass, students have to write a sentence using two antonyms, e.g. *The test was very difficult, but I studied a lot so it was easy.*

Practice
Resource Bank: Literary Term Printout
Student's App: Reading Practice; Literary Term Practice

Get Ready to Read

Lesson Objectives

- to activate prior knowledge about forest fires
- to practice the reading skill of understanding the sequence of events

Warm Up

To introduce the reading skill of understanding the sequence of events, play a version of *Backs to the Board* (see TB p. 25). Display one of the following actions: make a sandwich, have a shower, make a sandcastle. The class describes the different stages involved in the process, e.g. *First, put two pieces of bread on a plate. Then spread butter on the bread. Put some cheese on one piece of bread. Put the other piece of bread on top.* The student at the front follows the instructions and guesses what the action is, e.g. *make a sandwich.*

A Think, write, and discuss. Look back at *Arthur's Adventures*. Write the events in the story map. Then retell the story using the transition words.

- With books closed, brainstorm key words from *Arthur's Adventures* with the class and write them on the board. Then elicit what happens in the story, inviting several students to tell part of the story.
- Display or copy the story map onto the board. Point out that a story map helps us put the story events in order. Ask *What happened in the beginning?* Elicit answers from the class, then complete the first section as an example.
- Tell students to look back at the reading to find the four main events in the story and write them in the story map. Draw the students' attention to the transition words: *In the beginning, Next, Then, Last.* Then have students retell the story in their own words using these or other transition words.
- Have students look at the reading skill box. Then ask questions to check comprehension, e.g. *What does the sequence of events tell us?* (when and in what order things happened; how much time has passed between each event) *How does this help us?* (We can remember the story more easily.)

Suggested Answers

In the beginning, Arthur is a young crab in a tide pool. He chooses his first shell with his dad.
Next, Arthur breaks his shell and meets Conrad, another crab, who helps him.
Then, Conrad and Arthur grow bigger together and they change their shells.
Last, Arthur chooses a good, strong shell and swims back to his parents' tide pool with his sister.

B Look at the diagram. Read and sequence the events.

- Draw the students' attention to the diagram. Ask students what they think each stage illustrates. Provide any useful vocabulary, e.g. lightning, fire, sunlight, seedling.
- Then have students read the sentences and decide which picture illustrates each one. Check answers as a class, having students read the sentences in order.
- You or the students may point out that the sequence is actually a cycle, which starts again as soon as it finishes.

Answers

4, 3, 2, 1

C Think and write. What do you know about forest fires? What do you want to know about them?

- This activity activates schema about the topic of the reading and generates interest.
- Ask *What is a forest fire?* and elicit ideas. Don't correct or give much feedback at this stage, as students will learn more about the topic in the next lesson.
- Give students two to three minutes to think about what they know about forest fires, either from reading or about their country. Ask students if forest fires are common where they live and encourage them to say if they have heard of one recently. Students can write notes about their ideas in their books. Then have groups share their ideas with the class. Set up a class KWL chart for this activity. A KWL chart has three columns: *Know, Want to Know,* and *Learn.*
- Have each student add their thoughts to the K and W columns in the KWL chart.

Answers

Students' own answers

Now read **Fire Ecology**

Nonfiction: *Fire Ecology*—Persuasive Text

Lesson Objectives

- to read a persuasive text about fire ecology
- to make a personal connection to the reading

Materials

Audio Tracks 10 and 11; picture of a forest fire (WU)

Warm Up

Show students a picture of a forest fire, like the one on p. 35. Ask students if they have ever seen news about forest fires in their country on TV. Have students predict three possible consequences of forest fires. Have students discuss their ideas in pairs and write them in their notebooks.

TRACK 10 TB p. 230 Reading Approach

Engage with the Text

- Using the Story Player in the TTL, project the opening spread of the reading Ask students what they notice first. Have them look at the infographic and other pictures and make predictions about the reading. Then have them read the title. Explain that *ecology* refers to the relationship between living things and their surroundings, so *fire ecology* explores how a fire can affect the life of the plants and animals that live in its environment.
- Play the audio and have students follow along in their books. Pause the audio to ask prediction questions, e.g. *How do you think forest fires start? What do you think happens to the animals?*

TRACK 11 TB p. 231 Words in Context

- After the first reading of the text, draw students' attention to the Words in Context box.
- Give students a few minutes to find and highlight each instance of each word in the reading. Then have them identify the type of word by looking at the form and the sentence.
- Write these strategies on the board: *pictures; surrounding words and sentences; positive/negative; contrasting ideas; world knowledge.*
- Have students work in pairs to discuss the words. Then elicit which strategies they didn't use (positive/negative).

accident (p. 34, noun) The surrounding clauses provide supporting explanation (they don't know what they did) and a contrasting idea introduced with the conjunction *but* (it's done on purpose). Strategies to use: surrounding words and sentences, contrasting ideas

natural disasters (p. 34 / p. 37, noun) Looking at the individual words in this open compound noun helps figure out its meaning, as well as referring to the pictures. Strategies to use: word building, world knowledge, using pictures

canopy (p. 34 / p. 35, noun) The preceding part of the sentence of the first occurrence of this word (leaves and branches) give us its meaning. Pictures will also provide guideance. Strategies to use: surrounding words and sentences, using pictures

benefit (p. 36, verb) The following sentence gives positive outcomes for the animals that survive. Strategy to use: surrounding words and sentences

deliberately (p. 36, adverb) The adverb *even* tells us that the action is surprising. The previous sentences in the paragraph explain why a forest fire can be a good thing for some birds looking for food. This word can be contrasted with *accident* from p. 34 and connected to the synonym *on purpose* in that same sentence. Strategies to use: surrounding words and sentences, contrasting ideas

scavengers (p. 37, noun) The second part of the sentence and the rest of the paragraph explain what scavengers do. Strategy to use: surrounding words and sentences

species (p. 37, noun) The sentence shows that *species* is something that is related to plants and animals, and that there are a lot. Strategies to use: surrounding words and sentences, world knowledge

- Go through each word to elicit the meaning and how they know. Play the audio to practice pronunciation.

Practice **Student's App:** Story Player

Analyze the Text and Features

- Have students read the text individually in their books. Tell them to look at the pictures as they read and see how each picture represents a part of the text.
- Have students find the orange callouts to discuss in pairs. Alternatively, use Group Time to discuss the questions after students have finished reading (see TB p. 21).
  - **Making Connections** (p. 35): *How might humans start a fire by accident?* Elicit suggestions from the class.
  - **Personalization** (p. 37): *How do you feel about forest fires now?* Review the positive and negative effects of forest fires with the class and write them on the board in two lists. Then ask *Do you think forest fires are necessary?*

Interact with the Text

- Have students work in pairs to prepare a presentation about the life cycle of a forest using the infographic to help them. Have pairs present to the class or to smaller groups.

Cool Down

Have students think of three things they remember from the reading and write them on sticky notes. Collect the sticky notes, remove any duplicates, and stick them on a poster on the wall. Students can come back to this in a later lesson to see if they still remember!

Explore the Reading

Lesson Objectives

- to understand and analyze *Fire Ecology* through reading comprehension activities
- to learn about science through CLIL: biology
- to make a personal connection to the reading

Warm Up

Play *Ten Words* (see TB p. 27). Have students write down ten words about the topic of forest fires.

A Think and write five things that happen in a forest fire. Then trade with a partner. Check (✔) Plants or Animals.

- Have students work in pairs to write three questions about the reading, e.g. *What can cause forest fires? How do forest fires help some plants and animals?* Then they trade questions with another pair and answer the questions. Students can look back at the reading in their books if they need to.
- Do the activity orally first. Elicit ideas about the different things that can happen in a forest fire and write them on the board. Try to elicit more than five so students can choose when they do the activity. For each one, ask *Does this affect plants or animals?*
- Have students write their ideas in their books individually. Check answers as a class.

Suggested Answers

Plants: sunlight reaches the ground, trees burn, seeds open, new plants grow
Animals: some try to escape, some die, some scavenge / take advantage of the fire

B Think, discuss, and write. What is the author's opinion of forest fires? How can you tell?

Students are going to make inferences to analyze the text in more detail. This reading skill is taught explicitly in Unit 10.

- Ask *Are forest fires a good thing or a bad thing?* Elicit opinions from the class. Ask *What makes you say that?* to encourage students to justify their answers. Then ask *What is the author's opinion?* Have students look back at the text to find out. Tell them that they don't need to read the whole text again. We can often find the author's opinion at the beginning and end of a text. Draw students' attention to the opening paragraph. Tell students that this paragraph introduces the topic or situation.
- Have students read the second paragraph. Ask *Does the author give an opinion here?* Highlight the sentence *For many years … they are also an important part of the life cycle of a forest.* Elicit that here the author's opinion is that forest fires are an important part of the forest's life cycle. Then tell students to read the last paragraph of the reading. Ask them to underline the words and phrases that help them identify the author's opinion.
- Have students discuss their ideas in pairs and then write them in their books. For the discussion, you could use a Numbered Heads Together routine (see TB p. 20).

Suggested Answers

The author thinks that forest fires are not a negative thing: "they are also an important part of the life cycle of a forest." "It's possible for people to see forest fires more as natural wonders than natural disasters." Forest fires can benefit some plants and animals: "Some plants need fire or smoke to produce young plants." "Fires give predators the chance to hunt insects and small animals that have to leave their hiding places to escape."

C Think and write. What happens to each part of a forest in a fire?

In this activity, students will explain what happens to different parts of a forest during a fire. This draws on the CLIL science area of biology and ecology.

- Have students look at the diagram and remember the different parts of a forest. Tell students to think about the plants and animals that inhabit each part of the forest and how the fire affects them. They can look back at the reading to help them.
- Have students write the explanations in their books individually. Then have them discuss their ideas in pairs or small groups.

Answers

1 Fire burns the dry branches and leaves. 2 Fire gets rid of overgrown plants and fallen leaves. Heat and smoke cause seed pods to open. 3 Burned plants feed the soil. Sunlight can reach the forest floor.

Cool Down

Play *Word Tennis* (see TB p. 27). Start each round with words related to the reading, e.g. *forest, fire, predators.*

Practice **Student's App:** Reading Practice

Think Together

Lesson Objectives

- to make connections between the readings
- to explore the key concept: How do life cycles represent change?
- to reflect on the unit and provide personal thoughts and opinions

Warm Up

Play *Odd One Out* (see TB p. 26). Write some of the words that appear in either reading, e.g. *canopy, leaves, shell, trunk*.

A Compare and contrast the life cycles in *Arthur's Adventures* and *Fire Ecology*. Think about the changes for a hermit crab and for a new tree.

- Elicit a brief summary of the two readings. Then ask *What changes happen to Arthur? What changes happen to a tree? How does a tree begin life?* Elicit that a tree starts with a seed.
- This activity requires students to think critically about the two readings. Review how to complete a Venn diagram: on one side they will write about a hermit crab, on the other side about a tree, and in the middle the changes that apply to both a hermit crab and a tree. Students can look back at the two readings to help them complete the diagram. Then check answers.

Suggested Answers

Arthur's Adventures: takes place in the ocean
Both: predators and prey (fish and octopus are predators to crabs; falcons and woodpeckers are predators to insects and small animals); life cycles (life cycle of a hermit crab, lifecycle of the forest); creatures living together in shared habitats
Fire Ecology: how plants grow and change; takes place in the forest

B What other life cycles do you know? How do they show change? Do an Inside-Outside Circle.

- Tell students to think about animals or plants that change during their lives. Elicit a few animals and write their names on the board, e.g. butterflies, frogs, birds, or other animals that lay eggs. Then have each student choose one ready for the Inside-Outside Circle routine.
- Set students up for an Inside-Outside Circle (see TB p. 21). Have students on the outside of the circle ask their partner about the life cycle of their chosen animal. When you think they are ready to move on, use a signal to direct students to rotate and change partners. Remind students to explain the different stages in the life cycle each time. Encourage students to choose a new animal when they change partners.
- Invite some students to share their ideas with the class.

Practice **Resource Bank:** Unit Test
Student's App: Key Concept Practice

C Choose one of the cycles from B. Draw, write, and number. What changes at each stage?

- Tell students they are now going to apply what they have learned about life cycles and write about a life cycle of their choice. It should be one they know if you want to do this activity in class. You could have them research at home beforehand.
- Have students look back at the infographic in *Fire Ecology* and notice how the arrows show the life cycle. Tell students to think about four different changes or stages that occur during their chosen animal or plant's life. They should draw pictures, number each stage, and write what happens.

Answers

Students' own answers

My Reading Journal

What life cycle would you like to learn more about?

This is a personalization question. Ask a student which life cycles he/she is interested in. Elicit ideas about what students learned about life cycles during the unit and any questions they may have.

Have students answer the question for themselves and then discuss with a friend.

Example Answer

I would like to learn more about the life cycle of a spider. I want to know how spiders are born.

Do you like learning about biology? Why or why not?

This is another personalization question. Ask the question and elicit a show of hands. Tell students to think about why they like it (or don't like it) and write this in their books.

Example Answer

I like learning about biology because you learn lots of interesting things about animals.

Go back to page 25. What new questions do you have?

Have students look back at the VTR picture on pp. 24–25. Using the TTL, project the image onto the board. Ask students how they think the picture connects to the two readings in the unit. Then repeat the Question Starts routine. If you recorded students' ideas in Lesson 1, display these. Encourage students to think of new questions and ideas they have now, e.g. *Do all insects have the same life cycle?*

Cool Down

Play *Mime It!* (see TB p. 26). Have students act out the life cycle of an animal or plant.

UNIT 3

Figure It Out

Unit Overview

Themes

Solving and preventing crime

Using clues to solve problems

Synopsis

In this unit, students will explore the concept of crime. They will learn about how to investigate and prevent crime. They will discuss how we can use our powers of observation to help prevent crime and how we use clues to solve problems. Students will plan and prepare a conversation about how engaged they are with their neighborhood and write a crime story.

Language Book

Vocabulary

alibi, clue, commit a crime, criminal, detective, fingerprint, interview, investigate, suspect, suspicious, thief

Pronunciation: word stress: first and second syllable

p. 80

Explore Language

Reported Speech: Statements

p. 81

Global Citizenship

Why is it important to be observant?

guilty, opportunity, prevent, report (v), *risk* (n), *solve, steal, track* (v), *victim, witness* (n)

p. 82

Explore Language

Reported Speech: Requests and Commands

p. 83

Talk About It

Conversation: showing interest and responding to what you hear

p. 84

Write About It

A Crime Story

Paragraph Building: organizing elements in a story

p. 85

Think It Over

Review and Reflection: Two Stars and a Wish

p. 86

Language and Literacy Connections

The connecting theme for Unit 3 is crime and problem solving.

	Language	Literacy
Vocabulary	**Set 1:** investigating crimes **Set 2:** committing and preventing crime	**Nonfiction:** fingerprint, solve, steal/stolen, track **Fiction:** clue, crime, detective, investigate
Grammar	**Reported Speech: Statements** Paco said you were looking for clues. I said he was the thief! Greg said that you spilled yours. The detective said he didn't have an alibi. **Reported Speech: Requests and Commands** She asked Greg to clean it up. She told Greg to take it outside. I told him not to use it until now.	**Fiction:** He told me to apply. My assistant said he would look after the shop.
Skills	**Pronunciation:** word stress: first and second syllable **Process Writing:** planning	**Reading:** drawing conclusions **Literary Term:** closed compound
International English		tire/tyre; GPS/SatNav; sidewalk/pavement

Vocabulary

Lesson Objectives

- to learn vocabulary related to investigating crimes: *alibi, clue, commit a crime, criminal, detective, fingerprint, interview, investigate, suspect, suspicious, thief*
- to say a rap about an ace detective
- to practice word stress: first and second syllable

Materials
Audio Tracks 27 to 31; Video

Warm Up

Ask students *Would you like to be a detective? What do you think makes a good detective?* Elicit ideas.

A TRACK 27 TB p. 218 **Listen. Who does Mrs. Karpov think stole the Zoomboard?**

- Using the TTL, display the picture on the opening spread. Say *Someone has committed a crime.* Have students speculate about what is happening in the picture. Ask them if they can spot any possible clues. Have students discuss ideas in pairs.
- Tell students that they are going to listen to some of the people in the picture talk about a crime. Remind students of the challenge from the end of Unit 2. Encourage them to infer what Susie is good at (looking for clues and solving problems).
- Play the audio and have students look at the picture.
- Ask the comprehension question *Who does Mrs. Karpov think stole the Zoomboard?* Play the audio again and check the answer.

Answer
Greg White

B TRACK 28 TB p. 218 **Find and number the words in A. Then listen and check.**

- Have students look at the list of vocabulary words. Point out the example (1) and have students find *commit a crime* in the picture. Have students complete the activity in pairs.
- Play the audio to check answers.

Answers
1 *commit a crime* 2 thief 3 criminal 4 alibi
5 detective 6 interview 7 suspect 8 investigate
9 fingerprint 10 clue 11 suspicious

C TRACK 29 TB p. 218 **Close your eyes. Listen, visualize, and say.**

- Prepare students for the visualization (see Visualization).
- Play the audio, allowing students to visualize the scenario as they listen. Pause the audio where necessary to give students time to think.

D What's the order of events when the police investigate a crime? Complete the list. Is your order the same as your friend's?

- Display the list using the TTL. Look at the first example together. Tell students to use their critical thinking skills to consider all the different things that happen when a crime has been committed.
- Point out that the word *suspect* is near the end of the list. Ask *How do the police decide who the suspects are?* Elicit that they use different strategies to find out, e.g. by collecting fingerprints or interviewing people.
- Explain that there are no correct answers. Have students complete the activity individually, then compare answers in pairs.

Suggested Answers
1 *commit a crime* 2 thief/criminal 3 detective
4 investigate 5 clue 6 fingerprint 7 interview
8 *suspect* 9 suspicious 10 alibi 11 criminal/thief

E TRACK 30 TB p. 218 **Listen and write. Then watch and say.**

- Play the video or audio of *Ace Detective* and allow students to enjoy the rap. To focus on pronunciation, play the audio track first.
- Give students time to read the lyrics and try to complete the blanks. Play the rap audio and have students check their answers.
- Play the video or audio again and have students join in.

Answers
1 *detective* 2 criminal 3 fingerprint 4 clue
5 investigate 6 interview 7 crime

F TRACK 31 TB p. 218 **Pronunciation. Listen and say. Copy the word stress. Find other examples in the rap.**

- Display the examples from the rap. Ask *How many syllables are there?* (three)
- Have students try saying the words. Then play the audio and have students repeat the words chorally. Then have students take turns saying a word and clapping the syllables in pairs.
- Have students look for further examples of words following the two example stress patterns in the rap. Play the video or audio again and then check answers.

Answers
Like *criminal*: fingerprint, interview
Like *detective*: investigate

Cool Down

Play *Backs to the Board* (see TB p. 25). Choose one of the words from the lesson.

Practice **Student's App:** Vocabulary Practice; Spoken Word Video

Explore Language

Lesson Objectives

- to learn how to use reported speech: statements
- to practice vocabulary related to investigating crimes

Materials
Audio Tracks 32 and 33

Warm Up

Have students discuss the case of the stolen Zoomboard in pairs. Ask *Who was in the lab when the Zoomboard disappeared? What clues can the detectives look for?* Then get feedback from the class.

A TRACK 32 TB p. 218 **Listen and read. Who had coffee last night?**

- Tell students they are going to listen to Susie talking to Mrs. Karpov about what happened last night. Play the audio and have students follow the dialogue in their books.
- Ask the gist question *Who had coffee last night?* and elicit the answer. Play the audio again for students to check. Ask *Did the thief take the Zoomboard out through the window?* (No, the window is too small.) Ask students if they think the coffee is an important clue and encourage them to give reasons for their answers.

Answer
possibly both Mrs. Karpov and Greg White

B Look at A. Complete the table. How do the verbs change when we use reported speech?

- Display the table using the TTL. Have students look at the sentences under *Direct Speech*. Elicit that these are things the characters in the dialogue said. Ask students who might say each sentence.
- Have students look at the sentences under *Reported Speech*. Elicit that these are the same sentences but expressed in a different way. Have students complete the table in pairs, referring to the dialogue in A.
- Check answers as a class. Ask *How do we start the sentences in reported speech?* Elicit that we need a subject (*I / He / The detective*) plus the verb *said*. Ask *How do the verbs change when we use reported speech?* Compare the verb in both sentences, e.g. *He's the thief / He was the thief.* Elicit that verbs in the simple present in direct speech change to the simple past in reported speech.
- Note that the Grammar tip *Look* shows *that* as optional between the two parts of a reported statement.

Answers
Said, didn't; were
Verbs in reported speech go back in time, so simple present verbs in direct speech become simple past in reported speech, present progressive verbs become past progressive, and so on.

Practice **Resource Bank:** Grammar Printout
Student's App: Grammar Practice

C Think and discuss. Then choose.

- Look at the first sentence together. Explain that *quote* means to use the exact words that another person used. Write an example of a quote on the board, in quotation marks.
- Have students work in pairs to discuss the sentences. Refer them to the table in B for examples of direct and reported statements. Encourage them to ask themselves questions to figure out when to use direct/reported speech, e.g. *Which sentences use the same words as the speaker?* This can be done in Language 1 (L1). Then check answers as a class.

Answers
1 direct 2 reported 3 direct

D TRACK 33 TB p. 218 **Listen and say.**

- Play the audio, having students repeat each sentence chorally.
- For ideas on how to vary the drill, see TB p. 23.

E Look and read. Then complete the reported sentences.

- This activity provides controlled practice of reported speech. Look at the example together. Ask *Who said this?* (Susie) Read her sentence in direct speech. Then have students look at the second sentence and notice what is different. Elicit that the verb *has* is now *had*.
- Have students complete the sentences individually. Remind them to look at the table in B to help them. Check answers as a class.

Answers
1 *had* 2 was 3 was interviewing 4 were working
5 didn't have 6 was

F Interview a friend. Then report your findings. How much do you remember?

- Brainstorm a few questions for each topic on the page and write them on the board. In groups of three, students will interview a friend by asking questions. Then they tell the other person in the group what their friend said.
- Look at the example together. Ask *What did Antonella say?* (My name is Antonella Gómez.) Have two students pretend to be Antonella and her friend and do the example. Then have students interview their friend and report their answers.

Answers
Students' own answers

Cool Down

Play *Pass the Whisper* (see TB p. 26). The final student has to say the sentence using reported speech.

Global Citizenship

Lesson Objectives

- to learn vocabulary related to committing and preventing crime: *guilty, opportunity, prevent, report* (v), *risk* (n), *solve, steal, track* (v), *victim,* witness (n)
- to explore the importance of being observant and how people can prevent crimes
- to practice listening for gist and detail

Materials
Audio Tracks 34 to 36; Audio Track C

Opening Question

Ask the opening question: *Why is it important to be observant?* Elicit ideas and encourage students to think about different things we can pay attention to. Write ideas on the board. Tell students that *observant* means looking at things around us and paying attention to detail.

A TRACK 34 TB p. 218 **Listen to Kim and Li Yong talk about a suspected crime. What happened to Kim's cell phone?**

- Ask students what things they have lost or have had stolen. Have a quick discussion with the class.
- Tell students that they are going to listen to a girl named Kim talking about her cell phone with her friend Li Yong. Ask the gist question *What happened to Kim's cell phone?* Play the audio and then check the answer with the class.

Answer
The server put it behind the counter for safety.

B TRACK 35 TB p. 218 **Look at the pictures and definitions in A and write. Then listen and check.**

- Point out the example answer for number 1, *witness*. Ask *What does a witness see?* (a crime) Refer students to the vocabulary box in B and have them write the words for each picture and definition in A in pairs.
- Play the audio for students to check their answers. Use the audio to drill the pronunciation of the words.

Answers
1 *witness* 2 report 3 steal 4 track 5 risk
6 victim 7 prevent 8 solve 9 guilty
10 opportunity

TRACK C TB p. 218 **Visualization**

- **The TTL has a visualization audio track for this vocabulary set. (See TB p. 21.)**

C Read and complete the advice in the blog post. Use the correct form of the words in B.

- Have students read the paragraph. Elicit its purpose (to inform us about how we can stay safe).
- Look at the example together. Explain that the word *no one* tells us that the sentence is about a person.
- Have students complete the sentences. Then check answers as a class.

Answers
1 *victim* 2 risks 3 opportunity 4 report
5 prevent 6 witness 7 solve

D TRACK 36 TB p. 219 **Now listen to police officer Pat Jones talk about a crime prevention program. Has the program worked?**

- Tell students they are going to listen to an interview with a police officer about a program he has set up. Have students look at the pictures and say what kind of program they think it is. Ask *Where do you think the teenagers are? Do they look happy?*
- Listening for gist: ask the gist question *Has the program worked?* and play the audio. Check the answer with the class.

Answer
Yes. Teenagers are having a lot of fun at the youth club, and they don't have time to do anything criminal.

E Listen again. Answer the questions.

- Listening for detail: have students read the questions before they listen again to see what they remember. Play the audio, pausing after each question to give students time to write their answers. Then play the whole audio once more.
- Check answers as a class. Ask students if they think the club is a good idea and why.

Answers
1 *It encourages young people to join after-school youth clubs.*
2 Because there were gangs of young people hanging out.
3 Iceland 4 Two of the following: They are bored. They don't always want to sit at home. They want to be part of a group. 5 Young people have more self-confidence. They plan for the future. They're too busy to commit any crimes. 6 He says they're encouraged to get involved and to spend time with their teenage children.

Discussion Questions

- Draw students' attention to the discussion questions. Have students discuss each question in pairs or small groups (see **ETB**). Guide students to conclude that sometimes a crime can be prevented or solved by simply having people around to notice things like someone acting suspiciously. Ask students if they have a neighborhood watch organization or something similar in their area.
- Return to the opening question to ask again: *Why is it important to be observant?* Revisit any ideas discussed at the beginning of the lesson and encourage students to share any new ideas.

Cool Down

Play *I Spy* (see TB p. 26) to test students' observation skills.

Practice **Student's App:** Vocabulary Practice; Listening Practice

Explore Language

Lesson Objectives

- to learn how to use reported speech: requests and commands
- to practice vocabulary related to committing and preventing crime

Materials
Audio Tracks 37 and 38

Warm Up

Ask students what they remember about the case of the missing Zoomboard. Display the opening spread of the unit (pp. 36–37) and elicit what happened. Ask *Who are the suspects? Who do you think stole the Zoomboard?*

A TRACK 37 TB p. 219 **Listen and read. Who does Susie think stole the Zoomboard?**

- Tell students that they are going to discover what happened to the missing Zoomboard. Ask *Will the crime will be solved?* Play the audio while students follow the dialogue in their books.
- Ask the gist question *Who does Susie think stole the Zoomboard?* and elicit the answer.

Answer
Mrs. Karpov

B **Look at A. Complete the table. What kind of words come after the reporting verb?**

- Display the table using the TTL. Have students find the missing words in A and complete the table.
- Check answers as a class. Have students notice the use of *to* before the main verb. Ask *What kinds of words come after the reporting verb?* Point out that when the verb is negative we use *not to* + verb, e.g. *I told him not to use it.* Explain that after this verb we need a noun (e.g. a name) or an object pronoun (e.g. *me/you/him/her/them*).
- Explain that object pronouns are the object of a verb or preposition, not the subject of the verb. Write some examples on the board, elicit which words are the object pronouns, and underline them, e.g. *I told <u>him</u> not to use it.*
- Draw students' attention to the Grammar tip *Watch Out.* Point out that the object pronouns also change.

Answers
to; told; told, not
Nouns or object pronouns come after the reporting verb.

C **Think and discuss. Then choose.**

- Write *command, instruction,* and *request* on the board and an example for each one, e.g. *Close the window. Write your name. Can you help me?*
- Have students discuss the sentences, referring to the dialogue in A for examples of reporting verbs in context.

Check answers. Elicit that a request is a question. Ask *Which reporting verb we use for questions?* (*ask*).

Answers
1 tell 2 ask

D TRACK 38 TB p. 219 **Listen and say.**

- Play the audio. Have students repeat each sentence chorally. For ideas on how to vary the drill, see TB p. 23.

E **Rewrite the dialogue in reported speech.**

- Have students say what they think is happening in the picture. Then have three students act out the dialogue.
- Read the example Ask *Is it a command or a request?* (a request)
- Have students do the activity individually. Check answers.

Answers
1 *The man asked the police officer to stop the woman.* 2 The police officer told the woman she wasn't going anywhere. 3 The woman asked the police officer what he wanted. 4 The man told the police officer not to tell her yet. 5 The boy said that woman was his favorite teacher. 6 The man told the boy to give her the flowers.

F **Do an Inside-Outside Circle. Make requests, give commands, and report them.**

- Do an Inside-Outside Circle routine for a more free practice of the grammar. Brainstorm a requests and commands together. Have two students read the examples on the page.
- Give students another command and a request, to check understanding. Review the use of *asked* for a request and *told* for a reported command, e.g. *Can you clean it up? She asked me to clean it up. Stand up! Maria told me to stand up.* If students are stil unsure, review the imperative or write a list of simple commands on the board.
- Set up the *Inside-Outside Circle* routine (see TB p. 21). The student on the outside of the circle makes a request or gives a command. The student on the inside follows the request or command. When students rotate, the student on the inside tell his/her new partner what the previous student said, using reported speech.

Answers
Students' own answers

Cool Down

Play a Chain Game (see TB p. 25). Have students say a command or request. The next student reports that command or request before adding another; for example:

Student A: Can you sit down, please?
Student B: Maria asked me to sit down. Close your book.
Student C: Maria asked Jon to sit down. Jon told me to close my book. Say please.

Practice **Resource Bank:** Grammar Printout
Student's App: Grammar Practice

Write About It

Lesson Objectives

- to learn how to plan (Process Writing: Step 2)
- to plan and write a crime story
- to learn how to organize elements in a story
- to learn how to use adjectives and adverbs for atmosphere

Materials
Support writing printout from the Resource Bank (F)

Warm Up

Ask students if they ever read books or watch shows about mysteries. Have students quickly discuss in pairs.

A Read this extract from the middle of a crime story. What do you think happened before and after this?

This text type is also modeled in the Literacy Book for this unit, The Red-Headed League.

- Using the TTL, display the picture. Ask *What's happening? Who are the people? How do you think they feel?*
- Have students open their books and read the extract. Ask the prediction question *What do you think happened before and after this?* Have students discuss their ideas in pairs.

Answers
Students' own answers

B Look at the structure of a crime story. Read and answer.

- Go through each element and ask students which are in the extract (c). Ask students where the other elements might appear, e.g. before or after the extract.
- Have students order the key elements in question 1 individually and answer question 2. Check answers.

Suggested Answers
1 d, c, a, b but there is no absolute fixed order. 2 Both. Direct speech makes the reader feel involved, while reported speech keeps the reader at a distance.

C Look at the language in the extract from the crime story. Read and respond.

- Have students find a description of a person in the extract. Write it on the board and highlight the adjectives. Elicit what an adjective is. Ask *What kinds of words do we use to describe actions?* Explain that *quickly* is an adverb.
- Have students answer the questions individually and then compare answers in pairs. Check answers as a class.

Answers
1 c 2 a 3 red (hair), long black (hair) 4 impatient, nervous, scared 5 How things are done: *quickly* – Pablo pulled Theo down behind the bush; *quietly* – how Gemma Barnes and Bruce Torrington were talking; *carefully* – how Pablo climbed through a window

- Draw students' attention to the callout. Have students find more adjectives and adverbs in the text and encourage them to identify the noun or verb described.

D Think and discuss. Choose a story idea or think of one of your own. Use a Generating Ideas technique and make notes.

- Review the different ways of generating ideas that students discussed in **Process Writing Step 1: Generating Ideas** on p. 140.
- Tell students that they are going to plan and write a crime story. They can choose a story idea from the page or think of a different idea. Tell students to think about their word choice, as well as the plot. Remind them to use adjectives and adverbs to describe the people, things, and events.
- Then have students share their ideas with a friend.

Answers
Students' own answers

Now ask students to turn to p. 141 to learn about Process Writing Step 2: Planning (see TB p. 212 for teaching notes). Students will need to do this lesson before they do E.

E Plan your crime story. What will you say in each paragraph? Use your ideas in D and make notes.

- After students have completed **Process Writing Step 2: Planning** on p. 141, they will now complete E.
- Tell students they now need to think about how the events fit together to create a story. Point out the four paragraphs in the graphic organizer and tell students that each paragraph should include one of the four key elements from B. Elicit what information they should include in each paragraph.
- Have students make notes about the story events and language they want to use, including adjectives and adverbs.

Answers
Students' own answers

F Now write and illustrate your crime story.

- Have students write a rough draft of their stories in their notebooks or using the Support printouts from the Resource Bank. When they're happy with it, they can write it up on paper and add illustrations or decoration.
- Have students read each other's stories and make positive comments about the stories.

Answers
Students' own answers

Cool Down

Go back to the extract in A and have students suggest how the story ends. Write their suggestions on the board and have a class vote on the best ending.

Practice **Student's App:** Writing Practice
Resource Bank: Writing Game, *Who Did It?*

Talk About It

Lesson Objectives

- to prepare and practice a conversation about how engaged you are with your community
- to learn how to show interest and respond to what you hear in a conversation

Materials
Video

Warm Up

Find out how well students know their neighbors. Have students tell a partner who their neighbors are and what they know about them. Then recap with the class, asking *Do you know your neighbor's names? Do you know what they do? Do you have any friends in the neighborhood?* If you like, you can have students use reported speech to speak about their partner.

A TB p. 239 **Watch and listen. Do you think Maria's plan is good? Why or why not?**

- Tell students they are going to watch a video of a conversation between two children named Maria and Wade talking about an event.
- Have students look at the picture of the house and the flyer. Ask students if they would like to go to a barbecue here and why.
- Draw students' attention to the question *Do you think Maria's plan is good?* Play the video once and have students listen to find out what Maria's plan is. Then ask them if they think it is a good plan. Ask *What makes you say that?* to encourage students to justify their answers.

Answers
Students' own answers

B **Watch again. How do Maria and Wade use these words or phrases? Write *Explain* (tell the story) or *Respond*.**

- Tell students that they are going to categorize phrases from the video. Some phrases are explanations—they tell us what is happening or why. Others are responses—what we say after someone speaks. Look at the example together. Elicit why it's an explanation (Maria is telling Wade what she's doing).
- Have students read the sentences before they rewatch the video. See if they remember which phrases are used to explain something and which are responses.
- Play the video and have students notice who says each phrase and whether they are explaining something new or responding to what the other person said. Check answers as a class.

Answers
1 *Explain* 2 Respond 3 Respond 4 Respond
5 Explain 6 Respond 7 Explain 8 Respond
9 Respond

C **Think about how engaged you are with your neighborhood. Make notes.**

- Ask *Is Maria engaged with her neighborhood?* Explain that *engaged* means that you care about and participate in something. Have students give examples of how Maria is engaged with her neighborhood (she's having a party; she's trying to make the neighborhood safer).
- Ask *Are you engaged with your neighborhood? Do you know your neighbors? Do you do anything together?* Tell students to work in pairs to brainstorm ideas they can use in their conversations. They should try to think of as many ideas as they can for things they do and don't do.
- Draw students' attention to both sections of the graphic organizer. Tell students to plan their conversations individually in their books. Planning will help students structure their conversations, but they will need to be able to respond to what their partner says spontaneously. Remind students that they only need to write notes to prompt them, not full sentences.

Answers
Students' own answers

D **Talk with your friends using phrases in B.**

- Have students have their conversations in pairs. Remind students that it is very important to listen to what your friend is saying and respond appropriately. Encourage them to use gestures and appropriate body language to show interest and excitement as they speak.
- Have students analyze their own performances individually. Then have them discuss their reflections in pairs and see if their partner agrees.

Cool Down

Play *What Was the Last Word?* (see TB p. 27). Use the video and pause it after a key or difficult word.

Practice **Student's App:** Speaking Skills Practice; Speaking Video

Think It Over

Lesson Objectives

- to review what has been learned in the unit
- to reflect on the unit and their own progress
- to think about learning strategies and how to continue learning at home

Warm Up

Do a quick quiz with the class about Unit 3. Ask questions about pictures, words, or information and have students find the answers in their books. Have students play in teams. Possible questions: *What is Mitch looking at on the computer on p. 36? What other inventions are in the lab? Who were the suspects in the Zoomboard theft? What did the detective say on p. 39? What's the word for picture 6 on p. 40?*

How well did you meet the challenge of Unit 3? Read and respond.

Two Stars and a Wish

- Give students time to think about and discuss activities in the unit before they complete each section of the graphic organizer. Tell students they are going to review what they learned in the unit and reflect on what they've done successfully and what they need to improve upon. Explain that this can help them think about what to focus on next time or what they need to practice more or do again.
- Have students work in small groups to make mind maps about what they have done in the unit. Encourage them to think about the different things they studied in the unit, including words, grammar, phrases to use in conversation, things they learned about stories, things they learned about detective work, facts, interesting ideas, and so on. They can also include ideas from the **Literacy Book**. Then have students display their mind maps on the wall. Have groups go around the classroom and look at each other's maps.
- When you have a variety of suggestions in the mind maps, refer students to the graphic organizer in their book and the prompt sentences: *I give myself a star for …, I give myself another star for …, I want to get better at …* Have students talk in pairs about the different sections. Remind students to give reasons for their answers by explaining why they have chosen these things. Encourage them to focus particularly on the third section and to discuss what outstanding questions they have about things they learned. Write some prompts on the board to support their conversation, e.g. *I found that easy/difficult; I got all the answers correct here; I think I did this well; I'd like to know / learn more about …; Next time, I'm going to …*
- Ask students how they can get better at the things they wrote in the third section. Elicit ideas from the class. Remind students about the online materials, such as the **Student's App** on **Navio**, but also encourage them to think of other ways in which they can practice English.
- When you feel they have enough ideas, have students work individually to fill in the graphic organizer. Remind them that they should write their own responses about themselves. Monitor to help as necessary. Look at what the students are writing so you can tailor your classes and any additional practice to their needs.
- If you feel it is appropriate for your class, have students share their ideas with a partner. Encourage them to think together of how they can improve or practice the thing they want to get better at.

Looking Forward

Draw students' attention to the character at the bottom of the page. Elicit who it is and what they remember about him. (Mitch appeared in Lessons 1, 2, and 4.) Ask *What did Mitch invent?* (the Zoomboard) Have students read the speech bubble and make predictions about what Mitch is going to do with the gadget. Tell them that they will find out in the first lesson of Unit 4.

Practice
Resource Bank: Unit Test
Student's App: Vocabulary and Grammar Review

Get Ready to Read

Lesson Objectives

- to activate prior knowledge about solving crimes
- to guide inquiry and deepen understanding through a Think, Pair, Share VTR
- to preview the reading skill of drawing conclusions

Materials

VTR printout from the Resource Bank (A, B, C)

Warm Up

Ask students if they are good at guessing games. Explain that the unit title *Figure It Out* means to understand something or solve a problem, e.g. in guessing games you have to pay attention to the clues or questions in order to figure out the answer. Play *Twenty Questions* (see TB p. 27).

Think, Pair, Share

A Look at the picture. What do the lines mean? Think about it.

- This VTR encourages individual students to participate and gives students time to think independently before contributing their ideas about the image of a DNA test. Start by asking students what they can see in the picture, providing vocabulary where necessary.
- Then write the question *What do the lines mean?* on the board. Give students one or two minutes to think so that they form their own ideas. Tell them to cross their arms when they have thought of some ideas.

B Talk with your partner.

- Divide the class into pairs and have students share their ideas. Encourage them to discuss any questions they might have and to think of possible answers together. Give students two or three minutes to do this.
- Circulate and encourage students to expand on their ideas by asking *What makes you say that?* Provide vocabulary where necessary.

C Share with the class.

- Ask pairs to share their ideas about the picture with the class. Encourage students to use *we*, as they are talking about their partner's opinion, too.

Here's an example of this part of the routine.

Teacher: What do you think about the picture?
Student A: We think that the person is a scientist.
Teacher: OK. Why do you think that?
Student B: Because we think these are results from an experiment.
Teacher: What makes you say that?
Student B: She's pointing the pencil at the lines. Maybe she is comparing the results.

Transition

Ask students how they think the picture might be connected to the police. Ask *What scientific evidence can we get from people?* Elicit that when we touch things, we leave behind fingerprints and our DNA. Students will find out more about this in the reading.

D Think and discuss. What do the police do when there is a crime? How do they try to solve it?

- Tell students to imagine there has been a crime. Something was stolen from the classroom. The police have come to investigate. Ask students what the police will do in order to try to solve the crime. Have students think and discuss their ideas in pairs.
- Have students share their ideas with the class.

Answers

Students' own answers

E Read, think, and write. Read the paragraph. Then describe Ann.

- This activity previews the skill of drawing conclusions. Read the paragraph aloud or display it on the board, without showing the picture. Then tell students to imagine what both Mrs. Higgins and Ann look like. You could have them draw a picture of each one.
- Have students open their books, read the paragraph, and look at the picture to check their predictions.
- Ask *What do you know about Ann?* and elicit ideas. Have students write a description of Ann in their books. Then check answers. Discuss how students describe Ann—does everyone describe her in the same way? Ask *Does the paragraph tell us what color Ann's eyes and hair are?* (No, we only know what color they *aren't*.)

Answers

Students' own answers

Now read **Solving Crime with Science**

Nonfiction: *Solving Crime with Science*—Informational Text

Lesson Objectives

- to read an informational text about forensic science
- to make a personal connection to the reading

Materials

Audio Tracks 12 and 13

Warm Up

Remind students of the crime they imagined had happened in the classroom from the previous lesson. Ask students what kind of evidence the police may have looked for. Have students work in groups to search an area of the classroom for evidence, e.g. footprints, fingerprints (on glass or shiny surfaces), stray hairs. Then have groups share their findings.

TRACK 12 TB p. 231 Reading Approach

Engage with the Text

- Using the the Story Player in the TTL, project the opening spread of the reading. Allow time to notice the title, text, and pictures on the page and make connections between the four people and the reading. Explain that this is an informational text, but the pictures illustrate a story to help contextualize the information.
- Play the audio for the first reading and have students follow along in their books.
- Ask prediction questions as you read, e.g. *What clues do criminals leave behind at a crime scene?*

TRACK 13 TB p. 231 Words in Context

- After the first reading of the text, draw students' attention to the Words in Context box. Play the audio to practice pronunciation.
- Have students brainstorm a list of strategies that they can use to find the meanings of the words, including strategies they use in L1 (e.g. pictures; surrounding words and sentences; positive/negative; contrasting ideas; world knowledge).
- Divide the class into pairs or groups to look at some of the words only, e.g. two words per group or pair. Have them find and highlight each instance of each word in the reading and identify the type of word.
- Have students swap and explain their words, saying which strategy they used.
- Elicit the meanings together. Discuss which strategies worked and if any didn't.

puzzle (p. 42 / p. 45, noun) The sentence explains this word by saying how a crime is like a puzzle ("you have to put pieces together"). Strategies to use: surrounding words and sentences, world knowledge

forensics (p. 42, noun) The rest of the sentence explains this word. The pictures show different types of forensic evidence. Strategies to use: surrounding words and sentences, pictures

amounts (p. 43, noun) This word is preceded by the adjective *small*, so we know it's a noun that is quantified by size. Strategy to use: surrounding words and sentences

unique (p. 43 / p. 44, adjective) The first clause of the sentence explains this word. Strategies to use: surrounding words and sentences, world knowledge

identify (p. 43 / p. 44, verb) The following pronoun *who* shows us that this verb is related to people. The preceding paragraph also provides context. Strategies to use: surrounding words and sentences, world knowledge

genetic (p. 44, adjective) The rest of the sentence and paragraph explains this word. Strategies to use: world knowledge, surrounding words and sentences

Analyze the Text and Features

- Have students read the text individually. Ask *How many different types of evidence are used in forensics?*
- Have students find the green callouts and discuss in pairs.
  - **Task** (p. 42): *Someone has stolen Mrs. Higgins' valuable painting. Can you follow the clues and solve the crime?* Have students note the evidence and share their ideas.
  - **Making Connections** (p. 43): *What are the fingerprint patterns of the four suspects?* Have students identify the patterns. (loop = Sarah, Mrs. Higgins) / circle (whorl = Ann) / wave (arch = Professor Roberts).
  - **Fun Fact** (p. 44): *Only 0.1% difference in DNA makes each person unique.* Ask *What's the same or different about you and your friends or family.*
  - **Critical Thinking** (p. 45): *Can you solve the puzzle? Who stole the painting?* Have students discuss, using their lists of evidence. Elicit that Mrs. Higgins is the most likely thief and why (same fingerprint as the one on the wall on p. 43, wearing heels that matched the footprints on p. 43, and they found a blond hair on p. 44).

International English

Encourage students to notice the spelling changes in *tire* and *tyre*. Point out that both words have the same pronunciation.

Interact with the Text

- Have them take turns saying a sentence summarizing each section of the reading, in pairs or small groups.

Cool Down

Ask students which type of evidence was the most important in the reading and list the top three, with the best clue first. Have them compare with a friend and justify their choices.

Practice **Student's App:** Story Player

Explore the Reading

Lesson Objectives

- to understand and analyze *Solving Crime with Science* through reading comprehension activities
- to learn about the CLIL area of forensics
- to make a personal connection to the reading

Materials

Tape measures or long rulers, one per group of four students; pictures of investigation tools (WU)

Warm Up

Display pictures of items or tools that detectives and forensic scientists use, e.g. magnifying glass, microscope, petri dish and pipette, forensics brush, ultraviolet light. Have students say what they think each item is used for.

A Read and choose the answers.

- Refer back to *Solving Crime with Science* in the **Literacy Book**. Give students 30 seconds to look back at the reading. Using the TTL, display the reading. Then hide the reading or have students close their books. Have students tell their partner what they remember about the reading.
- Draw the students' attention to the questions and do the first one together. Encourage students to refer to the reading for support.
- Have students do the rest of the activity individually. Check answers as a class.

Answers

1 c 2 b 3 b 4 a 5 a 6 c

B Think and discuss. Why do you think detectives use so many different tools?

- Remind students of the pictures you showed them in the Warm Up and review how detectives might use the tools. Say *Are there any other tools that detectives use?* Elicit ideas and write the names on the board. Students may need to use L1 for this.
- Ask *Why do you think they use so many different tools?* Give students a few minutes to think. You could do a Think, Pair, Share routine to help generate ideas.
- Have students discuss their ideas in pairs or small groups.

Suggested Answer

Detectives use different tools to do different things. Some tools are used to look for clues, e.g. ultraviolet light and forensics brushes. Others are used to analyze clues, e.g. microscope. Some tools, like a camera or evidence bags, are used to record or save clues.

C Complete the table with your fingerprints. Label whorls, loops, and arches.

- Students are going to make connections between the reading and their own lives by examining their own fingerprints and those of their friends. This draws on the CLIL focus of forensics, as students notice differences between themselves and their friends.
- The objective of this activity is for students to examine their own fingerprint and find out what type of fingerprint they have. Have them use ink or paint to practice on paper or in their notebook before doing their fingerprint in the table in the book. Check that students understand the words for different fingers, e.g. *pinky* is another word for a little finger.
- Make sure students use contrasting colors, e.g. white paper and black ink. Tell them that they only need a thin layer of paint. If they use too much paint, they won't be able to see the details of their fingerprint.
- They can then examine their fingerprints in more detail. Have them label whorls, loops, and arches.

Answers

Students' own answers

D Think and share. What do you notice about the fingerprints?

- Tell students that they are going to analyze the fingerprints in their tables. Ask *What type of fingerprint do you think you have?*
- Have students work in small groups to compare their fingerprints. Encourage them to find similarities and differences between their fingerprints and their friends' fingerprints.

Cool Down

Play *Detectives* (see TB p. 25).

Practice **Student's App:** Reading Practice

Get Ready to Read

Lesson Objectives

- to activate prior knowledge about famous crimes
- to practice the reading skill of drawing conclusions

Materials

Pictures or realia of the following items: school bag, pencil case, notebook, sneakers and gym bag, lunchbox, calculator (WU)

Warm Up

Display the pictures or realia from the materials list. Tell students that these items all belong to a child and are inside the child's school bag. Ask *What inferences can you make about the child? Where is the child going?* Elicit that the child is going to school. Ask *What subjects is the child going to study today?* Encourage students to justify their answers by asking *What makes you say that?* (The child probably has gym class and math, and is staying at school for lunch.)

A Read the article and answer the questions.

- With books closed, write the newspaper headline on the board and display or draw a picture of a house. Review the meaning of *suspect* (this appears on **Language Book** p. 36). Elicit the meaning of *break* and elicit that a break-in is when thieves enter a home to steal things. Ask *Why do thieves break into homes? What do you think they stole?*
- Give students one minute to read the article quickly. Then ask students what details they remember about the break-in.
- Look at the first question together, *Why didn't the family hear the thieves last Friday night?* Ask students where the family was (on vacation). Have students answer the other questions individually. Then check answers as a class.
- Have students look at the reading skill box. Then ask questions to check comprehension, e.g. *What things can help us draw conclusions?* (clues, evidence, inferences, prior knowledge) Point out that students used their prior knowledge of the type of equipment we use in different lessons to draw conclusions about the subjects the child was studying in the Warm Up.

Answers

1 The family was away on vacation. 2 They found lots of fingerprints on a jewelry box and footprints and tire tracks on the concrete. 3 They used the suspects' fingerprints.

B Read. Then draw a conclusion and write.

- Have students read the text. Then have them look at the picture and identify each character.
- Have students read the text again. Ask *Who is Sherlock Holmes? Why does Mr. Wilson go to see Sherlock Holmes?* Make sure students understand that Mr. Wilson's assistant was active in helping him get another job. Guide students to think about why Mr. Wilson might be looking for another job when he already owns a shop.
- *What do you think Mr. Wilson's problem is?* Have students discuss their ideas in pairs. Then have a few students share their answers with the class.

Suggested Answer

Mr. Wilson's problem is that the office where he has a new job has suddenly closed and he doesn't know why.

C Think and discuss. What famous crimes do you know about?

This activity activates prior knowledge about the topic of the reading and generates interest.

- Ask students what crimes they know. Elicit ideas and write them on the board. Tell students that sometimes people make TV shows or movies about famous crimes.
- Give students a few minutes to discuss what famous crimes they know about in real life or from fictional works such as TV or books.
- Have Group Time (see TB p. 21) to discuss ideas as a class.

Answers

Students' own answers

Now read The Red-Headed League

Fiction: *The Red-Headed League—Story*

Lesson Objectives

- to read a story based on one of Sherlock Holmes' cases
- to make a personal connection to the reading

Materials

Audio Tracks 14 and 15

Warm Up

Show students an appropriate clip, image, or trailer from a Sherlock Holmes movie or TV show. Ask *Who is he?* (a famous detective) *What's special about him?* (He's very clever and good at solving mysteries.) *Who does he work with?* (Dr. Watson)

TRACK 14 TB p. 231 Reading Approach

Engage with the Text

- Using the TTL, project the opening spread of the reading or use the Story Player. Ask students what they notice first. Elicit that in a comic the pictures are very important. Have students look at the first page and predict what the story is about. Ask students what they understand by *The Red-Headed League*. Elicit that *a league* is like a team or club. Ask *What do you think members of the league need to have?* (red hair)
- Play the audio and have students follow along in their books. Pause the audio to ask prediction questions, including the green callout question on p. 51: *Do you know what the crime is?*

TRACK 15 TB p. 232 Words in Context

- After the first reading of the text, draw students' attention to the Words in Context box.
- Give students a few minutes to find and highlight each instance of each word in the reading.
- Have them identify the type of word by looking at the form and the sentence.
- Write these strategies on the board for students: pictures; surrounding words and sentences; positive/negative; contrasting ideas; world knowledge.
- Have students work in pairs to discuss the words.

apply (p. 48, verb) The sentence explains the result of applying for a job, e.g. *try to get the job*. Strategies to use: surrounding words and sentences, pictures

dictionary (p. 49, noun) We know from the sentences that a dictionary is something with words in it, and the next frame shows a picture of an open dictionary. Strategies to use: pictures, surrounding words and sentences

serious (p. 51, adjective) This adjective describes the word *crime*, so it's unlikely to be a positive adjective. Strategies to use: positive/negative, surrounding words and sentences

vault (p. 52, noun) The sentence tells us where the vault is (in the basement of a bank), and the following pictures show the men inside it. Strategy to use: pictures

trick (p. 53, noun) The rest of the sentence explains why the Red-Headed League was a trick. Strategy to use: surrounding words and sentences

- Go through each word to elicit the meaning and how they know. Play the audio to practice pronunciation.

Analyze the Text and Features

- Have students read the text individually in their books. Tell them to look at the pictures as they read and see how each picture represents a part of the text.
- Tell students to find the green callouts and the text focus question in blue, and discuss them with a partner. Alternatively, use Group Time to discuss the question after students have finished reading (see TB p. 21).
  - **Language Note** (p. 48): *What are clues?* Review the different clues that appeared in *Solving Crime with Science*. *Ask Are the clues the same here?*
  - **Personalization** (p. 53): *Did you draw the same conclusion as Mr. Holmes?* Ask students if they had the same ideas as Mr. Holmes or different ones. Encourage students to share the ideas they had and say why they thought this.
  - **Text Focus** (p. 48): *A flashback is when a story breaks its normal order and goes back into the past. It tells the reader about something important that happened.* Ask *Where is Mr. Wilson when he remembers this?* (in Sherlock Holmes' apartment) Tell students that we can use flashbacks to show the reader things that happened before our story starts.

Interact with the Text

- Have students act out an interview in pairs. One student will be Mr. Smith (the thief/assistant), and the other will be the detective. The detective prepares some questions about what happened, e.g. *Where were you last night?* Mr. Smith prepares an alibi. Then have students act out their interviews.
- Have some groups perform the story for the class. Keep a record of who performs and make sure that all students get to perform over the course of the year.

Cool Down

Play *Flashbacks* (see TB p. 25). Have students choose a scene from the story.

Practice **Student's App:** Story Player

Explore the Reading

Lesson Objectives

- to understand and analyze *The Red-Headed League* through reading comprehension activities
- to explore the SEL self-awareness objective of recognizing own strengths and limitations
- to make a personal connection to the reading

Warm Up

Play *Who Said It?* (see TB p. 27) with phrases from *The Red-Headed League*.

A Read and complete. What did Sherlock Holmes learn from these clues?

- Have students look at the table. Do the first question together. Point out that at the beginning of the story we don't know why the assistant showed Mr. Wilson the newspaper advertisement. Later we learn that the assistant wanted to dig a tunnel from Mr. Wilson's shop to the bank. Ask *What conclusions can we draw? What did Sherlock Holmes learn?* (that the assistant wanted Mr. Wilson to stay away from the shop)
- Have students write their ideas in their books individually. Encourage students to look back at the reading to help them. Check answers as a class.

Suggested Answers

1 The assistant wanted Mr. Wilson out of his shop. 2 The criminals wanted to get into the bank from the shop. 3 There was a tunnel underneath it. 4 Before he came into the shop, the assistant was digging in the tunnel. 5 The criminals were ready to rob the bank.

B Think and write. How did Holmes use these skills to solve the crime? Give examples from the story.

Students are going to analyze the reading in more detail and explore the SEL competency of self-awareness by recognizing strengths and limitations.

- Ask *What skills does Sherlock Holmes have?* Elicit ideas from the class. Then have students compare their ideas with the four skills on the page.
- Ask students how Sherlock used these skills, e.g. *When did he listen carefully?* (He tapped the sidewalk and listened to the sound.) Ask students how this helped him solve the crime. (He could hear that the sidewalk wasn't solid and discovered the tunnel.)
- Give students a few minutes to think about the skills, looking back at the story to help them, and write them in their books. Then check answers as a class.

Suggested Answers

1 He tapped the sidewalk. 2 He saw that there was a bank next to Mr. Wilson's shop. He also noticed the assistant's dirty knees. 3 He thought about what each clue meant. 4 He connected the different clues together.

C Think and discuss. Do you have the skills to make a good detective? Why or why not?

In this activity, students will explore the SEL self-awareness competency of recognizing their own strengths and limitations. They will think about the skills needed to be a good detective and evaluate their own skills and abilities.

- Ask *What skills does a good detective have?* Elicit the skills from B and any others that students come up with. Write the skills on the board. Other possible skills may be IT skills, communication skills (speaking and writing), patience, interpersonal skills (e.g. being friendly and kind).
- Ask *Do you have these skills? Which ones?* Tell students to think about the skills and to try to think of examples when they have shown them.
- Have students discuss their ideas in pairs or small groups. Encourage students to ask each other questions, e.g. *What makes you say that? When did you use that skill?*

Answers

Students' own answers

Literary Term: Closed Compound

Read and write.

- Draw students' attention to the explanation of *closed compounds*. Sometimes these are called *compound nouns*. Look at the words together with the class and elicit the compound nouns. For each one, ask students if they can guess what each new word means. Students may already know the meaning of the closed compounds. In this case, have students think about where the words come from, e.g. *playground* is a place (or piece of ground) where you play.
- Have students write the compound words in their books.
- Have students find more examples of closed compounds in the reading. Check answers as a class and discuss the meaning of each one.

Answers

1 chopstick 2 keyboard 3 sunlight 4 clownfish 5 stomachache 6 playground
Compound words in the reading: flashback, newspaper, notebook, outside, sidewalk

Cool Down

Have students invent new closed compounds. They should use their imaginations. You could provide a list of random nouns for students to choose from. Students choose a new compound and decide what its new meaning is, e.g. raindog (a multicolored rainbow dog).

Practice **Resource Bank:** Literary Term Printout
Student's App: Reading Practice; Literary Term Practice

Think Together

Lesson Objectives

- to make connections between the readings
- to explore the key concept: How do we use clues to solve problems?
- to reflect on the unit and provide personal thoughts and opinions

Warm Up

Ask students whether the story of *The Red-Headed League* is set now or in the past. Have students give reasons for their answers. Students may notice the clothes, furniture, and the low wages of the job. Tell students that the Sherlock Holmes stories were written around 120 years ago.

A Read and check. Then discuss. Who might use these techniques?

Students are going to use critical thinking skills to compare and contrast elements of the two readings and explore the key concept in the unit: *How do we use clues to solve problems?*

- Quickly review the different techniques that appear in *Solving Crime with Science* and write them on the board. Then elicit the techniques that Sherlock Holmes uses in *The Red-Headed League*.
- Have students look at the list and do the activity in their books. Check answers as a class, encouraging students to give examples of how each technique could be used. Ask *Why couldn't Sherlock Holmes use the techniques from the 1st reading?*
- Ask the key concept question: *How do we use clues to solve problems?* and elicit ideas from the class.

Answers

Checking an email trail on a laptop (Modern Forensic Scientist); Studying a footprint in the dirt (both); Testing the DNA found on a glass (Modern Forensic Scientist); Studying a person's clothes (both); Problem solving (both); Looking at the GPS on a cell phone (Modern Forensic Scientist); Investigating a fingerprint on a window (both)

B Read the puzzle. Do a Think, Pair, Share.

- Tell students to follow clues to solve a puzzle and think about all the possible answers at each stage. The options will become more limited as they find the clues, so they shouldn't worry if there are a lot of possible answers at the beginning.
- When everyone has finished, have students share their answers with a friend. Ask *Do you have the same answer?* If students have different answers, encourage them to go through the puzzle again together.
- Elicit the answer from the class. Go through each clue, asking students what the possible answers were at each stage.

Answer

Kiera's house is number 45.

C Write your own puzzle. Trade and solve.

- Brainstorm different types of puzzles with the class. These could be logic puzzles, word puzzles, riddles, and so on. Tell students that they are going to write a puzzle for their partner. They must write the puzzle and write the answer on a separate page.
- One simple puzzle idea is a coded message. Students create a code (e.g. reversed alphabet, or letter = number) and write a message.
- Have students make their puzzles. Students then trade puzzles with their partner and try to solve them.

My Reading Journal

Questions I still have after the unit are …

This is a self-evaluation question that encourages students to think about what else they want to learn. Give students time to think and write their answer, then discuss in pairs or small groups.

Ask students to say a question they'd like to know the answer to. Encourage other students to answer.

Suggested Answer

How do detectives find out people's passwords on computers?

What did you find surprising about solving crime?

This is a personalization question. Give students time to look back in their books and find things they found surprising. Have them share their ideas with a friend.

Ask if any students would like to share their answers with the class.

Suggested Answer

I think it's surprising that only 0.1% of our DNA is different.

Go back to page 41. What new thoughts do you have to share?

Have students look back at the VTR picture on pp. 41–42. Using the TTL, project the image onto the board. Ask students how they think the picture connects to the two readings in the unit. Then repeat the Think, Pair, Share routine. If you recorded students' ideas in Lesson 1, display these. Encourage students to think of new ideas and questions they have now, e.g. *I think this is a DNA test. A forensic scientist is looking for a criminal.*

Cool Down

Play *Draw It!* (see TB p. 25). Have students draw a forensic technique or tool.

Practice
Resource Bank: Unit Test
Student's App: Key Concept Practice

UNIT 4

When I Grow Up

Unit Overview

Themes

Unusual jobs and skills

Jobs and why we do them

Synopsis

In this unit, students will explore the topic of jobs. They will learn about the qualifications and skills required in different jobs. They will discuss the importance of all jobs and how businesses are useful to society. Students will plan and prepare a job interview and write a biography.

Language Book

Vocabulary

architect, challenging, comedian, creative, degree, party planner, pet psychologist, qualifications, rewarding, stressful, talented, underwater photographer

Pronunciation: intonation in yes/no questions

p. 96

Explore Language

Infinitive of Purpose

p. 97

Global Citizenship

Why are all jobs important?

ambition, boss, business, experience, independent, inspired, observant, reliable, resourceful, skills

p. 98

Explore Language

Tag Questions

p. 99

Talk About It

Conversation: using fillers to buy time to think in an interview

p. 100

Write About It

A Biography

Paragraph Building: support reasons with facts and details

Word Study: adjective collocations

p. 101

Think It Over

Review and Reflection: My Planning Sheet

p. 102

Think Together
Why do we work?
p. 109

Visible Thinking
Question Starts
p. 103

Literacy Book

Nonfiction
Biography: *The Hero of Lime Rock*

Words in Context: *row, rescues, took place, capsized, official*
p. 107

Fiction
Story: *Delivery Dan*

Words in Context: *ushers, audition, opera, starving, tip*
p. 104

Reading Skill
Understanding points of view
p. 106

Literary Term
Synonyms
p. 105

Language and Literacy Connections

The connecting theme for Unit 4 is jobs and skills.

	Language	Literacy
Vocabulary	**Set 1:** jobs and qualifications **Set 2:** work and skills	**Nonfiction:** skills **Fiction:** boss, rewarding, talented
Grammar	**Infinitive of Purpose** I ask the clients questions to find out what they want. We have a detailed schedule to make sure everything happens on time. **Tag Questions** You can't take pictures under water with it, can you? That was dangerous, wasn't it? You need to be observant, don't you? You'll need your camera, won't you?	**Nonfiction:** Lewis used all her strength to row out to the boat. Lewis rescued the men and brought them to safety. Hundreds of people came to visit her. **Fiction:** I sang really well, didn't I? I delivered lobster soup to you last week, didn't I?
Skills	**Pronunciation:** intonation in incomplete yes/no questions **Process Writing:** planning	**Reading:** understanding points of view **Literary Term:** synonym
International English	realized/realised; in college/at university	

Vocabulary

Lesson Objectives

- to learn vocabulary related to jobs and qualifications: *architect, challenging, comedian, creative, degree, party planner, pet psychologist, qualifications, rewarding, stressful, talented, underwater photographer*
- to say a poem about choosing a job
- to practice intonation in incomplete yes/no questions

Materials
Audio Tracks 39 to 43; Video

Warm Up

Play *Last Letter, First Letter* (see TB p. 26) using job names.

A TRACK 39 TB p. 219 **Listen. Which job do you think Gina likes best?**

- Display the the opening spread with the TTL. Tell students that the children are visiting a job fair. Have students work in pairs to explore the picture and say what jobs they think they can see. Ask further questions about the picture to encourage students to make general observations as well as pointing out details about the picture. Ask *What else can you see? What makes you say that?*
- Tell students that they are going to listen to some of the people in the picture talking about jobs. Remind students of the challenge from the end of Unit 3. Have students find Mitch in the picture and say why Mitch took the gadget out of the lab (to show the children at the job fair).
- Play the audio and have students point to the picture.
- Ask the comprehension question *Which job do you think Gina likes best?* Play the audio again and check the answer.

Answer
comedian

B TRACK 40 TB p. 219 **Find and number the words in A. Then listen and check.**

- Have students look at the list of vocabulary words. Point out the example (1) and have students find the matching person in the picture (Dan from the **Literacy Book** story, as he is a talented singer). Tell students to find the other words in the picture and to write the corresponding numbers in their books.
- Play the audio for students to check their answers. Point out the silent *p* in *psychologist*.

Answers
1 *talented* 2 qualifications 3 underwater photographer 4 party planner 5 degree 6 architect 7 creative 8 stressful 9 pet psychologist 10 challenging 11 comedian 12 rewarding

C TRACK 41 TB p. 219 **Close your eyes. Listen, visualize, and say.**

- Prepare students for the visualization (see Visualization).
- Play the audio, allowing students to visualize the ideas.
- Have students discuss the things they imagined in pairs.

D **Would you like to do any of the jobs when you're older? Complete.**

- Ask students which words from A they would like in a job. Elicit responses from the class, e.g. *I want to be a party planner. I want a creative job.*
- Note that there are no correct answers for this activity. Ask students which other words from A describe characteristics that they would or wouldn't like in a job. Have students complete the activity then discuss in pairs.

Answers
Students' own answers

E TRACK 42 TB p. 219 **Listen and write. Then watch and say.**

- Ask students what they want to do when they're older. Tell students that it doesn't matter if they don't know what job they want to do! Suggest thinking of things they like to think of a job that might be interesting.
- Play the video or audio of the poem and have students watch or listen and enjoy it. If you want to focus on the pronunciation, you may want to use just the audio initially.
- Have students read the lines and try completing the blanks. Play the poem video or audio to check answers.
- Play the video or audio again and encourage students to join in, copying the intonation.

Answers
1 *rewarding* 2 Challenging 3 talented 4 creative 5 pet psychologist 6 degree 7 party planner 8 underwater photographer

F TRACK 43 TB p. 220 **Pronunciation. Listen and say. Copy the intonation. Find two more questions like these in the poem.**

- Display the examples on the board. Have students notice how the arrow points upward at the end of the question. Have students try saying the questions. Play the audio and have students repeat the questions chorally.
- Point out that the questions are incomplete—elicit that we usually say *Do you want the chance to travel?* Have students ask each other the questions in pairs.
- Have students look for more examples of yes/no questions in the poem. Play the video or audio again and check answers. Play the poem again and have students join in.

Answers
Something that's rewarding?; Challenging too?; Imaginative too?; Want to get yourself a plan?

Cool Down

Play *Mime It!* (see TB p. 26). Choose one of the jobs from the lesson.

Practice **Student's App:** Vocabulary Practice; Spoken Word Video

Explore Language

Lesson Objectives

- to learn how to use infinitives of purpose
- to practice vocabulary related to jobs and qualifications

Materials
Audio Tracks 44 and 45

Warm Up

Tell students to imagine they're planning a party. Have them work in pairs or small groups to make a list of all the things they need to do to organize a great party. Encourage them to think about food, games, and decorations.

A TRACK 44 TB p. 220 **Listen and read. What does a party planner do?**

- Tell students they are going to listen to Eva talking about her job as a party planner. Have students look back at the picture on pp. 48–49 to find Eva and predict what she does in her job. Play the audio and have students follow the text in their books.
- Ask the gist question *What does a party planner do?* and elicit the answer. Ask *What things does she organize?* and play the audio again (food, music, decorations, prizes, games, possibly the venue).

Answer
They organize everything for a party.

B **Look at A. Complete the table. What verb form comes after *to*?**

- Refer students to the table and have them look for the sentences in A. Have them work in pairs to complete the table with the missing words.
- Check answers as a class. Ask students which word we need in both sentences (*to*). Then ask *What kind of word comes after "to"?* (a verb) and the question *What verb form comes after "to"?*
- Draw students' attention to the Grammar tip *Look*. Have students notice that *to* and *in order to* have the same meaning. Tell students that they can choose whether to use just the infinitive with *to* or the connector (*in order to*). Have students say the sentences in the table using *in order to*.

Answers
to, find out; make sure
The infinitive of purpose comes after *to*.

C **Think and discuss. Then choose.**

- Have students look at the sentences and options. Refer them to the table in B and the text in A to help. Have students work in pairs to discuss the sentences and choose.
- Check answers as a class. Have students think of *Why …?* questions that could have the answers in the table, e.g. *Why do you ask clients questions?* Elicit the answer *To find out what they want*. Then elicit a *Why …?* question for the second sentence. This should help students understand how to use the infinitive of purpose more clearly.

Answers
1 give a reason for doing 2 Why …?

D TRACK 45 TB p. 220 **Listen and say.**

- Play the audio, having students repeat each sentence chorally.
- For ideas on how to vary the drill, see TB p. 23.

E **Match the questions to the answers to make jokes. Then underline the infinitives of purpose.**

- Draw students' attention to the instructions and elicit the meaning of *jokes*. If necessary, explain why the first one is a joke (*planet* sounds the same as *plan it*). Ask students if they like to tell jokes. Remind students of the phrase *to have a sense of humor* from the Visualization on p. 48.
- Have students do the controlled practice activity individually. If students find it difficult to understand the jokes, allow them to do the activity in pairs. Tell students to look for words that are related in the questions and answers. Check answers as a class, explaining the joke where necessary.
- Have students work in pairs to try to come up with a joke of their own using the infinitive of purpose. If this is too challenging, have them find another similar joke online instead and share it with the class.

Answers
1 d 2 a 3 e 4 f 5 b 6 c
Infinitives of purpose: organize, tell, have, get, reach, C (see)

F **Play a chain game in teams. How long can you continue the chain?**

- This activity provides freer oral practice of infinitives of purpose. Brainstorm a few ways of using the verbs on the page. Divide the class into two teams. In teams, each student repeats the previous sentence and adds one more idea to the chain, using the infinitive of purpose.
- Have three students read the examples on the page. Then have students play in pairs. The pair that continues the chain for the longest wins.

Answers
Students' own answers

Cool Down

Play *Pass the Whisper* (see p. 26). The final student has to say the sentence using an infinitive of purpose.

Practice **Resource Bank:** Grammar Printout
Student's App: Grammar Practice

Global Citizenship

Lesson Objectives

- to learn vocabulary related to work and skills: *ambition, boss, business, experience, independent, inspired, observant, reliable, resourceful, skills*
- to explore why jobs are important and how business can be useful to society
- to practice listening for gist and detail

Materials

Audio Tracks 46 and 48; Audio Track D; a map of the world (Activity D); pieces of paper (Cool Down)

Opening Question

Ask the opening question: *Why are all jobs important?* Elicit ideas and encourage students to think about different jobs and how they might be important or useful. Record students' ideas in some way, e.g. in a spidergram, and come back to these at the end of the lesson.

A TRACK 46 TB p. 220 **Listen to Tyrone and Cody talk about starting a small business. What are they going to sell?**

- Ask *Why might someone want to start a business?* Elicit examples of small businesses. Ask *Do you know anyone who runs their own business?*
- Tell students they are going to listen to two children talking about starting a small business. Ask the gist question *What are they going to sell?* Play the audio and check the answer.

Answer

frozen bananas

B TRACK 47 TB p. 220 **Look at the pictures and definitions in A and write. Then listen and check.**

- Point out the example answer for number 1, *ambition*. Refer students to the vocabulary box in B and have them write the words for each picture and definition in A.
- Play the audio for students to check their answers.

Answers

1 *ambition* 2 observant 3 resourceful 4 experience 5 inspired 6 boss 7 independent 8 reliable 9 skills 10 business

TRACK D TB p. 220 **Visualization**

- The TTL has a visualization for this vocabulary set. (See TB p. 21.)

C Read and complete the paragraph.

- Have students read the text silently. Elicit the purpose of the email (to explain the girl's work experience and how it is relevant to becoming a pet psychologist).
- Look at the example together. Ask *What is her ambition?* (be a pet psychologist) Remind students that sometimes a definition or explanation comes after a word.
- Have students complete the sentences. Check answers.

Answers

1 *ambition* 2 experience 3 business 4 reliable 5 observant 6 skills 7 boss

D TRACK 48 TB p. 220 **Now listen to Nia Cole. What does she do?**

- Tell students they are going to listen to a girl from New Zealand talking about her business. Ask students what they know about New Zealand. See if they can find it on a map.
- Have students guess what kind of business it is.
- Listening for gist: ask the gist question *What does she do?* and play the audio. Check the answer with the class.

Answer

She's the boss of a company that makes cases for cell phones.

E Listen again. Put the sentences in order.

- Have students read the sentences and try re-ordering them before listening again. Elicit that the example sentence introduces the main idea. Give students time to read and order the sentences.
- Play the audio and have students check and amend their answers. Then check answers as a class. Elicit that Nia is the girl from the documentary that Tyrone watched. Have students remember what Tyrone said about her (she had to learn a lot, she was really enthusiastic, and she inspired him).

Answers

1 c 2 g 3 h 4 a 5 d 6 b 7 f 8 e

International English

Have students notice the different spellings. Tell students that the pronunciation is the same. Point out that this spelling difference that many words follow these spelling patterns. You could have students look in a dictionary for more words that end in *–ize* / *–ise*.

Discussion Questions

- Draw students' attention to the discussion questions. Have students discuss each question in pairs or small groups (see **ETB**). Encourage students to recognize that a good boss needs all kinds of skills. Help students understand the importance of small businesses to the community and how both large and small companies have their place.
- Return to the opening question to ask again: *Why are all jobs important?* Revisit any ideas discussed at the beginning of the lesson and encourage students to share any new ideas.

Cool Down

Give each student a slip of paper. Have students write one thing they learned from the lesson and one thing they enjoyed. Students hand in their completed papers as they leave the classroom.

Practice **Student's App:** Vocabulary Practice; Listening Practice

Explore Language

Lesson Objectives

- to review tag questions
- to practice vocabulary for work and skills

Materials
Audio Tracks 49 and 50

Warm Up

Ask students if they have ever been to the ocean. Ask students what sea creatures they know and brainstorm a list on the board.

A TRACK 49 TB p. 220 **Listen and read. Does Nancy-Yu have qualifications or skills as an underwater photographer?**

- Tell students that they are going to listen to Nancy-Yu talking to a boy named Tareq about her job. See if students can find Nancy-Yu and Tareq on other pages in the unit (Nancy-Yu appears on pp. 48–49, and Tareq appears on p. 50).
- Ask the gist question *Does Nancy-Yu have qualifications or skills as an underwater photographer?* and have students predict the answer. Play the audio for students to check. Ask *Would you like to get close to a shark?*

Answers
She has a biology degree, and she is a good photographer. She is observant and resourceful, and she solves problems quickly.

International English

Have students notice the different phrases in American and British English. Point out that in British English college often refers to a type of school for students aged 16–18, who may be studying to go to university or to get a job.

B **Look at A. Complete the table. When do we use the verb *do* in the tag question?**

- Review the use of auxiliary verbs in tag questions from Unit 10 of **Language Book** 4. Elicit and write auxiliary and modal verbs on the board (*do, be, have, can, should, will*). Write sentences on the board and elicit the tag question, e.g. *You're good at math, (aren't you)?*
- Have students find the sentences in A and complete the table in pairs.
- Check answers as a class. Have students notice how the auxiliary verbs are the same in the phrases and the tag questions (*can't/can, was/wasn't, 'll/won't*). Remind them that when the verb in the sentence is affirmative, the tag question is negative and vice versa. Ask *When do we use the verb "do" in the tag question?* and elicit the answer.
- Point out that in simple present and simple past affirmative sentences there's no auxiliary or modal verb and then elicit which auxiliary is used in the negative and question form (*do/did*).
- Draw students' attention to the Grammar tip *Watch Out*. Point out that in this exception, the form of the verb in the tag question is different from the form of the verb in the sentence. Explain that this is because it is very difficult to say *amn't!* Elicit that *aren't* is the second-person verb form but we use it for first person in this case.

Answers
can; That was, wasn't; need, you; won't
We use *do* in a tag question when the main part of the sentence doesn't have an auxiliary or modal verb.

C **Think and discuss. Then choose.**

- Have students work in pairs to discuss the sentences. Check answers as a class. Ask *Does Tareq know the answer to the questions he asks?* (probably—he's just checking). *What kind of answer do the questions need?* (yes/no).

Answers
1 think 2 keep the conversation going 3 *yes* or *no*

D TRACK 50 TB p. 220 **Listen and say.**

- Play the audio, having students repeat each sentence chorally. Make sure that students use the correct rising intonation.
- For ideas on how to vary the drill, see TB p. 23.

E **Read and complete the tag questions.**

- Look at the example together. Ask *What is the verb in the sentence?* (gets) *Is it an auxiliary or modal verb?* (no) Elicit that we need to use *does* because *gets* is the third person.
- Have students do the controlled practice activity individually. Then check answers as a class.

Answers
1 *doesn't he?* 2 aren't I? 3 won't it? 4 have we?
5 weren't there? 6 didn't you?

F **How well do you know your friend? Ask and answer 20 tag questions. Make a tally chart to keep score of your correct guesses.**

- Look at the topics on the page and brainstorm a few tag questions with the class. In this freer oral practice, students make tag questions to check what they know about their friend. Have two students read the examples on the page.
- Have students play in pairs, keeping a tally of how many they get right. The student with the most correct answers wins.

Answers
Students' own answers

Cool Down

Play a version of *Funniest Sentence* (see p. 25). Have students make tag questions instead of sentences.

Practice **Resource Bank:** Grammar Printout
Student's App: Grammar Practice

Write About It

Lesson Objectives

- to plan and write a biography
- to learn how to support reasons with facts and details
- to learn how to use adjective collocations
- to learn to generate ideas to help your writing

Materials

Support writing printout from the Resource Bank (F)

Warm Up

Ask *Do you know any famous businesspeople? Are there any famous businesspeople in your country? What skills do you think the owners of large companies have?*

A Read the biography. Why do you think the writer chose to write about this person?

This text type is also modeled in the Literacy Book for this unit, The Hero of Lyme Rock.

- Look at the picture together. Elicit who the person is and what he is doing. You could do a quick See, Think, Wonder routine (see TB p. 20) .
- Have students read the title. Explain that an *entrepreneur* is someone who starts a new business. Ask *Why do you think the writer chose to write about this person?* Have students discuss in pairs.
- Elicit the meaning of *admire* in the final paragraph, encouraging students to use reading strategies. The text doesn't give the exact answer to the question: students should infer this. Ask students who they admire and why.

Suggested Answer

because the writer admires him and his achievements

B Look at the structure of the biography. Read and check (✔) the features that appear in it.

- Go through each feature and check understanding. Elicit the meaning of key words, e.g. *achievements*, *facts*, and *aims*. Explain *chronological order*.
- Do an example with the class. Then have students look for and check the features individually. Check answers.

Answers

1; 2; 4; 8

C Look at the language in the biography. Read and respond.

- Have students find words a–d in the text and notice which words come after them. Ask *What kinds of words are they?*
- Have students work individually. Check answers together.

Answers

1 a good **at** studying b interested **in** creating
c proud **of** his achievements d excited **by** his ideas
Prepositions and nouns or gerunds (verb + *–ing*) come after these adjectives. 2 Students' own answers

- Draw students' attention to the callout. Have students find one more example of adjectives followed by a preposition + noun or gerund (*famous for starting*).

D Think and discuss. Research the life of someone successful whom you admire. Find out as much information as you can using one of the Generating Ideas techniques.

- Review different ways of generating ideas discussed for **Process Writing Step 1: Generating Ideas** on p. 140.
- Tell students that they are going to plan and write a biography about someone they admire. Draw students' attention to the mind map on the page and tell them to think about these questions.
- Give students time to think about the questions and make notes. Students can compare their ideas with a friend.

Answers

Students' own answers

E Plan your biography. Look at your ideas in D and decide what to include. Make notes in the table.

- Review how to plan by eliciting ideas from **Process Writing Step 2: Planning** on p. 141. Students can look back at the page if necessary.
- Ask students to think about how they should organize their content. Look at the table together. Explain how important it is to support ideas with facts and details.
- Have students complete the table with their ideas. Students will probably need to do some online research to find out more information about their chosen person.

Answers

Students' own answers

F Now write your biography.

- Remind students to keep in mind who they are writing for and what will be interesting for their readers. Remind students they don't need to include all the information that they find, only the most important and most interesting information. They should think carefully about how to justify their statements and opinions with facts.
- Give students time to write their biographies or have them do it as homework, using the Support printout from the Resource Bank. Encourage them to write a rough draft before writing the final version in their notebooks.

Answers

Students' own answers

Cool Down

Have students think of a question they had when reading the biographies and write it on a slip of paper. They should give their question to the person who wrote the biography and see if they can answer it. If not, they should try to find out the answer for homework.

Practice **Student's App:** Writing Practice
Resource Bank: Writing Game, *Who Am I?*

Talk About It

Lesson Objectives

- to prepare and practice an interview
- to learn how to use fillers to buy time to think in an interview

Materials
Video

Warm Up

Ask students what they know about the process of applying for a job. Elicit the different stages (sending in your resumé or filling out an application form, going to an interview, possibly taking an entrance exam or physical test for some jobs).

A TB p. 239 **Watch and listen. Do you think Wade will get the job?**

- Tell students they are going to watch a video of a boy being interviewed for a job.
- Have students look at the picture on the TV screen. Explain that all these things are sections on a person's resumé. Elicit examples of the different types of information, e.g. Contact Details: name, address, phone number, email.
- Draw students' attention to the question *Do you think Wade will get the job?* Play the video once and have students listen to see how well Wade performs in the interview. Then ask them if they think he will get the job. Ask *What makes you say that?* to encourage students to justify their answers.

Answers
Students' own answers

B Watch again. Check (✔) to answer the questions.

- Students are going to think about why Wade uses some of the words and phrases he does. Have students read the questions before they rewatch the video. See if they can remember any of the answers.
- Play the video once and have students answer the questions. Check answers as a class. Discuss how fillers are useful to give us time to think about what we want to say. You may also wish to discuss the different phrases in question 3 and when we might use each one. Point out that a and b are more polite and therefore more suitable for a job interview.

Answers
1 b 2 a, b, e 3 a, b

C What job can you do in your school? Plan what you will say at your interview. Then plan some interview questions.

- Ask students if there is a school magazine at their school. Then ask if there are any other activities that students at school help with. Some ideas may be running a school chess club, class representatives, and peer reading programs.
- Tell students to choose a job and think about what kinds of things they could say at an interview. Draw students' attention to the notepaper and text in C. Remind them to think about why they want the job, their experience, and their skills. Tell them that they have to plan both sides of the interview, so they need to think of some questions to ask another student who wants the job. They should try to include phrases from B in their conversations.
- Students plan their interview responses and questions individually. Planning will help students structure their conversations, but they will also need to be able to respond to their friend's questions spontaneously. Remind students that they only need to write notes to prompt them during the conversation and not full sentences.

Answers
Students' own answers

D Take turns interviewing each other. Use the fillers in B.

- Remind students that it is very important to listen to what your friend is saying and respond appropriately. Encourage them to use gestures and appropriate body language as they speak.
- Then have students practice their conversations in pairs. Have one or two pairs demonstrate their conversation in front of the class.

Answers
Students' own answers

Cool Down

Play *Bingo!* (see TB p. 25). Students draw a 3 x 2 grid and write in it some expressions from B. Draw an example on the board. Have two students come to the front and act out their interview. The others cross out the phrases as they hear them. If no one calls out *Bingo!*, another pair acts out their interview, and so on.

Practice Student's App: Speaking Skills Practice; Speaking Video

Think It Over

Lesson Objectives

- to review what has been learned in the unit
- to reflect on the unit and their own progress
- to think about learning strategies and how to continue learning at home

Warm Up

Do a quick quiz with the class about Unit 4. Ask questions about pictures, words, or information and have students find the answers in their books. Have students play in teams. Possible questions: *How many gadgets did Mitch take to the job fair? How many children are watching the comedian? What food is on the party planner's list? What's the word for picture 2 on p. 52? What color are Tareq's shoes? When was Richard Branson born?*

How well did you meet the challenge of Unit 4? Read and respond.

My Planning Sheet

- Give students time to think about and discuss activities in the unit before they complete each section of the graphic organizer. Tell students they are going to review what they've successfully learned and what they need to improve. They will then make a plan outlining what they will do next in order to continue learning.
- Tell students to imagine they have to tell a new student what they have done during the unit. Have students work in pairs or small groups to come up with a list or mind map of activities they have done and things they have learned. They can look back through the unit to help them.
- Refer students to the graphic organizer in the book and the prompt sentences and give an example for each one, e.g. *We're all good at some things. I'm good at writing a biography.* Have students talk in pairs about the different sections. Encourage them to focus particularly on the second and third sections and to discuss what they can do to learn more about or how they can practice the areas they have problems with. Remind students about the online materials, such as the **Student's App** on **Navio**, but also encourage them to think of other ways they can practice English. Write some prompts on the board to support their conversation, e.g. *I'm going to … / I plan to … / I can try to …*
- When you feel they have enough ideas, have students work individually to fill in the graphic organizer. Remind them that they should write their own responses about themselves. Monitor to help as necessary. Look at what the students are writing so you can tailor your classes and any additional practice to their needs.
- If you feel it is appropriate for your class, have students share their ideas with a friend. Encourage them to think together of how they can put their plans into practice.
- Discuss the last two sections with the class before you have students write about them. Ask *How will you know if your plan works?* Elicit that students will be able to do some of the things they wrote about in the second section without looking in their books. Ask students what they will do if their plan works. Encourage students to think of other areas they would like to practice. Remind them again about the **Student's App** on **Navio** and online materials. Then have students fill out the final two sections of the graphic organizer.

Looking Forward

Draw students' attention to the character at the bottom of the page. Elicit who it is and what they remember about her. (Nancy-Yu appeared in Lessons 1, 2, and 4.) Ask *What did Nancy-Yu study at college?* (biology) Have students read the speech bubble and make predictions about where Nancy-Yu is going. Tell them that they will find out in the first lesson of Unit 5.

Put It Together

To further review and recycle the language in Units 3 and 4, play *The Detective Game* on pp. 60–61. See TB p. 207 for teaching notes.

Practice **Resource Bank:** Unit Test
Student's App: Vocabulary and Grammar Review

Get Ready to Read

Lesson Objectives

- to activate prior knowledge about unusual jobs
- to guide inquifry and deepen understanding through a Question Starts VTR
- to preview the reading skill of understanding points of view

Materials

VTR printout from the Resource Bank (A, B, C)

Warm Up

To activate schema and introduce the theme of the lesson, have a *Board Race* (see TB p. 25) about the pets. Then ask students if any of them have any equipment for their pets and supply vocabulary as needed, e.g. dog bowl, kennel.

Question Starts

A Look at the picture. Then brainstorm questions for a pet furniture designer. Write a list.

This VTR encourages students to think of a variety of interesting questions to explore their ideas about the image of a pet furniture designer. Start by asking students what they can see in the picture, providing vocabulary where necessary.

- Note that the man is a pet furniture designer. Ask *What do you think he studied to become a pet furniture designer?*
- Draw students' attention to the question words. Ask *What questions do you have for a pet furniture designer?*
- Give students a few minutes to think and write questions in their notebooks, individually or in pairs. Encourage students to write as many questions as they can think of.
- Elicit questions from the class and write them on the board.

Here's an example of this part of the routine.

Teacher: What questions do you have for a pet furniture designer?
Student A: What kind of furniture do you make for pets?
Teacher: Good question! Do you have any other questions?
Student B: Where do you get your ideas?
Student C: What do you like about your job?

B Look at your list from A. Which questions seem most interesting? Discuss them with the class.

- Ask students to look at their list of questions and choose the questions they are most curious about.
- Tell students that they are going to practice negotiation skills. Have them work in groups of three to decide which three questions they want to ask, then review the questions and discuss possible answers. Have students write the questions in their notebooks.

C What new ideas or questions do you have now? Talk about your ideas with your partner.

- Encourage students to use the picture to ask questions about pet furniture designers. They shouldn't limit their ideas to what they see in the picture.
- Allow students to ask as many questions as they want to and express their ideas. Students can be as imaginative and creative as they like. Encourage students to discuss together, not just with you.

Here's an example of this part of the routine.

Teacher: What other questions do you have about pet furniture designers? Do you agree with your partner?
Student A: We wonder what you have to study to be a pet furniture designer.
Teacher: What an interesting question! Do other groups have the same question?
Student B: We want to know if they use computers to make their designs.

Transition

Ask students if they would like to be a pet furniture designer. Why or why not? Have students think of the positive and negative aspects of the job. Discuss with the class.

D Think and discuss. Do you know any unusual jobs?

- Elicit that a pet furniture designer is an unusual job and that not many people have it. Ask students to think of and discuss any other unusual jobs they know in pairs.
- Have students share their ideas and write answers on the board. Have students vote on which is the most unusual.

Answer

Students' own answers

E Read and answer. Scan *The Hero of Lime Rock* on the next pages for specific information.

Students are going to preview the skill of understanding points of view.

- Have students read the questions. Ask *What information do you need to find?* Review the skill of scanning by asking *How do you scan a text? Do you read all the words? What words will you look for?* (a name, pronouns that refer to a person)
- Have students do the activity and write the answers in their books. Then check answers as a class. Make sure that students are aware that the narrator is someone who tells the story. They can also be a character in the story, but they don't have to be.

Answers

1 Ida Lewis 2 an unknown narrator 3 no

Now read **The Hero of Lime Rock**

Nonfiction: *The Hero of Lime Rock*—Biography

Lesson Objectives

- to read a biography about a woman who lived in a lighthouse
- to make a personal connection to the reading

Materials
Audio Tracks 16 and 17

Warm Up

Ask students if they have ever been on a boat. Ask questions to encourage them to give more details, e.g. *What kind of boat was it: a large cruise ship, a ferry, or a small boat? Where did the boat travel: at sea or on a river? Where did the boat take you? Did the water move a lot? Did you feel sick?*

TRACK 16 TB p. 232 Reading Approach

Engage with the Text

- Project the opening spread of the reading with the Story Player. Ask students what they notice on the page and how they think the pictures and text are connected. See what students can predict about the text.
- Play the audio and have students follow along in their books. Pause the audio to ask prediction questions, e.g. *How do you think Ida Lewis saved people's lives? How do you think she felt?*

TRACK 17 TB p. 232 Words in Context

- After the first reading of the text, draw students' attention to the Words in Context box.
- Give students a few minutes to find and highlight each instance of each word in the reading.
- Have them identify the type of word by looking at the form and the sentence.
- Write these strategies on the board *pictures*; *surrounding words and sentences*; *positive/negative*; *contrasting ideas*; *world knowledge*.
- Have students work in pairs to discuss the words.

row (p. 58 / p. 59, verb) We know it's a verb because it's preceded by *to*. The picture shows how Ida moves the boat. Strategies to use: pictures, world knowledge

rescues (p. 58, noun / p. 59, verb) This word is used as a noun and a verb. In the first instance, as a noun, it is contrasted with opposing situations, *shipwrecks and drownings*. Strategies to use: contrasting ideas, surrounding words and sentences, pictures

took place (p. 59, verb) This phrasal verb is followed by a time and a date, which explains that it means the time and setting of an event. Strategy to use: surrounding words and sentences

capsize (p. 59, verb) The surrounding words and sentences show it's a negative action. Strategies to use: surrounding words and sentences, world knowledge of what happens to boats during storms

official (p. 59, adjective) The clause that follows explains this adjective. Strategy to use: surrounding words and sentences

- Go through each word to elicit the meaning and how they know. Play the audio to practice pronunciation.

Analyze the Text and Features

- Have the students read the text individually. While they read, have students look for the main idea in each paragraph and underline or highlight it.
- Tell students to find the red callouts and to discuss the questions with a partner.
  - **Critical Thinking** (p. 58): *Why do boats need lighthouses?* Have students look at the pictures. Ask students where the lighthouse is. Have them discuss what dangers there might be to boats. Ask students why they can't see the rocks.
  - **Personalization** (p. 59): *Would you like to live in a lighthouse?* Have students discuss this in pairs, giving reasons for their choices.
  - **Text Focus** (p. 30): The most exciting part of the plot is called the climax. Read the paragraph at the top of p. 30 again up until the text focus and ask Why is this part exciting? Elicit that Arthur is scared and we don't know what is behind him.

Interact with the Text

- Now that students are very familiar with the text, have them imagine they are making a movie of Ida Lewis' life. Tell them to write a summary in the style of a movie trailer, highlighting the most dramatic moments of her life. They can then read their "trailers" aloud to the class.

Cool Down

Play *What's the Next Word?* (TB p. 27). Read aloud sentences from the text.

Practice **Student's App:** Story Player

Explore the Reading

Lesson Objectives

- to understand and analyze *The Hero of Lime Rock* through reading comprehension activities
- to learn about the CLIL area of future careers
- to understand synonyms
- to make a personal connection to the reading

Warm Up

Find out what students remember about the reading. Have students work in pairs to write three sentences about the reading, but one of the sentences must be false. Then they get together with another pair and read their sentences aloud. The other pair has to guess which sentence is false.

A Read and match. Then put in order.

- Draw the students' attention to the questions and look at the example together. Have students match the beginnings and endings of the sentences.
- Elicit that the sentences are not in order. Ask *How we know that the example is number one?* (the reading is about Ida, so it starts with her birth).
- Have students put the sentences in order. Check answers. Note that these provide the most important information about Ida Lewis' life.

Answers
1 Ida Lewis was born … in 1842. 2 Her family moved to live … in the lighthouse on Lime Rock. 3 She rescued … two soldiers. 4 She received … a medal for saving the soldiers' lives. 5 She died … in 1911. 6 Lime Rock became … Ida Lewis Rock.

B Read and complete the biographical summary.

- Ask *What needs to be included in the Graphic Organizer?*
- Ask *Do you need to write full sentences?* Elicit that a summary is similar to a fact file. Personal information such as name or date of birth or death don't need full sentences, but questions like *Why was she famous?* and *Interesting Facts* sections do.
- Have students complete the summary in their books.

Suggested Answers
Name: Ida Lewis; **Born**: February 25, 1842; Lived: Rhode Island, USA; Occupation: Lighthouse keeper
Why was she famous?Why was she famous?: Because she was very brave. She saved at least 18 people's lives, possibly more. She was also the first female lighthouse keeper at Lime Rock. She received a medal for her bravery.
Interesting facts: She once rescued a sheep!; She met the President of the USA.; After she died, Lime Rock became Ida Lewis Rock.
Died: October 24, 1911

C Think and discuss. What are some unusual jobs people had in the past? What did they do? Why were those jobs unusual?

Students are going to make connections between the reading and their own prior knowledge of the world.

- Ask students if they know of any unusual jobs from the past. You could suggest a few, e.g. it was once someone's job to wake people up in the morning by knocking on their window; rat catcher; lamp lighter, etc.
- Do an Options Explosion routine to help students think of ideas. See TB p. 20 for the procedure.
- Then have students share their ideas with the class. You could then take a vote on the most imaginative or interesting job.

Answers
Students' own answers

Literary Term: Synonym

Think and write. What are the synonyms for the underlined words?

- Draw students' attention to the definition of *synonym*. Compare it with *antonym*, which students learned about in Unit 2. Elicit some synonyms from the class and write them on the board. Common examples are *enormous/huge*; *small/little*; *great/awesome*; *pretty/beautiful*.
- Look at the words in the colored lozenges with the class and elicit meanings. Ask students if they know any synonyms of these words. Then have them read the sentences and match the synonyms. Check answers as a class.
- Have students find more examples of synonym pairs in the reading. Check answers as a class.

Answers
1 discovered 2 correct 3 wonderful 4 silent
Words and their synonyms in the reading: trouble/danger, save/rescue, rough (waves) / strong (waves)

Cool Down

Have students work in pairs to make three sentences about Ida Lewis or her story, each using a synonym from the Literary Term section; for example, *Ida was a wonderful rower!* Elicit sentences from all the pairs in the class.

Practice **Resource Bank:** Literary Term Printout
Student's App: Reading Practice; Literary Term Practice

Get Ready to Read

Lesson Objectives

- to activate prior knowledge about jobs and activities we do for fun
- to practice the reading skill of understanding points of view

Warm Up

To introduce the reading skill of understanding points of view, ask students if they remember the story *The Red-Headed League*. Tell students that you are going to call out some things that the characters are thinking. They must decide who it is—Sherlock Holmes, Dr. Watson, or Mr. Wilson—and call out the person's name.
Suggested ideas: *Sherlock is very clever!* (Dr. Watson or Mr. Wilson) *I think there is a tunnel under the pavement!* (Holmes) *Oh, no! The office is closed!* (Mr. Wilson) *I wonder why his pants are dirty.* (Holmes) *I wonder what Sherlock is thinking.* (Dr. Watson)

A Read and underline the pronouns. Then discuss. Which text has a first-person narrator and which has a third-person narrator? What do they tell us about the characters in each text?

- Using the TTL, display the texts or have students look at the texts on the page. Have students read the two texts quickly for gist. Ask students what the texts are about.
- Point out the first pronoun, *He*. Say *He* is a pronoun that tells us who the text is about. Elicit other subject pronouns (*I, you, she*, etc.). Tell students that other pronouns can also give us this information, e.g. object pronouns (*me, you, him, her*, etc.) and possessive pronouns and adjectives (*my, your, his, her*, etc.).
- Give students one or two minutes to find and underline the pronouns.
- Then ask the questions *Which text has a first-person narrator and which has a third-person narrator? What do they tell us about the characters in each text?* Elicit ideas from the class and check answers.
- Have students look at the reading skill box. Then ask questions to check comprehension, e.g. *What pronouns does a first-person narrator use? Which pronouns does a third-person narrator use? What is the difference between the two?* (The first-person narrator only shows us the ideas and feelings of that character, but a third-person narrator can give us information about lots of characters.)

Answers

1 *He, he, He, he, he, they, him, They, him*
2 *My, me, they, I, I, I, my, I, I, I*
The first text has a third-person narrator, the second text has a first-person narrator. Both texts tell us how the characters feel, but the second one is more dramatic.

B Scan *Delivery Dan* and underline the pronouns. What is the point of view? Is it first person or third person? Answer and write three examples.

- Give students one or two minutes to scan the reading and underline the pronouns. Check the answer to the first question, *What is the point of view?*
- Have students look at the reading again and find three example sentences from the reading. Have students write these in their books. Then have students compare their examples with a partner.

Answers

The point of view is third person.
Suggested answers: 1 "Yeah," Dan replied, trying to smile. 2 He sang day and night. 3 He wanted to be an opera singer.

C Think and discuss. Look at the pictures in *Delivery Dan*. What jobs can you see? Why do you think some people do more than one job?

This activity activates prior knowledge about the topic of jobs people enjoy and helps students think about the importance of working hard to reach your goals.

- Give students a few minutes to look at the pictures and discuss the jobs they can see with a partner.
- Have Group Time (see TB p. 21) to discuss the second question as a class. Ask questions to help students with the discussion, e.g. *Do people always have a job they enjoy? Can you choose to do any job you like? Why is it sometimes hard to get the job you want? Can you make money from your hobbies? How important is it to get the right training for your job?*

Answers

Students' own answers

Now read Delivery Dan

Fiction: *Delivery Dan—Story*

Lesson Objectives

- to read a story about a man who dreams of being an opera singer
- make a personal connection to the reading

Materials

Audio Tracks 18 and 19

Warm Up

Ask *What kind of food do you order? Does someone bring it to your house?* Elicit students' experiences.

TRACK 18 TB p. 232 Reading Approach

Listen and Engage

- Project the opening spread of the reading with the Story Player in the TTL. Ask students to notice the position of the text on the page and how this is different from other stories they have read. Ask students what they learn about Dan from the pictures.
- Play the audio and have students follow along in their books. Pause the audio to ask prediction questions, e.g. *Do you think Dan will be an opera singer one day?*

TRACK 19 TB p. 232 Words in Context

- After the first reading of the text, draw students' attention to the Words in Context box.
- Have students brainstorm a list of strategies that they can use to find the meanings of the words.
- Divide the class into pairs or groups and have each pair or group look at all of the words. They should highlight each instance of each word, then identify the type of word by looking at the form and the sentence.
- Have students swap pairs or groups to explain the words, and share strategies.
- Elicit the meanings of the words as a class. Ask *Which strategies worked? Which didn't?*

ushers (p. 62, noun) The picture shows what an usher is. Strategies to use: pictures, world knowledge

audition (p. 62 / p. 68, noun) The surrounding sentences on p. 62 and p. 68 show it's like a test that you can pass or fail (p. 62, "I didn't get the part;" p. 68, "you already passed …") Strategies to use: surrounding words and sentences, world knowledge of the world of theater and how people get a job.

opera (p. 63 / p. 68 / p. 69, noun) The pictures show this is related to music. On p. 63, the following sentence tells us that this refers to old songs. The picture on p. 69 also gives us context. Strategies to use: surrounding words and sentences, pictures

starving (p. 65, adjective) The previous sentence shows it's a response to an invitation to eat. The previous paragraph helps us understand that Dan is probably hungry after working a lot ("he rode his bike many kilometers") Strategies to use: surrounding words and sentences, personal experience

tip (p. 66 / p. 67, noun) The pictures show the tip being offered. The preceding adjectives *nice* and *big* tell us it's something positive and also quantifiable. Strategies to use: pictures, surrounding words and sentences, world knowledge

- Go through each word. Play the audio to practice pronunciation.

Analyze the Text and Features

- Have students read individually, thinking about how each picture represents a part of the text as they read.
- Have students find the red callouts and discuss in pairs. Alternatively, use Group Time to discuss the question after students have finished reading (see TB p. 21).
    - **Making Connections** (p. 63): *Why do you think Dan wanted to take Italian lessons?* Ask *What language are many operas are in?*
    - **Personalization** (p. 69): *Have you ever listened to opera music?* Have students discuss in pairs. If possible, play a clip of opera music.
    - **Text Focus** (p. 62): *Hyperbole is exaggeration which may make a story funnier or more interesting.* Ask students how many times they think Ella said this to Dan. Ask *Did she really say it a million times? Can you find any other examples of hyperbole?* Have students look for more examples of hyperbole (*the unhappiest guy in the world*, p. 62; *day and night*, p. 63; *more than anything in the world*, p. 63; *hundreds of hungry kids*, p. 65; *starving*, p. 65).

Interact with the Text

- Have students draw a timeline of the plot, labelling key events. Elicit the beginning (Dan is working as an usher at the theater) and end (he is singing in the opera).

Cool Down

Have students do a Circle of Viewpoints routine to identify and explore the different possible perspectives in the story. Have students choose one of the following viewpoints: Ella, Antonia Allegro, one of Dan's customers, or a member of the audience at the opera. Say *I am thinking about Dan from the point of view of …* Have students write their thoughts about Dan from the point of view of their chosen character. This could be done in groups, with each member of the group taking on the role of a different character.

Practice **Student's App:** Story Player

Explore the Reading

Lesson Objectives

- to understand and analyze *Delivery Dan* through reading comprehension activities
- to explore the SEL competency of by planning and working toward goals
- to make a personal connection to the reading

Warm Up

Play *What's the Scene?* (see TB p. 27) with the pictures from *Delivery Dan*.

A Think and write. Imagine you're Dan. Answer the questions from a first-person point of view. Remember to add Dan's thoughts and feelings.

- Students are going to check their comprehension of the reading and practice the skill of understanding points of view. Have a Group Time discussion (see TB p. 21) to help students to remember the key ideas from the story. Ask questions to prompt students where necessary, e.g. *What was Dan's dream? Why did he need money?*
- Tell students to imagine they are Dan. Read the first question, *Where were you working at the beginning of the story? How did you feel?* Elicit responses from a few students. Ask *Why did you feel this way?* Tell students to read the questions and write their responses in their books.
- Have students write their ideas in their books individually. Encourage students to look back at the reading to help them. Check answers as a class, having students say how they felt after each one.

Suggested Answers

1 I was working in a theater but I didn't earn any money. I was unhappy.
2 I wanted to be an opera singer.
3 I needed to earn money for singing and Italian lessons, so I started a new job as a bicycle delivery man.
4 I started singing when I delivered food to customers.
5 I delivered lobster soup to the big house on the river. I sang a song, but the woman didn't give me a tip.
6 I went to the Opera House because I got a text inviting me there. The woman who ordered the lobster soup turned out to be the director. She gave me a part in a new opera.
7 I felt so happy and proud at the end of my first performance because my dream had come true. I was also very nervous because there were so many people.

B Think and write. Which adjectives describe Dan in each sentence?

Students are going to analyze the reading in more detail and think about the skills and qualities that Dan displays.

- Ask *What kind of person is Dan?* Elicit ideas from the class and write their suggestions on the board. Then have students look at the adjectives on the page.
- Ask *How did Dan show these qualities in the story? How was he hardworking?* (He had three jobs.) Point out that the answer to the first question could be *hardworking* but that for some of the questions more than one adjective could be correct.
- Give students a few minutes to match the adjectives to the sentences and write them in their books. Then check answers as a class.

Suggested Answers

1 hardworking, busy 2 fit 3 talented 4 resourceful, creative, excited 5 talented, excited 6 nervous, proud

C Think and discuss. Dan followed his dream to become an opera singer. What is one of your dreams? What is your plan to make it happen?

In this activity, students will explore the SEL competency of self-management by setting plans and working toward goals. They will think about their own dreams and the steps they can take to try to make their dreams come true.

- Ask *What dreams do you have?* Give students two or three minutes to think about their dreams and discuss with a friend.
- Ask *What skills do you need to do this? What can you do to make your dream happen?* Tell students to think about the skills, qualities, and qualifications they need to reach their goal. Do an example with the class, e.g. *If you want to be a doctor, you will have to study a degree in medicine. To do this, you need to get good grades in science, so you will have to work hard in science class.*
- Have students discuss their ideas in pairs or small groups. Encourage students to ask each other questions, e.g. *What is your dream? Why do you want to do this? What can you do to make it happen?*

Answers

Students' own answers

Cool Down

Play *Mime It!* using the adjectives from p. 70 (see TB p. 26).

Practice Student's App: Reading Practice

Think Together

Lesson Objectives

- to make connections between the readings
- to explore the key concept: Why do we work?
- to reflect on the unit and provide personal thoughts and opinions

Warm Up

Remind students of Ida Lewis from *The Hero of Lime Rock* and Dan from *Delivery Dan*. Tell them to think of two similarities and one difference between the two characters. (Similarities: They both worked very hard; They both helped people; Their jobs were rewarding; They both became famous / Differences: Ida saved lives; They lived in different periods; Ida learned her skills, whereas Dan had talent.)

A Think and discuss. Look back at *The Hero of Lime Rock* and *Delivery Dan*. Complete the table.

Students are going to use critical thinking skills to analyze elements of the two readings. Ask students what jobs the two characters did in the readings. Then ask *Why did Ida do this job?*

- Students complete the rest of the table. Allow them to look back at the readings. Check answers as a class, highlighting how the characters' qualities and skills influence their choice of job.

Answers

Ida Lewis: Lighthouse keeper; 1 She loved the ocean. 2 She loved working in the lighthouse. 3 She was brave and good at rescuing people.
Dan: Volunteered at the theater, 1 He wanted to work in a theatre in order to meet people and watch performances.; Delivery Man, 2 He needed money.; Opera Singer: 3 He loved singing and it was his dream.

B What different jobs do you know? Do a Round Robin. Then make a list.

- Put students in groups of four. Tell students that they are going to brainstorm all the jobs they know. Remind students how to do a Round Robin (see TB p. 20). Then give students two minutes to make a list of the jobs they came up with.
- Elicit ideas from the class and make a list on the board. Students can then add any jobs they didn't have to their lists.

Answer

Students' own answers

C Think and discuss. Look at the jobs in B. Why do people do these different jobs? What skills and qualities do people need to do these jobs?

Students are now going to identify the skills and qualities required in different jobs and discuss the key concept, *Why do we work?*

- Have each group call out one job from their lists and write these as headings on the board. Ask *Why do people do these jobs?* Elicit ideas from the class and write them on the board, e.g. vet—because they love animals. Elicit more than one reason for each job.
- Ask *What skills and qualities do you need to do these jobs?* Encourage students to use adjectives from p. 70 in their responses. Provide examples of skills, e.g. being able to drive.
- Have students discuss in small groups and then elicit ideas.

My Reading Journal

What did you learn about the jobs in the readings in this unit?

This question focuses on self-evaluation and encourages students to think about what they have learned. Give students time to think and write their answer, then discuss in pairs or small groups.

Have a few students share their ideas with the class.

Suggested Answer

I learned that you meet lots of people if you are a delivery man.

What do you want to be when you grow up? Why?

This question focuses on personalization. Give students time to think about why they want to do the job of their choice before they write their answers. Have them discuss with a friend. Ask if any students would like to share their answers with the class.

Suggested Answer

I want to be an architect because I like drawing and designing.

Go back to page 57. What new questions do you have?

Have students look back at the VTR picture on pp. 56–57. Using the TTL, project the image onto the board. Ask students how they think the picture connects to the two readings in the unit. Then repeat the Question Starts routine. If you recorded students' questions in Lesson 1, display these. Encourage students to think of new questions they have now, e.g. *What skills do you need to be a pet furniture designer?*

Cool Down

Play *I'm the Expert* (see TB p. 20). Have students choose one of the jobs from the unit.

Practice **Resource Bank:** Unit Test
Student's App: Key Concept Practice

UNIT 5

Express Yourself

Unit Overview

Themes

Coping with emotions and challenging situations

How to manage our emotions

Synopsis

In this unit, students will explore the concept of emotions. They will learn about positive and negative feelings and how to manage them. They will learn about how to improve their mood and discuss how feelings can affect how they learn. Students will plan and prepare a presentation and write an acrostic poem.

Language Book

Vocabulary

confused, delighted, determined, disappointed, enthusiastic, furious, optimistic, pessimistic, upset, worried

Pronunciation: sentence stress: content words

p. 112

Explore Language

Modal Verbs of Deduction

p. 113

Global Citizenship

How do our emotions affect our learning?

confident, fail, frustrating, improve, insecure, make mistakes, negative, positive, succeed

p. 114

Explore Language

Adverbs of Probability

p. 115

Take the Stage

Presentation: offering encouragement and dealing with nerves

p. 116

Write About It

An Acrostic Poem

Paragraph Building: using expressive language in poetry

Word Study: similes and metaphors

p. 117

Think It Over

Review and Reflection: My Favorite Mistakes

p. 118

Literacy Book

Think Together
How do we identify emotions?

p. 125

Visible Thinking
Step Inside

p. 119

Nonfiction
Instructional Text: *Using Your Emotional Toolbox*

Words in Context: *expect, deal with, strategies, contagious, mood*

p. 123

Fiction
Poems: *How I Feel*

Words in Context: *never mind, dare, attack, swoops, hanging out*

p. 120

Reading Skill
Identifying sensory details

p. 122

Literary Term
Metaphor

p. 124

Language and Literacy Connections

The connecting theme for Unit 5 is feelings and emotions.

	Language	Literacy
Vocabulary	**Set 1:** emotions 1 **Set 2:** emotions 2	**Nonfiction:** confused, upset, worried, positive
Grammar	**Modal Verbs of Deduction** It can't be a person, can it? It could be a bear. It must want our food. It might be a wild animal. **Adverbs of Probability** I'll probably forget about him in a week. Maybe I'll miss him a bit. Santiago's definitely going to miss you. Obviously you should be in the picture.	**Nonfiction:** See what the feeling may have to tell you. It could help you work through the difficult feelings.
Skills	**Pronunciation:** sentence stress: content words **Process Writing:** planning	**Reading:** identifying sensory details **Literary Term:** metaphor
International English	pretty sure/quite sure; recognize/recognise	jumping jacks/star jumps, sailboat/sailing boat, couch/sofa

Vocabulary

Lesson Objectives

- to learn vocabulary related to emotions: *confused, delighted, determined, disappointed, enthusiastic, furious, optimistic, pessimistic, upset, worried*
- to say a poem about being positive
- to practice sentence stress: content words

Materials
Audio Tracks 51 to 55; Video

Warm Up

Discuss students' experiences of outdoor activities or other challenges. Ask *Do you enjoy going to the countryside? Why or why not?*

A TRACK 51 TB p. 220 **Listen. Is Tyler leading the team well?**

- Display the opening spread with the TTL. Have students discuss what is happening in pairs, giving reasons. Elicit that the children are working in teams to follow clues.
- Tell students that they are going to listen to a conversation between some of the children in the picture. Remind students of the challenge from the end of Unit 4. Ask *Where was Nancy-Yu going? What is she doing there?* (She is behind the bushes and trees in the top right-hand corner. She is organizing an orienteering activity for the children.)
- Play the audio and have students look at the picture.
- Ask the gist question *Is Tyler leading the team well?* Play the audio again and check the answer.

Answer
Yes, he's doing his best to encourage everyone, and he's making sure that everyone is all right.

B TRACK 52 TB p. 221 **Find and number the words in A. Then listen and check.**

- Point out the example (1). Have students find the girl who looks *determined*. Do the activity together, asking questions to guide students, e.g. *What is she determined to do?*

Answers
1 *determined* 2 upset 3 furious 4 delighted
5 optimistic 6 pessimistic 7 disappointed
8 worried 9 enthusiastic 10 confused

C TRACK 53 TB p. 221 **Close your eyes. Listen, visualize, and say.**

- Prepare students for the visualization (see Visualization).
- Play the audio, allowing students to visualize as they listen.
- Encourage students to believe they are really in a forest, imagining all of the colors in the forest, smells, sounds, and how the earth feels under their feet.
- Encourage them to use facial expressions to show the emotions described in the visualization.

D Look and write. Then write three more adjectives in each category.

- Display the graphic organizer and have students notice the faces. Check understanding of *positive* and *negative*. Elicit that *delighted* is a positive emotion.
- Students use critical thinking to complete the organizer individually. Then have them compare their answers with a partner. Ask students to call out their extra adjectives; write these on the board for the class to see, and check understanding.

Suggested Answers
Adjectives for positive emotions: *delighted*, optimistic, determined, enthusiastic, students' own answers
Adjectives for negative emotions: confused, disappointed, furious, pessimistic, upset, worried, students' own answers

E TRACK 54 TB p. 221 **Listen and write. Then watch and say.**

- Play the video or audio of the poem and allow students to enjoy it. If you want to focus on the pronunciation, you may want to use just the audio initially. Ask students what they think the title means. Tell students that *to feel blue* is an idiom that means "to feel sad." Then ask why someone might be feeling sad when going on a trip.
- Give students time to read the poem and try to complete the blanks. Play the poem video or audio and have students check their answers.
- Play the video or audio again and have students join in. Encourage students to copy the rhythm and pronunciation.

Answers
1 *pessimistic* 2 confused 3 upset 4 determined
5 worried 6 optimistic

F TRACK 55 TB p. 221 **Pronunciation. Listen and say. Copy the sentence stress. Find other sentences in the poem and notice the stress patterns.**

- Point out that some words in the poem have a stronger stress than others. Have students try saying the phrases. Then play the audio and have them listen and repeat, noticing the stressed and weak words.
- Have students identify the stressed words in other sentences from the poem. Play the poem again, pausing after each sentence to have students repeat it chorally. Write some of the sentences on the board and mark the stressed syllables.

Answers
Stressed words in sentences are nouns, adjectives, verbs, question words, and some prepositions (*off* in *started off*).

Cool Down

Play *Freeze!* (see TB p. 26). Play the poem video again and have students act it out. They should try to show the emotions as they act out the scenes, using gestures and facial expressions.

Practice **Student's App:** Vocabulary Practice; Spoken Word Video

Explore Language

Lesson Objectives

- to learn how to use modal verbs of deduction
- to practice vocabulary related to emotions

Materials

Audio Tracks 56 and 57; recording of sounds from the forest (Warm Up)

Warm Up

Ask *Do you ever go to the forest?* Tell students to imagine they are in the forest. It's getting dark. Play the recording of forest sounds (you could use a sound effects app or look up forest sounds online). Ask *What did you hear?* Have students compare their ideas in small groups.

A TRACK 56 TB p. 221 **Listen and read. What was making the scary noise in the forest?**

- Tell students they are going to listen to two girls, Katie and Yukiko, talking in the forest. Have students find them in the picture on pp. 62–63 and say how they were feeling. Play the audio and have students follow the story.
- Ask the gist question *What was making the scary noise in the forest?* and elicit the answer. Play the audio again for students to check. Ask *What did they think was making the noise?* (a bear)

Answer

Mason was!

International English

Have students notice the similarities and differences between the two phrases. Elicit that the adjective *sure* is the same in both varieties but the adverb is different. The American English phrase *pretty sure* is also commonly used in the UK.

B Look at A. Complete the table. Which verb form comes after the modal verb?

- Display the table using the TTL.
- Students should now have the skills and strategies to be able to discuss and complete the grammar table themselves using the story. When they have completed the table, invite students to come up to the board and fill in one word each. Ask if everyone agrees. Discuss the word order, form, and patterns together, but let your class guide the discussion. For more support, use the notes in the **ETB**.
- Draw students' attention to the Grammar tip *Look*. Have students notice that we use *must* and *could* for affirmative sentences. We don't use *can* or *mustn't* to express deduction. Have students look at the table again and elicit that we use *can't* for negative sentences.

Answers

be; could, be; may; must, be; want

The infinitive without *to* comes after the modal verb.

C Think and discuss. Then choose and complete.

- Have students discuss the first statement in pairs, referring to the table in B for examples of modals of deduction. Elicit that we don't use modal verbs when we are sure. Yukiko would say *It's a bear* if she knew it was a bear.
- Draw students' attention to the arrow on the page for number 2. Elicit that it is a scale that shows being sure something is true (left) to being sure it isn't true (right). Have students work in pairs to look at the arrow diagram and complete with modal verbs. Check answers.

Answers

1 believe 2 sure it's true: must; possibly true: *may*, might, could; sure it isn't true: can't

D TRACK 57 TB p. 221 **Listen and say.**

- Play the audio, having students repeat each sentence chorally.
- For ideas on how to vary the drill, see TB p. 23.

E Complete the deductions. Sometimes more than one answer is possible.

- Look at the example in the controlled practice activity together. Tell students to think about whether the person in each sentence is sure or if it is just possibly true. Have them think about whether there is evidence to back up the idea.
- Have students complete the sentences individually. Check answers as a class. Explain that *may*, *might*, and *could* have very similar meanings and are interchangeable.

Answers

1 *can't* 2 must 3 can't 4 might / may / could
5 might / may / could 6 might / may / could

F Make deductions about the picture. Ask and answer.

- Have students look at the picture and say what they see. In this freer oral practice, students are going make deductions about the picture, saying what they think and using the picture as evidence.
- Have two students read the examples on the page. Ask *Why do you think the backpack is heavy?* Elicit that it's very big. Remind students to use modal verbs in their guesses. Have students ask and answer in pairs.

Answers

Students' own answers

Cool Down

Play *Twenty Questions* (see TB p. 27). After every five questions, students must make a deduction, e.g. *It might be a tiger* or *It can't be a snake because it has four legs.* When they are sure, they say *It must be …*

Practice **Resource Bank:** Grammar Printout
Student's App: Grammar Practice

Global Citizenship

Lesson Objectives

- to learn more vocabulary related to emotions: *confident, fail, frustrating, improve, insecure, make mistakes, negative, positive, succeed*
- to explore how our emotions affect our learning and how we can change our feelings
- to practice listening for gist and detail

Materials
Audio Tracks 58 and 60; Audio Track E; a map of the world (D)

Opening Question

Ask the opening question: *How do your emotions affect our learning?* Elicit ideas and encourage students to think about how they feel at school. Ask students if they work well when they feel tired or upset. Encourage personal responses.

A TRACK 58 TB p. 221 **Listen to an interview with Dr. Hernández, a child psychologist. What problem does he talk about?**

- Tell students they are going to listen to a child psychologist talking about a problem. Ask students why people might go to see a psychologist and what problems children might have. Discuss briefly with the class.
- Ask the gist question *What problem does he talk about?* Play the audio and have students look at the pictures as they listen. Check the answer with the class. Ask students how they feel when they make mistakes.

Answer
He talks about people believing that if they make mistakes, they've failed.

B TRACK 59 TB p. 221 **Look at the pictures and definitions in A and write. Then listen and check.**

- Point out the example for number 1, *succeed*. Refer students to the vocabulary box in B and have them write the words for each picture and definition in A in pairs.
- Play the audio for students to check their answers. Use the audio to drill the pronunciation of the words.

Answers
1 *succeed* 2 fail 3 positive 4 make mistakes 5 frustrating 6 improve 7 insecure 8 negative 9 confident

TRACK E TB p. 221 **Visualization**

- The TTL has a visualization audio track for this vocabulary set. (See TB p. 21.)

C Read and complete the letter asking for advice.

- Tell students they are going to read a letter from a girl who needs advice. Have students read the letter to find out what the girl's problem is (her friend can't deal with failure).
- Look at the example together. Ask *How do you know the experience was negative?* (Fran's friend made a mistake.) Elicit that you have to continue reading to find out what happened.
- Have students complete the sentences. Then check answers as a class.

Answers
1 *negative* 2 mistakes 3 improve 4 succeed 5 fail 6 positive 7 confident

D TRACK 60 TB p. 221 **Now listen to Erik. What disadvantage of living in Tromsø in Norway does he mention?**

- Tell students they are going to listen to an interview with a boy from Norway about the place where he lives.
- Have students look at the picture and say what they can see. Ask students what they know about Norway. Have them find Norway (or ideally, Tromsø) on a map and find out how far away it is from your country.
- Listening for gist: ask the gist question *What disadvantage of living in Tromsø does he mention?* Play the audio and check answers.

Answer
the 60 Polar Nights when people never see the sun

E Listen again. Choose the correct answer.

- Have students read the sentences again before they listen again and try to choose the right answer for each sentence. Play the audio and check answers.
- Ask students to imagine how they would feel if they lived in Tromsø. Link back to the opening question and ask students if they think their learning might be affected.

Answers
1 *24 hours* 2 winter 3 feel very tired 4 want to see their 5 should 6 talking to people 7 Positive

Discussion Questions

- Draw students' attention to the discussion questions. Have students discuss each question in pairs or small groups (see **ETB**). Guide students to conclude that our feelings can affect many different areas of our lives and it is important to try to control our emotions and have a positive outlook on life.
- Return to the opening question to ask again: *How do our emotions affect our learning?* Revisit any ideas discussed at the beginning of the lesson and encourage students to share any new ideas.

Cool Down

Have students write messages for the Positive Post Box (see **ETB**, Unit 4, Think Together Extension). They can write advice for their classmates based on observations they have made, e.g. *Sometimes I think you need help with an activity. I would like to help you!*

Practice **Student's App:** Vocabulary Practice; Listening Practice

Explore Language

Lesson Objectives

- to learn how to use adverbs of probability

Materials

Audio Tracks 61 and 62

Warm Up

Display the picture from p. 68 or have students use their books. Give students 30 seconds to look at the picture and remember as much as they can. Hide the picture and ask: *How many children are there?* (eight) *How many people are wearing blue caps?* (five) *What does the boy on the left have around his neck?* (a camera)

A TRACK 61 TB p. 222 **Listen and read. How does Mason feel?**

- Tell students that they are going to listen to Mason talking to the team leader, Jalen. Have students remember what Mason did in Lesson 2 (he made animal noises and frightened the girls). Play the audio and have students follow the dialogue in their books.
- Ask the gist question *How does Mason feel?* and elicit the answer. Ask *Why does he feel this way?* Elicit answers.

Answers
He's sad, but at the beginning he pretends he isn't. He's trying to be positive and says he's delighted for Santiago.

B Look at A. Complete the table. Which adverb can come at the beginning of the sentence or before the main verb?

- Write or display the table on the board.
- Students should now have the skills and strategies to discuss and complete the grammar table themselves using the dialogue. When they have completed the table, invite students to come up to the board and fill in one word each. Ask if everyone agrees. Discuss the word order, form, and patterns together, but let your class guide the discussion. For more support, use the notes in the **ETB**.
- Draw students' attention to the Grammar tip *Look*. Elicit that *maybe* and *perhaps* are synonyms. Have students look at the sentences in the table and find out where these two adverbs go (at the beginning of the sentence).

Answers
definitely, going; Maybe, miss; Perhaps, can; Obviously, should, be
Obviously can come at the beginning of the sentence or before the main verb.

C Think and discuss. Then choose and complete.

- Have students work in pairs to discuss the first sentence. Check the answer and elicit that we use these words in a similar way to the modal verbs of deduction—*may, might,* and *could*—to talk about things that we think are true.
- Have students work in pairs to complete the arrow diagram with the missing words. Then elicit which words we use when we are sure about something and which words we use when we are not sure.

Answers
1 sure 2 *perhaps*, maybe; probably; *definitely*, obviously

D TRACK 62 TB p. 222 **Listen and say.**

- Play the audio. Have students repeat sentences chorally.
- Play it again. Have students use facial expressions and gestures to show how sure they feel for each sentence.
- For ideas on how to vary the drill, see TB p. 23.

E Read and choose.

- Look at the example in the controlled practice activity. Elicit why *maybe* is incorrect in this sentence (it should be at the beginning of the sentence). Tell students to think about the position and meaning of the adverbs to help them choose the correct answer.
- Have students circle the words individually. Then check answers as a class.

Answers
1 *probably* 2 obviously 3 definitely 4 Perhaps
5 definitely 6 Maybe

International English

Have students notice the different spellings. Tell students that the pronunciation is the same. You may wish to point out that this spelling difference is a frequent one and many words follow these patterns. Elicit a word with the same pattern from Unit 4 (*realize/realise*).

F Play *What's the Chance?* Discuss with a friend.

- This activity provides freer oral practice of adverbs of probability. Have students look at the pictures and name the activities. Have students read the time prompts and check understanding of each one. Then have two students read the examples on the page.
- Have students play the game in pairs. Circulate, monitor, and help as necessary. Afterward, highlight any common mistakes on the board.

Answers
Students' own answers

Cool Down

Play a variation of *Word Sneak* (see TB p. 27). This time, instead of giving students words to use, give them a sentence containing an adverb of probability, e.g. *You'll obviously find the answer.*

Practice **Resource Bank:** Grammar Printout
Student's App: Grammar Practice

Write About It

Lesson Objectives

- to plan and write an acrostic poem
- to learn how to use expressive language in poetry
- to learn how to use similes and metaphors
- to learn how to select and organize ideas to help your writing

Materials
Support writing printout from the Resource (F)

Warm Up

Ask students if they can think of any poems that they know. Remind students of the poems in Lesson 1 of Unit 2 (p. 23) and Unit 4 (p. 49). Have students choose one, and play the video.

A Read the acrostic poems. What six things does the writer compare himself to?

This text type is also modeled in the Literacy Book for this unit, How I Feel.

- Display the first picture using the TTL. Ask *What's happening? Who is the boy? How do you think he feels? How does the picture make you feel?* Repeat with the picture from the second poem.
- Have students read the two poems. Ask *What six things does the writer compare himself to?* Give students a minute or two to answer. Ask *Which poems do you prefer?*

Answers
duck, kitten, bear, mice, balloon, snowflake

B Look at the structure of the acrostic poems. Read and answer.

- Look at the first question together. Have students notice that the first letter of the title is not included.
- Give students time to work individually, then check answers together. Ensure students notice the types of words used at the start of the sentences.

Answers
1 RELAXED, OPTIMISTIC 2 They are all images of things that make you feel good; they are all positive images. 3 No, because each line has to start with the correct letter. 4 No, sometimes there are gerunds, subject pronouns, and so on. 5 It doesn't start a word—it means a kiss.

C Look at the language in the acrostic poems. Read and respond.

- If you have not yet done the **Literacy Book** unit, refer students to A. Ask *How does the writer compare himself to a duck?* (the way of moving through the water like a duck paddling its feet). Point out that similes use *as* or *like*. Have students find more in the poem. Tell students that more direct comparisons, e.g. *I'm a balloon*, are called *metaphors*.
- Have students work in pairs. Then check answers together.

Answers
1 any phrase with *like*, e.g. like a duck, like a kitten; any phrase with *as* … *as*, e.g. as sleepy as a bear, as quiet as mice 2 b 3 c 4 Today I'm a balloon; I'm a snowflake 5 c

- Draw students' attention to the callout. Have students choose their favorite simile or metaphor from the poems.

D Think and discuss. Choose an adjective or think of one of your own for an acrostic poem. Brainstorm some ideas for each of the headings using a Generating Ideas technique.

- Review the different ways of generating ideas that students discussed in **Process Writing Step 1: Generating Ideas** on p. 140.
- Tell students to choose an adjective from the page or think of a different one. Then have students choose a way of generating ideas and to use it to brainstorm words and images they can use in their poem, using the headings to help them.

Answers
Students' own answers

E Plan your acrostic poem. Use your notes in D and a Planning technique.

- Review the planning techniques students have looked at in **Process Writing Step 2: Planning** on p. 141.
- Have students think about the words and images they want to use and how they can fit these together.
- Have students make notes in the space provided.

Answer
Students' own answers

F Now write your acrostic poem.

- Remind students to give their poem a title. Alternatively, this can be done once they have written the poem. Have students write a rough draft of their poems in their notebooks or using the Support printout from the Resource Bank. When they're happy with it, they can write it up on paper and add illustrations or decoration.
- Give students time to write and illustrate their poems or have them do it for homework.
- Display the poems on the classroom walls. Have students go around the room reading each other's poems. Remind students to make positive comments about the writing

Answers
Students' own answers

Cool Down

Choose one of the key words from the unit, e.g. *succeed*. Write the letters down the side of the board like an acrostic. Give students one minute to think of a word beginning with each letter in pairs.

Practice **Student's App:** Writing Practice
Resource Bank: Writing Game, *Unfortunately, Fortunately*

Talk About It

Lesson Objectives

- to prepare and practice a presentation giving advice
- to learn how to offer encouragement and deal with nerves

Materials
Video

Warm Up

Tell students you have a problem, e.g. your pet is sick. Write the problem on the board and ask students what advice they can give you. Write their suggestions on the board and then take a class vote on the best piece of advice.

A TB p. 239 **Watch and listen. Have you ever felt nervous about giving a presentation?**

- Tell students they are going to watch a video of a girl named Linda giving a presentation about giving presentations. Ask a prediction question: *What emotions do you think she will talk about?* Elicit suggestions from the class. Then play the video.
- Draw students' attention to the question *Have you ever felt nervous about giving a presentation?* Have students discuss the question with a friend.

Answers
Students' own answers

B Watch again. Check (✔) the expressions Linda uses to encourage her audience.

- Have students read the sentences before they rewatch the video and see if they remember which phrases Linda used.
- Play the video once and have students check their answers and complete. Then play the video again and check answers as a class. Then play the video again and have students repeat the phrases, copying Linda's pronunciation and intonation.

Answers
1; 2; 4; 6; 8; 9; 10

C Think of a time when you were nervous. Research and prepare a presentation to encourage people who are in a similar situation.

- Ask *What things make you nervous?* Brainstorm a few situations with the class, e.g. exams, competitions, sporting tournaments, or performances such as plays.
- Draw students' attention to the questions on the notepad paper in C. Have students think and write notes answering the questions in their notebooks individually. Give students time to do some research to find tips they can include in their presentations. They could ask family members, friends, or other teachers for ideas, or they could do research online. If necessary, they could do this for homework before the lesson.
- Tell students to try to use some of the phrases from B to encourage their audience. Remind students that they only need to write notes to prompt them during the presentation and not full sentences. Remind them that speaking spontaneously is more engaging than just reading full sentences from their notes.

Answers
Students' own answers

D Practice with your friends using phrases in B. Then share with the class. Make notes.

- Have students practice their presentations as many times as they like. Remind students that the more times they practice, the more familiar they will be with what they are going to say and the more comfortable they will feel.
- Have some students give their presentations in front of the class. While they are speaking, the other students should make notes. You could have them draw a table in their notebooks with the following columns: *Name*, *Topic*, *Things I Learned*, *Questions I Have*. When they have finished, students can compare their notes about their friends' presentations.

Cool Down

Play *I'm the Expert* (see TB p. 26). Have students choose an emotion and pretend to be a psychologist, giving advice on how to deal with that emotion.

Practice **Student's App:** Speaking Skills Practice; Speaking Video

Think It Over

Lesson Objectives

- to review what has been learned in the unit
- to reflect on the unit and their own progress
- to think about learning strategies and how to continue learning at home

Warm Up

Do a quick quiz with the class about Unit 5. Ask questions about pictures, words, or information and have students find the answers in their books. Have students play in teams. Possible questions: *What animals can you see on p. 62? What is the boy taking a picture of on p. 62? What are the two girls' names on p. 64? What illness does Erik mention on p. 67? What's the word for definition 7 on p. 66?*

How well did you meet the challenge of Unit 5? Read and respond.

My Favorite Mistakes

- Tell students they are going to think about what they learned during the unit and how they can improve. Remind students of the listening activity on p. 66 (A). Ask students to remember what Dr. Hernández said about making mistakes. Elicit that making mistakes can actually help you improve. Tell students that they are going to think about the mistakes they made in the unit, as well as what they have learned. Let them know that it's important that they don't worry about what other people think or say, as different students will have made different mistakes. Point out that everyone can find some way of improving, even if they think they didn't make any mistakes!
- Have students work in groups to think about the activities they did during the unit. Give each group a pack of sticky notes and have them write an idea on each one. Encourage students to think about the different things they studied in the unit, including grammar, presentation phrases, poems, vocabulary for emotions, facts, interesting ideas, and so on. Then have students stick their notes onto a board or a poster and display it on the wall. Have groups go around the classroom and look at each other's sticky note board.
- Draw students' attention to the acrostic: MISTAKES. Elicit the meaning of the words and explain that this means that we learn from our mistakes. Refer students to the different sections in the graphic organizer: *Two mistakes that I made in this unit that moved my learning on are …, Two things (knowledge) that I learned about emotions are …, Two things (experience and skills) I learned to say or do in English are …* Have students talk in pairs about the different sections. Write some prompts on the board to support their conversation, e.g. *I didn't know how to do this; I got this answer wrong; I didn't do this very well; I learned about …*
- Ask students what they would like to work on to improve. Refer students to the final section of the graphic organizer (*One thing I want to work on next month is …*) and the notes below it. Have students think about their ideas and then discuss them with a friend. The following prompts may be useful: *I'd like to know / learn more about …; Next time, I'm going to …*
- When you feel they have enough ideas, have students work individually to fill in the organizer. Remind them that they should write their own responses about themselves. Monitor and help as necessary. Look at what students are writing so you can tailor your classes and any additional practice to their needs.
- Ask if anyone has the same goals as their friend. Point out that goals should be personal and each student should choose those they think they would benefit from most. Remind students that everyone learns differently, so they will all have different answers.

Looking Forward

Draw students' attention to the character at the bottom of the page. Elicit who it is and what they remember about him. (Santiago appeared in Lessons 1, 2 and 4.) Ask *Where is Santiago moving to?* (Mexico) Have students read the speech bubble and make predictions about what Santiago's family does in Mexico. Tell them that they will find out in the first lesson of Unit 6.

Practice **Resource Bank:** Unit Test; Mid-year Test
Student's App: Vocabulary and Grammar Review

Get Ready to Read

Lesson Objectives

- to activate prior knowledge about emotions
- to guide inquiry and deepen understanding through a Step Inside VTR
- to preview the reading skill of identifying sensory details

Materials

VTR printout from the Resource Bank (A, B, C)

Warm Up

Divide the class into two groups. Tell one group to imagine a family camping trip with cold, wet weather. Tell the other group to imagine a warm, sunny camping trip. Ask questions, e.g. *What did you do? Did you enjoy yourself? How did you feel?* Pair students from each group to compare their ideas. Ask the class *How does the weather affects our feelings?*

Step Inside

A Look at the picture. Choose a person or thing. What can they see?

- This VTR encourages students to step inside a person or object that they can see and imagine their point of view. Ask students what they can see in the picture of a family that is camping. Provide vocabulary where necessary.
- Ask students to imagine that they are one of the people or things in the photo. Explain the concept of putting themselves in someone or something else's shoes.
- Ask students *What can you see (from that person, animal, or thing's viewpoint)?* Encourage them to think about the surroundings. Ask them, e.g. *What is she doing? What is she wearing? How is she feeling?*
- Have students discuss their ideas in pairs and then as a class.

B What do you think they believe?

- Tell students again that they need to imagine what's happening in the head of the person or thing they chose. Check students understand that *believe* means to have an opinion about something.
- Say *I think the man believes that camping is a fun activity. What does your person, animal, or thing believe?*
- Give students time to think about the person, animal, or thing they have chosen and their thoughts and opinions. Have students discuss their ideas in pairs and then as a class.

Here's an example of this part of the routine.

Teacher: Who did you decide to be in in the picture?
Student A: The girl with the cell phone.
Teacher: OK, so what does she believe?
Student A: She believes that sleeping in a tent is exciting.
Teacher: Great. What makes you say that?
Student B: Because she looks happy and she's taking a picture of the tent.

C What do you think they care about?

- Say *I care about the environment, so I always recycle.* Then ask students *If you care about something, is that thing important to you or not?* (yes)
- Ask students to think about what is important to the people, animals, or things in the picture. Give students time to think, then discuss in pairs. Elicit ideas.

Here's an example of this part of the routine.

Teacher: What does your person, animal, or thing care about?
Student A: The big girl cares about animals.
Teacher: Does she care about the countryside?
Student B: Yes, because lots of animals live there.

Transition

Ask students how they would feel if they went on a camping trip like the one in the picture. Ask them if they think they would have a good time. Elicit ideas and encourage students to give reasons for their ideas.

D Think and discuss. What is a feeling? What different emotions can you name? Then make a list.

- Elicit that *feeling* and *emotion* are synonyms. Ask students what feelings or emotions they mentioned in the Step Inside routine.
- Have students make a list of emotions in their notebooks in pairs. The pair with the most emotions on their list wins. Check answers by having the pair with the most answers read their list aloud.

Answers

Students' own answers

E Think and discuss. Look at the pictures in *Using Your Emotional Toolbox*. What are the people feeling? What makes you think that?

Students are going to preview the reading skill of drawing conclusions.

- Tell students to look at the pictures on pp. 74–77 and think about how the people are feeling. Give them one or two minutes to discuss the pictures and identify the emotions in pairs. Remind students to look at the people's body language as well as their facial expression.
- Elicit ideas and encourage students to give reasons.

Answers

Students' own answers

Now read **Using Your Emotional Toolbox**

Nonfiction: *Using Your Emotional Toolbox*—Instructional Text

Lesson Objectives

- to read an instructional text about dealing with emotions
- to make a personal connection to the reading

Materials

Audio Tracks 20 and 21

Warm Up

Have students choose an emotion and try to express that emotion silently using facial expressions and body language. In pairs they should guess what each emotion is.

TRACK 20 TB p. 233 Reading Approach

Engage with the Text

- Project the opening spread of the reading with the Story Player on the TTL. Ask students what they notice first. Students may find the images and speech bubbles attractive. Have students make predictions.
- For the first reading, have students read the text individually in their books. Before they start, ask prediction questions, e.g. *Which emotions do you think will be in the reading?* Give students plenty of time to read the text.

TRACK 21 TB p. 233 Words in Context

- After the first reading of the text, draw students' attention to the Words in Context box.
- Give students a few minutes to find and highlight each instance of each word in the reading.
- Have them identify the type of word by looking at the form and the sentence.
- Write these strategies on the board: *using pictures*; *using prefixes*; *surrounding words and sentences*; *positive/negative*; *world knowledge*; *personal experience*. Tell students there is one strategy they won't need to use (using prefixes).
- Have students work in pairs to discuss the words.

expect (p. 74, verb) The sentences that follow give a definition of the verb. Strategies to use: surrounding words and sentences, personal experience

deal with (p. 74 / p. 75, verb) This phrasal verb is the key concept of the article. On p. 75, there is a synonym, *handled* / *to handle*, in point 3. Strategies to use: personal experience, surrounding words and sentences

strategies (p. 76 / p. 77, noun) The singular form of this noun is on p. 76 followed by a synonym *plan*. Strategy to use: surrounding words and sentences

contagious (p. 76, adjective) The following phrase, *spread quickly*, acts as a synonym. Other examples are *'peace and quiet*. Strategies to use: surrounding words and sentences, world knowledge

mood (p. 76, noun) The adjective *positive* before this noun tells us that it's a state that can be good or bad. The context of the article tells us this is a feeling. Strategies to use: surrounding words and sentences, personal experience, positive/negative

- Go through each word to elicit the meaning and discuss strategies. Play the audio to practice pronunciation.

Analyze the Text and Features

- Play the audio and have students follow along in their books, or use the Story Player.
- Tell students to find the blue callouts and to discuss the questions with a partner.
  - **Personalization** (p. 74): *How many emotions have you felt today?* Tell students to think of the different things that have happened to them during the day and how they felt at each time.
  - **Fun Fact** (p. 76): *Smiling causes brain activity that actually makes you feel happier.* Have students smile and see if they notice any change in their mood.
  - **Personalization** (p. 77): *Which of these tools might you find useful?* Have students discuss how useful each tool might be for them. Then elicit opinions and find out which tools are most popular with the class.

International English

Encourage students to notice the similarities and differences between the two phrases. Elicit that *jump* is in both phrases. Elicit why (the exercise is a kind of jump). Ask students why they think it is called *star jumps* in British English (because your body looks like a star).

Interact with the Text

- Now that students are very familiar with the text, have them make a simple infographic in pairs including the key strategies from the text. Alternatively, they could make a poster for just one of the strategies.

Cool Down

Ask students which tools from the reading they think are the most useful in different situations. Call out a few situations where students may need to control their emotions, e.g. *the evening before a big test or an argument with their best friend.* Have students choose a strategy and then compare with a friend, justifying their choice.

Practice **Student's App:** Story Player

Explore the Reading

Lesson Objectives

- to understand and analyze "Using Your Emotional Toolbox" through reading comprehension activities
- to learn about the CLIL area of psychology
- to make a personal connection to the reading

Warm Up

Quickly review the different strategies from the reading by playing *Mime It!* (see TB p. 26). Have students choose one of the strategies and act it out.

A Think and write. Complete the outline with the main ideas and details from each heading.

- Refer back to Using Your Emotional Toolbox B in the **Literacy Book.** Review the reading skill of identifying the main idea and details. Remind students that a text usually has one or more main ideas and then includes other details to support that idea so that we understand more. This skill helps us summarize the key ideas in a text to show our understanding.
- Have students open their books and read the instructions. Elicit the two main headings from the reading: *Get to Know Your Emotions* and *Encourage Positive Emotions*. Give students a minute to skim the part of the text under the first heading and identify the main idea. Then draw students' attention to the example. Tell students to look back at the reading to find two supporting details for the first sentence.
- Have students complete the second part of the activity individually. Check answers as a class.

Suggested Answers

I *It's important to handle emotions in a healthy way.*
A Name the feeling
B Find the cause
II Encourage Positive Emotions
A Positive emotions can make us healthier and happier
B Having strategies can help us handle difficult feelings

B Complete the table. Think of a situation from your life for each emotion. Write what you did or would like to do next time. Use strategies from *Using Your Emotional Toolbox*.

- Tell students to think of a time when they were angry about something. Ask students what they did to deal with their anger. Elicit a few ideas and ask *Do you think this is the best thing to do? What else can you do?* Elicit ideas and write the tools and strategies on the board.
- Refer students to the table and tell them to use their own personal experiences to help them complete it. Remind them they can choose to write about the strategy they used or one that they would like to try.
- When students have completed their table, have them discuss their ideas in pairs or small groups.

Answers
Students' own answers

C Think, brainstorm, and write. Then discuss. Why do you think positive emotions can make us healthier and happier?

- Brainstorm positive emotions with the class and write them on the board.
- Draw the students' attention to the mind map and ask *Why do positive emotions make us healthy and happy?* Tell students to think of reasons why this might be true, drawing on their own experiences and lives. Give students a few minutes to think and write their ideas in the mind map.
- Have students compare and discuss their ideas in small groups.

Answers
Students' own answers

Cool Down

End the lesson by having students write messages for their classmates for the Positive Post Box (see TB p. 114).

Practice **Student's App:** Reading Practice

Get Ready to Read

Lesson Objectives

- to activate prior knowledge about our senses
- to practice the reading skill of identifying sensory details

Warm Up

To introduce the reading skill of identifying sensory details, give students two minutes to write down three things they see, two things they hear, and one thing they can smell. Have students compare their 3–2–1 lists with a friend and see if the items they wrote are the same or different.

A Read the poem. Underline the details that describe feelings and senses.

- Display the poem illustration and do a quick See, Think, Wonder routine. Then tell students that the picture illustrates a poem called *The Wish*. Have students predict what the boy in the picture wishes.
- Have students read the poem quickly to find out what the boy wishes. Then ask students why he wishes to be home and have them read the poem again.
- Refer students to the instructions and do an example with the class. Ask *How did Dima's boots feel?* (heavy and wet) Tell students that sometimes they may need to underline phrases, not just individual words.
- Have students look at the reading skill box. Then ask questions to check comprehension, e.g. *What do sensory details describe?* (how something looks, sounds, tastes, feels, or smells) Point out that these kinds of details help us imagine the scene and help us understand how the characters are feeling.

Suggested Answers

Walking through snow, boots heavy and wet; worries (were) sour in his throat; shivered inside his coat; small and alone; foolish, weak boy; thick gray fur; Sharp, pointed teeth, all yellow; home, warm inside.

B Complete the mind map with the words you underlined in A. Some words can appeal to more than one sense.

- Have students look at the mind map and think of one example for each box. These do not necessarily have to be words from the poem.
- Have students look back at A and write the phrases they underlined in the mind map. They can then compare their answers with a friend. Check answers as a class.
- Ask students if they think Dima really saw a wolf. Point out the use of *imagined* and elicit that this suggests that the wolf is just in Dima's imagination and is one of his *worries*. Ask students why they think Dima might imagine there is a wolf nearby. (He is alone and has a long journey ahead. He feels scared, and any sounds he hears might contribute to those feelings.)

Suggested Answers

Hear: boots heavy and wet; walking through snow
Smell: home
Touch: boots heavy and wet; thick gray fur, warm inside
Taste: sour in his throat
See: thick gray fur; Sharp, pointed teeth, all yellow

C Think and write. Draw something that makes you feel each of these emotions. Then write a sentence for each using sensory details.

- Explain that *joy* is a feeling of happiness. Ask students what makes them feel happy and elicit examples.
- Give students a few minutes to think about what makes them feel the three emotions and draw pictures. Tell students that their pictures do not need to be works of art and they should not spend too long drawing.
- Have students complete the sentences in their books. Then have them share their ideas with a friend.

Answers

Students' own answers

Now read **How I Feel**

Fiction: *How I Feel—Poems*

Lesson Objectives

- to read acrostic poems highlighting different emotions
- to make a personal connection to the readings

Materials

Audio Tracks 22 and 23

Warm Up

Elicit some emotions and write them on the board. Choose one and have students do a Rally Robin (see TB p. 20) naming things that make them feel that way.

Genre Focus

An acrostic poem is where the first, last, or other letters in a line spell out a word or phrase, which is usually the theme of the poem. The most common form of an acrostic poem is where the first letters of each line spell out the word or phrase, as in the poems in this lesson.

TRACK 22 TB p. 233 **Reading Approach**

Engage with the Text

- Project the opening spread of the reading with the Story Player in the TTL. Ask students to look at the opening page and predict what the poems are about. Elicit that this reading is made up of several poems all on the theme of feelings. Students may notice that the poems are acrostic (see Background Information in the **ETB**).
- Play the audio. Have students read along. Have students make predictions before they read.

TRACK 23 TB p. 233 **Words in Context**

- After the first reading of the text, draw students' attention to the Words in Context box.
- Give students a few minutes to find and highlight each instance of each word in the reading.
- Have them identify the type of word by looking at the form and the sentence.
- Write these strategies on the board: *pictures; surrounding words and sentences; positive/negative; contrasting ideas; world knowledge; personal experience.*
- Have students work in pairs to discuss the words.

never mind (p. 80, phrase) This phrase is in direct speech. We can see from the context that it's an expression used to cheer someone up. Strategy to use: surrounding words and sentences

dare (p. 81, verb) A contrasting idea to *do you dare* comes in the second clause of the sentence. We know it's contrasting because of the conjunction *or*. Strategies to use: contrasting ideas, surrounding words and sentences

attack (p. 82, verb) The second part of the sentence describes the attack. Strategies to use: pictures, surrounding words and sentences

swoops (p. 82, verb) The words *down low* describe this action, and we can also see the monster swooping in the picture. Strategies to use: surrounding words and sentences, pictures

hanging out (p. 85, verb) The following words *with friends* tell us that this phrasal verb is something you do with people. Strategies to use: pictures, surrounding words and sentences, personal experience

- Then go through each word to elicit the meaning and how they know. Play the audio to practice the pronunciation.

Analyze the Text and Features

- Assign each poem to a group of students. Play the audio again and have the students in the group say their poem along with the audio. At the end of each poem, discuss what makes the writer feel the emotion in each poem.
- Have students discuss the blue callouts with a partner.
  - **Language Focus** (p. 80): *What words can we use to describe emotions?* Have students look at the words spelled out in the acrostic poems. Elicit that some are adjectives and some are nouns. Elicit the nouns for the adjectives and vice versa, e.g. *sadness/sad; surprise/surprised*. Tell students that we usually use the noun *fear* with *scared/afraid*.
  - **Text Focus** (p. 81): *Internal rhyme is when a word in the middle of a line rhymes with a word in the middle or at the end of another line.* Ask students which word in the poem rhymes with *prey* (way). Have students find another example in the same poem (dare/scared). Point out that in this case the rhyme is in the same line.
  - **Text Focus** (p. 82): *Can you find the end rhymes in this poem?* Tell students that end rhyme is when the final words in each line have the same sound. Elicit examples from this poem. Elicit which other poems use end rhyme (*Escape to the Park*, *Joy*, and *My Favorite Things*).
  - **Personalization** (p. 85): *Which poem do you think describes an emotion best?* Have students look back at the poems and choose, justifying their choices.

Interact with the Text

- Have students choose one of the poems and practice reading to a partner. Remind students to include pauses between lines. Play the poems again and have students notice the rhythm.
- When they are ready, have some volunteers perform their poem for the class.

Cool Down

Play *What's the Scene?* (see TB p. 27). Have students choose a picture from one of the poems.

Practice **Student's App:** Story Player

Explore the Reading

Lesson Objectives

- to understand and analyze *How I Feel* through reading comprehension activities
- to explore the SEL competency of self-awareness by recognizing and labeling our own and others' emotions
- to make a personal connection to the reading

Warm Up

Play *Odd One Out* (see TB p. 26) with things from the poems, e.g. sandcastles, bikes, sailboats, salt water (bikes); teeth, eyes, shadows, feet (shadows); rain, sun, clouds, yard (yard); sadness, scary, angry, warm (sadness)

A Answer the questions.

- Have students work in groups to remember details from the poems. One student names a poem (and shows the illustration), and the other students try to remember things about the poem, e.g. *Party* (it was a surprise, it was in the living room, it was dark, everyone was behind the couch).
- Have students open their books. Do the first question together. Elicit that they go to ride bikes in the park.
- Have students write their ideas in their books individually. Encourage students to look back at the text to help them. Check answers as a class.

Suggested Answers

1 They go outside. 2 She is afraid. 3 He was tagged out in baseball. 4 They feel love. 5 any three of the following: hanging out with friends at the zoo, a fresh pizza, painting a picture, purple, a sound in a seashell, new books, a theater, popcorn, sunshine, warm socks

B Read and complete with sensory details from the poems. Write the emotion the lines describe. Trade and discuss the emotions.

- Students are going to analyze the text in more detail and think about the SEL competency of self-awareness by recognizing and labeling their own and others' emotions.
- Ask students what sensory details from the poems are things we can see. Go through the first two poems and elicit ideas from the class, e.g. *dark gray cloud, razor-sharp teeth.*
- Ask students which emotions they describe and elicit ideas (dark gray cloud—sad; razor-sharp teeth—scared).
- Give students a few minutes to look back at the poems to find at least one line for each sense, write them in their books, and decide which emotion it describes. Then discuss answers with the class. Students may have different answers to those below.

Suggested Answers

See: Razor-sharp teeth, hard eyes like stones; scared
Hear: Crunching its scary red jaws; scared
Touch: Sitting in the sunshine, enjoying the heat; happiness/satisfaction
Taste: cheesy melted goo; happiness/satisfaction
Smell: A fresh pizza from the oven; happiness/satisfaction

C Choose two of the poems. Write how each one made you feel. Then discuss.

- Ask students which poems they liked. Then tell students to choose two poems and think about how they felt when they were reading the poems.
- Give students a few minutes to reread some of the poems and write their ideas.
- Have students discuss their ideas in pairs or small groups. Encourage students to ask each other questions, e.g. *Which words made you feel scared?*

Answers

Students' own answers

Literary Term: Metaphor

Read and match.

- Draw students' attention to the explanation of *metaphor*. Look at the example together. Elicit that the classroom isn't really a circus, but it has some things that are similar to a circus. Have students suggest how a classroom might be compared to a circus. Then have them find the matching explanation (c).
- Have students read the remaining sentences and identify the metaphor.
- Have students match the sentences with the explanations.
- Have students find more examples of metaphors in the poems. Check answers as a class and discuss the meaning of each one.

Answers

1 c 2 d 3 a 4 b
Metaphors in the reading: I'm down and feeling blue; A dark, gray cloud blocks my view; her usual sunny smile

Cool Down

Have students invent a new metaphor for how they are feeling right now. Write the prompt *I am …* on the board. Do an example, e.g. *I am a flower in the sunshine*, and have students try to guess how you are feeling.

Practice **Resource Bank:** Literary Term Printout
Student's App: Reading Practice; Literary Term Practice

Think Together

Lesson Objectives

- to make connections between the readings
- to explore the key concept: How do we identify emotions?
- to reflect on the unit and provide personal thoughts and opinions

Warm Up

Show students some of the pictures from both of the readings. Have students describe each picture in pairs, saying which emotion or action it represents and why, e.g. the picture of the boy raking snow on p. 77—*the boy is doing something kind to help him feel better when he is sad.*

A Think, write, and discuss. Identify the emotions from the poems in *How I Feel*. Choose a tool from *Using Your Emotional Toolbox* and give advice.

- Have students look at the box and remember the techniques from *Using Your Emotional Toolbox*. Do the example together.
- Have students read the lines from the poems, identify the emotion, and choose the best tool for each emotion. Check answers as a class, encouraging students to give examples of how each technique could be used, e.g. *Yoga is good if you're sad, as it helps you think positive thoughts.*

Suggested Answers
1 *Sadness; Practice Yoga* 2 Anger; Count to 10
3 Love; Smile 4 Surprise; Do Something Kind
5 Happiness; Do Something Kind 6 Fear; Breathe Deeply

B Think and discuss. What are the signs that someone is having strong feelings? Do a Roundtable.

- Elicit examples of strong feelings from the class and write them on the board. Tell students to think about how people show those feelings. Remind them to think about verbal and nonverbal cues such as negative comments, tone of voice, body language, and facial expressions.
- See TB p. 20 for how to set up a Roundtable. Students are going to take turns writing their ideas on the paper. After two or three minutes, have students stop writing and look at their ideas together in their groups.
- Elicit answers from the class. Encourage students to share details and explanations, including personal stories to illustrate their ideas.

Answers
Students' own answers

C Play a game of Emotional Charades. Take turns, act, and guess.

- Students are going to apply what they have learned in the unit and discuss the key concept question: *How do we identify emotions?*
- Tell students that they are going to play a game in groups. This game is similar to *Mime It!* (see TB p. 26). One student chooses an emotion and tries to demonstrate it without speaking, using only facial expressions and body language. The other students have to guess the emotion.
- Ask students the key concept question: *How do we identify emotions?* Review all the ideas you have discussed in the unit. You could have students write their ideas on a class poster.

My Reading Journal

Do you think this unit has helped you understand your emotions better? Why or why not?

This question focuses on self-evaluation and encourages students to think about what they have learned. Give students time to think and write their answer, then discuss in pairs or small groups.

Suggested Answer
I know that I feel angry sometimes, but now I have some new ideas about what I can do to feel calm.

What do you think was the best part of the unit? Which part did you like the least?

This is a personalization question. Give students time to look back in their books and find things they enjoyed or found interesting and things they didn't enjoy. Have them share their ideas with a friend.

Suggested Answer
I enjoyed reading the poems because they made me think about my feelings. I didn't like the discussion on p. 86 very much because it was difficult to think of ideas.

Go back to p. 73. Do the routine again.

Have students look back at the VTR picture on pp. 72–73. Using the TTL, project the image onto the board. Ask students how they think the picture connects to the two readings in the unit. Repeat the Step Inside routine. Encourage students to choose a different person, animal, or thing from the picture. Have them compare their answers from the first time they did the routine to notice how the perspective changes, e.g. *Before, I chose the little girl and I thought she cared about animals. This time, I chose a tree. It was cold at night and windy. It's fall and my leaves are falling, so I was cold.*

Cool Down

Play *Word Tennis* (see TB p. 27). Give emotions as a starter and have students name things that make them feel that way, e.g.

Teacher: Happiness.
Student A: Friends.
Student B: Ice cream.

Practice **Resource Bank:** Unit Test; Mid-year Test
Student's App: Key Concept Practice

UNIT 6

Go Green

Unit Overview

Themes

Eco-tourism and sustainable living

Helping the environment

Synopsis

In this unit, students will explore the concept of being environmentally friendly. They will learn about how our lifestyle affects the environment and what we can do to look after our planet. They will learn about the consequences of plastic to people and animals. Students will plan and prepare a presentation and write a persuasive essay.

Language Book

Vocabulary

carbon footprint, conservation, damage (v), *eco-friendly, environment, impact* (n), *pollution, public transportation, tourism, waste* (v)

Pronunciation: word stress: third and fourth syllable

p. 128

Explore Language

First Conditional With Modal Verbs: *May, Might,* and *Be able to*

p. 129

Global Citizenship

How do our lifestyle choices affect the environment?

global, global warming, local, natural resources, organic, recycle, reduce, self-sufficient, sustainable, symbol

p. 130

Explore Language

Too + Adjective + Infinitive; Adjective + *Enough* + Infinitive; *Enough* + Noun + Infinitive

p. 131

Take the Stage

Presentation: appealing for help

p. 132

Write About It

A Persuasive Essay

Paragraph and Sentence Building: organizing and presenting information to argue a case

p. 133

Think It Over

Review and Reflection: Monthly Goal Reflection

p. 134

Think Together
What can we do in our own lives to help the environment?
p. 141

Visible Thinking
Explanation Game
p. 135

Nonfiction
Persuasive Text: *Not-So-Fantastic Plastic*

Words in Context: *biodegradable, overuse, disaster, estimate, ban, garbage patches, ignore*
p. 139

Fiction
Poem: *A Greener Life*

Words in Context: *surrounded, possessions, miserable, generates, wind turbine, solar panels*
p. 136

Reading Skill
Understanding the author's purpose
p. 138

Literary Term
Word Choice: Variety
p. 137

Language and Literacy Connections

The connecting theme for Unit 6 is the environment.

	Language	Literacy
Vocabulary	**Set 1:** eco-tourism **Set 2:** sustainable living	**Nonfiction:** environment, pollution, global, recycle, waste **Fiction:** self-sufficient
Grammar	**First Conditional With Modal Verbs** Turtles may become extinct if we don't protect them. If we protect the turtles' nests, there might be more babies. If we see some baby turtles, will I be able to take a photo? **Too and Enough** It's too hard to be eco-friendly. The wind is always strong enough to make electricity. Wind turbines make enough energy to power entire buildings.	**Nonfiction:** If we eat fish, we might be eating tiny amounts of plastic, too. If we all make changes, we can help the environment. If we don't take action now, our planet will be in great danger in the very near future. **Fiction:** If we care about this planet, we should live a greener life. The wheel turns and generates enough power to run the refrigerator each and every hour. We collect enough rain to cook, wash, and drink.
Skills	**Pronunciation:** word stress: third and fourth syllable **Process Writing:** drafting	**Reading:** understanding author's purpose **Literary Term:** word choice: variety
International English	public transportation/public transport	

Vocabulary

Lesson Objectives

- to learn vocabulary related to eco-tourism: *carbon footprint, conservation, damage, eco-friendly, environment, impact, pollution, public transportation, tourism, waste*
- to say a chant about protecting our world
- to practice word stress: Third and Fourth Syllable

Materials
Audio Tracks 63 to 67; Video

Warm Up

Have students work in groups to make a mind map of words they associate with the word *green*. Elicit that *green* means doing things to help our planet. Compare students mind maps for similar ideas.

A TRACK 63 TB p. 222 **Listen. What is HOP?**

- Display the picture on the opening spread with the TTL. Encourage students to make general observations, giving reasons for their ideas.
- Have students work in pairs to think of questions they have about the picture, e.g. *I wonder …*
- Tell students that they are going to listen to Santiago. Remind students of the challenge from the end of Unit 5. Have students find Santiago and ask *What does his family do?* (They run a vacation company that organizes eco-friendly activities.)
- Explain that each letter in the name HOP is the first letter of a word. Have students guess the words. Play the audio
- Ask the comprehension question *What is HOP?* Play the audio again and check the answer.

Answer
HOP is a green vacation company for people who want to help our planet.

B TRACK 64 TB p. 222 **Find and number the words in A. Then listen and check.**

- Point out the example (1) and have students find *tourism* in the picture. Ask *How does each word matche the picture?*
- Play the audio for students to check their answers.

Answers
1 *tourism* 2 conservation 3 eco-friendly 4 impact
5 carbon footprint 6 pollution 7 damage 8 waste
9 environment 10 public transportation

International English

Draw students' attention to the two words and ask which is American English and which is British English. Elicit the difference between the two words.

C TRACK 65 TB p. 222 **Listen and say. What do you think of when you hear these words? Talk with your friend.**

- From this unit on, the visualization prompts become shorter to help students develop as independent learners. This means that students need to use their own imagination.
- Play the audio, allowing students to visualize the words or ideas as they listen. Pause the audio where necessary. Have students discuss what they imagined in pairs.

D Look and complete the diagram.

- Display the Venn diagram. Review the meaning of *green* and point out that we don't have an opposite for this. Elicit an example and where it should go in the diagram.
- Have students complete the activity individually then compare answers in pairs.

Suggested Answers
Green: conservation, eco-friendly, public transportation
Both: impact, tourism
Not good for the *environment*: carbon footprint, damage, pollution, waste

E TRACK 66 TB p. 222 **Listen and write. Then watch and say.**

- Point to the title and have students say what they think a "green world" would be like.
- Play the video or audio. If you want to focus on the pronunciation, use just the audio initially.
- Give students time to complete the blanks, ordering the letters to form words. Play the audio to check answers.
- Play the video or audio again. Have students join in and encourage them to copy the rhythm and intonation.

Answers
1 *Pollution* 2 damage 3 environment
4 Conservation 5 Eco-friendly 6 waste 7 Tourism
8 carbon footprint

F TRACK 67 TB p. 222 **Pronunciation. Listen and say. Copy the word stress. Think of other words with three or four syllables. Where's the stress?**

- Display the examples on the board. Have students try saying the phrases. Then play the audio and have them listen and repeat. Ask *Which two words have the same pattern?* (*explanation* and *conservation*)
- Have students think of other words with three or four syllables. Have them write their words in their notebooks and highlight the stressed syllable.

Answers
Students' own answers

Cool Down

Play *Board Race* (see TB p. 25) with vocabulary from the lesson. Play the chant audio again and pause after one of the key words. Students race to the board and write the word they hear. Spelling must be correct to get a point.

Practice **Student's App:** Vocabulary Practice; Spoken Word Video

Explore Language

Lesson Objectives

- to learn how to use the first conditional with modal verbs
- to practice vocabulary related to eco-tourism

Materials
Audio Tracks 68 and 69

Warm Up

Ask students to remember what activities you can do at HOP Green Vacations (plant trees, clear trash from beaches, help sea turtles, help baby crocodiles). Ask students which activity they would prefer to do.

A TRACK 68 TB p. 222 **Listen and read. What activity is the group going to do?**

- Tell students they are going to listen to Javier talking to a girl named Adele about a problem on the beach. Play the audio and have students follow the dialogue in their books. Ask *What is the problem?* (Turtles may become extinct.)
- Ask the gist question *What activity is the group going to do?* and elicit the answer. Play the audio again for students to check. Have students find the turtle's nest in the picture.

Answer
They're going to look for a turtle's nest.

B **Look at A. Complete the table. When do we use a comma?**

- Display the table using the TTL.
- Students should now have the skills and strategies to be able to discuss and complete the grammar table themselves using the story. When they have completed the table, invite students to come up to the board and fill in one word each. Ask if everyone agrees. Discuss the word order, form, and patterns together, but let your class guide the discussion. For more support, use the notes in the **ETB**.
- Have students find another example of the first conditional in the dialogue that isn't in the table (*If we find one that isn't marked, we'll call the conservation experts*).
- Draw students' attention to the Grammar tip *Look*. Have students notice that the future form of *can* is *will be able to*, not *will can*.

Answers
if; If, protect, might; will, be able to
We use a comma when the *if* clause comes first in the sentence.

C **Think and discuss. Then choose.**

- Have students work in pairs to discuss the sentences. Refer them to the table in B for example sentences and have them think about each one to help them decide.
- Check answers as a class. Ask students if each situation is possible. Elicit if the speaker is sure in each one and how we know this.

Answers
1 possible 2 not sure

D TRACK 69 TB p. 222 **Listen and say.**

- Play the audio, having students repeat each sentence chorally. Then have them say the sentences to each other in pairs.
- For ideas on how to vary the drill, see TB p. 23.

E **Complete the first conditional sentences with your own ideas.**

- Look at the example in the controlled practice activity together. Tell students to think of a way to end the sentence. They should think about whether they are sure about what will happen or if it is just a possible idea. Remind students to look at the subject of the sentence to see to whom the sentence relates and to use the same pronoun in the other part of the sentence.
- Have students complete the sentences individually. Remind them to look at the table in B to help them. Check answers by having some students call out their sentences.

Answers
Students' own answers

F **Think and discuss. Where do you want to go on vacation? Predict what might happen.**

- This activity provides freer practice of the first conditional with modal verbs. Have students look at the pictures and name the places. Tell students they are going to discuss where they can go on vacation with a friend. They should think of things that might happen there.
- Have two students read the examples on the page. Have students work in pairs. Tell students to talk about all the places in the pictures and then try to find a place that they both think it would be a good idea to visit. Have students do the activity in pairs.

Answers
Students' own answers

Cool Down

Play a Chain Game (see TB p. 25). Students must make sentences using the first conditional, e.g. *If I go to the beach, I might see a shark.*

Practice **Resource Bank:** Grammar Printout
Student's App: Grammar Practice

Global Citizenship

Lesson Objectives

- to learn vocabulary related to sustainable living: *global, global warming, local, natural resources, organic, recycle, reduce, self-sufficient, sustainable, symbol*
- to explore how our lifestyle choices affect the environment and how we can look after the environment
- to practice listening for gist and detail

Materials

Audio Tracks 70 and 72; Audio Track F

Opening Question

Ask the opening question: *How do our lifestyle choices affect the environment?* Encourage students to think about the things they do that may have consequences for the environment. Examples include things like garbage, use of water, use of electronic devices, and different modes of transportation.

A TRACK 70 TB p. 223 **Listen to Sandra and Ekaterina talk about being green. What two things does Ekaterina say she's going to do?**

- Tell students that they are going to listen to two girls talking about being green. Have students predict things the girls might talk about.
- Ask the gist question *What two things does Ekaterina say she's going to do?* Play the audio and check the answer.
- Ask further comprehension questions and play the audio again, then check answers as a class.

Answer

She's going to reuse a bottle and fill it with water for tomorrow, and she's going to stop taking showers.

B TRACK 71 TB p. 223 **Look at the pictures in A and write. Then listen and check.**

- Point out the example for number 1, *sustainable*. Refer students to the vocabulary box in B and have them write the words for each picture in A in pairs or individually.
- Play the audio for students to check their answers. Use the audio to drill the pronunciation of the words.

Answers

1 *sustainable* 2 organic 3 local 4 symbol 5 global 6 reduce 7 recycle 8 self-sufficient 9 global warming 10 natural resources

TRACK F TB p. 223 **Visualization**

- The TTL has a visualization audio track for this vocabulary set. (See TB p. 21.)

C **Read and complete the poster.**

- Look at the poster and the example together. Ask *How can we stop global warming?* Elicit ideas from the class. Have students read the poster to check their ideas.
- Have students complete the sentences individually and check answers together. Ask students if the ideas on the poster are the same as their own.

Answers

1 *global warming* 2 sustainable 3 natural resources 4 organic 5 self-sufficient 6 symbol 7 Reduce 8 Recycle

D TRACK 72 TB p. 223 **Now listen to an interview with Lorena Rossi. What issue does she talk about?**

- Tell students they are going to listen to an interview with a conservation expert about a problem. Have students look at the pictures and say what they can see. Prepare students for the audio by asking students to guess what the pictures are of.
- Ask the gist question *What issue does she talk about?* Play the audio. Check the answer with the class. Point out the symbol for palm oil and ask what other symbols help you make an informed decision on what to buy, e.g. fair trade, organic, gluten-free, vegan.

Answer

She talks about the production of palm oil and its impact on the environment.

E **Listen again. Answer the questions.**

- Have students read and try to answer the questions. Then play the audio again, pausing for students to write their answers. Check answers as a class. Help students make the connection between the ideas in A and E and choosing a more sustainable lifestyle.

Answers

1 *Pizzas, cakes, cookies, soap, make-up, and shampoo.* 2 It causes climate change. / It adds to global warming. 3 It destroys the habitats of important animals and plants. 4 We can buy products made by companies that produce palm oil in a sustainable way. 5 There is a palm leaf symbol on the packaging.

Discussion Questions

- Have students discuss each question in pairs or small groups (see **ETB**). Guide students to conclude that every little bit helps and that we can contribute to help the environment.
- Return to the opening question: *How do our lifestyle choices affect the environment?* Revisit any ideas from the beginning of the lesson. Encourage students to share any new ideas.

Cool Down

Have students make pledges to help the environment and write down one thing that they plan to change.

Practice **Student's App:** Vocabulary Practice; Listening Practice

Explore Language

Lesson Objectives

- to learn how to use *too* and *enough* with the infinitive

Materials

Audio Tracks 73 and 74

Warm Up

Ask students if they ever do quizzes in magazines or on social media. Elicit that this type of quiz is a series of questions that usually have two or more answer options. Write a short quiz related to the topic on the board and have students ask and answer in pairs for a couple of minutes, e.g. *1) Do you recycle? Always/Sometimes/Never; 2) How do you get to school? Public transportation/Walking/Car; 3) Do you think tourism is good for the environment? Yes / I'm not sure / No.*

A TRACK 73 TB p. 223 **Listen and read. What kind of quiz is Adele doing with Lola?**

- Tell students that they are going to listen to Adele talking to her friend Lola. See if students remember what Adele did in Lesson 2 (she learned about protecting turtles). Play the audio and have students follow the dialogue in their books.
- Ask the gist question *What kind of quiz is Adele doing with Lola?* Elicit the answer. Ask *Is it too hard to be eco-friendly?*

Answer

It's a quiz about the environment and being eco-friendly.

B **Look at A. Complete the table. Which word can we use with a noun or an adjective?**

- Display the table using the TTL.
- Students should now have the skills and strategies to discuss and complete the grammar table independently, using the dialogue. When they have completed the table, elicit answers. Discuss the word order, form, and patterns together, but let your class guide the discussion. For more support, use the notes in the **ETB**.
- Then ask the question *Which word can we use with a noun or an adjective?* Check answers as a class.
- Draw students' attention to the Grammar tip *Look*. Point out that we can include *for* + noun/pronoun before the infinitive. We can also omit the second part of the sentence if it is obvious what we are talking about, e.g. *This jacket is too small (for me).*

Answers

too, to be; too, crowded; big, to grow; enough, electricity; to be

We can use *enough* with a noun or an adjective.

C **Think and discuss. Then choose.**

- Check understanding of *the right amount*. Have students discuss the sentences in pairs.
- Check answers and elicit examples by saying *I can't do this activity. It's too … (hard); This classroom is big enough for us to …* (students' own answers). Elicit that we need an adjective after *too* but we put the adjective before *enough*, and that we can also follow *enough* with a noun.

Answers

1 more than is needed 2 the right amount
3 a reason

D TRACK 74 TB p. 223 **Listen and say.**

- Play the audio, having students repeat each sentence chorally.
- Play it again and have students do actions as they repeat each sentence.
- For ideas on how to vary the drill, see TB p. 23.

E **Look and complete the sentences with *too* or *enough*.**

- This activity provides controlled practice of *too* and *enough* + the infinitive. Have students look at the picture and describe the scene. Tell them to imagine that they are the boy in the blue T-shirt and white shorts. Ask *How do you feel? Do you want to run?* Elicit that the boy is very hot. Draw students' attention to the example *It's too hot to run.*
- Remind students to think about whether the blank is followed by a noun or an adjective. Have students do the activity individually. Then check answers as a class.

Answers

1 *too* 2 enough 3 too 4 enough 5 too
6 enough

F **Play a memory game. Close your book. Talk with your friend. Who remembers the most?**

- If possible, display an enlarged version of the picture in E. Give students one minute to look at the picture to remember as much as they can.
- In pairs, students take turns making as many sentences as they can, describing the picture using the target language. Write any language students may need on the board to prompt them. Have a student read the example from the page.
- Have students play the game in pairs. Then they open their books and check their memory together.

Answers

Students' own answers

Cool Down

Play *Funniest Sentence* (see TB p. 26). Have students write a sentence using *too* or *enough*, e.g. *The elephant didn't have enough money to pay for the movie tickets.*

Practice **Resource Bank:** Grammar Printout
Student's App: Grammar Practice

Write About It

Lesson Objectives

- to plan and write a persuasive essay
- to learn how to organize and present information to argue a case
- to learn how to draft (Process Writing: Step 3)

Materials

Support writing printout from the Resource Bank (F)

Warm Up

Have students think about the food they usually eat. Ask *Do you know where it is grown or manufactured? Do you eat foods from other countries? Do you eat fish and meat?* Where is it from? Discuss as a class.

A Read the persuasive essay entry for the Green Living Competition. How many changes does the writer suggest we make?

This text type is also modeled in the Literacy Book for this unit, Not-So-Fantastic Plastic.

- Write the title of the essay on the board. Ask *What does Eating Green mean?* Elicit ideas.
- After reading the persuasive essay, ask *How many changes does the writer suggest we make?* Have students scan the text to find the answer.

Answers

Three changes: buy local food, buy food which doesn't come in plastic packaging, and grow our own food

B Look at the structure of the persuasive essay. Read, discuss, and answer.

- Look at the first question together. Have students identify the four paragraphs and match to letters a–d.
- Have students answer the questions. Check answers, discussing each feature. Point out that statistics show that we are using facts as well as opinions to support our ideas.

Answers

1 b, a, d, c 2 They grab your attention; they give us the writer's main message. 3 Cited Statistics: Producing one kilo of pineapple creates one kilo of carbon dioxide. Some plastic bottles will still be around as trash 450 years from now. Reason: They make the writer's argument stronger.

C Look at the language in the persuasive essay. Read and respond.

- Have students work in pairs, then check answers as a class.

Answers

1 simple present and present progressive, imperatives, modals; present verb forms: because the writer is stating facts and talking about habits; imperatives and modals to encourage people to do things 2 On the one hand, (But) on the other hand 3 In my opinion, I strongly believe

- Look at the callout. Have students choose three phrases from A that they would like to use in their essays.

D Think and discuss. Brainstorm some ideas for an eco-friendly city using one of the Generating Ideas techniques.

- Reviewways to generate ideas discussed in **Process Writing Step 1: Generating Ideas** on p. 140.
- Tell students that they are going to plan and write their own persuasive essay about an eco-friendly city. Ask *How can a city be eco-friendly.*
- Have students choose a way of generating ideas and think of ideas for their essay. Have them copy the mind map into their notebooks and add ideas with a partner.

Answers

Students' own answers

E Plan your persuasive essay. Use your ideas in D and one of the Planning techniques.

- Review the planning techniques students have looked at in **Process Writing Step 2: Planning** on p. 141.
- Have students choose ideas the best ideas from D to use in their essays. They should copy the headings into their notebooks and decide where to put each idea.

Answers

Students' own answers

Now ask students to turn to p. 142 to learn about Process Writing Step 3: Drafting (see TB p. 213 for teaching notes). Students will need to do this lesson before they do F.

F Prepare to write a first draft for your persuasive essay. Complete the plan. Then think about the language you used and revise it.

- After students have completed **Process Writing Step 3: Drafting** on p. 142, they will now complete F.
- Look at the plan on the page. Remind students to think about how to introduce each new section.
- Remind students that the best pieces of writing are rewritten more than once.

Answers

Students' own answers

G Now write your persuasive essay.

- Give students time to write their essays. Students can write in their notebooks or use a Support printout from the Resource Bank.
- Have students exchange essays with a friend for a peer review. Remind students to be positive.

Cool Down

Tell students to imagine sharing their essay on social media. They need to give readers the key idea, but only in ten words. Have students write their summaries on a sticky note.

Practice **Student's App:** Writing Practice
Resource Bank: Writing Game, *Going Green*

Talk About It

Lesson Objectives

- to prepare and practice a presentation about an environmental problem
- to learn how to appeal for help

Materials
Video

Warm Up

Remind students of the presentation they gave with a partner in Unit 2. Ask *How did you structure the presentation?* Elicit that they asked and answered questions. Tell students to imagine they are giving a presentation about going green. Ask *How can we save water?* and have students tell a partner their answer. Then have students ask each other questions in pairs.

A TB p. 240 **Watch and listen. What problem do Maria and Wade describe?**

- Have students look at the picture on the TV screen. Do a See, Think, Wonder routine to talk about the picture (see TB p. 20).
- Tell students they are going to watch a video of Maria and Wade giving a presentation about a problem. Ask a prediction question: *What do you think they're going to talk about?* Elicit suggestions from the class. Then play the video.
- Draw students' attention to the question *What problem do Maria and Wade describe?* Check the answer with the class. Ask students why they are giving the presentation.

Answer
Students at their school create too much trash.

B Watch again. Complete the sentences Maria and Wade use to ask for help.

- Have students read the sentences before they rewatch the video and see if they remember the missing words.
- Play the video once and have students complete the blanks. Check answers as a class. Then play the video again and have students repeat the phrases, copying the children's pronunciation and body language.
- You may wish to point out that we sometimes use *do* in the present simple affirmative for emphasis (as in question 5). However, students should be careful not to use it all the time, as that would not sound natural.

Answers
1 ask 2 on our own 3 looking; part
4 support; difference 5 do; join

C Choose a topic or use one of your own. Research and prepare visuals for a presentation. Think and plan.

- Have students look at the three ideas on the page. Tell students that they can use one of these or choose an idea of their own. Tell students that they are going to make visuals to use in a presentation.
- Take the first idea as an example. Brainstorm some types of visuals, e.g. photographs of endangered animals, photographs that explain why these animals are endangered (e.g. of their habitat being destroyed), a mind map of reasons why some animals are endangered and where, or a poster or cartoon showing what we can do to help.
- Draw students' attention to the questions on the notepad in C. Tell students to copy these questions into their notebooks and think of ideas. Remind students that they only need to write notes to prompt them during their presentation and not full sentences. Students can choose whether they want to give an individual presentation or work with a partner.

Answers
Students' own answers

D Practice with your friends using phrases in B. Then share with the class. Make notes.

- Have students practice their presentations as many times as they like. Remind students to think about when they should show their visuals to the audience. Their visuals need to support what they are talking about.
- Have some students give their presentations in front of the class. While they are speaking, the other students should make notes. You could have them draw a table in their notebooks with the following columns: *Name*, *Topic*, *Things I Learned*, *Questions I Have*. When they have finished, students can compare their notes about their friends' presentations.
- Have students analyze their own performances in pairs, making positive comments but also making suggestions.

Cool Down

Have students choose one of the presentations they saw and decide what they are going to do to help. They should try to find other students who also want to help with the same idea and discuss what they can do together.

Practice **Student's App:** Speaking Skills Practice; Speaking Video

Think It Over

Lesson Objectives

- to review what has been learned in the unit
- to reflect on the unit and their own progress
- to think about learning strategies and how to continue learning at home

Warm Up

Do a quick quiz with the class about Unit 6. Ask questions about pictures, words, or information and have students find the answers in their books. Have students play in teams. Possible questions: *What animals can you see on p. 74? How many people are on the bus on p. 74? What is the guide's name on p. 76? What's the Grammar tip, Look box, on p. 77? What problem does Lorena talk about on p. 79? What food can you see on p. 81?*

How well did you meet the challenge of Unit 6? Read and respond.

Monthly Goal Reflection

- Tell students they are going to review what they learned in the unit and also think about their own learning and whether they have reached their goals from for Unit 6. This time students are also going to evaluate how hard they worked and think about whether they need to do more in order to progress in their learning.
- Review what students have done in the unit with an Inside-Outside Circle routine (see TB p. 21). Have students on the outside of the circle start by remembering something they did. Students can have their books with them and show their partner the page they are referring to, if necessary. The students on the inside of the circle then say something different that they did. On the signal, students rotate and try to think of something new. Encourage students to remember information they learned, as well as activities they did. After a few minutes, stop the routine and move on to the next stage.
- Draw students' attention to the heading: *Monthly Goal Reflection*. Have students look back at the end of Unit 5 and remember what their goal was. Ask students if they think they have worked hard to reach their goal and whether they feel they have succeeded. Have them think about what they have done in order to achieve their goal.
- Allow students to work individually to fill in the first two parts of the graphic organizer. Remind them that they should write their own responses about themselves. Monitor to help as necessary. Look at what the students are writing so you can tailor your classes and any additional practice to their needs.
- Ask students what they would like to work on and improve upon in the future. Refer students to the final section in the graphic organizer. Tell students to think about whether they still need to work more to achieve their goal or, if they have succeeded, they will choose a different one. Have them look back through the unit and evaluate their learning in each lesson. Then have them write their ideas about their plans for their next goals. They can then share their ideas with a friend.
- Ask if anyone has the same goals as their friend. Point out that goals should be personal and each student should choose those they think they would benefit from most.

Looking Forward

Draw students' attention to the character at the bottom of the page. Elicit who it is and what they remember about her. (Lola appeared in Lesson 4 and was looking at a magazine with Adele.) Have students read the speech bubble and make predictions about what Lola does in her free time. Tell them that they will find out in the first lesson of Unit 7.

Put It Together

To further review and recycle the language in Units 5 and 6, play *Picture Puzzles* on pp. 86–87. See TB p. 208 for teaching notes.

Practice **Resource Bank:** Unit Test
Student's App: Vocabulary and Grammar Review

Get Ready to Read

Lesson Objectives

- to activate prior knowledge about eco-living
- to guide inquiry and deepen understanding through an Explanation Game VTR
- to review the reading skill of understanding the author's purpose

Materials

VTR printout from the Resource Bank (A, B, C, D)

Warm Up

Ask students if they have ever climbed a tree. Ask questions, e.g. *How tall was it? Were you scared? How did you climb it? What could you see from the top?* Have students discuss their ideas in pairs.

Explanation Game

A Look at the picture. Choose a thing or idea. What is it?

This VTR encourages students to identify interesting features in an object and explore the reasons why it is this way, through observation, questioning, and hypothesis. Start by asking students what they can see in the picture of the special garden. Provide vocabulary where necessary.

- Say *I think that bridge looks interesting.* Tell students to choose something interesting in the picture or that they would like to know more about. Have students look at the picture and choose an object together in pairs.

B What do you notice about it? Tell your partner.

- Say *I notice that the bridge is curved. What do you notice about it?* Encourage students to share any detail, even seemingly obvious ones. Ask *What do you notice about your object?*
- Give students time to think about what they noticed about their chosen object and share their ideas in pairs and write their ideas in their notebooks.

C Why do you think it is that way?

- Ask *Why do you think the bridge is curved?* Elicit one or two ideas from the class.
- In pairs, have students look at their list of ideas and think about the following questions: *Why do you think it is that way?* Encourage students to ask *What makes you say that?*
- Students should make visually note their ideas.

D What are some other reasons it might be that way? Share with the class.

- Tell students that they are going to share their ideas with the class. They need to say (a) what the object is, (b) what they noticed about it, (c) why they think it is this way, and (d) their reasons for thinking this.
- Have students share their ideas with the class. Encourage the class to think of and add more ideas about the explanations and reasons for these.

Here's an example of this part of the routine.

Teacher: What did you choose?
Student A: I chose the tallest tree.
Teacher: What did you notice about it?
Student B: I noticed that it has different plants from the other trees.
Teacher: Why do you think it is this way?
Student B: I think this tree was the first.
Teacher: What makes you say that?
Student B: Well, the plants are bigger and the tree is the tallest. So I think the plants have been growing for longer.
Teacher: Does anyone else have any ideas about this?
Student C: I think each tree has a different kind of plant because the leaves are different.
Student D: Maybe they represent different species of trees. The people who visit can learn about all the types of trees.

Transition

Ask students if they would like to visit the place in the picture. How would they feel? What do they think they would learn about there?

E What do you do to help the environment? Make a list. Then discuss.

- Have students work in pairs to make a list of things they can do to help the environment. The pair with the most ideas on their list wins. Check answers by having the pair with the most answers read their list aloud.
- Elicit ideas from the class, encouraging students to explain how and why they do these things.

Answers

Students' own answers

F Think and discuss. Scan *Not-So-Fantastic Plastic* on the next pages. What do you think the author's purpose is?

- Students are going to preview the reading skill of understanding the author's purpose.
- Tell students to scan the reading to find out why the author wrote it. Remind them that they can look at the title, headings, and pictures as well as the text. Give students two or three minutes to scan the reading.
- Elicit ideas from the class, encouraging students to give reasons for their answers.

Suggested Answer

The author's purpose is to persuade the reader of the negative effects of plastic on the environment and encourage him/her to take action.

Now read **Not-So-Fantastic Plastic**

Nonfiction: *Not-So-Fantastic Plastic*—Persuasive Text

Lesson Objectives

- to read a persuasive text about how plastic can be harmful
- to make a personal connection to the reading

Materials

Audio Tracks 24 and 25

Warm Up

Ask students what kinds of things they usually recycle. Ask them if they can identify the correct colors for each type of recycling. Draw three boxes on the board using the same colors and have students suggest items for each trash can.

TRACK 24 TB p. 233 **Reading Approach**

Engage with the Text

- Project the opening spread of the reading using the Story Player in the TTL. Have students predict what the text might be about. Ask students if they think the reading will say positive or negative things about plastic.
- For the first reading, have students read the text individually. Before they start, ask a prediction question, e.g. *How do you think plastic can be dangerous?* Have them fold their arms when they have finished reading.

TRACK 25 TB p. 234 **Words in Context**

- After the first reading of the text, draw students' attention to the Words in Context box.
- Give students a few minutes to find and highlight each instance of each word in the reading.
- Have them identify the type of word by looking at the form and the sentence.
- Write these strategies on the board for: *pictures; surrounding words and sentences; contrasting ideas; world knowledge; word building; using prefixes; making connections.*
- Have students work in pairs to discuss the words.

biodegradable (p. 91, adjective) You can break this word down: the prefix *bio–* (natural) and the suffix *–able* shows it's an adjective. The meaning of the word *degrade* is given in the second clause of the sentence. Strategies to use: prefixes, word building, surrounding words and sentences, world knowledge

overuse (p. 91, noun) This word can also be broken down into two parts: the prefix *over–* (too much) and *use*. Strategies to use: prefixes, word building

disaster (p. 91, noun) The noun *disaster* was used in the context of natural disasters in the article *Fire Ecology* in Unit 2 (pp. 34–37). The general context of the article and the photos show this is a negative word. Strategies to use: making connections, pictures

estimate (p. 91, verb) The number that follows shows this verb is associated with numeracy and math. The number is large but also a round number, showing it isn't exact. Strategy to use: surrounding words and sentences

ban (p. 91, verb) The preceding sentences help introduce the idea and support the writer's opinion. Strategy to use: surrounding words and sentences

garbage patches (p. 91, noun) The phrase can be broken down in the two parts. The surrounding words and the photo tell us there can be multiple areas of garbage. Strategies to use: pictures, word building

ignore (p. 93, verb) This is the concluding part of the article, and it summarizes what has come previously. We now know the writer's opinion of plastic, so we can deduce the meaning of the problem the writer thinks is "too serious." Strategies to use: surrounding words and sentences, making connections

Analyze the Text and Features

- Play the audio and have students follow along in their books, or use the Story Player.
- Have students find the orange callouts and discuss in pairs.
  - **Personalization** (p. 90): *What are some things that are made of plastic in your life?* Ask students what plastic they use in their everyday lives.
  - **Fact** (p. 92): *According to a recent report, our demand for plastic is growing every year and by 2050, there will be more plastic than fish in the ocean.* Ask students what consequences of this they can think of.
  - **Making Connections** (p. 93): *How much can you recycle and reuse?* Challenge students to come up with a list of as many things as they can. Give a time limit for this.

International English

Draw students' attention to the words. Elicit that *garbage* is American and *rubbish* is British English. Drill the pronunciation.

Interact with the Text

- Now that students are very familiar with the text, have them role-play a reporter and a volunteer, to think about solutions to the problems in the reading. The reporter interviews the volunteer, asking questions about how plastic can be harmful.

Cool Down

Have students do a variation of Two Stars and a Wish. This means that students should think of two problems from the reading and one solution. Have them write their ideas on sticky notes or in their notebooks, then share with a friend.

Practice Resource Bank: Story Player

Explore the Reading

Lesson Objectives

- to understand and analyze *Not-So-Fantastic Plastic* through reading comprehension activities
- to learn about the CLIL science area of ecosystems
- to understand word choice and variety in vocabulary
- to make a personal connection to the reading.

Warm Up

Play *Board Race* (see TB p. 25). Have students write as many words or ideas as they can remember from the reading.

A Read and write *Fact* or *Opinion*.

- Refer back to *Not-So-Fantastic Plastic*. Have a Group Time discussion to help students remember the reading. Ask questions to prompt students to retell the main ideas of the reading in their own words, e.g. *What kinds of things can be made of plastic? What is plastic made of?* Students can look back at the reading in their books if they need to
- Review the reading skill of identifying fact and opinion (Students studied this in Levels 2, 3, and 4). Remind students that a fact is something that is true and an opinion is what someone thinks.
- Have students open their books and look at the first sentence. Elicit whether this is a fact or an opinion (a fact). Ask students how they know this and elicit that the text provides supporting details, including photographic evidence.
- Have students do the other questions individually. Check answers as a class.

Answers

1 Fact 2 Opinion 3 Fact 4 Opinion 5 Fact
6 Opinion

B Think and complete the graphic organizer. What problems do you think plastic causes? How can we solve those problems?

This activity practices critical thinking skills by having students think of different ways of solving problems.

- Refer students to the graphic organizer and elicit one problem plastic causes from the class, e.g. *plastic hurts animals*. Copy the graphic organizer onto the board and fill out one of the boxes. Ask students if they can think of any solutions to this problem and write their ideas on the board.
- Have students complete their table in their books. Then have them discuss their ideas in pairs. Check answers as a class.

Suggested Answers

Problem 1: Plastic hurts animals
Solutions: Take the plastic out of the ocean; stop throwing away plastic bags
Problem 2: Plastic is in many of the things we use
Solutions: Use a different material, like paper; use reusable cups and bowls

C Think and discuss. Imagine that in 2050 there is more plastic than fish in the water. What might happen to the ecosystem of the oceans?

- This activity explores the CLIL science area of ecosystems. Elicit what an ecosystem is (a community made up of living organisms and its environment). Then ask students what kinds of living organisms inhabit the ocean. Write their ideas on the board.
- Then tell students to imagine that it is the year 2050 and there is now more plastic in the ocean than fish. Encourage students to visualize this for a moment. Ask students what they think might happen to the ecosystem of the oceans. Encourage them to think about what different types of sea creatures will eat and how that moves through the food chain.
- Have students discuss their ideas in groups. Then have groups share their ideas with the class.

Answer

Students' own answers

Literary Term: Word Choice: Variety

Think of a situation for each sentence. Choose the best word for it. Then discuss.

- Draw students' attention to the explanation of *variety*. Tell students that sometimes the same thing can make us feel different ways. Look at the first sentence together. Ask students when they might think honey tastes delicious. Why might it taste gross? (if someone doesn't like honey) Ask students which word they would choose.
- Then have students choose a word for each sentence, imagining a situation each time.
- Have students compare their answers with a friend and discuss any differences. Encourage them to explain why they chose their words for the situations they imagined.

Answers

Students' own answers

Cool Down

End the lesson by having students tell their partner something they have learned in that lesson. They can start their sentence by saying *Did you know that …?* and then have their partner respond.

Practice **Resource Bank:** Literary Term Printout
Student's App: Reading Practice; Literary Term Practice

Get Ready to Read

Lesson Objectives

- to activate prior knowledge about a different lifestyle
- to review the reading skill of understanding the author's purpose

Materials

Books and other different reading materials (letter, birthday card, instructions, travel brochures, catalog, etc.) (Warm Up)

Warm Up

To introduce the reading skill of understanding the author's purpose, show students the different reading materials you have brought in and ask students why they would read each one, e.g. travel brochure—to find a place to go on vacation. Then ask students why the writer wrote each text, e.g. the travel brochure was written by a travel agent because the agent wants to sell vacations.

A Read these summaries. Why did the authors write these texts? Think and discuss. Then check (✔).

- Quickly review the three texts by having students look at the pictures and titles and use their own words to say what each text was about.
- Tell students they are going to read a summary of each text. Tell students that a summary is a short text that tells us the main ideas. Have students read the first summary quickly and then ask students why the author wrote it. Point out the three options—inform, persuade, and entertain—and check the meaning of each one.
- Have students read the summaries and check the author's purpose for each one. Then check answers as a class.
- Have students read the reading skill box. Then ask questions to check comprehension, e.g. *What does "The Hero of Lime Rock" teach us? How does the writer of "Not-So-Fantastic Plastic" try to change our opinion? Why is "The Red-Headed League" entertaining?* Point out that some texts may have more than one purpose, e.g. *Not-So-Fantastic Plastic* informs us as well as persuades. Have students think about the other texts and try to identify alternative purposes. (*The Hero of Lime Rock* could also be to entertain us. We often choose biographies about people who interest us.)

Suggested Answers

1 entertain 2 inform 3 persuade

B Think and discuss. What different things have you read recently? How did they inform, persuade, or entertain you?

- Have students look at the instructions and think for a minute about all the different things they have read recently. Tell them that all texts have a purpose, however small, even a text message from a friend.
- Have students discuss their ideas in pairs, identifying the purpose of each one.
- Have some students share their ideas with the class.

C Read and check (✔). Then discuss. Read the first stanza of *A Greener Life*. What do you think the author's purpose is? Why?

- Have students read the stanza. Ask *What kind of text is it?* and elicit that it's a poem. Ask *What makes you say that?* and encourage students to give reasons, e.g. *It rhymes.* Remind students that a *stanza* is a section of a poem. It is also called a verse and is similar to a paragraph.
- Have students read the stanza again and decide what the author's purpose is. Have them compare their answers with a friend.
- Check answers as a class. Encourage students to back up their answers with reasons and examples. Elicit that the stanza may have more than one purpose (to persuade us to live a greener life as well as to entertain).

Answer

persuade

Now read **A Greener Life**

Fiction: *A Greener Life—Poems*

Lesson Objectives

- to read a poem about a family who chooses to change their lifestyle and move to the countryside
- to make a personal connection to the reading

Materials

Audio Tracks 26 and 27

Warm Up

Ask students whether they prefer living in the town or countryside and why. Have them discuss in pairs.

TRACK 26 TB p. 234 **Reading Approach**

Engage with the Text

- Project the opening spread of the reading using the Story Player in the TTL. Ask students to use the information on the opening page to predict what the poem is about. In Unit 5, students read a collection of poems. Tell students that this time they are going to read a long poem.
- Play the audio and have students read along in their books. Ask *Will the family like living in the countryside?*

TRACK 27 TB p. 234 **Words in Context**

- After the first reading of the text, draw students' attention to the Words in Context box. Play the audio to practice pronunciation.
- Have students brainstorm a list of strategies that they can use to find the meanings of the words, including strategies they use in L1 (e.g. using pictures; surrounding words and sentences; positive/negative; contrasting ideas; world knowledge).
- Divide the class into pairs or groups and have each group look at certain of the words only, e.g. two words per group or pair.
- Have them find and highlight each instance of each word in the reading and identify the type of word by looking at the form and the sentence.
- Have students swap pairs or groups and explain their words to each other, saying which strategy they used.
- Bring the class together and elicit the meanings of the words. Discuss which strategies worked and if any didn't.

surrounded (p. 96, verb) The previous line sets the context for where the writer is (the city) and the picture shows the tall apartment buildings. The second clause in the line provides a contrasting idea, suggesting the verb is used negatively. Strategies to use: using pictures, surrounding words and sentences

possessions (p. 97, noun) The possessive adjective *our* denotes belonging, and the sentence shows these are things you can sell. Strategies to use: using pictures, surrounding words and sentences

miserable (p. 97, adjective) The second clause of the sentence tells us this is a negative feeling. Students can use personal experience to think how they would feel in the same situation. Strategies to use: personal experience, surrounding words and sentences

generates (p. 97, verb) The surrounding sentences say what is generated (power) and what it does (run the refrigerator). Strategies to use: surrounding words and sentences, using pictures

wind turbine / solar panels (p. 98, nouns) These words can be broken into their two parts. The surrounding words and phrases help identify them in the picture (*as tall as a tree / on the roof*). Knowledge of different types of natural energy and surrounding words tell us how they are used. Strategies to use: word building, using pictures, surrounding words and sentences, world knowledge

Analyze the Text and Features

- Play the audio again and have students say the poem along with the audio, stanza by stanza. After each stanza, have students look at the picture and find the things that were mentioned.
- Have students find the orange callouts and discuss in pairs. Alternatively, use Group Time to discuss the questions after students have finished reading (see TB p. 21).
  - **Making Connections** (p. 98): *How did the sheep give them their coats?* Have students think about how clothes are made. Elicit where wool comes from. Ask students if they are wearing anything made of wool.
  - **Personalization** (p. 99): *Have you ever tried to grow fruit or vegetables? Was it easy?* Have students talk about their experiences of growing food. Ask students if anyone in their family grows their own vegetables.
  - **Text Focus** (p. 97): *Rhythm is the time it takes to say a line of poetry. It depends on the number of stressed syllables, not on the total number of syllables.* Have students count the number of stressed syllables in the first line of the second stanza. Write it on the board and underline the stressed syllables (We <u>sold</u> all our po<u>ssess</u>ions, all we <u>had</u> ex<u>cept</u> the <u>car</u>). There are five stressed syllables.

Interact with the Text

- Have students take turns reading the poem in pairs, each reading a stanza. Encourage students to pay attention to the rhythm. Play the audio again and have students repeat the rhythm.

Cool Down

Play *What's the Scene?* (see TB p. 27). Have students choose a part of the picture from the poem.

Practice **Resource Bank:** Story Player

Explore the Reading

Lesson Objectives

- to understand and analyze *A Greener Life* through reading comprehension activities
- to explore the SEL competency of self-awareness by identifying own needs and values and how they are met in students' lifestyles
- to make a personal connection to the reading

Warm Up

Have students play *What Are They Saying?* with people from the pictures in the poem. Students play in pairs, taking turns to point at the people in each poem and guess what they think that person is saying.

A Read and answer.

- Play a team game to have students remember details from the poem. Divide the class into teams. One team thinks of a true or false sentence about the poem, e.g. *The family have cows* (false; they have sheep and goats), and challenges another team to say whether it is true or false. Teams get a point for each correct answer.
- Have students open their books and look at the questions. Do the first one together. Have students look back at the poem to find the answer.
- Have students answer the questions in their books individually. Encourage students to look back at the poem to help them. Check answers as a class.

Suggested Answers

1 They were tired of the city; they wanted to live a different, greener life. 2 They had a water wheel, a wind turbine, and solar panels on the roof of the house. 3 They bought chickens for eggs, sheep for wool, and goats for milk. 4 It comes from their farm. 5 They like it because they have more time to do other things, like read. 6 They learn about food and where it comes from: they work on the land, collect eggs, plant vegetables, milk the goats, and feed the sheep.

B Read and complete the table. Then discuss. Describe the family's life in the city and on the farm. Which do you think is better? Support your answers with reasons.

- Tell students that they are going to compare the family's life before and after they moved. Ask *What was their life like in the city? Was it good or bad?* Try to elicit that there are positive and negative aspects to life in the city and the country.
- Draw students' attention to the table and the headings. Give students a few minutes to look back at the poem to find ideas and write them in the table.
- Then ask *Which is better—their life in the city or in the country?* Tell students to discuss the question in pairs, using the information in the table to support their answers.
- Then have some students share their opinions with the class.

Suggested Answers

In the City: (Good) They used to live in a modern apartment; They used to have lots of possessions and gadgets;
(Bad) They used to buy all their food from the supermarket; They were often tired; They spent a lot of time inside buildings.
On the Farm (Good) They keep bees for honey. They don't buy sugar now; Their food is home-grown. They don't go to the supermarket; They're very happy. They live a greener life; They're outside in the fresh air a lot of the time; They welcome city kids to their farm and show them country life. They have more time to read.
(Bad) They live in an old cottage; They don't have many possessions or gadgets.

C Think and discuss. Is your life more like the family's life before or after their move to the country? Look at B. Which sentences are true about your life?

Students are going to explore the SEL competency of self-awareness by recognizing own needs and values by thinking about what their life is like and what is important to them.

- Refer students to the question and give students a few minutes to look at their sentences in B and make connections to their own lives.
- Have students discuss their ideas in pairs or small groups. Encourage students to ask each other questions, e.g. *Do you buy all your food at the grocery store?* When students have finished, ask some students to share their ideas with the class. Ask students if their life is more like the family's life before or after their move and elicit a show of hands. Ask students if they would like to change their lifestyle in any way or have a different lifestyle when they are older.

Answers

Students' own answers

Cool Down

Play *What's the Next Word?* (see TB p. 27) with sentences from *A Greener Life*.

Practice **Student's App:** Reading Practice

Think Together

Lesson Objectives

- to make connections between the readings
- to explore the key concept: What can we do in our own lives to help the environment?
- to reflect on the unit and provide personal thoughts and opinions

Warm Up

Have students do 30-second speeches about the two readings in pairs. They each have 30 seconds to tell their partner as much as they can about one of the readings.

A Think and write. What does each reading say about these topics?

- Tell students to look at the topics in the table and find these things in each reading. They will need to scan the readings for the words in the topics column and find what each reading says about them. They can write in note form or copy phrases or sentences from the readings.
- Give students enough time to go through the two readings and write their ideas in their books individually. Then check answers as a class.

Suggested Answers

water: There are chemicals in the water; there is plastic waste in the oceans. The family collects rain; they don't use much water; the solar panels heat water.
clothes: Clothes can be made of plastic. The family makes clothes out of wool (from sheep).
animals: Some animals think the plastic bags are prey and eat them. The family uses animals for food, like chickens (for eggs) and goats (for milk).
supermarkets: Some supermarkets charge customers for plastic bags. The family avoids shopping in supermarkets by growing their own food.
helping the environment: Some stores and cafés ask customers to bring their own bags and cups. The family uses a wind turbine to make their own electricity.

B What changes can you make for a greener life? Do a Rally Robin. Make a list.

- Elicit one or two examples of things we can do to have a greener life. Using the topics in A, ask students to think about different areas of their life, e.g. how they travel, what they do with their trash, and the food they eat
- Give students a couple of minutes to do the Rally Robin (see TB p. 20) to generate ideas. Students take turns thinking of an idea and write it in the space in their books.
- Elicit ideas and encourage students to talk about things they already do as well as changes they would like to make.

Answers

Students' own answers

Practice Resource Bank: Unit Test
Student's App: Key Concept Practice

C Choose one idea from B. Think and write. What steps can you take to make this change?

- Students are going to apply what they have learned in the unit and discuss the key concept question: *What can we do in our own lives to help the environment?*
- Tell students that they are going to choose one idea to help make their life greener. They need to think about what steps they can take to make that change.
- Have students write their ideas in their books and then compare with a friend.
- Ask students the key concept question: *What can we do in our own lives to help the environment?* Review all the ideas you have discussed in the unit. Encourage students to really go through with their ideas and follow the steps they have outlined.

My Reading Journal

Did anything in the two readings in this unit surprise you?

This question focuses on personalization and encourages students to think about what they have learned. Give students time to think and write their answer, then discuss in pairs or small groups.

Suggested Answer

I was surprised that humans might sometimes eat small pieces of plastic when they eat fish.

Do you think it's possible to live a completely green life? Why or why not?

Give students time to think about how practical the life of the family in the second reading is. Have them discuss their ideas with a friend, then write in their books.

Ask if any students would like to share their answers with the class.

Suggested Answer

I think it's very difficult to have a completely green life because we need to travel to school and people need to work and earn money to live well.

Choose an object from the unit. Then play the Explanation Game.

Using the TTL, project the instructions onto the board. Tell students to choose something from another page this time. Then repeat the Explanation Game routine.

Cool Down

Have students talk in pairs about their favorite things from the unit. This could be an activity, a reading, an extension task, or just an image.

UNIT 7

In Safe Hands

Unit Overview

Themes

Emergencies and first aid

Literacy Book: Helping in an emergency

Synopsis

In this unit, students will explore the concept of emergencies. They will learn about first aid and how to help in an emergency. They will learn about the importance of volunteers and discuss how they can help others locally. Students will plan and prepare a presentation telling a story and write a flyer.

Language Book

Vocabulary

accident, allergic reaction, Band-Aid, burn (n), concussion, cut (n), disinfect, faint, ice pack, injured, rash, swell

Pronunciation: connected speech: consonant-vowel linking with /r/

p. 144

Explore Language

Simple Present Passive

p. 145

Global Citizenship

How do volunteers contribute to our well-being?

call for help, drill, emergency exit, evacuate, first responder, keep calm, panic, prepare, rescue, sound the alarm

p. 146

Explore Language

Reflexive Pronouns

p. 147

Take the Stage

Presentation: adding suspense to a story

p. 148

Write About It

An Informational Flyer

Paragraph Building: researching, organizing, and presenting information

p. 149

Think It Over

Review and Reflection

3.2.1

p. 150

Literacy Book

Think Together
What can we do to help in an emergency?
p. 157

Visible Thinking
Step Inside
p. 151

Nonfiction
Instructional Text: *First Aid for Beginners*
Words in Context: *gauze, bleeding, soft tissue, inject, venom*
p. 155

Fiction
Story: *The Chopper*
Words in Context: *wheezed, paramedic, stretcher, shivering, blades*
p. 152

Reading Skill
Understanding main ideas and details
p. 154

Literary Term
Similes
p. 156

Language and Literacy Connections

The connecting theme for Unit 7 is first aid and emergencies.

	Language	Literacy
Vocabulary	**Set 1:** injuries and first aid **Set 2:** preparing for an emergency	**Fiction:** call **Nonfiction:** allergic reaction, Band-Aid, cut, ice pack, injured, rash
Grammar	**Simple Present Passive** No one's allowed in the water. Glasses aren't allowed around the pool. Where's the first aid kit kept? And are Band-Aids kept in the first aid kit? **Reflexive Pronouns** She hurt herself on a ski trip. I can't hear myself think! We've been teaching ourselves to play the guitar.	**Fiction:** She felt worried and hugged herself. She felt herself beginning to relax. **Nonfiction:** It's sometimes difficult to know if a bone is broken. Sometimes a stinger is left in the skin.
Skills	**Pronunciation:** connected speech: consonant-vowel linking with /r/ **Process Writing:** drafting	**Reading:** understanding main ideas and details **Literary Term:** similes
International English	Band-Aid/plaster; first aid tent/first-aid tent; waterwings/armbands; first aid kit/first-aid kit; pharmacy/chemist; sound the alarm/raise the alarm; first responder/emergency services; fire marshal/fire warden	high school/secondary school; scrapes/grazes

Vocabulary

Lesson Objectives

- to learn vocabulary related to injuries and first aid: *accident, allergic reaction, Band-Aid, burn, concussion, cut, disinfect, faint, ice pack, injured, rash, swell*
- to say a rap about first aid
- to practice connected speech: consonant/r/ vowel linking

Materials
Audio Tracks 75 to 79; Video

Warm Up

Ask students to remember a time they hurt themselves. Ask them *What happened? Did you have any bruises or scars?* Have students discuss their experiences in pairs.

A TRACK 75 TB p. 223 **Listen. Which problem is real?**

- Using the TTL, display the picture on the opening spread. Have students discuss in pairs about the picture and what each child is doing. Encourage students to explain their ideas. Ask students further questions to provoke discussion, e.g. *Who looks like they are in pain?*
- Tell students that they are going to listen to a conversation between some of the children in the picture. Remind students of the challenge from the end of Unit 6. Ask *Where is Lola? What does she do in her free time?* (She volunteers in a first aid tent / teaches children about first aid.)
- Play the audio and have students look at the picture as they listen. Ask the gist question *Which problem is real?* Play the audio again and check the answer. Ask students if they think Neerav and Amira responded well to Tanya's problem. Elicit that students should always try to find an adult or emergency services when someone is hurt.

Answer
the allergic reaction

B TRACK 76 TB p. 224 **Find and number the words in A. Then listen and check.**

- Have students look at the list of vocabulary words. Point out the example (1) and have students find *injured* in the picture. Have students do the activity in pairs.
- Play the audio for students to check their answers.

Answers
1 *injured* 2 ice pack 3 swell 4 accident 5 faint
6 allergic reaction 7 rash 8 concussion 9 burn
10 cut 11 Band-Aid 12 disinfect

International English

Draw students' attention to the two International English features on pp. 88–89. Check understanding of vocabulary and then elicit the differences between the American English and British English words.

C TRACK 77 TB p. 224 **Close your eyes. Listen, visualize, and say.**

- Prepare students for the visualization (see Visualizations).
- Play the audio. Have students visualize the scenario.
- Have students discuss and act out what they imagined.

D Look and write.

- Display the table. Look at the example together. Elicit that students have to write health problems or injuries in the *What's wrong?* column and the treatments in the *Things that help* column.
- Have students complete the critical thinking activity individually. Then have students say which things help which problems, e.g. *an ice pack helps stop swelling.*

Suggested Answers
What's wrong?: *accident*, allergic reaction, burn, concussion, cut, faint, injured, rash, swell
Things that help: Band-Aid, disinfect, ice pack

E TRACK 78 TB p. 224 **Listen and write. Then watch and say.**

- Point to the title. Elicit that the picture scene shows a first aid tent. Ask *What happens in a first aid tent?* (people treat minor injuries). *Where might you find a first aid tent?*
- Play the video or audio and allow students to enjoy the rap. To focus on pronunciation, use just the audio initially. They can follow along in their books.
- Have students read the lyrics and try to complete the blanks. Then play the rap audio to check answers.
- Play the video or audio again and have students join in. Encourage students to copy the rhythm and intonation of the rap.

Answers
1 *injured* 2 cut 3 burn 4 accident 5 ice pack
6 Band-Aid

F TRACK 79 TB p. 224 **Pronunciation. Listen and say. Copy the linking. Think of other phrases like these.**

- Display the examples and elicit that the curved lines show linking. Have students try saying the phrases. Play the audio and have students repeat the phrases chorally.
- Elicit that the *r* at the end of the word runs into the vowel at the beginning of the next word. Drill the pronunciation of the /r/, especially if the sound is softer in students' L1.
- The rap has three examples of *r* + vowel linking. Have students try to come up with some examples of their own.

Answers
Students' own answers

Cool Down

Play *Shark* (see TB p. 26) using vocabulary from the lesson.

Practice **Student's App:** Vocabulary Practice; Spoken Word Video

Explore Language

Lesson Objectives

- to learn how to use the simple present passive
- to practice vocabulary related to injuries and first aid

Materials
Audio Tracks 80 and 81

Warm Up

Ask students if they enjoy swimming. Then ask *How can we make sure that everyone is safe at the pool?* Elicit ideas.

A TRACK 80 TB p. 224 **Listen and read. Are Neerav and Alex well prepared?**

- Tell students they are going to listen to two boys, Neerav and Alex, talking by the pool. Play the audio and have students follow along in their books. Ask *What are Neerav and Alex doing?* Elicit that they are lifeguards.
- Ask the gist question *Are Neerav and Alex well prepared?* Elicit the answer. Play the audio again to check.

Answer
Yes, they are; the pool party rules are on a poster; if anyone breaks the rules, they're told to leave the pool; there is a first aid kit by the pool; ice packs are in the fridge; Neerav's parents are in the house, so Neerav and Alex can call them if anything serious happens.

International English

Draw students' attention to the International English features on p. 90 and p. 91. Elicit which words are American English, which British English, and highlight the differences. Have students find the items in the picture. Ask *Which words do you want to use?*

Comprehension Check: Ask the following questions: *Can people swim if Neerav and Alex aren't there?* (no) *What can't they have near the pool?* (drinking glasses) *What happens if someone breaks the rules?* (That person has to leave the pool.) *Where are the ice packs?* (in the fridge) *Who will they ask for help if something serious happens?* (Neerav's parents)

Discussion: Ask students to look at the picture. Elicit the rules on the poster. Ask why these rules are important at a swimming pool and what accidents might happen if they are not followed.

B Look at A. Complete the table. Which verb form comes after the auxiliary verb (*be*)?

- Display the table using the TTL. Students should now have the skills and strategies to discuss and complete the grammar table themselves using the dialogue. Have them complete the table, then invite students to come up to the board and fill in a word each. Discuss the word order, form, and patterns, leting your class guide the discussion. For more support, use the notes in the **ETB**.

Practice **Resource Bank:** Grammar Printout
Student's App: Grammar Practice

- Look at the Grammar tip *Look*. Elicit that we only use the auxiliary verb in short answers, not the main verb.

Answers
allowed; aren't; 's/is; Are, kept; are
The past participle comes after the auxiliary verb (*be*).

C Think and discuss. Then choose.

- Have students work in pairs to discuss the sentences. Refer them to the table in B and the dialogue in A to see examples in context. Check answers as a class, asking questions to check comprehension, e.g. *Is it important who does the actions?*

Answers
1 the action 2 a routine or repeated process

D TRACK 81 TB p. 224 **Listen and say.**

- Play the audio. Have students repeat the sentences chorally.
- For ideas on how to vary the drill, see TB p. 23.

E Read and complete the dialogue.

- Have students look at the verbs in the box and check understanding. Have students give an example collocation with each verb, e.g. *use an eraser, call my mom.*
- Explain the dialogue is between two girls practicing for a first aid exam. Look at the example together. Have students read Rona's response. Elicit that you keep ice packs in the freezer, so the correct verb is *keep*.
- Have students complete the sentences individually. Remind them that the table in B will help them use the simple present passive forms correctly. Check answers as a class.

Answers
1 *are kept* 2 are bought 3 's/is disinfected 4 is used
5 are called 6 are written

F Think and discuss. Make some rules for a class camping trip. Whose rules are the best?

- Tell students they are going think about rules to stay safe on a camping trip. First, brainstorm things they will need to take on a camping trip. Then have students look at the colored boxes. Ask *What rules can we make about these things?*
- Have students read the examples on the page. Ask *Are these are good rules? Why?* Have students work in pairs to write at least one rule for each word, then share their rules with the class.

Answers
Students' own answers

Cool Down

Play the *Yes/No Game* (see TB p. 27). Call out true or false statements in the simple present passive, e.g. *Vegetables are bought at the pharmacy.*

Global Citizenship

Lesson Objectives

- to learn vocabulary related to preparing for an emergency: *call for help, drill, emergency exit, evacuate, first responder, keep calm, panic, prepare, rescue, sound the alarm*
- to explore how volunteers contribute to our well-being and what we can do to help others
- to practice listening for gist and detail

Materials
Audio Tracks 82 and 84; Audio Track G

Opening Question

Ask students if they remember the Level 3 unit about volunteers and elicit what a volunteer does. Ask the opening question: *How do volunteers contribute to our well-being?* Encourage students to think about the different types of volunteer work. Ask *Is anyone a volunteer? Do you know any volunteers?* Remind students of Lola from Lesson 1.

A TRACK 82 TB p. 224 **Listen to Mary and Isaac talk about volunteer roles. Why do you think the colored jackets are important?**

- Tell students that they are going to listen to two children talking about volunteer roles.
- Ask the gist question *Why do you think the colored jackets are important?* Play the audio and have students look at the pictures.
- Play the audio again to check the answer.

Answer
People can see them easily and know what role that person does.

B TRACK 83 TB p. 224 **Look at the pictures and definitions in A and write. Then listen and check.**

- Point out the example answer for number 1, *emergency exit*. Refer students to the vocabulary box in B. Have them write the words for each picture or definition in A.
- Play the audio for students to check their answers. Use the audio to drill the pronunciation of the words.

Answers
1 *emergency exit* 2 sound the alarm 3 first responder 4 rescue 5 call for help 6 prepare 7 keep calm 8 panic 9 drill 10 evacuate

International English

Draw students' attention to the different terms and ask which are American English and which are British English. Drill the pronunciation.

TRACK G TB p. 224 Visualization

- The TTL has a visualization audio track for this vocabulary set. (See TB p. 21.)

C Read and complete the blog post.

- Tell students they are going to read a blog post by a girl who volunteers as a fire marshal at her school. Then have students read the rest of the blog post.
- Look at the example together. Ask students why *prepare* is the correct answer and elicit that you have to continue reading to find supporting ideas.
- Have students complete the sentences and check answers.

Answers
1 *Prepare* 2 emergency exits 3 drill 4 keep calm 5 panic 6 first responder 7 rescue 8 sound the alarm

D TRACK 84 TB p. 224 **Now listen to a podcast about the origins of the first aid kit. What was the happy accident?**

- Tell students they are going to listen to a podcast about how the first aid kit was made. Tell students that a podcast is like an online radio show.
- Have students guess what's happening in the picture.
- Ask the gist question *What was the happy accident?* Play the audio. Check answers together.

Answer
a business person talking to another passenger, a doctor, on a train journey

E Listen again. Choose the correct answer.

- Have students read the sentences and try the activity. Play the audio to check answers.
- Ask students what connections there are between what Mary says in A and the podcast. (Mary says that it's really important to have the right things in a first aid kit. The podcast tells us how they decided what to put in it).

Answers
1 *1880* 2 weren't 3 business person 4 disinfect an injury 5 have been adapted 6 before

Discussion Questions

- Look at the discussion questions. Have students discuss each question (see **ETB**). Encourage students to recognize that even small actions can have a large impact over time and that we can all contribute to making the world a better place.
- Return to the opening question to ask again: *How do volunteers contribute to our well-being?* Revisit any ideas discussed at the beginning of the lesson and encourage students to share any new ideas.

Cool Down

Have students think of a global problem that they would like to fix. See if they can think of different ideas of how to fix it.

Practice Student's App: Vocabulary Practice; Listening Practice

Explore Language

Lesson Objectives

- to learn how to use reflexive pronouns

Materials
Audio Tracks 85 and 86

Warm Up

Tell students to imagine they have a broken leg and have to stay home and rest for two weeks. Ask *What would you do to pass the time?* Elicit ideas from the class.

A TRACK 85 TB p. 225 **Listen and read. How has Archie helped his sister?**

- Tell students that they are going to listen to Archie talking to his friends about his sister. Have students remember where Archie was in Lesson 2 (he was at the pool party). Have students find Archie in the picture. Play the audio and have students follow the dialogue in their books.
- Ask the gist question *How has Archie helped his sister?* and elicit the answer. Ask *What are they learning?* and elicit answers from the class (to play the guitar).

Answer
by spending time with her and helping her recover mentally from the shock of breaking her leg

B Look at A. Complete the table. How does the spelling of the reflexive pronoun change in the last sentence? Why?

- Display the table with the TTL. Students should now have the skills and strategies to discuss and complete the grammar table themselves using the dialogue. When they have completed the table, invite students to come up to the board and fill in a word each. Discuss the word order, form, and patterns together, letting your class guide the discussion. For more support, use the notes in the **ETB**.
- Point out that reflexive pronouns can also be used when describing doing something without help from other people, e.g. *No one would help me, so I did it myself.*
- Draw students' attention to the Grammar tip *Watch Out.* Look at the examples together. Tell students that the verbs *wash* and *get up* are not usually used reflexively. This is true for many verbs for daily routine. If these verbs are reflexive in the students' L1, remind them of this difference in English that they will need to remember.

Answers
yourself; herself; ourselves
–self changes to *–selves* because it's plural.

C Think and discuss. Then choose.

- Check understanding of *subject* and *direct object*, writing an example sentence from the table in B on the board and highlighting these. Then have students work in pairs to discuss the sentences.
- Check answers as a class. Ask students which verbs are not used with reflexive pronouns (*wash, get up*).

Answers
1 the same 2 Not all

D TRACK 86 TB p. 225 **Listen and say.**

- Play the audio, having students repeat each sentence chorally.
- Play it again and have students use facial expressions and gestures to demonstrate the meaning of each sentence, e.g. covering their ears while saying *I can't hear myself think!*
- For ideas on how to vary the drill, see TB p. 23.

E Read and choose.

- Have students look at the picture and say what is happening.
- Look at the example together. Ask *Is the alarm clock a person or a thing?* (a thing) Elicit that we use *it* to talk about things, so *itself* is the reflexive pronoun for an alarm clock.
- Have students do the controlled practice activity individually. Then check answers as a class.

Answers
1 *itself* 2 myself 3 ourselves 4 himself 5 yourself
6 themselves 7 yourselves

F Play *Tic-Tac-Toe*. Make sentences to win the squares.

- Students are going to play *Tic-Tac-Toe* (see TB p. 27). Students have to make sentences using the verbs in the squares with reflexive pronouns. This activity provides freer practice of reflexive pronouns.
- You could have students use their spinners to play. Write a number 1–6 next to each reflexive pronoun on the board. Students spin their spinner and have to use the reflexive pronoun with the number they land on.

Answers
Students' own answers

Cool Down

Play a variation of *Word Sneak* (see TB p. 27). Give students a sentence containing a reflexive pronoun, e.g. *I've cut myself.*

Practice **Resource Bank:** Grammar Printout
Student's App: Grammar Practice

Write About It

Lesson Objectives

- to plan and write an informative flyer
- to learn how to research, organize, and present information
- to review imperatives for giving instructions

Materials

Support writing printout from the Resource Bank (F)

Warm Up

Ask students what to do if a friend has fallen and hurt herself. Elicit a Dos and Don'ts list on the board in two columns, e.g. *Dos: Ask her if she's OK. Don'ts: laugh*

A Read the flyer about helping people. What are the three points to remember?

This text type is also modeled in the Literacy Book for this unit, First Aid for Beginners.

- Ask *What are the three points to remember?* Have students scan the text, then check answers as a class.
- Have students read the text more closely. Ask *Is this flyer about physical injuries?* (No, it's about injuries on the inside.)

Answers

Look, Listen, Follow Up

B Look at the structure of the flyer. Why does the writer use these features?

- Remind students that features are characteristics or things that the text has, e.g. headings. Do the first question together. Ask *Why does the writer use headings in the flyer?*
- Have students answer the other questions in pairs. Have students point out examples of features as you check answers together. Ask *How were these features helpful?*

Answers

1 to guide readers and tell them what the next section is about 2 to help organize the information clearly and in short, easy-to-read chunks 3 to make the important information stand out and be more memorable

C Look at the language in the flyer. Why does the writer use these features?

- Have students highlight or underline the verbs in the flyer.
- Have students answer the questions in pairs. Then check answers as a class.

Answers

1 b 2 c 3 a

- Look at the callout. Discuss why imperative forms and clear language are important in flyers like this.

D Think and discuss. Choose one of these situations. Brainstorm lots of ideas using one of the Generating Ideas techniques.

- Review **Process Writing Step 1: Generating Ideas** on p. 140.
- Tell students that they are going to plan and write their own flyer about one of the topics. In groups, have students choose, discuss, and find out about one of the topics.
- Have the groups draw a big mind map on poster paper and brainstorm ideas about their chosen topic. They can share their ideas with other groups with the same topic.

Answers

Students' own answers

E Plan your flyer. Use some of your ideas in D and one of the Planning techniques.

- Tell students they need to think about how to organize their ideas. Review the planning techniques students looked at in **Process Writing Step 2: Planning** on p. 141.
- Have students think about the ideas they want to use and how they can organize them logically. Encourage them to think of a heading for each main point and decide which ideas fit under each heading.
- Have students make notes in the table or copy the table into their notebooks and complete it. Students will plan and write their flyers individually.

Answers

Students' own answers

F Do a fast-writing draft of your flyer. Then think about how you've organized the information and revise it.

- Review the technique of fast writing that students looked at in **Process Writing Step 3: Drafting** on p. 142.
- Give students a few minutes to write their drafts. Remind students that they will need to review what they've written, so they shouldn't worry about making mistakes or having to start again.
- Have students use the checklist on p. 142 for their drafts. Encourage them to make notes on their drafts about things they want to change or move.

Answers

Students' own answers

G Now write and design your flyer.

- Have students write their flyers in class or for homework, either in their notebooks or using the support printout from the Resource Bank.
- Have students exchange flyers with a friend to read and check for clarity. Remind students to be positive and say what they liked about it.

Cool Down

Have students write messages for their classmates for the Positive Post Box (see **ETB**, Literacy Book Unit 4 Think Together) about how they help and listen to each other in class or outside, e.g. *You always ask me if I had a good weekend. Thank you!*

Practice **Student's App:** Writing Practice
Resource Bank: Writing Game, *Emergency Consequences*

Talk About It

Lesson Objectives

- to prepare and practice a presentation about a personal story
- to learn how to add suspense to a story

Materials
Video

Warm Up

Write the title *The Story of My Scar* on the board and have students guess what the story is about. Check understanding of *scar*. Ask students if they can think of any famous people or characters who have scars and if they know how they got them. Have them discuss this in pairs.

A TB p. 240 **Watch and listen. What was Maria's accident?**

- Tell students they are going to watch a video of a girl named Maria giving a presentation where she tells the story of how she got a scar. Ask a prediction question: *Where do you think her scar is?* Elicit suggestions from the class. Then play the video.
- Draw students' attention to the question *What was Maria's accident?* Have students discuss the question with a friend. Ask them how old Maria was when she had the accident (five).

Answer
She was standing on her brother's snowboard on the stairs and fell off and cut her head.

B **Watch again. Check (✔) the phrases Maria uses to involve the listeners in her story.**

- Tell students that they are going to look at some of the phrases Maria uses in the video. Have students read the sentences before they rewatch the video and see if they remember which phrases Maria used.
- Play the video once and have students check the phrases. Check answers as a class. Then play the video again and have students repeat the phrases, copying Maria's pronunciation and intonation.

Answers
2; 3; 4; 5; 6; 8; 9

C **Think of an accident you had or a scar you have now. Plan how you can tell the story.**

- Ask *What accidents have you had? Do you have any scars?* Brainstorm a few situations that might have happened to students, e.g. falling over while running, falling from a tree, or falling off a bike.
- Draw students' attention to the headings on the graphic organizer. Have students think and write notes under each heading, working individually. Encourage them to try to use some of the phrases from B to engage their audience. Remind students that they only need to write notes to prompt them and not full sentences.

Answers
Students' own answers

D **Practice with your friends using phrases in B. Then share with the class. Make notes.**

- Have students practice their presentations as many times as they like. Remind students to work on their intonation, body language, and eye contact, as well as what they are saying.
- Have some students give their presentations in front of the class. While they are speaking, the other students should make notes about the content (e.g. what happened) and the performance (e.g. did they ask questions, did they look at the audience).
- Have students analyze their own performances individually, thinking about whether they included all their ideas and if they organized their ideas well. Ask students if they used any of the phrases in B.

Cool Down

Have students make up a chain story about an accident. Have students sit in a circle. Give a story starter, e.g. *Did I ever tell you about the time when I broke my arm?* and have each student add a sentence. When you get to the last students, they must think of a way to end the story. With large classes, have students play in groups.

Practice **Student's App:** Speaking Skills Practice; Speaking Video

Think It Over

Lesson Objectives

- to review what has been learned in the unit
- to reflect on the unit and their own progress
- to think about learning strategies and how to continue learning at home

Warm Up

Do a quick quiz with the class about Unit 7. Ask questions about pictures, words, or information and have students find the answers in their books. Have students play in teams. Possible questions: *What happened to the girl with the sore hand on p. 88? How many people are there in the first aid tent on pp. 88–89? What are the two girls doing on p. 91? What's the word for picture 2 on p. 92? Name three verbs used with reflexive pronouns.*

How well did you meet the challenge of Unit 7? Read and respond.

3–2–1

- Tell students they are going to review what they learned in the unit and also think about their own learning.
- Have students work in small groups to make mind maps of what they have done in the unit. Encourage them to think about the different things they studied in the unit, including grammar, presentation phrases, writing techniques, vocabulary, facts, interesting ideas, and so on. They can also include ideas from the **Literacy Book**. Then have students display their mind maps on the wall. Have groups go around the classroom and look at each other's maps.
- Refer students to the graphic organizer in the book and the prompt sentences: *3 things I learned in this unit, 2 questions I have, 1 opinion I now have.* Have students talk in pairs about the different sections. Encourage them to focus particularly on the second section and to discuss what outstanding questions they have about things they learned.
- When you feel they have enough ideas, have students work individually to fill in the graphic organizer. Remind them that they should write their own responses about themselves. Monitor and help as necessary. Look at what students are writing so you can tailor your classes and any additional practice to their needs.
- If you feel it is appropriate for your class, have students share their ideas with a friend. Encourage them to think together of how they can improve or practice the thing they struggled with.

Looking Forward

Draw students' attention to the character at the bottom of the page. Elicit who it is and what they remember about him. (Aziz appeared in Lessons 1, 2, and 4.) Ask *Who is Aziz friends with?* (Archie and Paul) Have students read the speech bubble and make predictions about where Aziz likes going on weekends. Tell them that they will find out in the first lesson of Unit 7.

Practice **Resource Bank:** Unit Test
Student's App: Vocabulary and Grammar Review

Get Ready to Read

Lesson Objectives

- to activate prior knowledge about emergencies
- to guide inquiry and deepen understanding through a Step Inside VTR
- to preview the reading skill of understanding main ideas and details

Materials

VTR printout from the Resource Bank (A, B, C)

Warm Up

Have students think about the job of a firefighter. Divide pairs into A and B. Have student As make a list of the different things firefighters do in their job and student Bs list the things firefighters wear and use. Then have students discuss their ideas with their partner.

Step Inside

A Look at the picture. Choose a person or a thing. What can they see?

This VTR encourages students to step inside a person or object that they can see and imagine their point of view. Ask students what they can see in the picture. Provide vocabulary where necessary.

- Ask students to imagine that they are one of the people or things in the photo. Ask students what they can see (from that person or thing's viewpoint). Encourage them to think about the surroundings. Ask, e.g. *What is he doing? What is he wearing? How is he feeling?*
- Have students discuss their ideas in pairs, then as a class.

Here's an example of this part of the routine.
Student A: The fire truck can see the car.
Teacher: Great. What else can the fire truck see?
Student A: It can see the firefighters. It's watching them do their job.
Teacher: OK, tell me more about that.
Student A: It can see the firefighter cutting the car.
Teacher: Which part of the car can it see? Can it see anyone inside?
Student B: It can see a person in the front of the car.

B What do you think they believe?

- Ask students to imagine what their chosen person or thing might believe, based on what they can see, feel, or hear.
- Say *I think the person in the car believes that the firefighter will help him/her get out. What does your person or thing believe?*
- Give students time to think about the person or thing they have chosen and their thoughts and opinions. Have students discuss their ideas in pairs and then as a class.

Here's an example of this part of the routine.
Teacher: Who did you decide to be in in the picture?
Student A: The badge around the firefighter's neck.
Teacher: OK, so what does it believe?
Student A: It believes that the person in the car is injured.
Teacher: Great. What makes you say that?
Student B: Because it's looking at the person in the car and it can see her sad face.

C What do you think they care about?

- Ask students to think about what is important to the people, animals, or things in the picture.
- Give students time to think and then discuss in pairs. Elicit ideas.

Here's an example of this part of the routine.
Teacher: What does your person or thing care about?
Student A: The firefighter cares about people.
Teacher: Does he care about the car?
Student B: No, because he is damaging it. He cares about the people inside.

Transition

Ask students how the firefighters are helping the person in the picture. Elicit that they are going to force open the car door. Ask *Why do they need to force open the door?* Elicit that someone is trapped inside and they need to get into the car to get the person out and to the hospital safely.

D Think and discuss. What is an emergency? What different kinds of help do people need?

- Ask *What is an emergency?* Brainstorm different situations with the class. Encourage them to think about all the emergency services (ambulance, fire department, police, coast guard, etc.) and write these on the board.
- Have students think about the type of emergencies each service deals with and discuss their ideas in pairs or small groups. Then have a few students share their ideas with the class.

E Think and predict. Then write. Look at the pictures from *The Chopper*. What do you think the story is about?

- Tell students to look at the pictures on pp. 106–111 and identify the main idea of the story. Give them one to two minutes to discuss the pictures and the situation in pairs.
- Elicit ideas from the class, encouraging students to give reasons for their answers.

Suggested Answer

I think the story is about someone getting hurt (because there is an ambulance).

Now read **The Chopper**

Fiction: *The Chopper—Story*

Lesson Objectives

- to read a story about a man who has a medical emergency
- to make a personal connection to the reading

Materials
Audio Tracks 28 and 29

Warm Up

Ask students what kinds of activities they do with different members of their family. Have them discuss in pairs.

TRACK 28 TB p. 234 **Reading Approach**

Engage with the Text

- Project the opening spread of the reading with the Story Player in the TTL. See if students notice the circled *H* in the title. Ask them to guess what it means, but don't correct answers yet.
- For the first reading, play the audio and have the students follow along in their books, or use the Story Player. Ask prediction questions before turning the page, e.g. *What do you think will happen to the girl's dad?*

TRACK 29 TB p. 235 **Words in Context**

- After the first reading of the text, draw students' attention to the Words in Context box. Play the audio to practice the pronunciation.
- Have students brainstorm a list of strategies that they can use to find the meanings of the words, including strategies they use in L1.
- Divide the class into pairs or groups and have each pair or group look at all of the words.
- Have them work together to find and highlight each instance of each word in the reading and identify the type of word by looking at the form and the sentence.
- Have students then swap pairs or groups and take turns explaining words to each other, saying which strategy they used. Encourage students to discuss different strategies and which work better.

wheezed (p. 107, verb) This word is onomatopoeic, so saying it out loud will help. Knowledge of what happens when you cough and/or have an asthma attack also help. Strategies to use: word sounds, world knowledge

paramedic (p. 108 / p. 109, noun) We know the paramedic is a person/job because her name is given and we can see a woman in the picture. Strategies to use: pictures, surrounding words and sentences, world knowledge

stretcher (p. 108 / p. 110, noun) The sentence tells us this is something Papa is lying on, so students can find it in the picture. Using knowledge of the equipment in an ambulance will also help. Strategies to use: pictures, surrounding words and sentences, world knowledge

shiver (p. 109, verb) The sentence says that the night breeze is making Sophia do this action. Students can think about how they might feel and react physically in a situation like this. Strategies to use: surrounding words and phrases, personal experience

blades (p. 109, noun) Each sentence where this word occurs describes in a different way how they work and shows that the word is related to the helicopter. Strategies to use: pictures, surrounding words and phrases, world knowledge

Analyze the Text and Features

- Have students read the text individually in their books. Give them plenty of time to read. Ask them to identify the climax (the most exciting part) of the story as they read.
- Have students find the purple callouts and discuss the questions with a partner.
  - **Making Connections** (p. 106): *Why do we need emergency services?* Elicit what types of things are considered emergencies. Brainstorm some situations with students and have them decide whether they should call emergency services in each case.
  - **CLIL Focus** (p. 107): *What number do you call in an emergency?* Ask students if they know the telephone number for emergency services in their country.
  - **Fact** (p. 108): *An asthma attack makes it difficult and painful to breathe.* Ask students if they know anyone who has asthma. Tell students that it is a common illness and people with asthma live normal and active lives.
  - **Personalization** (p. 111): *Do you know a story about an emergency? What happened?* Have students discuss this in pairs. If they don't know any stories, have them talk about a movie they have seen featuring an emergency.
  - **Text Focus** (p. 107): *What caused Papa's asthma attack? What are its effects?* Have students look at the two pages to find out how Papa's asthma attack started and what the symptoms were.

Interact with the Text

- Now that students are very familiar with the text, have them act out the story in pairs.

Cool Down

Ask students which scene from the story they liked best and why. Have them discuss with a friend.

Practice **Resource Bank:** Story Player

Explore the Reading

Lesson Objectives

- to understand and analyze *The Chopper* through reading comprehension activities
- to learn about the SEL competency of self-management by managing personal and interpersonal stress
- to review the reading skill of understanding main ideas and details
- to understand the use of similes

Warm Up

Play *Who Said It?* (see TB p. 27) with phrases from *The Chopper*.

A Read and sequence the events.

- Refer back to *The Chopper*. Use a Group Time discussion to review the story with the class. Ask questions to help students remember the story, e.g. *What were Sophia and Papa doing? Why did Papa feel ill? What did Sophia do?*
- Ask students what the very first event in the story was (Sophia put on some music and she and Papa started to dance). Tell students they are going to put the story events in order. Have students open their books and find the first event (*Sophia pushed play and the music started*).
- Have students do the ordering activity individually. Encourage them to order the sentences from memory. They can then look back at the reading to check their answers. Check answers as a class.

Answers

8, 4, 6, 5, 3, 1, 7, 2

B Complete the table with the missing cause or effect.

- Review the reading skill of identifying cause and effect. Remind students that the *cause* is what makes something happen, and the *effect* is what happens because of that.
- Refer students to the table and look at the first effect. Ask *What caused this?* Elicit that Papa was dancing. Ask students why they think dancing caused Papa's asthma attack (see Background Information in the **ETB**).
- Have students complete the table individually. Then check answers as a class.

Suggested Answers

Missing causes: Papa and Sophia were dancing; The last boat had already left.

Missing effects: Sophia helped him sit down on the sofa; The ambulance came/arrived; The chopper lifted up. It went higher and higher.

C Think and discuss. Think about a time when you felt stressed like Sofia. How did you calm yourself down?

- Check the meaning of *stressed* and ask students how you feel when you're stressed. Elicit that you feel worried or nervous about a situation, and this can be caused by complicated things happening in your life.
- Brainstorm situations that can make people stressed and write these on the board, such as work, studies, exams, moving to a new house, bullying, peer pressure, or being too busy. Ask students what the symptoms of stress are and elicit ideas, e.g. losing your temper, not sleeping well, headaches, stomach problems, feeling overwhelmed, difficulty concentrating.
- Ask students why Sophia felt stressed (her dad couldn't breathe; she couldn't find his inhaler, and he was getting worse). Tell students to think of a time when they felt stressed and what happened. Ask *Could you calm down?*
- Have students discuss their ideas in pairs and then share with the class.

Literary Term: Simile

Read and underline the similes.

- Draw students' attention to the explanation of *simile*. Remind students about metaphors, which they studied in Unit 5, p. 86. Point out that a metaphor compares two things directly, whereas a simile says that something is similar to another thing.
- Look at the first sentence together and have students identify the simile. Ask *Are foxes clever?* Point out that foxes have useful skills and abilities that not all animals have, and for this reason, we consider them to be *clever*.
- Have students work in pairs to identify the similes.
- Have students find more examples in the reading. Check answers and discuss the meaning of each one.

Answers

1 like a fox 2 as loud as a lion's roar 3 as quiet as a mouse 4 tall like a giant 5 as noisy as a zoo 6 like a cheetah

Similes in the reading: like a giant, flying monster; like red eyes

Cool Down

End the lesson by having students choose a phrase or sentence they liked or found interesting from the reading. Have them write their phrase on a sticky note and then stick them on the wall.

Practice **Resource Bank:** Literary Term Printout
Student's App: Reading Practice; Literary Term Practice

Get Ready to Read

Lesson Objectives

- to activate prior knowledge about injuries and first aid kits
- to review the reading skill of understanding main ideas and details

Warm Up

Tell students to imagine that their friend was climbing a tree and fell to the ground. Have students quickly think of three things they can do to help. Then discuss their answers as a class. (Suggested answers: call an ambulance, talk to the patient, cover the patient with a blanket or clothes, try to stop any bleeding using your clothes, put the patient in the recovery position)

A Read and write. What is the main idea? What are two details?

- Display the picture using the TTL and have students say what they think is happening (people are learning about first aid, more specifically, CPR).
- Have students read the text quickly to find out what it is about. Then ask students what the main idea is and elicit the answer.
- Tell students to find two details from the text and write them in their books. Check answers as a class.
- Have students read the reading skill box. Then ask questions to check comprehension, e.g. *Which sentence has the main idea?* (the topic sentence) *Why do details help the reader understand more?* (because they provide supporting information that helps create a complete picture) Remind students that they looked at topic sentences and supporting details in the Write About It lesson in Unit 6 of the **Language Book** (pp. 82–83).

Suggested Answers

Main idea: CPR is a life-saving method for people who are having breathing or heart emergencies.
Detail 1: It was invented in the 1700s.
Detail 2: People learn CPR by taking training courses.

B Read the paragraph from *First Aid for Beginners*. Then write the main idea and details.

- Have students read the paragraph, identify the main idea and details, and write them in their books. Then check answers as a class.
- Ask students if they have ever had a soft tissue injury such as a sprain, bruise, or strain. How did they get this injury? Did they get treatment? Have students discuss their experiences in pairs.

Suggested Answers

Main idea: Sprains, bruises, and strains are soft tissue injuries.
Detail 1: They can happen in many different places.
Detail 2: They might cause minor pain and swelling.

C Think and discuss. What first aid skills do you know? What do first aid kits usually contain?

- Elicit the meaning of *first aid*. Explain that *aid* means help, so *first aid* means the basic help or treatment given to people when they become sick or have an injury.
- Draw the students' attention to the two questions. Tell students to think about what to do in different situations where someone has gotten hurt and what equipment they might need to help. Give students a few minutes to think about and discuss their ideas in small groups. You could have students write their ideas in their notebooks.

Now read **First Aid for Beginners**

Nonfiction: *First Aid for Beginners*—Instructional Text

Lesson Objectives

- to read an instructional text about first aid
- to make a personal connection to the reading

Materials
Audio Tracks 30 and 31

Warm Up

Play *Cross the Circle*. Give students a number 1–4. Call out a number and give them instructions containing different medical problems or injuries, e.g. *Number 1s! Cross the circle as if you have a sprained ankle.* Then repeat with different medical problems or injuries.

TRACK 30 TB p. 235 Reading Approach

Engage with the Text

- Project the opening spread of the reading with the Story Player in the TTL. Ask students to predict what kind of information is in the reading. Elicit that the reading provides instructions about what to do in emergencies.
- Play the audio and have students follow along in their books. Ask prediction questions before they read each section, e.g. *What do you think the ice pack is for?*

TRACK 31 TB p. 235 Words in Context

- After the first reading of the text, draw students' attention to the Words in Context box.
- Give students a few minutes to find and highlight each instance of each word in the reading.
- Have them identify the type of word by looking at the form and the sentence.
- Write these strategies on the board: *pictures; positive/negative, surrounding words and sentences; contrasting ideas; word families; world knowledge*. Tell students there is one strategy they won't need to use, and they need to find which one it is (positive/negative).
- Have students work in pairs to discuss the words.

gauze (p. 114 / p. 115, noun) This item is labeled in the first aid kit picture. The surrounding words and personal experience will also help. Strategy to use: pictures

bleeding (p. 115, noun) This word is in a word family with *blood*. It can also be used as a verb. Personal experience of having a cut will also help. Strategies to use: word families, personal experiences

soft tissue (injuries) (p. 115, adjective) The following sentence tells us the different types of soft tissue there are in the body. Reading on to the next section about bones provides a contrasting idea. Strategies to use: surrounding words and sentences, contrasting ideas

inject (p. 116, verb) The surrounding sentences explain how and what is injected. The pictures also show the meaning. Strategies to use: pictures, surrounding words and sentences, world knowledge

venom (p. 116, noun) The second clause of the sentence explains this. Knowledge of stings and allergies will also help. Strategies to use: pictures, surrounding words and sentences

- Then go through each word to elicit the meaning and how they know. Play the audio to practice the pronunciation.

Analyze the Text and Features

- Have students read the text in pairs. They can take turns to read aloud a section of the reading to each other.

International English

Have students notice the two different words. Remind students that they can choose the variety of English they want to use but they must be consistent.

- Tell students to find the purple callouts and discuss them with a partner. Alternatively, use Group Time to discuss the question after students have finished reading (see TB p. 21).
  - **Gist** (p. 114): *What is first aid?* Students discussed this in the Get Ready to Read lesson. Elicit that first aid is what the first person to help someone does.
  - **Fun Fact** (p. 116): *Wasps won't leave a stinger, but they can sting more than once. Bees can only sting once.* Ask students if they have been stung by a wasp or a bee. Did they see the sting? Ask if it was painful.
  - **Personalization** (p. 117): *Do you feel more prepared for an emergency now?* Ask students to answer the question in pairs. Then ask students how they would help if someone had an injury at school.

Interact with the Text

- Now that students are very familiar with the text, have them work in groups with each student choosing a different section of the reading. Play the audio again and have students listen for the pronunciation of difficult words in their section of the reading and make a note in their books. Have students practice reading their section of the text.
- Have one or two groups read and present the text for the class.

Cool Down

Play *Backs to the Board* (see TB p. 25). Have students choose an item from the first aid kit.

Practice **Resource Bank:** Story Player

Explore the Reading

Lesson Objectives

- to understand and analyze *First Aid for Beginners* through reading comprehension activities
- to practice the reading skill of understanding main ideas and details
- to explore the CLIL science concept of first aid
- to make a personal connection to the reading

Warm Up

Play *Odd One Out* (see TB p. 26) with words from the reading, e.g. gauze pad, Band-Aid, ice pack, stinger (stinger), rash, ice pack, swelling, tight feeling (ice pack), broken bone, sprain, bruise, strain (broken bone).

A Think and discuss. Write five questions about the reading to ask your partner.

- Have students work in groups to try to remember details from the reading. One student names an injury, and the other student tries to remember what kind of first aid treatment should be given, e.g. *hypothermia* (give the patient clothes and a blanket; give the patient a warm drink and food).
- Tell students that they have to write the questions about the reading for a partner to answer. Look at the example question and answer together. Tell students to try to write open questions (i.e. not yes/no questions). Write question words on the board as prompts: *What / Where / When / How / Which / Why / Who.*
- Have students write their questions and answers in their books individually. Encourage students to look back at the reading for reference.
- When they have finished, have them ask and answer their questions in pairs. Tell students to let their partner look back at the reading to find the answer if needed.

Answers
Students' own answers

B Read and complete the table.

- Tell students they are going to practice the reading skill again. Ask *What are the main ideas in the reading?* Elicit one or two. Then have students look at the table. Have a student read the first main idea and then ask students what details they can find about this. Have them look back at the reading to find one detail.
- Give students a few minutes to look back at the reading to find the missing information and write it in the table. Then check answers as a class. Students may have different answers to those below.

Suggested Answers
Missing main ideas: It can be hard to tell if a bone is broken. Hypothermia can happen when someone has been cold for a long time.
Missing details: The first-aider should clean the wound carefully. Put an ice pack on the sting.

C Think, write, and discuss. Check (✔) to choose an injury. What do you need to treat it? Make a list. Then share how you treat it.

Students are going to connect the reading to their own knowledge. This draws on the CLIL science focus of first aid.

- Pretend that one of the injuries has just happened to you, e.g. that you have sprained your ankle. Tell students what has happened (pretend that it hurts and start limping!) and ask them if they know what to do. Elicit ideas from the class.
- Have students choose one of the injuries and think about what they need to treat it. Give them a few minutes to write down what they need and how they will treat injury.
- Have students discuss their ideas in pairs or small groups. Encourage students to ask each other questions, e.g. *What do you do first?*

Answers
Students' own answers

Cool Down

Play *Mime It!* (see TB p. 26) with the injuries from the reading.

Practice **Students' App:** Reading Practice

Think Together

Lesson Objectives

- to make connections between the readings
- to explore the key concept: What can we do to help in an emergency?
- to reflect on the unit and provide personal thoughts and opinions

Warm Up

Remind students of both of the readings and ask students what they have in common. Give students a minute to look back through their books and make connections between the two readings. (Suggested answers: both are about emergencies, acting quickly is important, Sophia learned about first aid at Scouts)

A Complete the table. What are some of the possible signs of these health problems? Look back at *The Chopper* and *First Aid for Beginners* to help you.

- Have students look at the table and remember which reading each health problem is from. Ask students if they remember any of the possible signs and elicit ideas.
- Then have students write their ideas in the table, using the readings to help them. Then check answers.

Suggested Answers

An asthma attack: shortness of breath, wheezing, chest pain

A broken bone: swelling (part of the body looks bigger than normal), if the skin around the injury has changed color, if the person can't use that part of their body, if there is a lot of pain

An allergic reaction: an itchy, red rash on the skin; a tight feeling in the throat and/or chest; difficulty breathing; swelling around the face, lips, tongue, throat or eyelids

B Think and discuss. What skills and strategies will help you in an emergency? Do a Numbered Heads Together routine.

- Students are going to apply what they have learned in the unit and discuss the key concept question: *How can we help in an emergency?*
- Review the different problems that may be considered emergencies. Allow students to look at the notes they made in the previous lesson.
- Do a Numbered Heads Together routine (see TB p. 20). As you review ideas with the class, focus on the key concept *How can we help in an emergency?* Elicit skills and strategies for specific situations, choosing a different number each time.

Answers

Students' own answers

C Imagine there's an emergency. You're there when it happens. What can you do to help? Work with your group and plan a role play. Take turns to act out your role play for the class.

- Tell students that they are going to role-play in groups. Tell students to choose an emergency and think about what they can do to help.
- Have students decide what will happen, who the characters are, what they will say, and the actions they will do. Encourage them to use all the ideas they have learned.

My Reading Journal

Have you ever been in an emergency? What happened? If you haven't, can you imagine what you would do?

This question focuses on personalization and encourages students to make a personal connection to the unit. Give students time to think and write their answer, then discuss in pairs or small groups.

Suggested Answer

I have never been in a fire, but I think I would stay calm and call the fire department.

Write a review of this unit. What were the best and worst parts?

This question focuses on self-evaluation and personalization. In pairs, have students think back to identify challenges, what they enjoyed or found interesting.

Invite students to share their answers with the class.

Suggested Answer

The best part was the reading about first aid because I learned what to do in an emergency. The worst part was the second reading because it was boring.

Go back to page 105. Do the routine again.

Have students look back at the VTR picture on pp. 104–105. Using the TTL, project the image onto the board. Ask students how they think the picture connects to the two readings. Then repeat the Step Inside routine. Encourage students to choose a different person or thing from the picture this time. Then have them compare their answers from the first time they did the routine and notice how the perspective changes, e.g. *Before, I chose the window and I thought it was hurting because it was broken. This time, I chose the helmet. I protected the firefighter because I care about his safety.*

Cool Down

Play *Word Tennis* (see TB p. 27). Use things from a first aid kit and have students name injuries it can be used for, e.g. Teacher: *Band-Aid.* Student A: *Cut.* Student B: *Scrape.*

Practice **Resource Bank:** Unit Test
Student's App: Key Concept Practice

UNIT 8

Way Back Then

Unit Overview

Themes

Discoveries and ancient civilizations

Ancient civilizations and mysteries

Synopsis

In this unit, students will explore ancient civilizations. They will learn about discoveries and inventions and how we have learned from past civilizations. They will learn about how we have developed knowledge and ideas to solve problems. Students will plan and prepare a presentation about the present from a future perspective and write an informative article about a historical place.

Language Book

Vocabulary

cross (v), *engineering*, *invent*, *practical*, *preserve*, *printing*, *record information* (v), *solution*, *stone*

Pronunciation: connected speech: elision, dropping the *t*

p. 160

Explore Language

Past Modal Verbs of Obligation

p. 161

Global Citizenship

Why do people like to learn about the past?

assess, *civilization*, *create*, *culture*, *develop*, *discover*, *knowledge*, *technique*

p. 162

Explore Language

Simple Past Passive

p. 163

Take the Stage

Structuring, Transitioning, and Concluding

p. 164

Write About It

An Informative Article

Genre Focus: recognizing fact and opinion

Sentence Building: phrases to link cause and effect

p. 165

Think It Over

Review and Reflection

My Favorite Mistakes

p. 166

Literacy Book

Think Together

How do we explain the mysteries from ancient civilizations?

p. 173

Visible Thinking

See, Think, Wonder

p. 167

Nonfiction

Informational Text: *Mysterious Malta*

Words in Context: *archaeological, constructed, architecture, researchers, hypothesize, ruts*

p. 171

Fiction

Fable: *The Great Race*

Words in Context: *current, sneaky, effort, slithered, diligent*

p. 168

Reading Skill

Recognizing genres

p. 170

Literary Term

Transition Words

p. 169

Language and Literacy Connections

The connecting theme for Unit 8 is ancient civilizations.

	Language	Literacy
Vocabulary	**Set 1:** discoveries and inventions **Set 2:** developing knowledge and ideas	**Fiction:** stone, cross (v) **Nonfiction:** create, preserve, civilization, discover
Grammar	**Past Modal Verbs of Obligation** So what did they have to do? They didn't have to carry stones. The bridges had to be strong enough for people and animals. Did the people have to be careful? **Simple Past Passive** Who was it used by? It was spoken by the ancient Romans. We were taught Latin. Modern languages weren't created out of nowhere.	**Fiction:** You had to use your skills and talents to cross the river. **Nonfiction:** The temples were built between 3100 and 2500 BCE. Hal Tarxien was discovered by local farmers in 1913. The main entrance was constructed of three huge stones. The temple walls were made of enormous stones that were transported to Tarxien from other parts of the island. Very hard stone was used for outside walls. Many carvings and paintings of plants, animals, or people were found inside the rooms. Floors were made of enormous flat stones. Small round stones were discovered under these stones. Perhaps they were used to hold doors open.
Skills	**Pronunciation:** connected speech: elision, dropping the ***t*** **Process Writing:** drafting	**Reading:** recognizing genres **Literary Term:** transition words
International English	civilization/civilisation	civilization/civilisation

Vocabulary

Lesson Objectives

- to learn vocabulary related to discoveries and inventions: *cross* (v), *engineering, invent, practical, preserve, printing, record information* (v), *solution, stone*
- to say a poem about famous inventions
- to practice connected speech: elision and dropping the *t*

Materials

Audio Tracks 87 to 91; Video

Warm Up

Ask students to think about all the technology they use and how it improves their life. Encourage them to think about different aspects of their life, e.g. for studying, cooking, leisure. Discuss as a class.

A TRACK 87 TB p. 225 **Listen. How did the Ancient Chinese improve their lives?**

- Display the picture on the opening spread with the TTL. Have students speculate about what is happening in the picture, including the pictures visible on the panel. Ask questions, e.g. *Which ancient cultures can you see?*
- Tell students that they are going to listen to a conversation between Aziz, Jasmin, and their guide, Liu Wei. Remind students of the challenge from the end of Unit 7. Ask *Where does Aziz like going on weekends?* (on history club field trips)
- Play the audio and have students look at the picture. Point out that a *field trip* is a visit to a place that gives students the chance to study something in a real environment rather than in a classroom or laboratory.
- Ask the gist question *How did the Ancient Chinese improve their lives?* Play the audio again and check answers. Ask *What three groups of people are the children learning about?* (the Ancient Egyptians, the Ancient Chinese, and the Incas) Ask *What do you know about these three civilizations?*

Answers

They invented the umbrella, matches, kites, fireworks, paper, printing using blocks of wood, and the compass. They were also famous for their engineering.

B TRACK 88 TB p. 225 **Find and number the words in A. Then listen and check.**

- Have students look at the list of vocabulary words. Point out the example (1) and have students find *stone* in the picture. Have students do the activity in pairs.
- Play the audio for students to check their answers.

Answers

1 *stone* 2 record information 3 cross 4 solution
5 practical 6 printing 7 engineering 8 preserve
9 invent

C TRACK 89 TB p. 225 **Close your eyes. Listen, visualize, and say.**

- Prepare students for the visualization (see Visualization).
- Play the audio, allowing students to visualize the scenario as they listen.
- Have students discuss the things they imagined in pairs.

D **Look and complete the phrases.**

- Display the activity with the TTL. Do the example together. Have students complete the phrases using words from A.
- Check answers by having half the class call out a word from A and the other half call out the rest of the phrase from D, e.g. Team A: *engineering.* Team B: *project.*

Suggested Answers

1 *engineering* 2 cross 3 preserve 4 solution
5 printing 6 stone 7 practical 8 invent
9 record information

E TRACK 90 TB p. 225 **Listen and write. Then watch and say.**

- Ask *What is your favorite invention?* Elicit responses. Play the video or audio. Have students follow along in their books.
- Have students read the poem and try completing the blanks. Play the poem video or audio to check answers.
- Play the video or audio again and have students join in, copying the rhythm and pronunciation of the poem.

Answers

1 *practical* 2 solutions 3 printing 4 engineering
5 stones 6 invent

F TRACK 91 TB p. 225 **Pronunciation. Listen and say. Copy the linking. Think of other phrases like these.**

- Display the examples and elicit that the curved lines show linking. Have students try saying the phrases. Then play the audio and have students listen and repeat.
- Elision is the omission of one or more sounds to make it easier to pronounce. In this case, we drop the *t* before the consonants *l, w,* and *d*. Have students notice how the *t* at the end of the word is dropped in each example.
- Have students try to come up with some examples of their own. Encourage them to look in their book for phrases that follow the same pattern.

Answers

Students' own answers

Cool Down

Play *3–2–1 Challenge*. Have students think of three things printed onto paper, two things designed by engineers, and one thing made of stone.

Practice **Student's App:** Vocabulary Practice; Spoken Word Video

Explore Language

Lesson Objectives

- to learn how to use past modal verbs of obligation
- to practice vocabulary related to discoveries and inventions

Materials

Audio Tracks 92 and 93

Warm Up

Ask students if they have ever built anything and then ask what kinds of things they have built. Tell them to think about outdoor constructions they have made using materials they have found outside; indoor tents and dens they have built using things found in the house; and buildings or structures made with construction bricks, models, and so on. Have them discuss their ideas in pairs.

A TRACK 92 TB p. 225 **Listen and read. What does Jasmin want to do?**

- Tell students they are going to listen to Caleb and Jasmin from Lesson 1 talking about a practical activity they can do at the museum. Play the audio and have students follow the dialogue in their books. Ask *What were the Incas good at?* (engineering)
- Ask the gist question *What does Jasmin want to do?* and elicit the answer. Play the audio again for students to check. Ask students if they would like to build a bridge.

Answer

She wants to build a bridge.

B Look at A. Complete the table. When do we use *did*?

- Display the table using the TTL.
- Students should now have the skills and strategies to discuss and complete the grammar table themselves using the dialogue. When they have completed the table, invite students to come up to the board and fill in one word each. Ask if everyone agrees. Discuss the word order, form, and patterns together, but let your class guide the discussion. For more support, use the notes in the **ETB**.
- Draw students' attention to the Grammar tip *Remember*. Have students notice that the modal verb is in its infinitive form because the past form is in the auxiliary verb.

Answers

have to; didn't have to; had to; Did, have to; did
We use *did* in the question and the negative form.

C Think and discuss. Then choose.

- Have students work in pairs to discuss the sentences. Refer them to the table in B and the story in A to see examples in context. Check answers as a class, encouraging students to give reasons and examples to explain their answers.

Answer

1 obligations 2 didn't have to

D TRACK 93 TB p. 225 **Listen and say.**

- Play the audio, having students repeat each sentence chorally.
- For ideas on how to vary the drill, see TB p. 23.

E Look and complete the sentences.

- Have students look at the pictures and ask them what they think is happening in each one. Draw their attention to the verbs under each picture and check understanding.
- Look at the example together of the controlled practice activity and have students look at the picture. Point out the water in the picture and elicit that the picture shows a good irrigation system. Then ask students what the woman is doing in the same picture (she is drying food). Ask *Did they have to dry their food to preserve it?* (yes)
- Have students complete the sentences individually. Remind them to look at the table in B to help them use the verb forms correctly. Check answers as a class.

Answers

1 *didn't have to carry* 2 had to dry 3 had to trade 4 didn't have to work 5 had to cook 6 didn't have to use

F Imagine you traveled back to ancient times with your family. What did or didn't you have to do?

- Tell students they are going to imagine what it was like to live in the past. Say *Imagine you lived in Ancient Egypt, Rome, or China for a week. What obligations did you have?* Brainstorm ideas about life in the past and support with vocabulary if necessary, writing key words on the board.
- Have three students read the examples on the page. Have students think of more ideas about what they had to do and didn't have to do. Have students work in pairs or small groups to discuss their ideas.
- Have some groups share their ideas with the class.

Answers

Students' own answers

Cool Down

Have students ask and answer questions in pairs about their obligations when they were five years old, e.g. *Did you have to clean your room? Did you have to wear a uniform?*

Practice **Resource Bank:** Grammar Printout
Student's App: Grammar Practice

Global Citizenship

Lesson Objectives

- to learn vocabulary related to developing knowledge and ideas: *assess, civilization, create, culture, develop, discover, knowledge, technique*
- to explore why people like to learn about the past and how we have learned from ancient civilizations
- to practice listening for gist and detail

Materials

Audio Tracks 94 to 96; Audio Track H; a map of the world (D)

Opening Question

Ask the opening question and elicit ideas: *Why do people like to learn about the past?* Encourage students to think about what we can learn from history. Ask *What skills have we learned from people in the past and which skills will we need when modern technology breaks down?*

A TRACK 94 TB p. 225 **Listen to Umeko and her dad talk about their yard. What solution do they find for their problem?**

- Tell students that they are going to listen to a girl and her dad talking about growing vegetables. Ask *Do you grow any vegetables at home?* Discuss briefly with the class.
- Ask *What problem do they have? What solution do they find?* Play the audio and have students identify the problem and solution. Ask students if they think it is a good solution.

Answer

They decide to grow plants on the sunny walls and in pots.

B TRACK 95 TB p. 226 **Look at the pictures and definitions in A and write. Then listen and check.**

- Point out the example for number 1, *assess*. Refer students to the vocabulary box in B and have them write the words for each picture and definition in A in pairs or individually.
- Play the audio to check answers. Drill pronunciation.

Answers

1 *assess* 2 discover 3 knowledge 4 create
5 technique 6 culture 7 develop 8 civilization

TRACK H TB p. 226 Visualization

- The TTL has a visualization audio track for this vocabulary set. (See TB p. 21.)

C **Read and complete the blog post. Use the correct form of the words in B.**

- Tell students they are going to read about why the writer likes learning about ancient civilizations. Have students read the blog post.
- Look at the example together. Elicit why *civilization* is the correct answer and elicit that it refers to a group of people.
- Have students complete the sentences and check answers.

Answers

1 *civilization* 2 knowledge 3 discovered
4 techniques 5 developed 6 created 7 culture
8 assess

International English

American: civilization

British: civilisation

Have students notice the different spelling. Tell students that the pronunciation is the same. See if students can remember any other words with these spelling patterns (*realize, recognize*).

D TRACK 96 TB p. 226 **Now listen to historian Dr. Abbas. Why do you think she's fascinated by the Ancient Romans?**

- Have students look at the pictures and say what they see. Find Italy on a map of the world together. Tell students they are going to listen to a radio show by a historian talking about the Ancient Romans.
- Listening for gist: ask the gist question *Why do you think she is fascinated by the Ancient Romans?* and play the audio. Check the answer with the class.

Suggested Answer

She likes learning about the past and thinks we can learn a lot from the Romans.

E **Listen again. Write *True, False,* or *Doesn't Say*.**

- Have students read the sentences and complete the activity. Play the audio. Then check and discuss answers.
- Elicit that the radio show is the same documentary that Umeko's dad listened to in A. Have students compare what Umeko's dad says about the Aztecs with what Dr. Abbas says about the Ancient Romans. Elicit that both civilizations found ingenious ways to solve their problems.

Answers

1 *True* 2 True 3 False 4 Doesn't Say 5 False
6 Doesn't Say

Discussion Questions

- Have students discuss the questions in pairs or small groups (see **ETB**). Focus on how we like to understand how things work and how knowledge and techniques have evolved over time. Guide students to conclude that many modern techniques were developed from ancient discoveries and solutions.
- Return to the opening question to ask again: *Why do people like to learn about the past?* Revisit any ideas discussed at the beginning of the lesson and encourage students to share any new ideas.

Cool Down

Have students choose their favorite discovery so far, then find another student who likes the same one.

Practice **Student's App:** Vocabulary Practice; Listening Practice

Explore Language

Lesson Objectives

- to learn how to use the simple past passive

Materials

Audio Tracks 97 and 98

Warm Up

Display the picture from p. 106. Have students read the Latin sentence on the stone and guess the meaning. Tell them to use the picture on the stone to help them. This is a Words in Context strategy from the **Literacy Book**. Have students discuss their ideas in pairs and write a sentence in English. Then ask some pairs for their translations and write them on the board. *(translation: In the picture is a girl.)*

A TRACK 97 TB p. 226 **Listen and read. Why do people learn Latin now?**

- Tell students that they are going to listen to Caleb talking to a woman named Juana about an ancient language. See if students remember where Caleb was in Lesson 2 (he was at a museum learning about ancient civilizations). Play the audio and have students follow the dialogue in their books.
- Ask the gist question *Why do people learn Latin now?* and elicit the answer. Ask *Which languages can Latin help you learn?* (French, Spanish, Italian, and Portuguese).

Answer

to help learn other languages

International English

Have students notice the different phrases and drill the intonation of both. Have the students practice saying these phrases sympathetically. If you have time, you could ask students to think of scenarios where it would be appropriate to use these phrases.

B Look at A. Complete the table. When do we use *by*?

- Write or display the table on the board.
- Students should now have the skills and strategies to discuss and complete the grammar table themselves using the dialogue. When they have completed the table, invite students to come up to the board and fill in one word each. Ask if everyone agrees. Discuss the word order, form, and patterns together, but let your class guide the discussion. For more support, use the notes in the **ETB**.

Answers

used; was, by; were; created
We use *by* with passives to say who did the action.

- Draw students' attention to the Grammar tip *Remember.* Elicit more examples of past participle forms of regular and irregular verbs and make a list on the board.

Practice **Resource Bank:** Grammar Printout
Student's App: Grammar Practice

C Think and discuss. Then choose.

- Have students discuss the sentences in pairs. Write an example from the table on the board and highlight the *subject* and the *object.*
- Elicit answers from the class. Point out that the subject can come after *by* at the end of the sentence, if it is important.

Answers

1 the past action 2 object

D TRACK 98 TB p. 226 **Listen and say.**

- Play the audio. Have students repeat each sentence chorally.
- Play it again and have students say each sentence to each other in pairs.
- For ideas on how to vary the drill, see TB p. 23.

E Find and correct the errors.

- Have students look at the picture and say what is happening. Tell students they are going to read some sentences with grammatical errors. This activity provides students with controlled practice of the language by having them identify the errors and correct them.
- Look at the example together and elicit the two errors (the verb *be* is in the simple present, and the past participle has *–ed* missing). Remind students to check the form of both the auxiliary verb and the past participle in all of the sentences.
- Have students find and correct the errors. Check answers as a class. You could make this into a competition by awarding points for correctly identifying and correcting the errors.

Answers

1 ~~*is develop*~~ *was developed* 2 ~~have~~ were
3 ~~built were~~ were built 4 ~~were~~ was
5 ~~creating~~ created 6 ~~trade~~ traded

F Write a *True or False* quiz. Use ideas from your book. Then test your friend.

- This activity provides freer practice of the grammar. In pairs, have students make a *True or False* quiz.
- Have two students read the examples on the page. Pairs then take turns saying their statements, and the other pair identifies and corrects any factual errors.
- Give students five minutes to look through the unit for facts about ancient history. They should write one true statement, and four statements with factual errors.

Answers

Students' own answers

Cool Down

Play *Mime It!* (see TB p. 26) using sentences in the simple past passive, e.g. *The pyramid was built by the Egyptians.*

Write About It

Lesson Objectives

- to plan and write an informative article
- to review how to recognize fact and opinion
- to learn how to use phrases to link cause and effect
- to learn to write drafts to improve your writing

Materials

Support writing printout from the Resource Bank (F)

Warm Up

Tell students to think about one of their favorite movies and the places that appear in it. Ask *Where was it filmed/ set? Which place from the movie would you like to visit?* Have students discuss ideas in pairs.

A Read the informative article about Tikal in Guatemala. What happened to the city in 900 CE?

This text type is also modeled in the Literacy Book for this unit, Mysterious Malta.

- Look at the article. Ask the question *What happened to the city in 900 CE?* Have students scan the article to find the answer then check the answer together.
- Have students read the article more closely. Ask *What did you learn about Tikal?* and elicit answers.
- Ask students if they would like to visit Tikal and why.

Answer

All the people left and the city died.

B Look at the structure of the informative article. Read and answer.

- Remind students that the structure is the information in a text and the way it is organized. Look at the first question together *What is the purpose of this article?*
- Have students answer the other questions in pairs. Check answers and have students identify facts in the text.

Answers

1 to give information about a place / Tikal 2 Yes. Because people are reading the article to get the facts. 3 No. The reader is interested in the facts and not the writer's opinions. 4 websites, encyclopedias, books, TV documentaries, etc.

C Look at the language in the informative article. Read and respond.

- Have students complete the table with causes and effects from the article. Then check answers.
- Look at the callout. Ask students which phrases are used to introduce a cause and which introduce an effect (Cause: *because of, is due to*; Effects: *as a result of this, consequently*).

Answers

1 Cause: The people of Tikal built reservoirs. Effect: They always had plenty of water.; Cause: Tikal traded with neighboring cities. Effect: The city became rich.; Cause: Tikal had many beautiful buildings. Effect: It's very popular with tourists.; Cause: It was a location in the first *Star Wars* film. Effect: More and more people want to visit it. 2 As a result (of this), Because of (its trade with neighboring cities), (Its popularity) is due to, Consequently, (more and more people want to visit it).

D Think, research, and discuss. Choose a historical place or think of one of your own. What do you want to know? Use one of the Generating Ideas techniques.

- Review **Process Writing Step 1: Generating Ideas** on p. 140.
- Tell students that they are going to plan and write their own informative article about a historical place. In groups have students choose a place. Give students time to research, collate their findings, and write down their ideas.

Answers

Students' own answers

E Plan your informative article. Use some of your notes in D and one of the Planning techniques.

- Review the planning techniques students looked at in **Process Writing Step 2: Planning** on p. 141.
- Have students think about logically organizing their ideas. Ask *Which ideas should go together? What order makes the most sense? How many paragraphs do you need?*
- Have students make notes in the table, then plan and write their article individually.

Answers

Students' own answers

F Write a first draft, then revise it. Use one of the Drafting techniques.

- Review **Process Writing Step 3: Drafting** on p. 142. Drafts may be written in notebooks or on support printouts from the Resource Bank.
- Have students use the checklist on p. 142 to check their draft and make notes about things they want to change.

Answers

Students' own answers

G Now write your final informative article.

- Have students write their articles.
- Have students peer review and give feedback on clarity.

Cool Down

Have students write messages for their classmates for the Positive Post Box (see **ETB**, Literacy Book, Unit 4, Think Together) with the most interesting facts they learned from reading the articles.

Practice **Student's App:** Writing Practice
Resource Bank: Writing Game, *Incas and Romans*

Talk About It

Lesson Objectives

- to prepare and practice a presentation about the past (from a future perspective)
- to learn how to structure, transition, and conclude a presentation

Materials
Video

Warm Up

Write *2050* on the board and tell students to think about what life will be like in the year 2050. Have them discuss in pairs the things that they think will be different from now.

A TB p. 240 **Watch and listen. What three things does Veronica talk about?**

- Tell students they are going to watch a video of a girl named Veronica giving a presentation where she talks about what life is like now to people in the future. Have students predict the things she might say. Elicit suggestions from the class. Then play the video. Check that students know that she is talking from a future perspective—she is in the year 2050 and is talking about what life was like in our own time.
- Draw students' attention to the question *What three things does Veronica talk about?* Elicit answers from the class.

Answers
how people lived in the USA 25 years ago, their architecture and inventions, and what we can learn from those times

B Watch again. Complete the phrases Veronica uses to structure her presentation.

- Tell students that they are going to listen to some of the phrases Veronica uses in the video. Point out the three headings and elicit that *Structuring* refers to how she organizes her ideas, *Transitioning* is how she moves from one section to the next, and *Summarizing* is how she ends her presentation.
- Have students look at the table before they rewatch the video and see if they remember how to complete any of the phrases.
- Play the video once and have students complete the phrases. Check answers as a class. Then play the video again and have students repeat the phrases, copying Veronica's pronunciation and intonation.

Answers
Structuring: *three*; that; talk
Transitioning: with; move; now
Summarizing: points; about; looked; discussed

C Plan your presentation. Imagine it's 2050. Think about three areas to talk about. Then organize your ideas.

- Tell students to imagine that they are now living in 2050 and they are going to give a presentation about life in the past (i.e. now). Brainstorm with the class the different areas of life students can include, e.g. transportation, school, work, free time, family life, fashion, the environment, buildings.
- Draw students' attention to the graphic organizer and tell them to choose three areas they want to talk about. Have students think and write notes in each section, working individually. Encourage them to try to use some of the phrases from B to organize their presentation. Remind students that they only need to write notes to prompt them and not full sentences. They should also decide if they need any visuals and prepare these.

Answers
Students' own answers

D Practice with your friends using phrases in B. Then share with the class. Make notes.

- Have students practice their presentations as many times as they like. Remind students to work on their communication with the audience, including eye contact, and to ensure the audience has time to process the information by adding pauses and speaking slowly.
- Have some students give their presentations in front of the class. While they are speaking, the other students should make notes about the content (e.g. what areas are mentioned) and the performance (e.g. did they speak slowly, did they look at the audience).
- Have students analyze their own performances in pairs.

Cool Down

Play *Draw It!* (see TB p. 25) but have students choose something from 2050 or from the present. Students have to decide whether the picture represents the present or the future.

Practice **Student's App:** Speaking Skills Practice; Speaking Video

Think It Over

Lesson Objectives

- to review what has been learned in the unit
- to reflect on the unit and their own progress
- to think about learning strategies and how to continue learning at home

Warm Up

Do a quick quiz with the class about Unit 8. Ask questions about pictures, words, or information and have students find the answers in their books. Have students play in teams. Possible questions: *What animals can you find on p. 100–101? What is the Ancient Egyptian woman holding on p. 100? How long were the Inca roads on p. 102? What's the word for picture 6 on p. 104? How did Ancient Romans bring water to their cities?* (p. 105)

How well did you meet the challenge of Unit 8? Read and respond.

My Favorite Mistakes

- Tell students they are going to review what they learned in the unit and how they can improve. Remind students not to worry about what other people think or say, as different students will have made different mistakes. Point out that everyone will have some way of improving, even if they think they didn't make any mistakes!
- Have students work in groups to think about the activities they did during the unit. Give each group a pack of sticky notes and have them write their ideas; one idea per sticky note. Encourage students to think about the different things they studied in the unit, including grammar, presentation phrases, poems, vocabulary, facts, interesting ideas, and so on. Then have students stick their notes onto a board or a poster and display it on the wall. Have groups go around the classroom and look at each other's sticky note board.
- Draw students' attention to the acrostic: MISTAKES. Students did this review activity in Unit 5. Refer students to the different sections in the graphic organizer: *Two mistakes that I made in this unit that moved my learning on are …, Two things (knowledge) that I learned about the past are…, Two things (experience and skills) I learned to say or do in English are …* Have students talk in pairs about the different sections.
- Ask students what they would like to work on to improve. Refer students to the final section in the graphic organizer (*One thing I want to work on next month is …*) and the notes below it. Have students think about their ideas and then discuss them with a friend. The following prompts may be useful: *I'd like to know / learn more about …; Next time, I'm going to …*
- When you feel they have enough ideas, have students work individually to fill in the organizer. Remind them that they should write their own responses about themselves. Monitor and help as necessary. Look at what students are writing so you can tailor your classes and any additional practice to their needs.
- Ask if anyone has the same goals as their friend. Point out that goals should be personal and each student should choose those they think they would benefit from most.

Looking Forward

Draw students' attention to the character at the bottom of the page. Elicit who it is and what they remember about her. (Juana appeared in Lesson 4.) Ask *What ancient language can Juana speak?* (Latin) Have students read the speech bubble and make predictions about what Juana does as a volunteer. Tell them that they will find out in the first lesson of Unit 9.

Put It Together

To further review and recycle the language in Units 7 and 8, play *Guessword* on pp. 112–113. See TB p. 209 for teaching notes.

Practice **Resource Bank:** Unit Test
Student's App: Vocabulary and Grammar Review

Get Ready to Read

Lesson Objectives

- to activate prior knowledge about ancient civilizations
- to guide inquiry and deepen understanding through a See, Think, Wonder VTR
- to preview the reading skill of recognizing genres

Materials

VTR printout from the Resource Bank (Activities A, B, C)

Warm Up

Ask students if they have ever visited any ruins. Ask what kind of ruins they were, what they used to be before, and where they were. Ask students what they liked about the visit. Have students discuss their answers in pairs.

See, Think, Wonder

A Look at the picture. What do you see?

This VTR encourages students to make predictions, observations, and interpretations about the image of the archaeological site. Start by asking students *What do you see?* Give students up to a minute to look at the picture and think silently.

- Guide students to focus their answers on what is visible, not how they interpret it. Have students share more answers in small groups or pairs. Then bring the groups together for a class discussion.
- Record the students' ideas from the VTR to revisit in the Think Together lesson.

B What do you think?

- Ask students *What do you think about the picture?* Give them one minute to think silently about the picture and then share their ideas in pairs before sharing with the class. Encourage students to discuss together, not just to you.

C What do you wonder?

- Say *I wonder who lived there.* Then ask *What do you wonder? What questions do you have?* Give students one minute to look at the picture and think.
- Have students discuss their ideas in groups or as a class.

Here's an example of this part of the routine.

Teacher: What do you wonder?
Student A: How old are the ruins?
Teacher: Good question—what do you think? Are they hundreds of years old?
Student B: No, I think they're thousands of years old!
Teacher: Which people do you think built it?
Student A: The Incas.
Student B: Why do you think that?
Student A: It looks like some other ruins I saw on TV.
Teacher: **Great.** What else do you wonder?

Transition

Tell students that Aguateca was built by the Mayans (see Background Information in the **ETB**). Ask students what they know about the Mayans. Do they know where they lived? Elicit ideas from the class.

Tell students to imagine that they are helping with the excavation of Aguateca. What kinds of objects would they expect to find?

D Think, write, and discuss. Which ancient civilizations do you know about? Which civilizations do you want to learn more about?

- Ask *What is an ancient civilization?* Elicit that it is a large group of people who lived long time ago and developed a culture and rules to live by. Brainstorm a few different ancient civilizations and write these on the board.
- Have students draw a KWL chart in their notebooks. A KWL chart has three columns: *Know, Want to Know,* and *Learn.* Students write what they know about ancient civilizations in the *Know* column. Then they write any questions they have in the *Want to Know* column. They don't write anything in the *Learn* column yet—they will have the opportunity to fill this out at the end of the unit.
- When students have finished writing, have them discuss and compare their ideas and questions in pairs or small groups.

Answers

Students' own answers

E Think and discuss. Look at the picture from *The Great Race*. Is it fiction or nonfiction? What kinds of characters are there?

- Tell students to look at the picture in E and say what they see. Preview the skill of recognizing genres by asking *Is it fiction or nonfiction?* Give them one to two minutes to discuss the picture and questions in pairs.
- Elicit ideas from the class, encouraging students to give reasons for their answers.
- Then ask students what kinds of characters are in the picture and have them share their ideas with the class.

Suggested Answers

I think it is fiction because the animals look like they can talk. The characters are both people and animals.

Now read **The Great Race**

Fiction: *The Great Race—Fable*

Lesson Objectives

- to read a fable about the origins of the Chinese zodiac
- to make a personal connection to the reading

Materials
Audio Tracks 32 and 33

Warm Up

Write the names of the animals from the story on the board. Ask students what skills they think each animal has. Can they swim? Which animals are strong/fast/smart? Have students discuss their ideas in pairs.

TRACK 32 TB p. 235 **Reading Approach**

Engage with the Text

- Display the opening spread of the story. Allow students time to look at the opening page of the story and use the information to predict ideas about the story. Elicit that the story is set in ancient China, encouraging students to use the pictures and text to infer this.
- For the first reading, play the audio and have students follow along in their books, or use the Story Player. Ask prediction questions before turning the page, e.g. *Which animal will win?*

TRACK 33 TB p. 236 **Words in Context**

- After the first reading of the text, draw students' attention to the Words in Context box.
- Give students a few minutes to find and highlight each instance of each word in the reading.
- Have them identify the type of word by looking at the form and the sentence.
- Write these strategies on the board for students to use to find the meaning of the words: *pictures; surrounding words and sentences; positive/negative; contrasting ideas; world knowledge.*
- Have students work in pairs to discuss the words.

current (p. 124, noun) The surrounding sentences tell us that this is a property of the river and that it's strong and takes great strength and effort to fight against it. Strategies to use: pictures, surrounding words and sentences, world knowledge

effort (p. 124, noun) The last clause of the sentence explains how *using all her effort* made Tiger feel, so we know that this is something difficult. Strategy to use: surrounding words and sentences

slithered (p. 125, verb) This is a movement verb because it is used with the adverb *quickly*. The sentence also tells us it's something Snake does when she gets to the ground. Strategies to use: pictures, surrounding words and sentences, world knowledge

sneaky (p. 125, adjective) The preceding sentences and the picture tell us how Snake beat Horse to sixth place in a not very sportsmanlike way. The suggestion is that it isn't a positive word. Strategies to use: surrounding words and sentences, pictures

diligent (p. 126, adjective) The first clause of the sentence explains the meaning of this adjective with a positive and a negative example. Strategies to use: positive/negative, surrounding words and phrases

Analyze the Text and Features

- Have students read the text individually in their books. Give them plenty of time to read. As they read, ask them to find out in which order the animals arrived and make a list in their notebooks.
- Tell students to find the blue callouts and to discuss the questions with a partner.
  - **Making Connections** (p. 122): *Are cats and rats usually friends?* Ask students what the typical relationship is between cats and rats, and elicit that usually cats are rat-catchers.
  - **Fun Fact** (p. 123): *The animals from the Emperor's guard are the same animals used to mark years and months on the Chinese calendar.* Ask students if they know anything about the Chinese zodiac and if they know what animals they are. If you have time, have students do research online to find out.
  - **Genre Focus** (p. 125): *Fables are stories that try to explain how something happened when we don't know the facts.* Ask students what this fable is trying to explain (why cats and rats don't get along, why 12 animals represent the years in the Chinese zodiac).
  - **Personalization** (p. 127): *Which animal in the story do you admire the most? Why?* Have students discuss this in pairs. Then have a show of hands to see which animal is the most popular. Elicit reasons from students.

Interact with the Text

- Now that students are very familiar with the text, have them work in pairs to choose a pair of animals whose paths cross in the story (or group of three), e.g. the horse and the snake, and together, imagine what happened.

Cool Down

Play *What's the Scene?* (see TB p. 27) using scenes from the story.

Practice **Student's App:** Story Player

Explore the Reading

Lesson Objectives

- to understand and analyze *The Great Race* through reading comprehension activities
- to learn about the SEL competency of social awareness by appreciating diversity
- to understand the use of transition words
- to make a personal connection to the reading

Warm Up

Play *Draw It!* (see TB p. 25) using the animals from the reading.

A Read and answer.

- Refer back to *The Great Race* in the **Literacy Book**. Before students open their books, check what students have retained. In pairs, have them write three sentences about the reading. Then have them read their sentences aloud with another pair. Ask *Did you remember similar things?*
- Have students open their books and look at the activity. Look at the first question together and give students 20 seconds to look back at the reading and find the answer.
- Then have students answer the rest of the questions individually. Encourage them to answer the questions from memory, using their own words. They can then look back at the reading to check their answers. Check answers.

Answers

1 13 2 Rat forgot to wake Cat, so she came last / didn't become the Emperor's guard. 3 It was difficult because the current in the river was strong. 4 Dragon stopped to help Rabbit cross the river. 5 Goat pushed, Monkey paddled, and Rooster steered the raft.

B Think, match, and write. How did each animal show its characteristics?

- Review ordinal numbers by counting around the class (first, second, etc.). Ask *Which animal was first in the race?* (Rat) *What characteristic did Rat show?* Have students look back at the reading to find what the Emperor thought about Rat (he admired how Rat cleverly crossed the river). Draw the students' attention to the example.
- Review the meaning of each adjective as a class. Then have students do the activity individually. Remind them to look back at the reading, find the sentences that tell them about each animal's characteristic and underline them in the text.
- Then check answers as a class.

Suggested Answers

Rat—clever—He cleverly traveled on Ox's back.
Tiger—strong—She swam across the river by herself
Rabbit—quick—He was pushed across by Dragon's smoke.
Dragon—kind—He helpfully blew Rabbit's log.
Snake—sneaky—He/She hid under Horse and made the Emperor laugh.
Horse—brave—She was frightened but she still tried.
Dog—playful—He had fun in the river.
Boar—diligent—He didn't give up.

C Think and discuss. Each animal had special characteristics. Which characteristic do you admire most in others? Why?

This activity draws on the SEL competency of social awareness by appreciating diversity, as students explore the characteristics and qualities of the different characters.

- Check the meaning of *admire* (to respect or look up to). Say *The Emperor admired all the different characteristics the animals showed. What characteristics do you admire?*
- Have students discuss the characteristics in B and say whether they admire them. Encourage them to think of additional characteristics. Students should say why they admire these characteristics, giving examples of behavior and people who have shown them, e.g. friends, family members, famous sports stars.
- Have students discuss in pairs, then share with the class.

Literary Term: Transition Words

Read. Then underline the transition words.

- Look at the explanation of *transition words*. Explain that we sometimes call these connectors or linking words.
- Write an example on the board and elicit the transition word, e.g. *Similarly, she was going to study art at university.*
- Have students work individually to read the paragraph and underline the transition words.
- Elicit the transition words students have already seen, e.g. *however, although, when.*
- Have students find more transition words in the reading. Check answers as a class and discuss how we use each one.

Answers

Suddenly, Then, Now, Of course
Transition words in the reading: But, Before, Now, Suddenly, Next, But, Soon, Then, Meanwhile, Now, but, Since then, Now

Cool Down

Play *Mime It!* (see TB p. 26), having students act out the adjectives in B.

Practice **Resource Bank:** Literary Term Printout
Student's App: Reading Practice; Literary Term Practice

Get Ready to Read

Lesson Objectives

- to activate prior knowledge about Malta
- to review the reading skill of recognizing genres

Materials

(Optional) Sentences to display on screen or on large pieces of paper (Warm Up)

Warm Up

Have a reading race to help students remember the different readings in previous units. Call out or display sentences summarizing the readings and have students find the title and the page on which they start. Possible sentences: *Learn how to follow clues such as fingerprints and DNA* (*Solving Crime with Science*, p. 42); *Find out how your use of plastic can be dangerous to the environment* (*Not-So-Fantastic Plastic*, p. 90); *A man wants to be an opera singer* (*Delivery Dan*, p. 62); *A family moves to the countryside to live a better life* (*A Greener Life*, p. 96); *Students play against the teachers in a sports competition* (*You're Out!*, p. 10)

A Look back at these four readings. Match them to the genres and complete the table.

- Have students find the readings in their books and discuss what they remember about each one in pairs.
- Ask students which of the four readings is a fable (*The Great Race*). Ask *Is it fiction or nonfiction?* (fiction) Elicit what students know about fables. They discussed this briefly in the reading lesson. Draw students' attention to the table and look at the features together.
- Have students read the reading skill box. Then ask questions to check comprehension, e.g. *What is genre?* (the kind of writing, e.g. story or instructional text) *Do we read all texts in the same way?* (No, we read stories in order, but we might not read other texts in order.) Elicit that we often skim or scan more when we read an instructional text, but we don't usually do this with fiction the first time we read—only if we have specific questions.

Answers

Fiction; The Great Race
Fiction; The Red-Headed League
Nonfiction; First Aid for Beginners
Nonfiction; The Hero of Lime Rock

B Think and discuss. Look at *Mysterious Malta*. What features does it have? What genre is it?

- Tell students that they are going to look at the next reading and try to find out which genre it is. Tell them to look at the features, using the table in A to help them. Point out that not all the genres are in the table. Give students a few minutes to do the activity and discuss their ideas with a friend.
- Check answers as a class. If possible, display the reading and have students point out the features.

Answers

Informational text. Features: contains facts, has headings, has pictures, has clear sections

C Scan *Mysterious Malta*. Write three facts about Malta.

- Tell students to scan the reading to find three facts. Remind students that they don't need to read every word when they scan. Before they read, have them predict ideas about the type of facts that may appear in the text.
- Have students scan the text and write three facts in their books.
- Check answers as a class, encouraging students to say where they found each fact.

Suggested Answers

1 The temples were built between 3100 and 2500 BCE.
2 Today Hal Tarxien and the other temples are recognized as a UNESCO World Heritage Site.
3 The temple walls were made of enormous stones.

Now read **Mysterious Malta**

Nonfiction: *Mysterious Malta—* Informational Text

Lesson Objectives

- to read an informational text about ancient ruins on the island of Malta
- make a personal connection to the reading

Materials

Audio Tracks 34 and 35; photos of monuments and ruins displayed together (Warm Up)

Warm Up

Show students photos of different monuments and ruins without telling them when they were built and have students guess which are the oldest, e.g. the Great Pyramid in Giza, Egypt (2560 BCE); the Great Wall of China (200 BCE); and Machu Picchu in Peru (1450 CE).

TRACK 34 TB p. 236 Reading Approach

Engage with the Text

- Project the opening spread of the reading with the Story Player in the TTL. Have students predict what kinds of ruins they will learn about in the reading.
- Have students read the text silently in pairs, stopping after each section to discuss what they learned. As they read, have them find the main idea of each paragraph.

TRACK 35 TB p. 236 Words in Context

- After the first reading of the text, look at the Words in Context box. Play the audio to practice pronunciation.
- Have students brainstorm a list of strategies that they can use to find the meanings of the words, including strategies they use in L1.
- Divide the class into pairs and have them look at *some* of the words only, e.g. two to three words per pair. Then, have students swap pairs and explain their words to each other, saying which strategy they used.
- Bring the class together and elicit the meanings. Discuss which strategies worked and which didn't.

archaeological (site) (p. 130, adjective) The paragraph gives many examples of archaeological sites and explains they are prehistoric. The picture below the paragraph shows the site. Strategies to use: pictures, surrounding words and sentences, world knowledge

constructed (p. 130 / p. 131, verb) A synonym, *built*, appears in the first clause of the sentence. Strategy to use: surrounding words and sentences

architecture (p. 131, noun) This is in the subheading, signalling it as the main idea of the following paragraph. Strategies to use: making connections, world knowledge

hypothesize (p. 131 / p. 133, verb) The sentence that follows gives an explanation of this verb: *(they) don't know for sure*. Strategy to use: surrounding words and sentences

researchers (p. 131, noun) The suffix *–er* shows it is a job. The previous sentence connects it to *scientists*. The verb *investigating* tells us what they do. Strategies to use: suffixes, surrounding words and sentences

ruts (p. 133, noun) The preceding sentence explains what these are. The picture also shows the ruts. Strategies to use: pictures, surrounding words and sentences

Practice **Student's App:** Story Player

International English

Have students notice the different spelling. Tell students that the pronunciation is the same. See if students can remember any other words that follow these spelling patterns (*realize, recognize*).

Analyze the Text and Features

- Play the audio. Have students follow along in their books. Pause the audio to ask comprehension questions and discuss the blue callouts. Alternatively, use Group Time for discussion after reading (see TB p. 21).
  - **Fact** (p. 130): *Hal Tarxien was built during a period called the Bronze Age.* Provide background information about the period or have students do research to find out more.
  - **Making Connections** (p. 132): *Why do you think the decorations showed plants and animals?* Have students discuss in pairs. (Possible answer: The artists saw the plants and animals in the world around them.)
  - **Imaginative Thinking** (p. 133): *Imagine the ancient civilization that created these temples. How do you think their lives were different from yours?* Have students discuss in pairs, then elicit ideas.
  - **Text Focus** (p. 131): *Nonfiction texts have features such as headings, subheadings, labels, and maps. How many can you find?* Have students work in pairs to find examples of these features in the text.

Interact with the Text

- Now that students are very familiar with the text, have them role-play tour guides and tourists visiting Malta. In groups, each student will be responsible for a different site. Assign each part of the classroom each site and have groups rotate, taking turns as the tour guide.
- Have one or two groups act out their role-play for the class.

Cool Down

Have students choose a photograph from the reading that they want to see in real life. Then have them find another student who wants to see the same thing and discuss why.

Explore the Reading

Lesson Objectives

- to understand and analyze *Mysterious Malta* through reading comprehension activities
- to explore the CLIL history concept of life in the Bronze Age
- to make a personal connection to the reading

Warm Up

Play *What's the Scene?* (see TB p. 27) with pictures from the reading, but have a student choose and describe the picture, e.g. *I can see one long rock and lots of smaller rocks next to it. There is grass on the ground.*

A Read and rewrite these false sentences to make them true.

- Have students work in groups to challenge each other to answer questions about the reading, e.g. *What were the floors made of?*
- Tell students that they are going to read false sentences about the reading and they have to correct the sentences so that they are true.
- Have students do the activity individually. Encourage students to look back at the text to help them check the facts. Check answers as a class.

Answers

1 Hal Tarxien temples were built before 2500 BCE but not discovered until 1913 CE. 2 The rooms are semi-circular. 3 The main entrance is made of three huge stones. 4 The small round stones were used to roll the floor stones into position. 5 The water at Hal Tarxien came from an underground spring.

B Think and write. Think about the mysteries of Malta. Hypothesize different answers. Give reasons.

Students are going to using critical thinking skills to make connections between the reading and their own prior knowledge. This draws on the CLIL history focus of life in the Bronze Age.

- Remind students of the meaning of *hypothesize*. Tell students that they are going to use what they know to try to draw conclusions about some of the mysteries of Malta. They can use information from the reading, but they must try to make connections with their own knowledge in order to come up with possible answers to the questions.
- Give students a few minutes to look back at the reading to find objects in the questions and discuss possible answers with a friend before writing their answers in their books. Remind students that there are no correct answers, as we don't know the answers to these questions.
- Then discuss answers with the class, encouraging students to give reasons for their hypotheses.

Answers

Students' own answers

C Choose one of the mysteries in B. Think and plan an experiment to test your hypothesis.

Students are going to use the critical thinking skills of analysis and evaluation to test out their hypotheses.

- Tell students that they are now going to analyze and evaluate one of their hypotheses from B. They should choose one and think about how they can test it. Discuss different ways of finding out information with the class. (They can do research online or in books to find out more about how people in that era lived, or they can do an experiment to see how the physical elements of the object are made, e.g. by making a model.)
- Have students choose one of their hypotheses and get together in groups with other students who have chosen the same one. They should think together about what they can do to test it. Give them a few minutes to discuss and write down their plan.

Answers

Students' own answers

Cool Down

Play *Different Uses* (see TB p. 25) with the picture of the clay pot from p. 133.

Practice **Student's App:** Reading Practice

Think Together

Lesson Objectives

- to make connections between the readings
- to explore the key concept: How do we explain the mysteries from ancient civilizations?
- to reflect on the unit and provide personal thoughts and opinions

Warm Up

Review what students know about the two ancient civilizations from the readings: the ancient Chinese and the ancient people of Malta.

A Think and write. How do *The Great Race* and *Mysterious Malta* help us to understand ancient civilizations?

- Have students look at the ideas in the box and check understanding. Ask *Which reading has characters?* (*The Great Race*) Tell students to think about which of the phrases apply to each reading.
- Have students write their ideas in the table, using the readings to help them. Then check answers.

Suggested Answers

Mysterious Malta: looks at evidence, uses photographs, presents hypotheses
The Great Race: tells a story, has characters, makes emotional connections

B Think about something that happens in nature. Decide how you would like to explain it with fiction or nonfiction. Write a fable or develop a hypothesis with a research plan.

Students are going to apply what they have learned in the unit and discuss the key concept question: *How do we explain the mysteries from ancient civilizations?*

- Have students brainstorm things that happen in nature, e.g. why rainbows appear after rain or why thunder and lightning happen together. Write their ideas on the board.
- Tell students they're going to explain their ideas either in a fable (fiction) or a hypothesis (nonfiction). Remind students that if they write a fable, they can make up a story about why this is the case. If they develop a hypothesis, they can come up with a research plan for how they will test to investigate or try to prove why this happens. Have students select idea an idea and choose the genre; ensure that at least three students choose an idea in order to make up the groups for C and D.
- Give students plenty of time to write their ideas, or let them do this stage for homework.

Answers

Students' own answers

C Ask your partner about their writing. Do a Three-Step Interview.

- Tell students that they are going to do a Three-Step Interview using their fable or hypothesis from B (See TB p. 20). Divide the class into two groups: fables and hypotheses, then divide these groups into pairs. Don't pair students with the same nature idea at this stage.
- Have students take turns asking questions about their fable or hypothesis. Then have them change partners.

D Think and discuss. How are your fables or hypotheses similar or different?

- Put students back into their fables and hypotheses groups (all the nature ideas together). Have them compare their ideas, looking for things that are the same and things that are different, summarizing their findings in two lists

My Reading Journal

What would you like to find out about life 5,000 years ago?

This question focuses on personalization and encourages students to make a personal connection to the unit. Give students time to think and write their answer, then discuss in pairs or small groups.

Suggested Answer

I would like to know if there was an ancient civilization living near my city.

What do you think people in the future will think about life now?

Students should use their existing knowledge to analyze and make predictions. Have them discuss in pairs and write their ideas. Elicit ideas from the class.

Suggested Answer

I think people in the future will think we didn't care about the environment because humans have caused so much pollution.

Go back to page 121. What new things do you see, think, or wonder?

Have students look back at the VTR picture on pp. 121–122. Using the TTL, project the image onto the board. Ask students *How does the picture connects to the two readings?* Then repeat the See, Think, Wonder routine. If you recorded students' ideas in Lesson 1, display these. Encourage students to think of new questions they have now, e.g. *I wonder what happened to the ancient civilization that lived there.*

Cool Down

Play *Twenty Questions* (see TB p. 27) and have a student choose an ancient civilization or building.

Practice **Resource Bank:** Unit Test
Student's App: Key Concept Practice

UNIT 9

Tell Me a Story

Unit Overview

Themes

Storytelling

Different ways of telling stories

Synopsis

In this unit, students will explore the concept of stories and storytelling. They will learn about the importance of stories and how they help us connect with people. They will learn about the different features of stories and think about different ways of telling stories. Students will plan and prepare a conversation and write a story.

Vocabulary

brave, characters, cliffhanger, cruel, enemy, hero, heroine, narrator, plot, suspense, terrifying, thrilling, villain

Pronunciation: sentence stress: weak form *to* /ə/ (Schwa)

p. 176

Explore Language

Second Conditional: Positive Statements

p. 177

Global Citizenship

How do stories bring people together?

anecdote, details, empathize, fascinating, imagination, moral, pass on, share, surprising, understand

p. 178

Explore Language

Second Conditional: Negative Statements and Questions

p. 179

Talk About It

Conversation: offering opinions, agreeing and disagreeing

p. 180

Write About It

A Story

Genre Focus: creating a narrative voice

Word Study: suffixes and prefixes

p. 181

Think It Over

Review and Reflection

My Planning Sheet

p. 182

Language Book

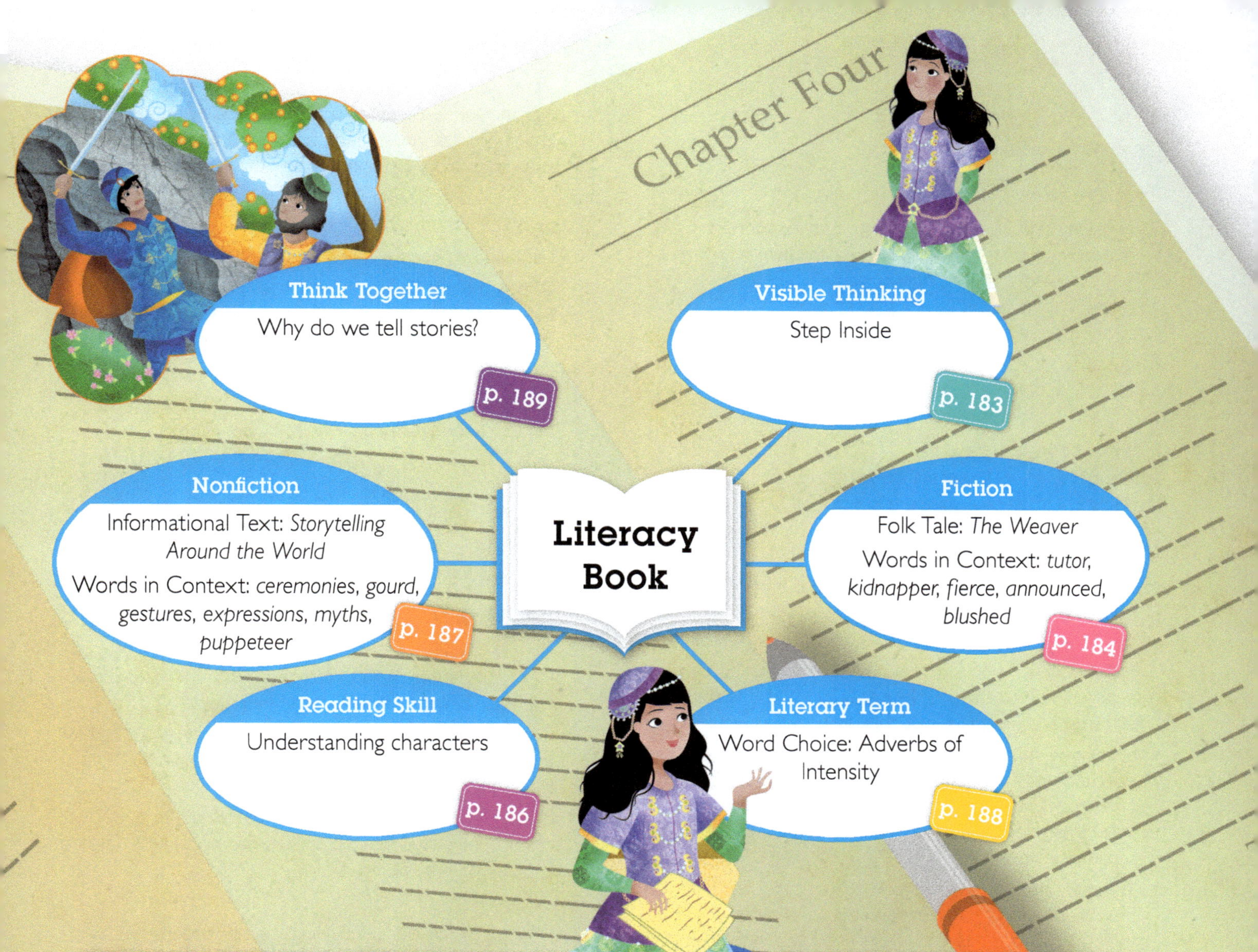

Language and Literacy Connections

The connecting theme for Unit 9 is stories.

	Language	Literacy
Vocabulary	**Set 1:** storytelling **Set 2:** sharing stories	**Nonfiction:** character, hero, plot, villain **Fiction:** brave, cruel
Grammar	**Second Conditional: Positive Statements** I'd forget about Gerda if I were you. If I were lost, Kay would look for me. If Gerda were my daughter, she'd stay with me forever. **Second Conditional: Negative Statements and Questions** If I came with you, I wouldn't be much help. If it weren't for him, she would be too late. What would she do if he didn't remember her? Would he be OK if she looked after him?	**Fiction:** If I had a choice, I would have my head in a book. If I were you, I would want to listen! If I were you, I would be extremely proud. And if I wrote a story like that, I would want to put it in a book!
Skills	**Pronunciation:** sentence stress: whith weak form *to*/tə/ **Process Writing:** editing and publishing	**Reading:** understanding characters **Literary Term:** word choice: adverbs of intensity
International English	empathize/empathise	

Vocabulary

Lesson Objectives

- to learn vocabulary related to storytelling: *brave, characters, cliffhanger, cruel, enemy, hero, heroine, narrator, plot, suspense, terrifying, thrilling, villain*
- to say a poem about listening to stories
- to practice sentence stress: Weak Form *to* (Schwa)

Materials
Audio Tracks 99 to 103; Video

Warm Up

Ask students if they know any fairy tales. Remind them that a fairy tale is a traditional children's story. Elicit some examples of fairy tales from the class, e.g. *Cinderella*. Ask students which of these stories have a princess.

A TRACK 99 TB p. 226 **Listen. Who did the princess turn into?**

- Display the picture on the opening spread with the TTL. Have students speculate about what is happening in the picture and who the people are. Ask *How do the characters in the picture feel?* Have students discuss ideas in pairs.
- Encourage students to predict what the story is about. Ask students if they know the story of the Snow Queen. (*The Snow Queen* is a Hans Christian Andersen story.) Have them discuss in pairs. The story continues over three separate lessons.
- Tell students that they are going to listen to Juana telling the children a story. Remind students of the challenge from the end of Unit 8. Have students find Juana in the picture and ask *What does she do as a volunteer?* (She reads stories to children at the library.)
- Play the audio and have students look at the picture.
- Ask the comprehension question *Who did the princess turn into?* Play the audio again and check the answer.

Answer
The Snow Queen

B TRACK 100 TB p. 226 **Find and number the words in A. Then listen and check.**

- Have students look at the list of vocabulary words. Point out the example (1) and have students find *cruel* in the picture. Do the activity as a class, asking students to explain why each word matches the picture.

Answers
1 *cruel* 2 brave 3 suspense 4 enemy 5 cliffhanger 6 thrilling 7 narrator 8 plot 9 terrifying 10 characters 11 villian 12 hero 13 heroine

C TRACK 101 TB p. 226 **Close your eyes. Listen, visualize, and say.**

- Prepare students for the visualization (see Visualization).
- Play the audio, allowing students to visualize as they listen. In this visualization, students are going to think about a story they know or make up their own story.
- Have students discuss the things they imagined in pairs, using the new vocabulary.

D Look and write.

- Display the graphic organizer. Check understanding of the three headings and look at the example together. Remind students that adjectives describe people and things.
- Have students complete the activity with words from A.
- Then have them compare their answers with a partner before checking answers with the class.

Suggested Answers
Features of a story: *characters*, cliffhanger, enemy, hero, heroine, narrator, plot, suspense, villain
Describing people: cruel, brave
Describing the story: thrilling, terrifying

E TRACK 102 TB p. 226 **Listen and write. Then watch and say.**

- Play the video or audio of the poem and allow students to enjoy it. They can follow along in their books.
- Give students time to read the poem and try to complete the blanks. Play the poem video or audio and have students check their answers.
- Play the video or audio again and have students join in. Encourage students to copy the pronunciation and intonation of the poem.

Answers
1 *plot* 2 heroine 3 terrifying 4 cliffhanger 5 characters 6 villain

F TRACK 103 TB p. 227 **Pronunciation. Listen and say. Copy the weak forms. Think of other phrases like these.**

- Display the examples on the board. Point to the word *to* and elicit its pronunciation.
- Play the audio and have students listen and repeat. Note the pronunciation of the schwa in the weak form of *to*. Point out that *going to* has an informal weak form *gonna* /ˈgɑːnə/ as in the poem here.
- Drill each sentence from the poem. Then play the poem again and have students say the phrases using weak forms.
- Have students think of more examples of weak forms. Remind students that these words may have different vowels but the weak form is always pronounced with the schwa.

Answers
Students' own answers

Cool Down

Play *Disappearing Sentences* (see TB p. 25) using the vocabulary from the lesson, but have students either give a definition of the word or use it in a sentence.

Practice **Student's App:** Vocabulary
Practice: Spoken Word Video

Explore Language

Lesson Objectives

- to learn how to use the second conditional: positive sentences
- to practice vocabulary related to storytelling

Materials

Audio Tracks 104 and 105; sentences from the Snow Queen on slips of paper (TB p. 227, Track 104), one copy per group (WU)

Warm Up

Prepare sentences from the story of the Snow Queen and cut them up so that students can order them. Divide the class into groups and have them put the sentences in the order they happened in *The Snow Queen*. The first group to correctly order the sentences wins.

A TRACK 104 TB p. 227 **Listen and read. Do you think Gerda will find Kay?**

- Tell students they are going to listen to the next part of *The Snow Queen*. Play the audio and have students follow the story in their books. Ask *Who is telling the story now?* (Nadeen, the girl with black hair) Elicit that Nadeen heard Juana tell the story and now she is telling another friend (Luca) the story.
- Ask the gist question *Do you think Gerda will find Kay?* and elicit the answer. Encourage students to give reasons for their answers by basing their predictions on what they know, e.g. *Gerda is very determined, so I think she won't stop looking for Kay.*

Answer

Students' own answers

B **Look at A. Complete the table. What verb form comes after *if*?**

- Display the table using the TTL.
- Students should now have the skills and strategies to discuss and complete the grammar table themselves using the story. When they have completed the table, invite students to come up to the board and fill in one word each. Ask if everyone agrees. Discuss the word order, form, and patterns together, but let your class guide the discussion. For more support, use the notes in the **ETB**.
- Draw students' attention to the Grammar tip *Look*. Have students notice the different spellings. Drill the pronunciation of the homonyms. Ask students how they know which word someone is saying and elicit that the context and grammar of the sentence will help them decide: *would* is a verb, and *wood* is a noun.

Answers

forget, if, were; If, were; stay
Were comes after *if*.

Practice **Resource Bank:** Grammar Printout
Student's App: Grammar Practice

C **Think and discuss. Then choose.**

- Have students work in pairs to discuss the sentence. Refer them to the table in B for example sentences and have them think about whether each situation is possible or real. Check the answer with the class. Remind students that we use first conditional for possible situations.

Answer

1 unreal or impossible

D TRACK 105 TB p. 227 **Listen and say.**

- Play the audio. Have students repeat each sentence chorally.
- Play it again and have students say repeat each sentence to a friend.
- For ideas on how to vary the drill, see TB p. 23.

E **Read and complete the sentences.**

- Look at the example together. Have students notice that the sentence starts with *if*, so the first verb must be in the simple past, and the verb in the other part of the sentence needs *would* before it.
- Have students complete the sentences individually. This activity provides students with controlled practice of the second conditional. Remind students to look at the table in B to help them. Check answers as a class.

Answers

1 *were; 'd win* 2 included; would be 3 were; 'd like 4 'd tell; knew 5 'd understand; explained 6 had; 'd read 7 played; 'd be able to 8 'd draw; were

F **Play the *What if ...?* game. How many sentences can you make?**

- Tell students they are going to make second conditional sentences using prompts and their own ideas. This activity allows for freer practice of the second conditional.
- Have two students read the examples on the page. Put the class into teams. Teams discuss the prompts and decide on a sentence featuring the second conditional for each one.
- After an allotted time, have teams read their answers one by one. They win a point for each grammatically correct answer and two points if they come up with a correct answer that no other team has.

Answers

Students' own answers

Cool Down

Play a Chain Game (see TB p. 25). Students must make sentences using the second conditional, e.g. *If I were an actor, I would play James Bond.*

Global Citizenship

Lesson Objectives

- to learn vocabulary related to sharing stories: *anecdote, details, empathize, fascinating, imagination, moral, pass on, share, surprising, understand*
- to explore how stories bring people together and why it is important to share stories
- to practice listening for gist and detail

Materials

Audio Tracks 106 to 108; Audio Track 1

Opening Question

Ask the opening question: *How do stories bring people together?* Encourage students to think about how we interact with stories and the connection between storyteller and listener. Record students' ideas to revisit at the end of class.

A TRACK 106 TB p. 227 **Listen to Harry talk to his grandpa about a local project. What stories does Harry's grandpa want to tell?**

- Tell students that they are going to listen to a boy named Harry talking to his grandpa about a storytelling project. Ask *What do you talk about with your grandparents? Do your grandparents tell you stories?*
- Ask the gist question *What stories does Harry's grandpa want to tell?* and play the audio. Check the answer with the class.
- Ask further comprehension questions. Play the audio again, then check answers as a class.

Answer

anecdotes/stories about when he was a construction worker

B TRACK 107 TB p. 227 **Look at the pictures and definitions in A and write. Then listen and check.**

- Point out the example answer for number 1, *understand*. Refer students to the vocabulary box in B and have them write the words for each picture and definition in A.
- Play the audio to check answers and drill pronunciation.

Answers

1 *understand* 2 imagination 3 empathize 4 fascinating 5 details 6 pass on 7 surprising 8 anecdote 9 moral 10 share

International English

Ask students to notice the spelling difference between *empathize* and *empathise*. Remind students that the pronunciation is the same.

TRACK 1 TB p. 227 **Visualization**

- The TTL has a visualization audio track for this vocabulary set. (See TB p. 21.)

C **Read and complete the diary. Use the correct form of the words in B.**

- Tell students they are going to read part of Harry's diary. Ask students what Harry's grandpa's nickname was (Spider) and why they think people called him this.
- Look at the example together. Ask students what Harry's grandpa tells (stories or anecdotes).
- Have students complete the activity and check answers. Ask *Why did Harry's grandpa get his nickname?* (because he ate a sandwich with a spider in it!).

Answers

1 *anecdotes* 2 details 3 imagination 4 fascinating 5 shared 6 understand 7 moral

D TRACK 108 TB p. 227 **Now listen to Zoë. What is the Memory Diaries project?**

- Tell students they are going to listen to an interview with a woman named Zoë talking about the Memory Diaries project. Elicit that the project is about their lives in the past.
- Look at the pictures. Ask *Where was the photo taken?*
- Ask the gist question *What is the Memory Diaries project?* and play the audio. Check answers.

Answer

The Memory Diaries project records family and community stories so that people in the future will know about life in the past.

E **Listen again. Answer the questions.**

- Have students discuss possible answers. Play the audio, pausing for students to write their answers.
- Check answers. Have students make connections between A and E: ask *Why is it important to share stories?* (Stories make Harry and Manu feel closer to their grandparents.)

Answers

1 *She was musical like him. She sang in a band.* 2 reading stories, hearing / listening to stories 3 Any one of: smartphones / cell phones, tablets / computers / laptops, technology, work, studying 4 We can pass them on. 5 everyone in the local community 6 People read the stories on the community website.

Discussion Questions

- Have students discuss each question in pairs or small groups (see **ETB**). Guide students to conclude that stories help us make sense of the world, help foster a sense of community, and emotional connections with other people.
- Return to the opening question to ask again: *How do stories bring people together?* Revisit any ideas from the beginning of the lesson and encourage students to share any new ideas.

Cool Down

Have students make pledges to become a better listener and write down one thing that they plan to do in order to listen better.

Practice **Student's App:** Vocabulary Practice; Listening Practice

Explore Language

Lesson Objectives

- to learn how to use the second conditional: negative sentences and questions

Materials
Audio Tracks 109 and 110

Warm Up

Recap the story of the Snow Queen so far as a class. Ask students what the cliffhanger was in Lesson 2 (Gerda came across some robbers). Then elicit descriptions, ideas, and opinions about the story and what will happen next or at the end of the story. Have students discuss this in pairs.

A TRACK 109 TB p. 227 **Listen and read. Who helped Gerda escape from the robbers?**

- Tell students that they are going to listen to the next part of *The Snow Queen*. Play the audio and have students follow the dialogue in their books.
- Ask the gist question *Who helped Gerda escape from the robbers?* and elicit the answer. Ask *Who is telling the story now?* and elicit that it is Luca, the boy who was listening to the story in the previous lesson. Elicit that the children are *passing on* the story.

Answer
a little girl who was one of the robbers

B **Look at A. Complete the table. What verb form comes after *would*?**

- Display the table using the TTL.
- Students should now have the skills and strategies to discuss and complete the grammar table themselves using the dialogue. When they have completed the table, invite students to come up to the board and fill in one word each. Ask if everyone agrees. Discuss the word order, form, and patterns together, but let your class guide the discussion. For more support, use the notes in the **ETB**.
- Draw students' attention to the Grammar tip *Watch Out*. Point out that we only use *would* in one part of the sentence and never after *if*.

Answers
be; weren't, would/'d; would, if, didn't; Would, be
The infinitive without *to* comes after *would*.

C **Think and discuss. Then choose.**

- Have students work in pairs to discuss the sentences. Refer them to the table in B for example sentences and have them think about whether the sentences and questions are about the past or the future. Check answers as a class.

Answers
1 second 2 future

D TRACK 110 TB p. 227 **Listen and say.**

- Play the audio, having students repeat each sentence chorally.
- Play it again and have students use facial expressions and gestures as they repeat each sentence.
- For ideas on how to vary the drill, see TB p. 23.

E **Read and complete the end of the story.**

- Have students look at the picture and predict how the story ends. Then have them read the story to find out.
- Remind students to read the phrase after the blank, as sometimes this contains the other part of the conditional sentence, and they will need this to understand the sentence. Look at the example together. Have students notice that the first sentence is a statement, not a question, because there is no question mark.
- Have students do the controlled practice activity individually. Then check answers as a class.

Answers
1 *if she didn't help Kay* 2 if his heart were warm
3 Would Kay remember her 4 I wouldn't be cold anymore 5 What would I do

F **Think and discuss. What happens next?**

- Divide the class into groups. Tell students they are going to think of questions using the second conditional about *The Snow Queen*. Have two students read the examples.
- Give students another example to help them get started, e.g. *What would the Snow Queen do if Kay fixed the mirror?* Encourage them to use negatives as well.
- Have students discuss their ideas in their groups. This activity provides students with freer practice of second conditional questions and statements.

Answers
Students' own answers

Cool Down

Play a version of *Funniest Sentence* (see TB p. 26). Have students ask questions using the second conditional and reply with a funny answer.

Practice **Resource Bank:** Grammar Printout
Student's App: Grammar Practice

Write About It

Lesson Objectives

- to learn how to edit and publish (Process Writing: Steps 4 and 5)
- to plan and write a story
- to learn how to create a narrative voice
- to learn how to use suffixes and prefixes
- to learn editing and publishing tehcniques to help your writing

Materials

Support writing printout from the Resource (F)

Warm Up

Write some story openers to well-known stories on the board. Have students guess which stories they are from, e.g. *One day, a little girl was walking through the forest to get to her grandmother's house* (*Little Red Riding Hood*).

A Read the opening of a story. How many people are mentioned?

This text type is also modeled in the **Literacy Book** for this unit, The Weaver.

- With books closed, write the opening question of the story on the board: *What would you do if you got lost in a dark forest?* Have students discuss in pairs.
- Have students open their books and read the story opening. Ask *How many people are mentioned?* Give students one minute to skim the text and find the answer.

Answer

five people

B Look at the structure of the opening of the story. Read and check (✔) all the correct statements.

- Have students read the statements and check understanding of key words, e.g. *introduce, at least*.
- Have students answer the questions. Check answers, discussing each feature.

Answers

1; 3; 5; 6

C Look at the language in the opening of the story. Read and respond.

- Have students work in pairs. Then check answers.

Answers

1 a unhappy b "no" or "not" c Students' own answers (unfair, unusual, untidy) 2 a confidently/excitedly/strangely b adverbs of manner c Students' own answers (quietly, slowly, bravely)

- Look at the callout. Remind them to use a wide range of vocabulary when writing their own stories.
- Have students choose a word with the prefix *un–* and a word with the suffix *–ly* to use in their stories.

D Think and discuss. You're going to write the opening of an adventure story. Brainstorm some ideas using one of the Generating Ideas techniques.

- Review **Process Writing Step 1: Generating Ideas** (p. 140).
- Tell students that they are going to plan and write the opening of an adventure story. Have students copy the headings in their notebooks. Have students write their ideas before discussing in pairs.

Answers

Students' own answers

E Plan the opening of your adventure story. Use your ideas in D and one of the Planning techniques.

- Review **Process Writing Step 2: Planning** (p. 141) to help students organize their ideas from D.
- Have students plan their stories in their notebooks.

Answers

Students' own answers

F Write a first draft. Then revise it using one of the Drafting techniques.

- Review **Process Writing: Step 3 Drafting** (p. 142). Tell students that the first line should hook readers' interest.
- Remind students to revise their writing. Drafts may be written in a notebook or on the writing printout.

Answers

Students' own answers

Now ask students to turn to p. 143 to learn about Process Writing Steps 4 and 5: Editing and Publishing (see TB p. 214 for teaching notes). Students will need to do this lesson before they do G.

G Now write the opening of your adventure story. Reread and edit it using these ideas to help you analyze it. Then publish it.

- After completing steps from **Process Writing Steps 4 and 5: Editing and Publishing** on p. 143, students will complete G.
- Have students write the opening of their adventure story, in class or for homework. Students may use the support printouts from the Resource Bank.
- Students should then reread and edit their stories using the strategies they learned on p. 143.
- Look at the interesting features checklist in the colored boxes. Have students check their story for these things. .
- Have students exchange stories with a friend. Remind students to say what they liked about the story.

Cool Down

Go back to the story in A and have students suggest how the story ends. If students know the real story, accept their suggestions but encourage them to use their imaginations to think of an alternative ending. Write their suggestions on the board and have a class vote on the best ending.

Practice **Student's App:** Writing Practice
Resource Bank: Writing Game, *Crazy Stories*

Talk About It

Lesson Objectives

- to prepare and practice a conversation about a story
- to learn how to offer opinions and agree or disagree

Materials
Video

Warm Up

Ask students to remember the last time they went to see a movie at the movie theater. Have them talk in pairs about which movie they saw and whether they liked it.

A TB p. 240 **Watch and listen. Did Gene and Lloyd both enjoy going to the movie?**

- Tell students they are going to watch a video of Gene and Lloyd having a conversation about a movie they both saw. Play the video on silent first and see if students can answer the question *Did Gene and Lloyd both enjoy going to the movie?* just by looking at the boys' body language.
- Play the video again. Check predictions and the answer with the class.

Answer
Yes, they did.

B Watch again. Which phrases do Gene and Lloyd use to say they share the same opinion, and which do they use to say they have a different opinion? Write *Same* or *Different*.

- Tell students that they are going to listen to some of the phrases the children use in the video. Have students read the sentences before they rewatch the video and think about whether they have the same opinion or a different opinion.
- Play the video once and have students write the answers. Check answers as a class. Then play the video again and have students repeat the phrases, copying the children's intonation and body language.

Answers
1 *Different* 2 Same 3 Different 4 Same 5 Same 6 Same

C Choose a movie, TV program, or book that you and your friend both know. Think and plan.

- Tell students that they are going to work in pairs to plan a conversation about a movie, TV program, or book that they both know. Give students one or two minutes to choose what to talk about.
- Draw students' attention to the questions on the notepad. Tell students to use these questions to plan their conversations. Remind students that they only need to write notes and not full sentences. Have students plan their conversations together.

Answers
Students' own answers

D Discuss with your friend using phrases in B. Do you agree with each other?

- Have students have their conversations in pairs. Remind students that it is very important to listen to what your friend is saying and respond appropriately. Encourage them to use gestures and appropriate body language to show interest and excitement as they speak.
- Encourage students to video their conversations in order to better analyze them afterward.
- Have students analyze their own performances in pairs.

Cool Down

Have students make opinion statements about anything they like in small groups. Brainstorm a few topics on the board first, e.g. horror movies, beach vacations, vegetables. One student chooses a topic and gives their opinion. The other students say whether they agree or disagree, using phrases from B.

Practice **Student's App:** Speaking Skills Practice; Speaking Video

Think It Over

Lesson Objectives

- to review what has been learned in the unit
- to reflect on the unit and their own progress
- to think about learning strategies and how to continue learning at home

Warm Up

Do a quick quiz with the class about Unit 9. Ask questions about pictures, words, or information and have students find the answers in their books. Have students play in teams. Possible questions: *What book titles can you see on p. 114? How many children are in the library on p. 114? Which words sound the same in the Grammar tip, Look, on p. 117? Name two words that have definitions on p. 118. Who is listening to the story on p. 120?*

How well did you meet the challenge of Unit 9? Read and respond.

My Planning Sheet

- Give students time to think about and discuss activities in the unit before they complete each section of the graphic organizer. Tell students they are going to review what they've successfully learned and what they need to improve. They will then make a plan outlining what they will do next in order to continue learning.
- Have students do a Chalk Talk routine (TB p. 20) to recap as many things that they have done during the unit as possible. Elicit categories from the class, e.g. speaking activities, facts and ideas, and stories. Write each one in the middle of a large sheet of paper. Give students a couple of minutes to do each stage of the Chalk Talk routine.
- When students have finished adding ideas to the Chalk Talk posters, have them stick the posters on the wall for reference. Then refer students to the graphic organizer in their book and the prompt sentences: *We're all good at some things. I'm good at …; And we all need to improve some things. I need to work on …; We can always work to improve. Even when we are good at something, we can get better! My plan to improve is …* Allow students time to talk in pairs about the different sections. Encourage them to focus particularly on the second and third sections and to discuss what they can do to learn more about or practice the areas they have problems with. Remind students about online materials, such as the **Student's App** on **Navio**, but also encourage them to think of other ways they can practice English. Write some prompts on the board to support their conversation, e.g. *I'm going to … / I plan to … / I can try to …*
- When you feel they have enough ideas, have students work individually to fill in the first three parts of the graphic organizer. Remind them that they should write their own responses about themselves. Monitor and help as necessary. Look at what students are writing so you can tailor your classes and any additional practice to their needs.
- If you feel it is appropriate for your class, have students share their ideas with a friend. Encourage them to think together of how they can put their plans into practice.
- Discuss the last two sections with the class before you have students write about them. Ask *How will you know if your plan works?* Elicit that students will be able to do some of the things they wrote about in the second section without looking in their books. Ask students what they will do if their plan works. Encourage students to think of other areas they would like to practice. Remind them again about the **Student's App** on **Navio** and online materials. Then have students fill out the final two sections in the graphic organizer.
- Have students share their goals with their friends.

Looking Forward

Draw students' attention to the character at the bottom of the page. Elicit who it is and what they remember about him. (Mostafa appeared in Lesson 4 and was listening to Luca tell the story of the Snow Queen.) Have students read the speech bubble and make predictions about where Mostafa is going. Remind them that they will find out in the first lesson of Unit 10.

Practice **Resource Bank:** Unit Test
Student's App: Vocabulary and Grammar Review

Get Ready to Read

Lesson Objectives

- to activate prior knowledge about storytelling
- to guide inquiry and deepen understanding through a Step Inside VTR
- to preview the reading skill of understanding characters

Materials

VTR printout from the Resource Bank (A, B, C)

Warm Up

Ask students if they have read any fiction recently. Have them talk in pairs about the name of the book, what genre it is, and what it is about.

Step Inside

A Look at the picture. Choose a person or thing. What can they see?

- This VTR encourages students to step inside a person or object that they can see and imagine their point of view. Start by asking students what they can see in the picture. Ask what story they think the scene is from (*Little Red Riding Hood*). Provide vocabulary where necessary.
- Ask students to imagine that they are one of the people or things in the picture. Ask students what they can see (from that person, animal, or thing's viewpoint). Encourage them to think about the surroundings. Ask, e.g. *What is she doing? What is she wearing? How is she feeling?*
- Have students discuss in pairs and then as a class.

B What do you think they believe?

- Tell students again that they need to imagine what's happening in the head of the person or thing they chose.
- Say *I think the wolf believes that the girl is scary. What does your person, animal, or thing believe?*
- Give students time to think about the person, animal, or thing they have chosen and their thoughts and opinions. Have students discuss in pairs and then as a class.

Here's an example of this part of the routine.

Teacher: Who did you decide to be in the picture?
Student A: The smaller wolf.
Teacher: OK, so what does it believe?
Student A: It believes that Red Riding Hood is angry.
Teacher: Great. What makes you say that?
Student B: Because it's looking at the ground—I think it's scared because she's shouting.

C What do you think they care about?

- Ask students to think about what is important to the people, animals, or things in the picture.
- Give students time to think and then discuss in pairs. Elicit ideas.

Here's an example of this part of the routine.

Teacher: What does your person, animal, or thing care about?
Student A: The girl cares about getting through the forest safely.
Teacher: Does she care about the wolves?
Student B: No, because she's shouting at them.

Transition

Ask students if they think the story in the picture is a good story and why or why not. Have students discuss their ideas in pairs. They could discuss what they like about the original story of *Little Red Riding Hood* or what they like about the version in the picture. Ask them how this picture differs from most accounts of *Little Red Riding Hood*.

D Think and discuss. What is a story? What does a good story need?

- Tell students they are going to think about what makes a good story. Ask *Do you remember any good stories? Why did you like them?* Have students discuss in pairs, drawing on stories they have read and heard before. Students may include stories from the **Literacy Book** or stories they have read or heard outside the classroom.
- Elicit ideas from the class and write them on the board, encouraging students to give examples of stories they particularly enjoyed. Tell students that movies are also stories told visually as well as with words.

Answer

Students' own answers

E Think of your favorite story. Who is the main character? What are some of their characteristics?

- This activity previews the reading skill of understanding characters.
- Tell students that the main character is a very important part of a story. Elicit a well-known story and ask students who is the main character. What do they know about this character? What words would they use to describe him/her? Remind students that a characteristic tells us what someone is like.
- Now have students think of their favorite story and the main character. What kind of person is he/she? What words can they think of to describe him/her? What actions does the character do to show these characteristics? Have students work individually to write a list of characteristics in their books.
- Ask some students to share their ideas with the class.

Answers

Students' own answers

Now read **Storytelling Around the World**

Nonfiction: *Storytelling Around the World*—Informational Text

Lesson Objectives

- to read an informational text about different storytelling techniques from around the world
- to make a personal connection to the reading

Materials
Audio Tracks 36 and 37; slips of paper containing sentences from each part of the reading, one set per group

Warm Up

Ask students if they know any traditional stories from their country. Ask students where they learned about this story. Have they read the book? Did they learn about it at school or at home? Did their parents or grandparents tell the story?

TRACK 36 TB p. 236, Reading Approach

Engage with the Text

- Display the opening spread of the reading. Ask students to use the title and pictures on the page to predict what the reading is about. Ask students which countries they think will be mentioned. Ask *What makes you say that?* to encourage students to give reasons for their ideas.
- For the first reading, play the audio and have students follow along in their books or use the Story Player. Pause the story to ask prediction questions, including the one in the yellow callout: *How do people around the world tell stories?*

TRACK 37 TB p. 236 Words in Context

- After the first reading of the text, draw students' attention to the Words in Context box.
- Give students a few minutes to find and highlight each instance of each word in the reading.
- Have them identify the type of word by looking at the form and the sentence.
- Write these strategies on the board: *using pictures; surrounding words and sentences; positive/negative; contrasting ideas; world knowledge.*
- Have students work in pairs to discuss the words.

ceremonies (p. 138, noun) The conjunction *such as* after the word tells us that an example of this word will follow. Strategy to use: surrounding words and sentences

gourd (p. 138, noun) Students can use world knowledge of musical instruments and how they look and the picture to discover the meaning of this word. Strategies to use: world knowledge, pictures

gestures (p. 139, noun) Students should know this word from the speaking lessons in the **Language Book**. The surrounding words, sentences, and following paragraph give many examples and synonyms of gestures. Strategies to use: making connections, surrounding words and sentences

expressions (p. 139, noun) The sentence tells us this is something you do with your face in conjunction with movement and gestures. Strategies: surrounding words or sentences, making connections

myths (p. 139, noun) This word is found in conjunction with a similar term, *ancient stories*, in the same sentence. Strategy to use: surrounding words and sentences

puppeteer (p. 141, noun) The preceding sentences talk about puppets. The –(e)*er* suffix tells us it's a person. Pictures can also be used for reference. Strategies to use: pictures, surrounding words and sentences, suffixes

- Go through each word to elicit the meaning and how they know. Play the audio to practice pronunciation.

Analyze the Text and Features

- Have students read the text. As they read, have them find the names of the different storytelling techniques.
- Ask comprehension questions to check understanding of the text, e.g. *How long have people been telling stories for?* (since prehistoric times)
- Tell students to find the yellow callouts and to discuss the questions with a partner.
  - **Fact** (p. 140): *"Oral" means using spoken words, or using the mouth.* Ask students which types of storytellers tell oral stories (Griots sing, Hakawati tell oral stories). Ask students if they prefer oral or written stories.
  - **Personalization** (p. 141): *What different ways do you use to tell stories?* Have students brainstorm different ways in which they tell stories. Point out that a story can be anything they want to share with other people, e.g. personal anecdotes. Encourage them to think about how they use technology to tell stories, e.g. with videos or social media.

Interact with the Text

- Now that students are very familiar with the text, have them reconstruct part of the reading. Write some of the sentences from each part of the reading on slips of paper and mix them up. Give each group a copy of the sentences. Then have them read the sentences, decide which part of the text they are from, and order accordingly. Alternatively, to save time, you could write these sentences on the board out of order.

Cool Down

Play *What's the Scene?* (see TB p. 27) using the pictures from the reading.

Practice **Resource Bank:** Story Player

Explore the Reading

Lesson Objectives

- to understand and analyze *Storytelling Around the World* through reading comprehension activities
- to learn through CLIL (social studies): storytelling traditions around the world
- to make a personal connection to the reading

Warm Up

Play *Board Race* (see TB p. 25). Have students write as many words or ideas they remember from the reading as they can.

A Think and complete the table.

- Refer back to *Storytelling Around the World* in the **Literacy Book.** Have a Group Time discussion to help students remember the reading. Ask questions to prompt students to retell the main ideas of the text in their own words, e.g. *How many different ways of telling stories are there in the reading? Where do people use dance to tell stories?* Students can look back at the reading in their books if they need to.
- Have students open their books and look at the table. Elicit what type of information should go in each column. Ask *Where do Griots tell stories?* (in West Africa) Have students write this example in their tables.
- Have students complete the table. Check answers.

Answers

Griot; West Africa; Oral/musical storytelling
Kathak; *India*; Dance
Hakawati; Middle East and North Africa; *Oral storytelling*
Wayang Kulit; Southeast Asia, Java; Shadow puppet theater

B Think, draw, and write. Then discuss. Create your own hero and villain. What characteristics do heroes and villains have?

- Divide the board into two and write the headings *Heroes* and *Villains* at the top of each side. Elicit that heroes are characters with good qualities and villains are the bad characters. Point out that heroes and villains can be male or female, although we can also use *heroine* for women. Brainstorm examples of heroes and villains with the class and write them on the board. Encourage students to think about characters in books, movies, TV shows, and video games.
- Refer students to the graphic organizer and tell students they are going to create their own hero and villain. They are going to draw pictures and write about their new characters. Copy the graphic organizer onto the board and do an example, eliciting suggestions from the class.
- Have students do the activity individually in their books. Then have them share their hero and villain with a friend, pointing out the characteristics they have chosen for each character.
- Have students share some of the characteristics they have chosen with the class.

Answers

Students' own answers

C Think and write. What problem do your hero and villain have? How do they solve it?

- Choose a story that all students know and elicit who are the hero(es) and villain(s). Point out that we usually consider the main character to be the hero, even if they don't always display heroic actions. Explain that the hero of the story is the person we are most engaged with.
- Then ask students what problem the hero and villain have. Elicit what the main conflict of the story is (e.g. In *Little Red Riding Hood*, the wolf eats or scares the grandmother and wants to eat or catch the girl, too). Then ask *How do they solve it?* In the case of *Little Red Riding Hood*, a third character (the hunter or woodcutter) appears to save both the girl and her grandmother.
- Give students time to think about the problems their hero and villain from B might have and write their ideas in their books.

Answers

Students' own answers

D Think and discuss. Who tells stories in your family? What kind of stories do they tell? What family traditions do they preserve?

This activity explores the CLIL social studies focus of traditions by having students think about the benefits of family traditions such as storytelling.

- Draw the students' attention to the questions and check understanding of *preserve*.
- Have students discuss their ideas in pairs or small groups.
- Elicit ideas and discuss as a class. Ask students if people in their family still tell them stories. Point out that stories are not just fictional tales; they can also be personal stories about the past.

Answers

Students' own answers

Cool Down

Put students in groups of five or six. Have students choose either the hero or villain they created in B and try to find another student in their group whose character has a similar trait. They take turns naming one characteristic their character has. When they hear a shared characteristic, they can call out *Snap!*

Practice **Student's App:** Reading Practice

Get Ready to Read

Lesson Objectives

- to activate prior knowledge about what makes a good storyteller
- to practice the reading skill of understanding characters

Materials

Pictures of characters from famous movies or stories students will know (Warm Up)

Warm Up

To introduce the reading skill of understanding characters, show students the different pictures you have brought in or looked up online and see if they can name the character and the movie or book they are from. You could do this as a team game, awarding points for each correct answer.

A Think and write. How would you describe the characters?

- Quickly review what students know about the four characters by having students remember what happened in each story. For each character, ask *What did X do?* Elicit answers.
- Tell students they are going to think about what these characters are like. Look at the clues in the table and tell them that this information will help them. Look at Sherlock Holmes together. Have a student read the clue aloud. Then ask *How can you describe Sherlock Holmes?* Elicit answers from the class.
- Tell students to use the clues to write a description of each character. Remind them that we are describing their personality and behavior, *not* their physical appearance.

Suggested Answers

Sherlock Holmes: Sherlock Holmes is creative and good at solving problems.
Camilo: Camilo is honest.
Sophia: Sophia is quick thinking. She remembers what she has learned. She acts when there is a crisis.
Delivery Dan: Dan works hard and doesn't give up on his dreams.

- Have students read the reading skill box. Then ask questions to check comprehension, e.g. *What does an author tell us about the characters?* (what they do, what they think, and what they say)

B Read, think, and write. Read the first page of *The Weaver*. How would you describe the character of Mariam?

- Have students look at the picture and predict basic characteristics of the girl. Ask questions, e.g. *Where do you think she lives? How old is she? What does she like doing?* and elicit ideas from the class.
- Tell students to turn the page and read the first page of the story on p. 144. Give students one or two minutes to do this.
- Ask students what they have learned about Mariam's character and elicit answers from one or two students. Then have students write their answers in their books.
- Have some students share their ideas with the class.

Suggested Answers

She's resourceful and determined. She doesn't want to do her work. She is creative. She likes to write stories.

C Think and discuss. What makes a good storyteller?

- Tell students that Mariam is going to write a story. Review what makes a good story. Students discussed this on p. 137.
- Then ask *What makes a good storyteller?* Elicit ideas. Tell students that a good storyteller makes you forget that you are in a room with other people and makes you feel like you are in the story. Have students think about a time when they were really involved when listening to a story. Ask them to try to remember what the storyteller did. Have students discuss their ideas in pairs.
- Discuss the question with the class. Elicit different storytelling techniques and write them on the board, e.g. *using your voice to show emotion, using gestures, interacting with the audience, using pauses to add suspense.*

Answer

Students' own answers

Now read The Weaver

Fiction: *The Weaver—A Folk Tale*

Lesson Objectives

- to read a folk tale about a princess who loves writing stories
- make a personal connection to the reading

Materials
Audio Tracks 38 and 39

Warm Up

Play a version of *Stand Up, Sit Down* (see TB p. 26). Call out different activities and hobbies and have students stand up if they do the activity or remain seated if they don't, e.g. *play video games, do homework, have a piano lesson.*

TRACK 38 TB p. 236 Reading Approach

Engage with the Text

- Display the opening spread of the story. Review the predictions students made about Mariam's character from p. 143. Ask *What will the folk tale will be about?*
- Play the audio. Have students follow along in their books.

TRACK 39 TB p. 237 Words in Context

- After the first reading of the text, look at the Words in Context box. Play the audio to practice pronunciation.
- Have students brainstorm a list of strategies that they can use to find the meanings of the words, including strategies they use in L1.
- In pairs, have students look at all of the words.
- Have them find and highlight each instance of each word in the reading and identify the type of word by looking at the form and the sentence.
- Have students swap pairs and explain words to each other, saying which strategy they used.
- Bring the class together and elicit the meanings. Discuss which strategies worked and which didn't.

tutor (p. 144 / p. 145, noun) The rest of the sentence explains what action is related to tutors—*teach.* Strategies to use: surrounding words and phrases, world knowledge

kidnapper (p. 145 / p. 147 / p. 148, noun) We know that this noun refers to a person because of the *–er* suffix. The preceding part of the sentence tells us what the kidnapper did, and the adjective *cruel* tells us that this is a bad person. Strategies to use: suffixes, surrounding words and sentences

announced (p. 146, verb) The quotation marks around the direct speech shows us this is a verb for reporting speech. The following direct speech shows this verb introduces a statement. Strategies to use: surrounding words and sentences, sentence structure

fierce (p. 146, adjective) This adjective describes the wolves. The following words and sentences say what physical attributes make them fierce, and that normally people are frightened. Strategies to use: pictures, surrounding words and sentences

blushed (p. 149, verb) You can see Mariam blushing in the picture, and the sentence describes how her face feels (*warm*) when she blushes. Strategies to use: pictures, surrounding words and sentences, personal experience

Analyze the Text and Features

- Have students silently read the text. Ask them to find examples of good storytelling.
- Ask comprehension questions to check understanding, e.g. *Does Mariam enjoy weaving?* (No, she prefers other lessons and activities.)
- In pairs, have students find and discuss the yellow callouts.
  - **Fun Fact** (p. 144): *An oud is a stringed instrument played in Africa and Asia. Can you find one on this page?* Have students look at the picture and say if they have ever seen one.
  - **Making Connections** (p. 144): *Where can stories take us?* Ask students what happens when they read or listen to a good story. Elicit that stories can take us to different places and different times and into imaginary worlds.
  - **Language Focus** (p. 146): *"The blink of an eye" is figurative language. What would be the literal equivalent?* Ask students *Did time pass quickly or slowly?* Elicit that the phrase means "very quickly."
  - **Making Connections** (p. 149): *What other story does this remind you of?* Ask students if they know any similar stories and elicit ideas.
  - **Text Focus** (p. 146) *Imagery is the vivid description an author uses to bring you into the story. What kinds of images does Mariam's story make you see?* Remind students that similes and metaphors are ways of using imagery. Have students read parts of Mariam's story again, imagine the scenes in their heads, and discuss in pairs.

Interact with the Text

- Play the parts of the audio where Mariam tells her story. Pause and have students copy the intonation and show similar emotion. Encourage them to gesture as though telling the story.
- Then have them work in pairs to each tell parts of Mariam's story, trying to use voice and gestures.

Cool Down

Play *Who Said It?* (see TB p. 27) using lines from the reading.

Practice Resource Bank: Story Player

Explore the Reading

Lesson Objectives

- to understand and analyze *The Weaver* through reading comprehension activities
- to practice the reading skill of understanding characters
- to explore the SEL competency of self-management by monitoring progress toward personal and academic short- and long-term goals
- make a personal connection to the reading

Warm Up

- Play a team game to have students remember details from the reading. Have students work in teams to think of true and false sentences about the reading and test each other, e.g. *Mariam has English lessons* (false; she has math, writing, music, and weaving lessons). Teams get a point for each correct answer.

A Complete the table. Describe the character and give an example from the reading.

- Have students look at the table. Do the first one together. Say *Mariam is determined. She wants to do what she wants.* Elicit phrases from the story that show this. Ask *What other things do you know about Mariam's character?* Elicit answers.
- Have students complete the table. Then check answers

Suggested Answers

Mariam: smart, clever, and intelligent; learns quickly but doesn't want to learn traditional subjects for girls, like weaving; not very patient; creative; loves writing stories; very determined. **Example:** "I use words instead of wool." "I don't want to weave. Can't I just have my normal lessons like math, writing, and music?"
Queen Ayeisha: kind and loving; understands her daughter and is proud of her. **Example:** "If I wrote a story like that, I would want to put it in a book!"
King Jahmal: loves his daughter; expects Mariam to do what he tells her; very powerful because he's the king. **Example:** "Well, I think your story is wonderful!"
the kidnapper: cruel, fierce, strong. **Examples:** "Never!"
Harun: strong (he beats the kidnapper in the end) and brave; a good, loving son because he rescues his father. **Example:** "I have you now!"
Farida: gentle and kind; loves Mariam and her stories; not a strict tutor **Example:** "As you wish, but please keep it short." "What a wonderful story! And it has a fine moral."

B Think and write. Which characters in A are heroes? What characteristics make them heroes?

- Ask student what they remember about heroes. Have them look back at their heroes from p. 142. Ask *What characteristics did they have?* and elicit answers.
- Have students suggest a character from A and say what characteristics make this person a hero. (Example: Harun: He is brave. He fought the kidnapper and saved his father.)
- Have students write their ideas about the different possible heroes in A. Have students share their ideas.

Suggested Answers

I think that Mariam and Harun are heroes. Mariam is a hero because she is resourceful and came up with a clever way to pursue her goal (of being a writer/storyteller). Harun is a hero because he rescues his father in the story.

C Think and discuss. Mariam preferred to study writing and music. What subjects and hobbies do you enjoy doing? How do you make time for them?

- Students are going to explore the SEL competency of self-management by monitoring progress toward personal and academic short- and long-term goals.
- Have students think about what they enjoy and make a list.
- Ask students if they have lots of time to do all the activities they enjoy and why. Do they feel that they need more time to do these activities?
- Have students discuss their ideas in pairs, then as a class.

Answers

Students' own answers

Literary Term: Word Choice: Adverbs of Intensity

Complete the table. Sort the adverbs by intensity.

- Draw students' attention to the explanation of *adverbs of intensity*. Tell students that sometimes we want to make something seem more important or less important. Have students compare *I was really angry* with *I was a little angry.* What might be the causes and consequences of each situation?
- Tell students that the adverbs in the box can be categorized into the three columns. *Low intensity* means not very strong, and *high intensity* means very strong.
- Have students complete the table individually. Check answers as a class. Then have students look for more examples in the reading and add them to the table.

Answers

Low Intensity: slightly, kind of, a bit
Medium Intensity: fairly, rather, pretty
High Intensity: extremely, not at all, completely, totally, absolutely, very
Adverbs as intensifiers in the reading: very, really, perhaps, extremely, really, very, extremely

Cool Down

Tell students to imagine a perfect day where they can spend as much time as they like doing their favorite activities. Tell them to write down what they will do and have them compare their day with a partner.

Practice **Resource Bank:** Literary Term Printout
Student's App: Reading Practice; Literary Term Practice

Think Together

Lesson Objectives

- to make connections between the readings
- to explore the key concept: Why do we tell stories?
- to reflect on the unit and provide personal thoughts and opinions

Warm Up

Have students do 30-second speeches about the two readings in pairs. They each have 30 seconds to tell their partner as much as they can about one of the readings.

A Look at *Storytelling Around the World* and *The Weaver* again. Write a paragraph that explains why people tell stories. Use some of these words to help you.

- Students are going to apply what they have learned in the unit about storytelling and discuss the key concept question: *Why do we tell stories?*
- Check that students know what each word in the box refers to and have them find the names of the different types of storytelling in the first reading.
- Have students think about whether each word in the box could be used to talk about *Storytelling Around the World* or *The Weaver.*
- Give students enough time to look back at the two readings and write their paragraphs in their books individually. Then ask *Why do we tell stories?* Elicit ideas.

Answers
Students' own answers

B What other entertaining stories do you know? Do they tell about your traditions and have a good moral message? Do a Numbered Heads Together routine.

- Elicit an example of an entertaining story from the class. Ask students if the story includes any traditions or aspects of their culture. Check that students remember the meaning of *moral message*. Then ask them which stories they know that have a moral message. Remind students that fables and folk tales often have a message that teaches us an important lesson.
- Set up the Numbered Heads Together routine (see TB p. 20) and ask the question. Give students a few minutes to discuss their ideas. They can take notes if they wish to.

C Think about your story from B. How would you tell that story? What type of storytelling would you use? Plan and share.

- Elicit the different ways of telling a story. Tell students to think about which method is best for the story they chose in their groups.
- Give students time to plan how they will tell their story in their groups. They will need to make simple notes about what happens in each part of the story.
- Have students tell their stories (see **ETB** for an extension) in groups.

Answers
Students' own answers

My Reading Journal

What are two questions you have after reading this unit?

This question encourages students to think about what else they want to learn. Give students time to think and write their questions, then discuss in pairs or small groups.

Suggested Answer
1 How do the Kathak dancers make people understand the story?
2 Will Mariam write a book of her story?

What's your favorite story with heroes and villains?

This question encourages students to give a personal response to the unit. Have them discuss their ideas with a friend, then write in their books. Ask if any students would like to share their answers with the class.

Suggested Answer
My favorite story with heroes and villains is *Harry Potter.* Harry is the hero because he is smart. The villain is Voldemort. He's evil and scary, but Harry always manages to stop him.

Go back to page 137. Do the routine again.

Remind students of how to do the Step Inside routine by looking back at pages pp. 136–137. Using the TTL, project the instructions onto the board. Then repeat the Step Inside routine. Encourage students to choose a different person, animal, or thing from the picture this time. Then have them compare their answers from the first time they did the routine and notice how the perspective changes, e.g. *Before, I chose the wolf and I thought it cared about finding a warm place to stay. This time, I chose the basket. It cared about keeping the food inside it safe.*

Cool Down

Have students talk in pairs about their favorite things from the unit. This could be an activity, a reading, an extension, or just an image.

Practice **Student's App:** Key Concept Practice

UNIT 10

Why Was It Made?

Unit Overview

Themes

Design

Design and problem solving

Synopsis

In this unit, students will explore the concept of design and problem solving. They will learn about the importance of good design and how it can affect different people. They will learn about why we need design and how it can help us solve problems. Students will plan and prepare a conversation and write a letter of complaint.

Language Book

Vocabulary

design (v), *evolve, heavy, light, man-made, original, portable, useful, useless*

Pronunciation: connected speech: intrusive /w/

p. 192

Explore Language

Reported Speech: Questions

p. 193

Global Citizenship

Why do we need design?

adapt, customize, effective, feedback, flexible, material, trial and error, user-friendly

p. 194

Explore Language

Agreeing With *Too, So, Either,* and *Neither*

p. 195

Talk About It

Conversation: exploring options and reaching agreement

p. 196

Write About It

A Letter of Complaint

Paragraph Building: letter-writing conventions

Sentence Building: formal and informal language

p. 197

Think It Over

Review and Reflection

Monthly Goal Reflection

p. 198

Think Together
How can design solve problems?
p. 205

Visible Thinking
Explanation Game
p. 199

Literacy Book

Nonfiction
Informational Text: *Designing Drones*
Words in Context: *aerodynamic, data, famine, fuel, touchscreen*
p. 203

Fiction
Science Fiction: *The Restore Key*
Words in Context: *elevator, ambitious, code, beam, backup*
p. 200

Reading Skill
Making inferences
p. 202

Literary Term
Word Choice: Degrees of Intensity
p. 204

Language and Literacy Connections

The connecting theme for Unit 10 is design.

	Language	Literacy
Vocabulary	**Set 1:** design **Set 2:** design to solve problems	**Nonfiction:** design, adapt, material **Fiction:** difficult
Grammar	**Reported Speech: Questions** First he asked how many of us wore a watch. This morning it asked me if I needed to do some exercise. But I asked you how it did that! **Agreeing With Too, So, Either, and Neither** I'd like one of those at home! Me, too! I don't have a skateboard at the moment. Neither do I. I want to get a new one soon. So do I. I really don't know which one is going to win. I don't either.	**Fiction:** They said it was destroyed in the accident.
Skills	**Pronunciation:** connected speech: intrusive /w/ **Process Writing:** editing and publishing	**Reading:** making inferences **Literary Term:** degrees of intensity
International English	yours truly/yours faithfully	elevator/lift

Vocabulary

Lesson Objectives

- to learn design vocabulary: ***design, evolve, heavy, light, man-made, original, portable, useful, useless***
- to say a rap about designing different objects
- to practice connected speech: intrusive /w/

Materials

Audio Tracks 111 to 115; Video

Warm Up

Draw students' attention to the unit title. Have them think about why different objects or devices in the classroom were made. Choose a variety of items, from basic tools like a pencil to technological devices like a projector or tablet. Have students discuss their ideas in pairs.

A TRACK 111 TB p. 227 **Listen. Why does Mostafa think Dubai is a good place for the Design Club to visit?**

- Display the picture on the opening spread with the TTL. Have students speculate about what is happening in the picture. All the characters from previous units can be found in this scene. Ask students what they think is going on and why they think that.
- Tell students that they are going to listen to Mostafa talking to Tareq and Jasmin. Remind students of the challenge from the end of Unit 9. Have students find Mostafa in the picture and ask *Where is he?* (in Dubai)
- Play the audio and have students look at the picture.
- Ask the comprehension question *Why does Mostafa think Dubai is a good place for the Design Club to visit?* Play the audio again and check the answer.

Answer

He feels really inspired by all the designs he has seen.

B TRACK 112 TB p. 228 **Find and number the words in A. Then listen and check.**

- Have students look at the list of vocabulary words. Point out the example (1) and have students find *evolve* in the picture. Have students do the activity in pairs.
- Play the audio for students to check their answers.

Answers

1 *evolve* 2 original 3 useless 4 portable 5 useful
6 design 7 man-made 8 heavy 9 light

C TRACK 113 TB p. 228 **Close your eyes. Listen, visualize, and say.**

- Prepare students for the visualization (see **Visualization**).
- Play the audio, allowing students to visualize the ideas as they listen.
- Have students draw pictures of the things they imagined.

D Look and write.

- Display the Venn diagram. Tell students that they are going to categorize the words depending on whether they are good (positive) characteristics or bad (negative) characteristics. Look at the example together and elicit why *light* is positive in this context (it is easy to carry).
- Have students complete the diagram. Then have them compare answers in pairs, then check answers as a class.

Suggested Answers

Positive: *light*, original, portable, useful
Both: design, evolve, man-made
Negative: heavy, useless

E TRACK 114 TB p. 228 **Listen and write. Then watch and say.**

- Play the video or audio for *Design's My Line*. Have students follow along in their books.
- Have students read the lyrics and complete the blanks. Play the rap audio and have students check their answers.
- Play the video or audio again. Encourage students to join in and copy the intonation and rhythm of the rap.

Answers

1 *heavy* 2 useless 3 light 4 portable 5 useful
6 original

F TRACK 115 TB p. 228 **Pronunciation. Listen and say. Copy the linking. Find three more phrases like these in the rap.**

- Display the examples and elicit that the curved lines show linking. Have students try saying the phrases. Play the audio for students to listen and repeat.
- Draw students' attention to the pronunciation of the two linked words, *you_a*, and have students notice the /w/ sound between *you* and *a*. Explain that when a word ends in a vowel and is followed by a word starting with a vowel, we often have a consonant sound "intruding" to help us say it, e.g. *do_it*. When a word ends in /uː/, /ʊ/, /oʊ/, or /aʊ/, it's easier to say if you add a /w/ sound. This /w/ is inserted in the middle of some words, such as doing /ˈduːwɪŋ/.
- Drill each phrase chorally. Then have students repeat in pairs.
- Have students look for more examples of intrusive /w/ in the rap. Have a few students write their answers on the board, showing the linking as on the page. Have the class say the phrase.

Answers

you_(w)_a phone; you_(w)_amused; you_(w)_a watch

Cool Down

Play *Draw It!* (see TB p. 25) using the vocabulary from the lesson. Remind students they will need to use their imaginations to think of how to draw the words.

Explore Language

Lesson Objectives

- to learn how to use reported speech: questions
- to practice vocabulary related to design

Materials

Audio Tracks 116 and 117

Warm Up

Ask students if they have a cell phone or tablet and which features they use regularly. Ask students why they think companies are constantly designing new models. Discuss and encourage students to give examples.

A TRACK 116 TB p. 228 **Listen and read. What does Archie's watch do at the end?**

- Tell students they are going to listen to Archie talking to his friend Miguel about his watch. Play the audio and have students follow the dialogue in their books. Ask *Does Archie have a normal watch?* and elicit answers (no—it's a smartwatch).
- Ask the gist question *What does Archie's watch do at the end?* and elicit the answer.

Answer

It tells him not to be lazy!

B Look at A. Complete the table. Do we use question marks at the end of reported questions?

- Display the table using the TTL.
- Students should now have the skills and strategies to discuss and complete the grammar table themselves using the story. When they have completed the table, elicit answers. Ask if everyone agrees. Discuss the word order, form, and patterns together, but let your class guide the discussion. For more support, use the notes in the **ETB**.
- Draw students' attention to the Grammar tip *Remember.* Point to the pronouns in the questions. Elicit how they have changed. Point out that the pronouns depend on who is speaking. So if you are telling someone what someone said to you, you say *He told* ***me***.

Answers

wore; if, needed; did

No, we don't use question marks at the end of reported questions.

C Think and discuss. Then choose.

- In pairs, have students discuss the sentences. Refer them to the table in B for example sentences. Check answers. Elicit which words change when it is reported (pronouns, verb forms). Ask students which question in B is a yes/no question and what other changes are made (*If/Whether* replaces the auxiliary verb).

Practice **Resource Bank:** Grammar Printout
Student's App: Grammar Practice

Answers

1 explain what someone asked 2 yes/no

D TRACK 117 TB p. 228 **Listen and say.**

- Play the audio. Have students repeat sentences chorally. Then have say the sentences to each other in pairs.
- For ideas on how to vary the drill, see TB p. 23.

E Find and correct the errors.

- Tell students that they have to identify the errors and correct them to practice the grammar in a controlled way.
- Look at the example together. Ask *What was the direct question?* (Is it man-made?). Elicit that it is a yes/no question, so it needs *if* or *whether* before the reported question. Point out that the verb form also needs to be changed to the simple past. Remind students to check the verb forms, reporting verbs, use of auxiliary verbs, and pronouns when they are forming reported questions.
- Have students do the activity individually, then check answers. Make this into a competition by awarding points for correctly identifying and correcting the errors.

Answers

1 *She asked me ~~is it~~* ***if it was*** *man-made.* 2 The teacher asked if we ~~need~~ **needed** more help yesterday morning.
3 His dad ~~said~~ **asked** him if the test ~~is~~ **was** difficult.
4 I asked her where ~~did you get~~ **she got** that backpack.
5 He ~~asked to me~~ **asked me** where I **was** going.
6 They asked ~~we~~ **us** whether we ~~are~~ **were** having fun.

F Think and discuss. Ask the designers questions. Then tell a friend.

- Tell students they are going to pretend to be designers and ask each other questions about their designs. Look at the pictures on the page. Elicit a few direct questions about the designs, e.g. *What is the T-shirt made of?*
- Divide the class into groups of three. Have students ask a question to one student and then tell the other student what they asked using a reported question. Have three students demonstrate using the examples on the page.
- Have students do the activity in their groups, taking turns to ask questions. Elicit reported questions from the class.

Answers

Students' own answers

Cool Down

Play a Chain Game (see TB p. 25). Have students ask a direct question. The next student reports that question before asking a question. For example:

Student A: What's your favorite color?
Student B: Maria asked me what my favorite color was. Did you do your homework?
Student C: Maria asked Jon what his favorite color was. Jon asked me if I did my homework.

Global Citizenship

Lesson Objectives

- to learn vocabulary related to using design to solve problems: *adapt, customize, effective, feedback, flexible, material, trial and error, user-friendly*
- to explore why we need design and how it can affect people
- to practice listening for gist and detail

Materials
Audio Tracks 118 to 120; Audio Track J

Opening Question

Ask the opening question: *Why do we need design?* Elicit ideas and encourage students to think about how design is important. Ask students what makes a design good or bad, encouraging them to give examples of things they own. Keep a record of students' ideas to revisit at the end of the lesson.

A TRACK 118 TB p. 228 **Listen to Inès talk to Rafael. Why is Rafael's backpack special?**

- Tell students that they are going to listen to a girl named Inès talking to a boy named Rafael about his backpack. Have students describe their own backpacks in pairs.
- Ask the gist question *Why is Rafael's backpack special?* and play the audio. Check the answer with the class.
- Ask further comprehension questions and play the audio again, then check answers as a class.

Answer
He designed it himself. / He customized it.

B TRACK 119 TB p. 228 **Look at the pictures and definitions in A and write. Then listen and check.**

- Point out the example answer for number 1, *adapt*. Refer students to the vocabulary box in B. Have them write the words for each picture and definition in A in pairs or individually.
- Play the audio for students to check their answers. Use the audio to drill the pronunciation of the words.

Answers
1 *adapt* 2 feedback 3 material 4 effective
5 flexible 6 trial and error 7 user-friendly
8 customize

TRACK J TB p. 228 **Visualization**

- The TTL has a visualization audio track or this vocabulary set. (See TB p. 21.)

C Read and complete the paragraph.

- Tell students they are going to read a paragraph about a place called Art Space. Have students predict what Art Space is for and imagine what it looks like. Then have them read the paragraph to check.
- Look at the example together. Ask students why they displayed the top three designs and elicit that they wanted people's opinions in order to choose the winner.
- Have students do the activity individually. Check answers as a class. Ask students what Art Space will be used for (painting lessons, exhibitions, children's activities).

Answers
1 *feedback* 2 flexible 3 adapt 4 material
5 effective 6 customize

D TRACK 120 TB p. 228 **Now listen to Sadie and Misha being interviewed. What is their project?**

- Tell students they are going to listen to two girls talk about their school project. Before playing the audio, have students describe the pictures. Ask them who they think will use the objects in the picture and elicit ideas from the class.
- Listening for gist: ask the gist question *What is their project?* and play the audio. Check the answer with the class.

Answer
to find design solutions to help children with learning difficulties at a weekend activity center in their community/town

E Listen again. Match the sentence halves.

- Have students read the sentence halves and try to match them from memory before they listen again. Then play the audio and have students check their answers. Check answers as a class.
- Help students make connections between A and E by asking them what the children considered when they were doing their designs. Elicit that in both activities the children wanted to make something practical that would help them or other people in their day-to-day lives.

Answers
1 c 2 f 3 g 4 e 5 b 6 d 7 a

Discussion Questions

- Draw students' attention to the discussion questions. Have students discuss each question in pairs or small groups (see **ETB**). Guide students toward the conclusion that bad design can have a hugely negative impact on people's lives and that good design can make our lives much easier.
- Return to the opening question to ask again: *Why do we need design?* Revisit any ideas discussed at the beginning of the lesson and encourage students to share any new ideas.

Cool Down

Have students work in pairs to write a meaningful sentence containing as many words from B as possible. The sentence that has the most key words (and makes sense) wins.

Practice **Student's App:** Vocabulary Practice; Listening Practice

Explore Language

Lesson Objectives

- to learn how to use *too, so, either,* and *neither*

Materials

Audio Tracks 121 and 122

Warm Up

Display the opening spread of the unit (pp. 126–127) and have students look for the different inventions in the picture. Remind students that the children are taking part in a Young Designer of the Year competition. Ask students which designs they think are in the competition.

A TRACK 121 TB p. 229 **Listen and read. Which two designs do Susie and Archie talk about?**

- Tell students that they are going to listen to two children talking about the designs. Play the audio and have students follow the dialogue in their books.
- Ask the gist question *Which two designs do Susie and Archie talk about?* and elicit the answers. Ask students whether Susie and Archie know who will win the competition.

Answers

the door that opens out to make a table tennis table and the skateboard parking unit

B **Look at A. Complete the table. Where in the sentence do *too, so, either,* and *neither* appear?**

- Display the table using the TTL.
- Students should now have the skills and strategies to discuss and complete the grammar table themselves using the dialogue. When they have completed the table, elicit answers. Ask if everyone agrees. Discuss the word order, form, and patterns together, but let your class guide the discussion. For more support, use the notes in the **ETB**.
- Draw students' attention to the Grammar tip *Look*. Point out the use of the auxiliary verb in *So do I* and *Neither do I*. Explain that we use these to respond to simple present phrases. If the original statement has an auxiliary or modal verb such as *be* or *can* then we use that same auxiliary verb in the response, *So can I*.

Answers

too; Neither; do I; don't either

So and *neither* appear at the beginning of the sentence. *Too* and *either* appear at the end of the sentence.

C **Think and discuss. Then choose.**

- Have students work in pairs to discuss the sentences. Refer them to the table in B for example sentences. Check answers.
- Elicit the two different ways of agreeing with positive sentences and then with negative sentences. Write the positive responses on one side of the board and the negative responses on the other. Ask students which word we can use with any sentence (*too*). Then elicit the difference between *either* and *neither* (we use *either* with a negative verb).

Answers

1 *too* or *so* 2 *either* or *neither*

D TRACK 122 TB p. 229 **Listen and say.**

- Play the audio, having students repeat each sentence chorally.
- Play it again and have students repeat each sentence to a friend.
- For ideas on how to vary the drill, see TB p. 23.

E **Read and respond in two ways.**

- Look at the example together. Point out the negative verb and the subject in parentheses. Explain that students have to respond using the words in parentheses, so in the second question possible answers could be *Ours was too / So was ours.*
- Remind students to look at the verb in the sentence and check whether it is an auxiliary or modal verb or if it needs *do*. They should then decide if the statement is positive or negative.
- Have students write the possible responses individually. Then check answers.

Answers

1 *Neither did I. / I didn't either.* 2 Ours was, too. / So was ours. 3 You will, too. / So will you. 4 Neither did our friends. / Our friends didn't either. 5 Neither did Ben. / Ben didn't either. 6 Her brother did, too. / So did her brother.

F **What do you have in common with your friends? Ask and answer.**

- Divide the class into small groups. Tell students they are going to find out what they have in common with their friends. Have students read the speech bubbles and notice how the different ways of agreeing are used.
- Have students ask and answer questions in their groups, writing down their answers in their notebooks. You could give a target of number of things to find, e.g. five, or leave it open to see which group finds the most things that they have in common. Encourage students to say the expressions with meaning.

Answers

Students' own answers

Cool Down

Have students vote on their favorite design from A to find out which item would win the competition if the class were the judges.

Practice **Resource Bank:** Grammar Printout
Student's App: Grammar Practice

Write About It

Lesson Objectives

- to plan and write a letter of complaint
- to learn how to use letter-writing conventions
- to learn how to use formal and informal language
- to learn editing and publishing tehcniques to help your writing

Materials

Support writing printout from the Resource Bank (F)

Warm Up

Ask students if they have ever bought something that broke. Discuss possible solutions, e.g. take it back to the store.

A Read Hubert Dronkin's letter of complaint. What problems has he had with the Exerdesk?

This text type (a letter) is also modeled in the Literacy Book for this unit, The Restore Key.

- Using the TTL, display the letter and have students skim to find out if Hubert is happy with the desk.
- Ask *What problems has he had with the Exerdesk?* Have students scan the text and underline the problems.

Answers

It's badly designed. It's too small. It only has one gear. The instructions were difficult. It took six hours to build. He cut himself on a pedal. The Customer Services person rudely refused to refund his money.

International English

American: Yours truly

British: Yours faithfully

Have students notice the different phrases and drill the intonation of both. Have the students practice saying these phrases sympathetically. If you have time, you could ask students to think of scenarios where it would be appropriate to use these phrases.

B Look at the structure of the letter of complaint. Read and put the features in order.

- Read the statements and check understanding of key words. Elicit the order of information: first, the address of the person we are writing to on the left, then our own address on the right. Have students find and number the features in order. Then check answers.

Answers

1 h 2 e 3 a 4 g 5 c 6 f 7 d 8 b

C Look at the language in the letter of complaint. Complete the table.

- Look at the callout. Ask *Why do we do this?*
- Explain that all the informal phrases in the table match a more formal form in the letter. Do the first one as an example. Draw attention to the second paragraph where the writer contrasts two ideas using *However*, and have students write them in the *Formal* column. Have students complete the table, then check answers.

Answers

Formal: However; It is very badly designed.; I was disappointed to discover …; How would you feel …?; I would be grateful if you could …; I look forward to hearing from you.

D Think and discuss. You're going to write a letter of complaint. Choose a problem or think of one of your own. Brainstorm lots of ideas using one of the Generating Ideas techniques.

- Elicit the problems in the pictures (jacket coming apart, deflating waterwings, leaking coffee cup). Have students choose one to write a letter of complaint, or to make up a problem.
- Have students choose a way of generating ideas, then discuss their ideas in pairs and make notes.

Answers

Students' own answers

E Plan your letter of complaint. Use some of your ideas in D and one of the Planning techniques.

- Have students think about how to organize their ideas from D and plan their letters in their notebooks.

Answers

Students' own answers

F Write the first draft of your letter. Then revise it using one of the Drafting techniques.

- Review the drafting techniques from **Process Writing Step 3: Drafting** on p. 142. Have students make a first draft in their notebook or using the writing printout and then revise it.

Answers

Students' own answers

G Now write your final letter of complaint. Then check it using one of the Editing and Publishing techniques. Publish it.

- Have students write their letter of complaint in class or for homework. Students may use the support printouts from the Resource Bank.
- Elicit and write on the board a checklist for students to check their work with. Have students reread and edit their letters with strategies from **Process Writing Steps 4 and 5: Editing and Publishing**.
- Have students exchange letters with a friend and give feedback.

Cool Down

Play *Stand Up, Sit Down* (see TB p. 26) but this time call out phrases from C and have students stand up if the phrase is formal and remain seated if it is informal.

Practice **Student's App:** Writing Practice
Resource Bank: Writing Game, *I'm Very Disappointed*

Talk About It

Lesson Objectives

- to prepare and practice a conversation where students make a decision together
- to learn how to explore options and reach an agreement

Materials
Video

Warm Up

Tell students to think about what kind of decisions they make every day, e.g. *I decide what to wear.* Have them work in pairs to make a list. Tell students not to worry if their ideas sound trivial. The idea is to make students realize that they are actually responsible for making lots of decisions in their lives.

A TB p. 240 **Watch and listen. Do you think Gene, Veronica, and Linda are going to choose the right thing?**

- Have students look at the pictures on the TV screen and predict what the children are going to talk about.
- Tell students they are going to watch a video of Gene, Veronica, and Linda trying to make a decision together. This is the first time students will see a video of three people talking. Play the video. Elicit that the children are the judges for the Young Designer of the Year competition.
- Draw students' attention to the question *Do you think Gene, Veronica, and Linda are going to choose the right thing?* Play the video again and elicit that they are going to choose the glasses. Then ask students if they think that is the right decision and encourage students to give reasons for their answers.

Answer
Students' own answers

B **Watch again. Put the sentences and phrases in order.**

- Have students read the sentences before they rewatch the video.
- Play the video once and have students order the phrases. Then play the video again so that students can check their answers. Check answers as a class.
- Finally, play the video again and have students repeat the phrases, copying the children's intonation and body language. Remind them that questions should go up at the end.

Answers
a 2 b 4 c 1 d 10 e 3 f 7 g 5 h 8 i 6 j 9

C **Think of a decision you and your friends need to make. What ideas do you have?**

- Tell students that they are going to work in pairs to plan a conversation where they make a decision in groups of three.
- Draw students' attention to the ideas in the colored boxes. Tell students to choose one of these ideas to talk about. They should then think of ideas or options that they can discuss. Do an example with the class, e.g. *where to go on Saturday.* Brainstorm with the class places to go and write the ideas on the board as a mind map.
- Then have students work in their groups to think of ideas and make notes.

Answers
Students' own answers

D **Talk with your friends using phrases in B. Do you agree?**

- Have students practice their conversations. Remind students that it is very important to listen to what your friend is saying and respond appropriately. Encourage them to direct the discussion positively by using gestures and using phrases to move the conversation along and try to reach agreement.
- Encourage students to video their conversations in order to better analyze it afterward.
- Have students analyze their own performances in pairs, thinking about whether they tried to reach an agreement.

Cool Down

Have students make opinion statements about anything they like in small groups. The other students say whether they agree or disagree, using phrases from B.

Practice **Student's App:** Speaking Skills Practice; Speaking Video

Think It Over

Lesson Objectives

- to review what has been learned in the unit
- to reflect on the unit and their own progress
- to think about learning strategies and how to continue learning at home

Warm Up

Do a quick quiz with the class about Unit 10. Ask questions about pictures, words, or information and have students find the answers in their books. Have students play in teams. Possible questions: *How many children are on pp. 126–127? What color is Susie's T-shirt on p. 126? Which words can be both positive and negative on p. 127? What four pictures are on p. 129? What is the British English phrase in International English on p. 132?*

How well did you meet the challenge of Unit 10? Read and respond.

Monthly Goal Reflection

- Tell students they are going to review what they learned in the unit and also think about their own learning and whether they have reached their goals from Unit 10. This time students are also going to evaluate how hard they worked and think about whether they need to do more in order to progress in their learning.
- Review what students have done in the unit with an Inside-Outside Circle routine (see TB p. 21). Have students on the outside of the circle start by remembering something they did. Students can have their books with them and show their partner the page they are referring to, if necessary. The students on the inside of the circle then say something different that they did. On the signal, students rotate and try to think of something new. Encourage students to remember information they learned, as well as activities they did. After a few minutes, stop the routine and move on to the next stage.
- Draw students' attention to the heading: *Monthly Goal Reflection*. Have students look back at the end of Unit 9 and remember what their goal was. Ask students if they think they have worked hard to reach their goal and if they feel they have succeeded. Have them think about what they have done in order to achieve their goal.
- When you feel they have enough ideas, have students work individually to fill in the first two parts of the organizer. Remind them that they should write their own responses about themselves. Monitor and help as necessary. Look at what students are writing so you can tailor your classes and any additional practice to their needs.
- Ask students what they would like to work on in the future. Refer students to the final section in the graphic organizer. Tell students to think about whether they still need to work more to achieve their goal or, if they have succeeded, they should now choose a different one. Have them look back through the unit and evaluate their learning in each lesson.
- Ask students what they can do over the summer vacation to continue to work toward their goals. Brainstorm ideas for things they can do over the summer and have students choose the ones they want to do. Then have them write their ideas their plans for their next goals, for the summer ahead or the next school year. They can then share their ideas with a friend.
- As this is the last unit in the book, encourage students to think about the progress they have made over the course of the whole school year. Ask them what they enjoyed most in the book. They can discuss in small groups. Then ask the groups to report back. Praise them for all their hard work this year.

Reflection

Draw students' attention to the characters at the bottom of the page. Elicit the names and what they remember about them. Encourage students to look back through the units and discuss in pairs which units and characters they liked best and why, and to imagine if the characters have changed over the year

Put It Together

To further review and recycle the language in Units 9 and 10, play *Build a Story* on pp. 138–139. See TB p. 210 for teaching notes.

Practice
Resource Bank: Unit Test; End-of-year Test
Student's App: Vocabulary and Grammar Review

Get Ready to Read

Lesson Objectives

- to activate prior knowledge about design
- to guide inquiry and deepen understanding through an Explanation Game VTR
- to preview the reading skill of making inferences

Materials

VTR printout from the Resource Bank (Activities A, B, C, D)

Warm Up

Ask students if they have a hot drink every day. Ask them what kind of drink it is, when they have it, and why they like it.

Explanation Game

A Look at the picture. Choose a thing or idea. What is it?

- This VTR encourages students to identify interesting features in an object and explore it, through observation, questioning, and hypothesis. Ask *What can you see in the picture?* Provide vocabulary where necessary.
- Say *I think the cup handle looks interesting.* Tell students to choose something interesting in the picture. Have students look at the object in the picture together in pairs.

B What do you notice about it? Tell your partner.

- Tell students again that they are going to notice something interesting about the object.
- Say *I notice that the handle is curved. What do you notice about it?* Elicit ideas and write them on the board. Then say *What do you notice about the object?*
- Have students think about the interesting things they notice about the object, share their ideas in pairs and write their ideas in their notebooks.

C Why do you think it is that way?

- Ask *I think the handle is curved because it makes it easier to hold in your hand. Why do you think it's curved?* Elicit ideas from the class. Encourage students to give reasons for their explanations, by asking *What makes you say that?*
- Have students take turns asking their partner *Why do you think it is that way?* about all the interesting things they noticed. Encourage students to ask each other *What makes you say that?*
- Students should make a mind map or other visual representation of their ideas.

D What are some other reasons it might be that way? Share with the class.

- Prepare students to share their ideas with the class. They need to say what they noticed about the object, why they think it is this way, and their reasons for thinking this.
- Have students share their ideas. Record their ideas in a table on the board or on a poster. Encourage the class to think of and add more ideas about the explanations.

Here's an example of this part of the routine.

Teacher: What do you think the object in the picture is?
Student A: I think it's something for tea.
Teacher: Yes, it looks like it. What did you notice about it?
Student B: I noticed that its head is outside the cup and its body is inside the cup.
Teacher: Why do you think it is this way?
Student B: I think the head stops it from falling in.
Teacher: What makes you say that?
Student B: Well, it's like a clip.
Teacher: Does anyone else have any ideas about the reindeer?
Student C: I agree. I also think that the tea comes out of the holes at the bottom.
Student D: Yes, and I think it's a reindeer because it's funny. Maybe it was a present or a souvenir from a place where there are reindeer.

Transition

Ask *Do you think the owner of the cup uses it every day? Why? Why not? Do you have a special cup that you always use?*

E Think and discuss. Think of an object you use every day. What is it for? What does it look like?

- Tell students to think of something they use every day. Have students discuss their ideas in pairs and say what their object is used for and what it looks like.
- Elicit ideas from the class, encouraging students to describe their objects and say what they use them for.

Answers

Students' own answers

F Read the paragraph. Make inferences.

- Remind students of the reading skill making inferences. *Inference* means using the information we have to draw conclusions about what we don't know.
- Have students read the paragraph and think of things the text doesn't tell them about, e.g. *What is a drone? What do they do in a drone club?* Ask *Can we infer the answers to these questions?* Point out that the text tells us that people race drones, so we can infer that drones move. Elicit that the text tells us that people build drones, so perhaps students build drones and/or race them in the club.
- Have students write one inference in their books.

Answers

Students' own answers

Now read **Designing Drones**

Nonfiction: *Designing Drones—* Informational Text

Lesson Objectives

- to read an informational text about how drones are designed
- to make a personal connection to the reading

Materials
Audio Tracks 40 and 41

Warm Up

Give students two minutes to work in pairs to make a list of all the objects they can think of that fly. The pair with the most items on their list wins.

TRACK 40 TB p. 237 Reading Approach

Engage with the Text

- Display the opening spread of the reading. Ask students to notice the title, text, tables, and pictures on the page. Ask students what jumps out at them first. Which part do they want to look at more closely? Point out that often we look at any diagrams and tables before reading the longer sections of text.
- For the first reading, play the audio and have students follow along in their books. Alternatively, use the Story Player. Pause the audio to ask prediction questions, e.g. *How do you think drones can save lives?*

TRACK 41 TB p. 237 Words in Context

- After the first reading of the text, draw students' attention to the Words in Context box. Play the audio to practice the pronunciation.
- Have students brainstorm a list of strategies that they can use to find the meanings of the words, including strategies they use in L1.
- Divide the class into pairs and have each pair look at *all of the words.*
- Have them find and highlight each instance of each word in the reading and identify the type of word by looking at the form and the sentence.
- Have students swap pairs and explain words to each other, saying which strategy they used.
- Bring the class together and elicit the meanings. Discuss which strategies worked and which didn't.

aerodynamic (p. 155, adjective) The prefix *aero–* is associated with the air and flying. The sentence goes on to explain the effect of being aerodynamic; we know this is an effect, as it's preceded by *so*. Strategies to use: prefixes, surrounding words and sentences, making connections

data (p. 155 / p. 156, noun) The first part of the sentence explains that data is a synonym for *information*. Strategies to use: surrounding words and sentences, world knowledge

famine (p. 156, noun) The direct definition of this word is given in parentheses afterward. Strategy to use: surrounding words and sentences

fuel (p. 156, noun) The sentence explains how the fuel is used. World knowledge should help students understand what is needed to cook food. Strategies to use: surrounding words and sentences, world knowledge

touchscreen (p. 157, noun) This word can be broken down into its two parts, and students can use their personal experience to help. Strategies to use: word building, pictures, world knowledge

Analyze the Text and Features

- Have students read the text individually. As they read, give them tasks to do: find the lightest drone, the longest flight time, and the drone with the longest range.
- Ask comprehension questions to check understanding of the text, e.g. *What are the main uses for drones mentioned in the article?* (farming, saving lives, and transporting people)
- Tell students to find the pink callouts and to discuss the questions in pairs.
  - **Personalization** (p. 154): *Have you ever played with a drone?* Ask students what they liked or didn't like about it. If they have never played with a drone, ask them if they would like to do so.
  - **Making Connections** (p. 155): *In what other ways do you think drones could help farmers?* Have students brainstorm different ways in which drones could help farmers. Encourage them to think about other styles of drone that can carry things, e.g. seeds or store things such as fruit.
  - **Personalization** (p. 157): *How could drones help in your life?* Have students work in pairs to come up with ideas about how drones could help them. Encourage them to be imaginative and think of how a drone could help them at home, at school, and so on.

Interact with the Text

- Now that students are very familiar with the reading, have them choose a section of it and work in pairs to write a summary. Remind them to include the most important ideas and to try to use their own words.

Cool Down

Play *I'm the Expert* (see TB p. 26), having students ask and answer questions about one of the drones from the reading.

Practice **Student's App:** Story Player

Explore the Reading

Lesson Objectives

- to understand and analyze *Designing Drones* through reading comprehension activities
- to learn through CLIL (science): engineering through analyzing problems and solutions
- to make a personal connection to the reading

Warm Up

Write the names of the five different types of drones on the board and have students quickly remember what each one is used for. Then have students choose their top three, ordering from most important to least important. Then have them compare their ranking with a partner.

A Think and complete the table.

- Refer back to *Designing Drones* in the **Literacy Book**. Have students write three questions about the reading in pairs. Then have them get together with another pair and read their questions aloud. See how many students can answer correctly without looking back at the reading.
- Have students open their books and look at the table. Elicit what type of information should go in each column. Ask *What problems did farmers have?* (checking crops took too much time and energy) Have students write this example in their tables. Ask *How do drones help?* and elicit ideas from the class.
- Have students complete the rest of the table individually, looking back at the reading to help them. Check answers as a class.

Suggested Answers

Farming: (Problem in the Past) Checking crops took too much time and energy. (How Drones Have Solved the Problem) They can fly quickly over large areas of land and gather data for farmers to analyze later.
Saving Lives: (Problem in the Past) Finding, helping, and rescuing people in disaster areas took a long time and was often dangerous. (How Drones Have Solved the Problem) They can find people very quickly and can take supplies to them. Rescue workers can control the drones from far away so their lives are not in danger.
Transporting People: (Problem in the Past) Traveling is slow and unpleasant because of the amount of traffic. (How Drones Have Solved the Problem) They can fly very quickly above the traffic. For short journeys they're more eco-friendly than cars.

B Think, brainstorm, and write. What are some other problems that a drone can help solve?

- Tell students that farming, saving lives, and transporting people are three ways in which drones solve problems. However, there are more ways. Have students work in small groups to think of other problems that a drone could help solve. You could have students do an Options Explosion routine to generate ideas. Then brainstorm ideas as a class.
- Have students write their ideas in their books.

Answers

Students' own answers

C Think, write, and discuss. Look at B. Choose one of the problems and solutions. Design a drone to help solve it. Share.

- This activity explores the CLIL science focus of engineering through the analysis of problems and possible solutions, and the design of a drone.
- Write all the problems students came up with in B on the board. Tell students that they are going to choose one of these problems and design a drone to help solve that problem. Choose a problem and do an example, e.g. delivering parcels to places with bad roads. Ask students what things they need to think about. Elicit that the drone needs to be big and strong enough to carry heavy parcels and have extended battery power and fairly long autonomy (flight time) to be able to travel long distances.
- Then draw the students' attention to the table and check understanding of each feature.
- Give students time to think about what their drone needs in order to solve the problem and write their ideas in their books.

Answers

Students' own answers

Cool Down

Put students in groups and have them compare the drones they designed in C and decide which is the most useful.

Practice **Student's App:** Reading Practice

Get Ready to Read

Lesson Objectives

- to activate prior knowledge about risks in design
- to practice the reading skill of making inferences

Warm Up

To introduce the reading skill of making inferences, have students look at the VTR image from Unit 9 on pp. 136–137. Ask questions, e.g. *Who is the girl? Where is she going? How do you think she feels? What time of year is it?* Then ask students if they know the answers to these questions or if they guessed. Ask students if there are any clues in the picture that helped them guess.

A Think and discuss. Look at the title and the picture. Predict what the paragraph is about. Then read.

- Have students read the title and look at the picture. Then have them discuss in pairs what they think the paragraph is about. If possible, display the title and picture on the board.
- Check answers as a class, encouraging students to give details about what kind of information they think is in the text, e.g. *I think it's about a bridge that looks like a wave. It will tell us where the bridge is.*

Answers
Students' own answers

- Have students read the reading skill box. Then ask questions to check comprehension, e.g. *When we make inferences, what do we do first?* (We read and look at the pictures and title.) *What helps us understand the text?* (evidence from the text and things we already know) Make sure students are clear that when they infer, they use ideas from the text and pictures to help them draw conclusions. This is different from the reading skill of prediction where they simply guess based on what they see.

B Think and answer the questions.

- Display the table using the TTL and check understanding of the headings. Do the first one together. Ask *What does the text say about the size of the bridge?* Elicit the answer and write it in the table. Then ask students what they can infer about this (e.g. there must be higher bridges for cars in Singapore).
- Have students complete the table individually in their books.
- Then have students compare their inferences in pairs and say what evidence and clues support their ideas.

Suggested Answers
The Author Said Directly... : Size: It's the "highest foot bridge in Singapore." Materials: It has "strong metal arches and pieces of curved wood." Design: "People can sit and enjoy views over the island while watching the birds and plants."
I Can Infer ...: There must be other foot bridges in Singapore. People took a lot of time and care in making this bridge. Singapore is an island.

C Read, think, and write. Look back at *Designing Drones*. Make an inference.

- Give students a few minutes to look back at *Designing Drones* and find and underline some useful facts or information about the drones. They should then try to think of some questions whose answers aren't directly stated in the reading. They need to look for clues that will help them find the answers.
- Have students think about the following questions: *What do I know? What don't I know? Are there any clues that help me find the answers?* Encourage them to make an inference for each type of drone.
- Tell students they will have to write down what the author said directly and what they can infer from this.
- Elicit answers from the class.

Answers
Students' own answers

D Think and discuss. Imagine you're a designer in 2043. What are you designing?

- Tell students to imagine that it is the year 2043. Ask students how they think life will be different from now and brainstorm ideas with the class. Then tell students to imagine they are designing a new object. Have students think about what kind of machine or device might be needed in 2043. They should think about what problems there might be in the future and what current problems might be solved or have gotten worse. Once students have identified a few problems, have them choose one in pairs and decide what they can design to solve it.
- If students are interested, they could draw a quick prototype of their design. Then have students share their ideas in groups. Take a vote for the best idea.

Answer
Students' own answers

Now read **The Restore Key**

Fiction: *The Restore Key*—Science Fiction

Lesson Objectives

- to read a science fiction story about a boy whose mother built a space elevator
- make a personal connection to the reading

Materials
Audio Tracks 42 and 43

Warm Up

Play the *Yes/No Game* (see TB p. 27). Make predictions about inventions and technology from the future, e.g. *Everyone will travel by drone* or *There will be a time machine.*

TRACK 42 TB p. 237 Reading Approach

Engage with the Text

- Display the opening spread of the reading. Have students use the information to predict ideas and make inferences about the reading.
- Play the audio. Have students follow along in their books. Ask prediction questions, e.g. *Will Sky get into his mom's computer? Will the space elevator work?*

TRACK 43 TB p. 238 Words in Context

- After the first reading of the text, draw students' attention to the Words in Context box.
- Have students find and highlight each instance of each word in the reading.
- Have them identify the type of word by looking at the form and the sentence.
- Write these strategies on the board: *pictures; surrounding words and sentences; contrasting ideas; world knowledge.* Tell students there is one strategy they won't need to use (contrasting ideas).
- Have students work in pairs to discuss the words.

elevator (p. 161 / p. 162 / p. 164, noun) Dad's speech about the elevator tells us this is an alternative way to travel into space. The pictures show the designs for it. Personal experience can be used to think of ways of going up and down in a building. Strategies to use: pictures, surrounding words and sentences, world knowledge

ambitious (p. 161, adjective) This adjective describes the dream. The paragraph describes the whole idea of transforming space travel and how exciting the dream was, which tells us this isn't an easy thing to do. Strategy to use: surrounding words and sentences

code (p. 163, noun) The pictures show this is related to computers. The surrounding words and sentences tell us it's something that can go wrong and can be updated. Strategies to use: pictures, surrounding words and sentences, world knowledge

beam (p. 164, noun) The first part of the paragraph tells us it's a bright light. We can use pictures to see where the pod appears. Strategies to use: surrounding words and sentences, pictures

backup (p. 165, noun) Students know from the events of the story what information the restore key has and what it does. Strategies to use: surrounding words and sentences, world knowledge of computers

Analyze the Text and Features

- Have students read the text. While they read, ask them to find words that refer to inventions or technology.
- Ask comprehension questions to check understanding, e.g. *Why are the boy and his dad sad?* (because they thought Mom had passed away)

International English

Have students notice the two different words. Remind students that they can choose which variety to use, but they should be consistent.

- Have students find and discuss the pink callouts. Alternatively, use Group Time for discussion after students have finished reading (see TB p. 21).
  - **Text Focus** (p. 161): *Mood is the feeling we get when we read a story. How does this story make you feel?* Have students discuss how they feel in the different scenes of the story.
  - **Text Focus** (p. 163): *Notice how the mood suddenly changes again. Why?* Have students compare the first few scenes where Sky is frustated that he doesn't know much about his past to Sky's enthusiasm to build and repair the elevator. Sky and his dad become hopeful and positive. Ask *Does your mood change with the boy's feelings?*
  - **Personalization** (p. 165): *What makes you appreciate your family?* Sky's mom is grateful to Sky for bringing her back home to be with her family. Explain that *appreciate* means to be thankful for. Ask *When do you feel glad to be with your family?.*

Interact with the Text

- Have students work in groups of three to act out part of the text. Assign each group a different part of the text or different pages and roles (in some parts there will be a narrator; in other parts there will be three characters). Play the audio again and have students repeat their lines.
- Have students tell the whole story as a class.

Cool Down

Have students think about what might happen next in the story. Will Sky travel into space in the elevator? Have students vote yes or no.

Practice **Student's App:** Story Player

Explore the Reading

Lesson Objectives

- to understand and analyze *The Restore Key* through reading comprehension activities
- to practice the reading skill of making inferences
- to explore the SEL competency of relationship skills by managing and expressing emotions in relationships and respecting diverse viewpoints
- to make a personal connection to the reading

Warm Up

Play *Flashbacks* (see TB p. 25) with scenes from the story.

A Read and answer.

- Play a team game to remind students of details from the reading. Divide the class into teams. One team thinks of a true or false sentence about the reading, e.g. *Sky found the designs for the elevator* (true). The team guesses. Teams get a point for correct answers.
- Have students read and answer the questions. Encourage students to look back at the reading to help them. Tell students that they might need to infer some of the answers, e.g. their feelings. Check answers as a class.

Answers

1 Sky found his mom's computer in the garage. The password was his birthday. 2 Sky felt upset that his dad didn't tell him sooner. 3 The restore key restores the backup code for the space elevator. 4 Sky's mom felt amazed and delighted.

B Think and write. What can you infer from each sentence?

- Tell students that they are going to practice the reading skill of making inferences. Display the table on the board. Elicit that the first column tells us what the characters said. Ask *What can we infer from this information?* Remind students to think about *What do I know? What don't I know? Are there any clues that help me find the answer?*
- Discuss the first one together. Ask *Why didn't Dad tell Sky what happened?* Elicit that he thought Sky was too young to understand. Write this in the second column. Ask students what they can infer from this.
- Have students complete the table in their books. Check answers as a class.

Suggested Answers

1 (I Already Know …) Dad couldn't tell Sky because he thought he was too young to understand / it would upset him. (I Can Infer …) Dad cares about Sky's feelings.
2 (I Already Know …) Sky wanted to build his mom's elevator. (I Can Infer …) Sky is good with technology.
3 (I Already Know …) Sky and his dad just rebuilt the elevator. (I Can Infer …) Someone is in the elevator and working it.

C Think and discuss. In the story, Sky and his dad disagree and talk about how they feel. How do you communicate difficult feelings with your friends and family?

- Students are going to explore the SEL competency of relationship skills by managing and expressing emotions in relationships and respecting diverse viewpoints.
- Ask students what Sky and his dad disagree about. Elicit that Sky was upset because his dad didn't tell him about his mom's project to build the elevator. Ask *Why didn't Sky's dad didn't tell him?* Elicit answers from the class (Sky's dad was sad that his wife had disappeared and he found it difficult to talk about her; he thought that Sky was too young to understand). Ask *How did Sky and his dad deal with their disagreement?* (they talked about their feelings).
- Ask *What kinds of uncomfortable feelings do you have? How do you discuss these feelings with your friends and family?* In pairs, have students talk about their personal experiences.
- Have some students share their ideas.

Answers

Students' own answers

Literary Term: Word Choice: Degrees of Intensity

Think and discuss the different meaning of each word choice.

- Look at the explanation of *degree of intensity*. Remind students that in Unit 9 they studied adverbs of intensity, which make words stronger or weaker. Tell students that sometimes we can choose different words to do the same thing.
- Have students look at the first question and the three options. Ask *Which word refers to the strongest light?* (dazzling). The words appear in order from less to more powerful.
- Have students work in pairs to discuss the meanings of the words and notice how the intensity increases.
- Check answers. Have students look for more examples.

Answers

Students' own answers
Examples showing degrees of intensity in the reading: went wrong/completely destroyed, surprised/horrified, big/huge/enormous, pleased/amazed/delighted

Cool Down

Tell students to imagine they travel in the space elevator. When they get to the top and come out of the elevator, what do they see? Have students draw a picture and/or describe what they imagine in pairs.

Practice **Resource Bank:** Literary Term Printout
Student's App: Reading Practice; Literary Term Practice

Think Together

Lesson Objectives

- to make connections between the readings
- to explore the key concept: How can design solve problems?
- to reflect on the unit and provide personal thoughts and opinions

Materials

A digital alarm clock or other everyday piece of technology (B)

Warm Up

Tell students to think of one similarity and one difference between the passenger drone and the space elevator. Encourage students to think creatively.

A Complete the table using the details from *Designing Drones* and *The Restore Key*.

- Have students think about the form and function of the inventions from the readings. Note that *form* refers to what something looks like and *function* means what it can do.
- Give students enough time to look back at the two readings and complete the table. Then check answers.

Suggested Answers

Form: The Passenger Drone: The passenger drone is small. It looks like a flying car. The Space Elevator: It has a door and a seat. It has a touchscreen. It is beautiful. It's very tall. It looks like a tower. There's a pod inside that goes up and down.
Function: The Passenger Drone: It can carry one person through the air to different places. It can travel at 100 km. per hour. It can stay in the air for a maximum of 30 minutes. The Space Elevator: It can carry passengers into space.

B Think about a piece of technology you use every day. Think about the form and function. What works well? What could be better? How could it be better? Do a Numbered Heads Together routine.

- Students are going to apply what they have learned in the unit about design and discuss the key concept question: *How can design solve problems?*
- Do an example with the class. Choose an everyday item, e.g. a digital alarm clock. Have students describe its form and function, e.g. (Form) *It's square and made of plastic.* (Function) *It makes a noise to wake you up in the morning.*
- Show students how it works, e.g. by setting the alarm and having it sound. Ask *Do you think it works well? How can it be improved?*
- Have students get into groups or four for the routine and choose a piece of technology.
- Set up the Numbered Heads Together routine (see TB p. 20) Have students discuss their ideas.

C Think about the piece of technology you talked about in B. Design a solution to improve the form and function.

- Tell students that they are going to think about how they can solve the problems they discussed in B.
- Students will work individually for the first step. Have them think and write down their ideas in note form.
- Have students get into their groups and compare ideas.

Answers

Students' own answers

My Reading Journal

How has reading these texts made you feel about the future?

This question encourages students to give a personal response to what they have learned. Give students time to think and write their questions, then discuss in pairs.

Suggested Answer

I am excited to know what kinds of machines people will design in the future. I would love to travel in a drone.

Which was your favorite unit in this book. Why?

This question encourages students to give a personal response to the whole book. Have students look back through the units and find things they enjoyed, then write about their favorite unit in their books. Elicit ideas.

Suggested Answer

My favorite unit was Unit 9 because I love reading stories and I enjoyed "The Weaver."
Congratulate students on the progress they have made this year. Remind them that they can now read, understand, and analyze long texts in English, so they should be proud of themselves!

Choose an object from the unit. Then play the Explanation Game.

Use the TTL to project the instructions for the Explanation Game onto the board. Tell students to choose something from another page. Then repeat the Explanation Game routine. Encourage students to notice as many things as possible about their new object and think about how it connects to the theme of the unit. Do an example first, e.g. *I pick the key from "The Restore Key." I notice that it is small and square, and it looks like a chip because it has lines and circles.*

Cool Down

Have students talk in pairs about their favorite things from the whole book. This could be an activity, a reading, an extension, or just an image.

Practice **Resource Bank:** Unit Test; End-of-year Test
Student's App: Key Concept Practice

I've Just ...

Lesson Objectives

- to review vocabulary from Units 1 and 2, focusing on sports and animals
- to review grammar from Units 1 and 2, focusing on indefinite pronouns and the present perfect with *already*, *just*, *yet*, *for*, and *since*
- to practice communication and fluency skills

Warm Up

Ask students *What is something you have just done?* Elicit as many different answers as possible starting with *I've just …* Encourage students to use their imaginations to think of as many ideas as they can.

How to Play

- Students are going to play a game in pairs in which they choose pictures from the page and make sentences or questions about them. Read through the instructions on the **Language Book** page as a class. More detailed instructions on how to play are given below.
- Students play in pairs, sharing one Student Book to play. No other materials are needed to play.
- Students take turns choosing a picture and saying a sentence about that picture. They should attempt to use at least one of the words in white from the page in their sentence.
- Their partner then asks a question and they continue the conversation with their friend for one minute, asking and answering questions about the picture.
- Have students write their name at the top of one of the points charts on p. 35. Each time they produce a correct sentence, students should color in another square on their points chart in whatever color they want.
- Before students start playing the game, have two students read the examples on the page. Point out the use of *just* and elicit that this sentence is worth two points. Explain that if they use one of the words in white from the middle of the page, they win two points. If they don't use one of the words, they get one point. Elicit that the example question is also worth two points, because the student has used *anything*.

Elicit a few more examples using different words from the page:

Student A: The horse has just had a baby horse! (2 points)
Student B: Oh, yes! Everyone will be so happy. (2 points)
Student A: I agree. Do you think it will have anything to eat? (2 points)
Student B: I don't know. Maybe it will drink milk. (1 point)

- Tell students that the winner is the student who gets to 20 points first. Students keep choosing pictures until one player reaches 20 points. If students have already attempted talking about all the pictures before either reaches 20 points, they can try making new sentences for pictures they have already tried.

Cool Down

Have students choose their favorite picture from the page. Then have students go around the class trying to find someone who likes the same picture. Encourage them to say why they like it.

The Detectives Game

Lesson Objectives

- to review vocabulary from Units 3 and 4, focusing on jobs, skills, and crime
- to review grammar from Units 3 and 4, focusing on reported speech, infinitives of purpose, and tag questions
- to practice communication and fluency skills

Materials

Spinner and Counters printout from the Resource Bank (one spinner per group; one counter per player)

Warm Up

Ask students to remember what a detective does in his/her job and what skills and equipment are needed. Write their ideas on the board in three columns.

How to Play

- Note: to save time, download and cut out the spinners and counters before the lesson. Ensure you have one spinner per group and one counter for each student.
- Students are going to play a board game where they move around the board and answer questions. They may move forward or miss a turn. Read through the instructions on the **Language Book** page as a class. More detailed instructions on how to play are given below.
- Students can play in pairs or in groups of three or four. Each student has a counter. Students should color their counter a different color from those of the other people in their group.
- Students take turns spinning the spinner and moving around the board, placing their counter. When they stop on a space, they must answer the question or follow the instructions. If they answer correctly, they move forward one space and then the next player goes (only one question or move per turn). If they don't answer correctly, they stay on that space. Tell students that if another player lands on the same square as someone before them, they must give a different answer or answer a different question.
- Tell students that the first player to reach the *Finish* wins.
- Before students start playing the game, write an example on the board: *Mrs. Slim and Mr. Slim are the victims. Explain what you think has happened.* Elicit possible answers. Encourage full sentences, e.g. *I think someone broke into their home and stole their money.*

Here is an example:

Student A: Four. One, two, three, four. You use this to … look for fingerprints!

Student B: That's right! Move forward one space.

Student C: OK. My turn. Two. One, two. Describe how the victims feel. Hmm. Well, I think they're angry because someone took all their personal things.

Cool Down

Have students look back at the game and find one square they found easy to answer and one they found difficult. Then have them compare with a partner.

Picture Puzzles

Lesson Objectives

- **to review vocabulary from Units 5 and 6, focusing on emotions, eco-tourism, and sustainable living**
- **to review grammar from Units 5 and 6, focusing on modal verbs of deduction, adverbs of probability, first conditional with modal verbs, and *too* + adjective + infinitive; adjective + *enough* + infinitive; *enough* + noun + infinitive**
- **to practice communication and fluency skills**

Warm Up

Tell students to draw something that makes them delighted, something that makes them disappointed, and something that makes them furious. Have them compare their pictures with friends and see if they have drawn similar things.

How to Play

- Students are going to play a game in pairs in which they choose a picture from the page and make sentences about it. Read through the instructions on the **Language Book** page as a class. More detailed instructions on how to play are given below.
- Students play in pairs, sharing one Student Book to play. No other materials are needed to play.
- Students take turns to secretly choose a picture and think of a sentence about it using one of the words from the jigsaw puzzle pieces. Student A says the sentence to Student B, who guesses which picture their partner is describing. If Student B correctly identifies the picture, they win a point. Then they choose a different picture and use a different prompt word to describe it.
- Have students write their name at the top of one of the points charts on p. 86 or p. 87. Each time they guess which picture their friend is describing, students should color in another puzzle piece on their points chart, in whatever color they want.
- Before students start playing the game, have two students read the examples on the page. Then elicit a few more examples using different words from the page:

Student A: Perhaps the boy is furious because his friend won't give him the ball.

Student B: Hmm … Picture 10.

Student C: Correct!

- The winner is the student who first gets to 20 points. Students keep choosing pictures until one player reaches 20 points. If students have talked about all the pictures before either have reached 20 points, students may try making new sentences for pictures that already been attempted.

Cool Down

Have students talk in pairs about how each picture makes them feel, e.g. *Picture 1 makes me feel nervous because I think the girl is worried about her test.*

Guessword

Lesson Objectives

- to review vocabulary from Units 7 and 8, focusing on first aid and emergencies and ancient civilizations
- to review grammar from Units 7 and 8, focusing on the simple present passive, reflexive pronouns, past modal verbs of obligation, and the simple past passive
- to practice communication and fluency skills

Materials

Playing Cards printout from the Resource Bank, one set of cards per group

Warm Up

Give pairs two minutes to remember as many things as they can about the Ancient Romans. Students should make a list in their notebooks. They should then compare their lists with another pair.

How to Play

- Note: to save time, download and cut out the cards and counters before the lesson.
- Students are going to play a card game. Print one copy of the accompanying printout cards for each group of four students. If possible, print the cards in different colors for each group. Cut out the cards and shuffle.
- Give each group of four a set of cards. Go through the instructions on the **Language Book** page. More detailed instructions on how to play are given below.
- Students play in teams of two. Student A takes a card, making sure that no one else sees what is written on the card. Student A gives a clue describing the word or phrase in capital letters on the card and tries to get the other three students to guess the word.
- Some cards have another word or phrase in lower case. In this case, students must use this word or phrase in their sentence. If their teammate doesn't guess after the first clue, they can give more clues.
- The first team to guess the word correctly moves forward two spaces on the game board. The first team to reach *Finish* wins the game.
- Students have only 30 seconds to guess. If no one guesses correctly, both teams stay where they are on the game board. Have one student in each group of four keeps time.

Here is an example:

Student A: This is a place that is evacuated when there is a disaster.
Student B: Hmm … Is it a house?
Student A: No, a house is one example.
Student C: It's a building!
Student A: Correct!

Cool Down

Play *Correct the Teacher* (see TB. 25). Call out sentences about the things on the cards or other vocabulary from Units 7 and 8, e.g. *A first responder is the last person to arrive at the scene of an accident.*

Build a Story

Lesson Objectives

- to review vocabulary from Units 9 and 10, focusing on storytelling
- to review grammar from Units 9 and 10, focusing on the second conditional, reported questions, and agreeing with *too*, *so*, *either*, and *neither*
- to practice communication and fluency skills

Warm Up

Have students sit in a circle and tell a collaborative, one-sentence story. Write the story opener *Once upon a time there was a …* on the board and have the first student call out a word to add, and then the second student, and so on. Write the words on the board. Each student around the circle adds one single word to keep the sentence going as long as possible, e.g. *Once upon a time there was a* (Student A) *girl* (Student B) *who* (Student C) *had* (Student D) *long* (Student E) *blond* (Student F) *hair* (Student G) *and …*

How to Play

- Students are going to play a game where they build a story by choosing elements from different sections on the page. Read through the instructions on the **Language Book** page as a class. More detailed instructions on how to play are given below.
- Students play in pairs. Students write a number from 1 to 4 in each of the boxes A to G. Make sure that students don't look at the rest of the page as they are doing this—their choices should be random.
- Students then look again at the boxes A to G on the page to see what basic elements their story has, according to the numbers they have chosen.
- Then they think of more details to add to their stories, discussing their ideas and making notes in their notebooks.
- When each pair has lots of ideas, they use their notes to tell the story to another pair of students.
- Before students start playing, do an example with the class. Have two students choose a number from 1 to 4 and use these to do an example with A and B.

Here is an example:

Student A: Three.

Student B: *A thoughtful chef called Bertie. No one was better at cooking than Bertie.* What does Bertie look like?

Student A: He's an old man with gray hair.

Student B: OK. Let's choose a place. (Student C), give me a number.

Student C: One.

Student B: *Under the bed.* So Bertie the chef is under the bed. What is he doing under the bed? Why is he there?

- When they have finished, they can play again to build another story.

Cool Down

Play *What's the Scene?* (see TB p. 27). Have students choose a picture from Unit 9 or 10.

Process Writing

Generating Ideas

Lesson Objectives

- to learn about process writing: generating ideas

This is the first in a series of lessons that help students develop their writing skills and become better writers. Process writing breaks down the stages of writing into carefully scaffolded steps. Process writing encourages students to write with better organization, structure, and accuracy.

In this lesson, students are going to learn different ways of generating ideas.

- Draw students' attention to the first sentence in the Generating Ideas explanation box. Elicit that the first stage in writing is thinking of ideas about the topic they are going to write about. When they have lots of ideas, they can then choose the best ideas to include in their writing. Explain that it is important to think of lots of ideas, even ideas we don't agree with, because sometimes we need to discuss different sides of a topic or argument.
- Then have students read the second sentence. Elicit different types of writing, e.g. stories, letters, articles, and who reads each one. Note that we need to think about what the reader needs to know. Tell students to imagine they are writing a party invitation. Elicit what the reader needs to know (the date, time, and place of the party).

A Think and discuss. *What are some ways you use to get ideas and how do you write them down?* Read and check (✔). What are the advantages and disadvantages of each one for you?

- Have students look at the different ways of getting ideas and choose the ones they use. Then have them compare with a friend.
- Brainstorm ideas about what each way of getting ideas might involve, e.g. having a conversation, doing a survey, having a formal debate.
- Ask students if they prefer to think of ideas by themselves or working with a friend. Point out that it may be useful to use all three methods of generating ideas. Students might want to spend some time thinking on their own first, then discussing their ideas with a friend, and then doing some research to find out the things they don't know.
- Then have students look at the three ways of noting the ideas and say which ones they like to use. Remind students that it is good to use a variety of different techniques.

Suggested Answers

Getting ideas

Advantages: discussing with a friend can help overcome an initial lack of ideas, and researching can help you find out things you don't know, especially when you don't know much about the topic. Some students might prefer to work alone and need thinking time to come up with ideas. Disadvantages: Some students have trouble generating ideas by themselves, some students don't enjoy discussing ideas with a partner, and research can take a long time.

Noting ideas

Advantages: a list is a quick and easy format, mind maps are visual and can help organize ideas, and pictures can be a simple way of expressing meaning. Disadvantages: in a list, your ideas are not organized, and pictures can take a long time and be difficult to do if you are not good at drawing.

B You're going to write a blog post with the title *Is My Life Like Yours?* Compare your life with the life of someone like you but in another country. Choose two ways from A to get and note ideas. Brainstorm as many as you can.

- Ask *What is a blog post? What kinds of things do people blog about? Elicit answers.*
- Give students plenty of time to think of ideas. They can work individually, in pairs, or in small groups. Remind them to try two different ways to get ideas.

Answers

Students' own answers

C Think and discuss. Which way of getting and noting ideas do you prefer? Why?

- Have students discuss their thoughts about and experiences with the two ways of getting and noting ideas they used in B.
- Have some students explain why they liked (or didn't like) the different ways of getting ideas and taking notes.

D Write a paragraph for your blog post comparing one part of your life with your friends'. Use your notes from your preferred method in B.

- Give students time to write their blog post using their notes. Remind them that they only need to write about one part of their life, e.g. the type of food they eat or their daily routine.
- Look at the writing callout. Ask students if their notes for B were in full sentences. Note that when we brainstorm, we just need to write down the key ideas and words we want to use.

Planning

Lesson Objectives

- to learn about process writing: planning
- to practice generating ideas

Materials

Sticky notes and large pieces of paper (C)

This is the second in a series of lessons that help students with process writing. In this lesson, students are going to learn how to plan their writing.

- Draw students' attention to the first sentence in the planning explanation box. Tell students that once they have lots of ideas, they need to choose the best ideas to include them in their writing. They will need to think about how to organize their ideas so that the reader can understand them.
- Then have students read the second sentence. Students are familiar with different types of texts from other levels: letter to a friend, email, postcard, book report, diary entry, experiment, poems, character profile, story, anecdote, description (of a place). Choose one or two of these and ask students what kind of information the reader needs to know for each.

A You're going to write an email to a friend with the subject line *The Funniest Thing That Has Ever Happened to Me*. Choose a way to get as many ideas as you can from p. 140 and make notes.

- Have students remember the different ways of getting ideas and choose the one they want to use. Give students a few minutes to brainstorm ideas, either individually or in groups. Remind them to choose a method of noting their ideas.
- Ask students which ways of generating ideas they used and if they think they made the right choice. Tell students that they can choose a new way of generating ideas during a brainstorming activity if they feel that the one way they chose is not working for them.

Answers

Students' own answers

B Look at your notes. Which ideas are good? Are there any ideas you don't want to include? Discuss your decisions with a friend. Does he/she agree with you?

- Ask students how they know which ideas are good. Elicit that the ideas they include should all be related in some way. If students have several possible ideas for the funniest thing that ever happened to them, they need to choose one and think about how they can tell the story. Have students look at their ideas and cross out any they don't want to include.
- Then have students discuss their ideas with a friend. They should try to explain how their ideas connect with each other, and why they decided not to use others. Encourage students to ask each other questions and make suggestions, e.g. *I think that idea is interesting. Why don't you include it?*

Answers

Students' own answers

C Think about the features of an email. Check (✔) the features that you will include.

- Have students discuss their ideas in pairs. Ask students if they have ever seen an email. Show students a real email, if necessary. Ask students what information we need to include in an email.
- Have students read the list and check the features they think should be in an email. Have them compare their answers in pairs before checking with the class. For those features that are not usually in emails, ask students in which kind of writing they might find them, e.g. rhyme and rhythm in poems.

Answers

3; 4; 5; 6; 8

D Complete the graphic organizer using your notes in B. Do you have enough details? Are the details in the best order?

- Elicit examples of what information should go in each section of the graphic organizer. Then give students time to write their ideas in the organizer.
- Have students compare their plans in pairs or groups. Specifically, encourage them to consider: *Does the plan make sense? Is there anything you could add to make it better?* If students think of more ideas, they can add them now.

Answers

Students' own answers

E Write the greeting and opening paragraph of your email.

- Give students time to write the beginning of their emails or have them write them for homework.
- Then ask students if they think the graphic organizer helped them organize their ideas.
- Have students tell each other about what they wrote in their emails in groups. Then have students in each group choose the funniest story.
- Draw students' attention to the writing callout. Have students look at their graphic organizers and check whether they have enough ideas in each section. Point out that they should probably have the most ideas in the *Details* sections.

Drafting

Lesson Objectives

- to learn about process writing: drafting
- to practice generating ideas and planning

This is the third in a series of lessons that help students with process writing. In this lesson, students are going to learn how to write a draft.

- Draw students' attention to the first two sentences in the drafting explanation box. Tell students that sometimes we plan some good ideas but realize that they don't fit when we do our writing. Point out that a draft is like a practice run and is always followed by a revision stage where we can insert new ideas, cross out any ideas we don't like, move ideas to a different place, or change words and expressions.
- Then have students read the last sentence and elicit that a draft does not have to be neat and tidy; in fact, your writing will probably be better if your revision has lots of changes!

A You're going to write a short persuasive essay with the title *Why My Family Is Important to Me*. Brainstorm lots of ideas (p140). Then choose which ones to include and make a plan (p141).

- Have students remember the different ways of getting ideas and choose the one they are going to use. Encourage them to try out different ones for each of these lessons.
- Then have students use a planning technique. Students could use a graphic organizer, table, or mind map. Give students time to decide which ideas to include and organize their ideas.

Answers
Students' own answers

B Write a first draft very quickly. Don't worry about spelling, grammar, or organizing your ideas. Try to write at least 50 words.

- Tell students they are going to do a fast-writing activity where they will write their ideas in their books individually. Do this activity at the same time as the students. They will appreciate you joining in and find it more fun.
- Tell students that it doesn't matter if they make mistakes in spelling or grammar at this stage—the important thing is to get their ideas down on paper.
- Give students up to three minutes to write their first drafts, using their ideas from A. Students should try to continue writing until the time is up.
- Have students discuss their drafts in pairs. Have students discuss which ideas they want to keep or why they got stuck. Encourage students to look back at their plans to check they have included all their ideas.
- Ask some students to share their ideas with the class. Make a point of praising inventiveness and detail.

Answers
Students' own answers

- Draw students' attention to the writing callout. Ask students if they enjoyed the fast writing activity. Were they able to think of ideas? Tell students that they only need to spend one or two minutes doing this.

C Read and revise your draft. Use a checklist like this.

- Go through the list of features and check understanding. Tell students to check the things that are true about their draft. Have students look at their draft and analyze the ideas and their order. Tell students that they can go through this checklist several times, making changes to their draft as necessary.

Answers
Students' own answers

D Think about your reader. Which topic sentence do you think is the most interesting for an essay about family? Think and discuss.

- Remind students about the basic structure of an essay (four paragraphs including an introduction, first idea, second idea, and conclusion). Ask them who the reader is and remind them to keep that reader in mind.
- Explain the need to grab the reader's attention at the beginning of the essay and also at the beginning of every paragraph. The first sentence should use the topic of the text or paragraph.
- Have students discuss the examples given for merit and interest. Students should notice the different styles and decide if they're all valid as topic sentences. Elicit what makes a good topic sentence.

Answers
1 The sentence is too generic and impersonal.
2 Starting with a question can encourage readers to read on to find the answer. 3 Starting with a story might make the reader want to know what happened and how the story is related to the title. 4 A gerund with a negative idea is a strong statement.
2, 3, or 4 would make a good topic sentence.

E Write a topic sentence for your essay, and rewrite your paragraph.

- Give students time to think of their own topic sentence, using their ideas from the brainstorm and planning, and then have them rewrite their paragraph based on their checklist in C.

Editing and Publishing

Lesson Objectives

- to learn about process writing: editing and publishing
- to practice generating ideas, planning, and drafting

This is the last in a series of lessons that help students with process writing. In this lesson, students are going to learn different ways of editing and publishing their writing.

- Draw students' attention to the first sentence in the editing and publishing explanation box. Point out that this is the stage at which they can add, delete, reorder, and replace words with more effective synonyms as necessary. Ask students what kinds of things they think they should check and elicit ideas from the class.
- Then have students read the other two sentences and elicit that the final draft should be neat and tidy. This is the piece of writing they will share with their readers. Highlight the importance of checking your own work. Explain that in order to do this, it's important to think differently—as though you were the reader, not the writer.

A Put on your editor's hat! Find and correct 16 more errors. What kind of errors are they?

- Point out that when we edit, we are looking for errors that we might not have noticed when we were writing our drafts.
- Look at the example together. Elicit that the student forgot to start his letter with *Dear*. Then have students read the letter and find 16 more errors. Give them a few minutes to do this and then have them compare their answers with a friend.
- Check answers as a class. Then draw students' attention to the table and the five columns. Point out that *Dear* is a text feature of letters. Then have students work in pairs to categorize the errors. They should write the **corrected** words or phrases in the table.
- Display the completed table for students to check their answers.

Answers

Dear Grandma,
How are you**?** I'm sorry I haven't writ**t**en sooner. I've be**e**n so busy! You know my friend Sam, who play**s** basketball? His team is in the final**.** **L**ast weekend I went to watch—it was very exc**i**ting! "Come on, Sam**!"** Sam**'**s team played well but the other team was to**o** good and they scored more **points**. **H**e's my best friend—we get **o**n really well. Have you and **G**randpa done anything inter**e**sting recently?
Table: Text feature: missing *Dear*; Spelling: writ**t**en, exc**i**ting, to**o**, inter**e**sting; Punctuation: How are you**?**, final**.**, **L**ast, Sam**!**, Sam**!"**, Sam**'**s, **H**e's, **G**randpa; Vocabulary: **points**, get **on**; Grammar: I've be**en**, play**s**

B You're going to write an article with the title *My Dreams and How I Can Make Them Happen*. Follow the steps of Process Writing (pp140–142).

- Tell students they are going to write an article using all the steps in process writing. Quickly review ways of generating ideas (p. 140), planning (p. 141), and drafting (p. 142).
- Give students plenty of time to follow all the steps. You may wish to assign stage 3, drafting, for homework. Remind students to use the checklist (p. 142) .

Answers

Students' own answers

C Read and edit your article. Check it for errors and text features.

- Ask students what text features should be in an article. Refer them back to the Write About It lesson (p. 108) to find out. Common features of an article include a title, facts, causes and effects, and phrases like *as a result of*, *because of*, *consequently*, and *due to*.
- Have students check their writing for the different types of errors in the table. The first few times, students can go through their writing several times, each time looking for a different type of error. .

Answers

Students' own answers

- Look at the writing callout. Have students read their article to a friend. Did they or their friend notice any errors? Note that our brains sometimes filter out errors as we read so we can't see them. If we try saying the words on the page, sometimes we can notice other errors.

D Rewrite your article using your best handwriting or the clearest electronic format. Now you're ready to publish!

- Ask students if they prefer to writing their final versions by hand or on a computer. Remind students that their writing must be very clear and easy to read. For some types of writing, they may wish to include illustrations, photos, or text boxes or use different colors and typefaces. All of these can be included by hand or on a computer.

Audio Scripts

Language Book

For the vocabulary drills, where an alternative exists in British English, this is noted in parentheses next to the corresponding American English word/phrase. Audio recordings of the British English pronunciation and words/phrases are available through the **Teacher's App** on **Navio**.

Language Review

TRACK 1

A Look and write what Miguel and his friends saw at the Viking Museum. Then listen to Miguel talking to his mom about the trip. Match the names to the people.

Mom: Who's the girl next to you in the photo, Miguel?
Miguel: The one who's talking to the trader? She knocked the bowls onto the ground. She looks so embarrassed! That's Anna!
Mom: The trader looks pretty stressed! … Oh, what's wrong with George? Why is he upset?
Miguel: He dropped his ice cream! It was OK. We got him another one. It was even bigger—he was very grateful!
Mom: Where's Daisy? Oh—she's lifting up that big sword.
Miguel: Yes, she was really nervous at first—but it didn't take long for her to feel more confident.
Mom: Who's the boy on his own? Don't you think he looks lonely?
Miguel: That's Rob. He just likes to be on his own sometimes. He was probably thinking about the presentation we have to do about our trip to the museum. He loves Vikings!
Mom: And who's that girl with the necklace?
Miguel: That's Katie. She loved wearing it. She felt so proud!
Mom: You had a great day at the Viking Museum, Miguel!
Miguel: Yes, we did!

TRACK 2

A Read and complete the tag questions. Listen and check.

Girl 1: You painted the background, didn't you?
Miguel: Yes—twice! First they said green—then they wanted it yellow!
Girl 2: I don't have to sing, do I?
Girl 1: No! You're our best dancer!
Boy 1: He should finish that later, shouldn't he?
Boy 2: Yes, he should! Aaaargh!
Girl 3: Eeeeeeeeek!
Boy 3: She won't do that tonight, will she?
Boy 4: I hope not …
Boy 5: We're all ready, aren't we?
Boy 6 and Girl 4: Yes, we are!

Unit 1

TRACK 3

Unit 1, Vocabulary
A Listen. Which sports do Nishi and Miguel try?

Mom: OK, kids, we've got an hour to explore. Try as many different activities as you can—and have fun … but be careful!
Nishi: Oh, look at those two trampolining!
Miguel: They're jumping so high!
Ugh, Rollerblading's a lot harder than it loooooooks! …Ouch!
Nishi: Here, let me help you up.
Miguel: Thanks, Nishi.
Nishi: Don't you just love a challenge?!
Miguel: Well, yes sort of … (sigh) I keep falling down. It's a good thing I have pads to protect my knees and elbows and a helmet for my head! But you're really good! How did you become such an expert?
Nishi: I've practiced—a lot! I think you're doing pretty well. As a beginner you just have to take your time and learn the moves. That way you'll build your confidence and get better more quickly.
Miguel: Hmm, maybe you're right.
Nishi: Hey, do you want to try something else now? Maybe the BMX racing, those bikes look cool!
Miguel: Hmm, it looks like the race has already started. What about rappelling?
Nishi: Oh! Swinging down the wall on a rope looks a bit scary to me…
Miguel: Don't worry, it'll be fun! Come on—keep your helmet and pads on. Here, you'll need a harness, too—it keeps you safe when you're high up. I'm an expert, you know!

TRACK 4

Unit 1, Vocabulary
B Find and number the words in A. Then listen and check.

1 rappelling (British English: abseiling)
2 BMX racing
3 trampolining
4 snowboarding
5 beginner
6 harness
7 rope
8 skiing
9 expert
10 pads
11 Rollerblading
12 helmet

TRACK 5

Unit 1, Vocabulary
C Close your eyes. Listen, visualize, and say.

You've arrived at the Sports Experience. There are so many great activities to try! Let's start with rappelling. Put on your harness. Is it on correctly? Make sure it's tight. Say "harness." Now, hold on to the rope. How does it feel as it moves through your fingers? Say "rope."
You're moving backwards, over the edge slowly, and then down, down, down … Say "rappelling."
What next? How about Rollerblading? Imagine you're a beginner. Stand up carefully … Oh, no! You fell over! Say "beginner."
Now get up and try again. Move slowly and carefully … now more quickly and confidently. Say "Rollerblading."
Ooooh! Let's try trampolining. Bounce slowly at first, then faster and harder so that it feels like you're flying. Say "trampolining."
Look! A BMX race is about to start … Choose a helmet and put it on—you need to be safe. Say "helmet." Next the pads. Put them on your knees—right, then left. Say "pads."
Now, get on your bike and go! Who's winning? Jump into the air with your bike—how does it feel? Say "BMX racing."
What about snow sports? Can you snowboard? Imagine standing on your board and sliding down on the snow. Say "snowboarding."
Finally, let's go skiing. Brrrrr, it's cold, but you'll soon be warm as you race down the hill. Say "skiing."
You're an expert at this—turn sideways to make yourself stop. Say "expert."

TRACK 6

Unit 1, Vocabulary
E Listen and write. Then watch and say.
Back to School Challenge

"Isn't that too hard for you?"
Too hard for me?! Says who?"

Never been on a trampoline?
Rollerblading might be more your scene.
Jump up high like a kangaroo.
Climb like a monkey. Try something new!

If snowboarding's the sport for you,
Pick up some pads, a helmet, too.
Just a beginner? Not for long.
Practice hard—get fit, get strong!

Is it skiing that you're into?
You're an expert—you know how to!
Hello, new year! Hello, new you!
Find the challenge that you want to do.

TRACK 7

Unit 1, Vocabulary
F Pronunciation. Listen and say. Copy the linking. Find other examples of linking in the rap.

been-on (2x),
jump–up (2x),
like a (2x)

TRACK 8

Unit 1, Explore Language
A Listen and read. What does Jordan learn about being good at sports?

Miguel: Wow, that was even faster than last time. I was watching you. You're an expert at skating, Jordan!
Jordan: I know.
Miguel: Wow, that was awesome! You're an expert at skiing, too, Jordan.
Jordan: I know.
But I'm looking for a new sport. Can I look at your snowboard?
Miguel: Oh, yes, of course. Snowboarding's difficult, but a lot of fun. I've done it for about two years.
Jordan: I haven't tried snowboarding before. But I'm really good at skating, skateboarding, and skiing. I'll find it easy, I'm sure …

Miguel: Why don't you give it a try?
Jordan: Aaaaaaaaah! Ouch! Maybe snowboarding isn't so easy …
Miguel: Are you going to go back to skiing?
Jordan: Oh, no—I love a new challenge! Where can I get some lessons, Miguel?
Miguel: Come and meet my snowboarding instructor!
Instructor: Good job, Jordan!
Jordan: I thought skiing was fun, but this is even better!
Miguel: I know!

TRACK 9
Unit 1, Explore Language
D Listen and say.
1 You're an expert at skiing.
2 I'm not taking off my harness.
3 Was she wearing a helmet? Yes, she was.
4 Have you ever tried Rollerblading? No, we haven't.
5 They're going to fall off!

TRACK 10
Unit 1, Global Citizenship
A Listen to Aida and Rahul talk about helping others. What does Rahul challenge Aida to do?
Aida: A man from Children Are Our Future came to talk to our school yesterday.
Rahul: Oh, what does Children Are Our Future do?
Aida: It's a charity that helps children all over the world. It raises money to buy educational equipment for schools. I'm going to help!
Rahul: Oh—are you going to do the fun run to raise money for them?
Aida: Fun run? What's that?
Rahul: You run for five kilometers and …
Aida: Run? No way! I'll give them some money.
Rahul: But they'll get a lot more money if you take part in the race and get people to sponsor you. You could ask people to give a certain amount of money for every kilometer you run.
Aida: Yes, but what if I have to give up before the end? Five kilometers is a very long way …
Rahul: I used to think that. Six months ago, I couldn't even run one kilometer! But I set myself a challenge and I started to train. I got better and better. Now I can run five kilometers easily!
Aida: That's great, Rahul! But you love sports and I'm not a good runner. **Rahul:** I can help you get fit. We can run as a team.
Aida: OK. Let's do it!

TRACK 11
Unit 1, Global Citizenship
B Look at the pictures and definitions in A and write. Then listen and check.
1 get fit
2 race
3 team
4 give up
5 train
6 raise money
7 sponsor
8 charity
9 fun run
10 take part in

TRACK A
Unit 1, Global Citizenship Listen and say. What do you think of when you hear these words? Talk with your friend.
Get fit. Say "get fit."
Race. Say "race."
Team. Say "team."
Give up. Say "give up."
Train. Say "train."
Raise money. Say "raise money."
Sponsor. Say "sponsor."
Charity. Say "charity."
Fun run. Say "fun run."
Take part in. Say "take part in."

TRACK 12
Unit 1, Global Citizenship
D Now listen to Elsa. How did she challenge herself?
My name's Elsa. I arrived here from Sweden last summer. Coming from a different country, it was an exciting change—but also a little scary!
We arrived at the start of summer vacation, so I didn't go to school at first. I was on my own a lot, and I actually felt quite lonely.
In my old town, I used to play basketball. I really missed my friends on the team—and going to train every week. Eventually, my mom told me to stop feeling sorry for myself and do something about it! So … My mom's always trying to get fit, so she suggested we put on our sneakers and go to the park. When we arrived, we saw some girls playing soccer. Suddenly, a girl fell over. "I hurt my leg," she said. "You'll need to find another player." I really wanted to volunteer, but I was too shy. Then a girl on the team called to me, "Do you play?" Before I could answer, my mom said yes, and I was on the team! I was nervous and I didn't play well at first, but I didn't give up. The team encouraged me, and I got better!
The girl who called out was Kerry—now she's my best friend! Next week, we're taking part in a sponsored fun run—I've never done one before, but Kerry says they're great fun. So, my advice is, if you want to make new friends, play a sport—it's great for bringing people together!

TRACK 13
Unit 1, Explore Language
A Listen and read. How does Casey feel about the fun run?
Runner 1: Hi there!
Runner 2: Over here!
Runner 3: Can you hold this …
Runner 4: I can't find my number…
Casey: Wow! This is great! Everyone's so colorful! I've never done a fun run before, but I think I'll be fine: no one has trained harder than me! And anyway, there's no chance of me giving up—so many people have sponsored me. Has anyone seen my dad? He has my camera to take pictures of us all, but I can't see him anywhere! Ooh, it's going to be a long race.
Jordan: Hey Casey, CASEY! I love your costume!
Casey: Thanks, Jordan. Yours too… I'm glad I had something to eat before we started—I'm going to need a lot of energy! I wonder how fast everyone will be.
Jordan: We'll soon find out—it's nearly time to start!
Everyone: Five, four, three, two, one!
Casey: Let's go, Jordan!

TRACK 14
Unit 1, Explore Language
D Listen and say.
1 Everyone's so colorful!
2 Don't worry—she's done everything.
3 No one was brave enough to do it.
4 Can anyone help me?
5 Our team needs somewhere to play.

Unit 2

TRACK 15
Unit 2, Vocabulary
A Listen. Which animal looks after its young longer?
Mrs. Davis: So, you've all had a chance to look at the winners of the Animal Photos of the Year Competition, which show the animals we were learning about in class. Who would like to tell us about one of them and how they look after their babies? Excellent, Faris! Which animal would you like to talk about?
Faris: Elephants, Mrs. Davis. Here goes … female elephants are pregnant for 22 months, and when the babies are born, they can't look after themselves. All the females in the group help look after the babies—it's like having a lot of aunts as well as a mom! The group changes its behavior to help the babies—they travel slowly, and they all protect the babies when they're in danger. They also teach them how to use their trunks—that takes a whole year!
Mrs. Davis: Good job, Faris. We have time for one more before we go to see the birds—any volunteers? Casey?
Casey: I researched seahorses, which was really interesting! The female seahorse lays eggs, which—surprisingly—the male seahorse looks after. He carries the eggs in his pouch, on the front of his body. It takes four weeks for the eggs to hatch, and seahorses don't look after their babies after they are born. For this reason, seahorses have as many as 1,500 eggs as sadly most of them die. The babies have to find their own food. Seahorses have eyes that work independently so that they can look forward and backward at the same time.

TRACK 16
Unit 2, Vocabulary
B Find and number the words in A. Then listen and check.
1 food chain
2 pouch
3 pregnant
4 be born
5 habitat
6 die
7 trunk
8 behavior (British English: behaviour)
9 female
10 male

TRACK 17
Unit 2, Vocabulary
C Close your eyes. Listen, visualize, and say.
You're on safari in Africa! Get in the truck and look around. What animals can you see in this habitat? Is it hot? Are there many trees? Say "habitat."
The guide points out the lions. There's a male lion sleeping under a tree. Look at the thick fur around its head. Say "male."
The female lion isn't lazy. She's chasing a zebra. Look at how fast she is! Say "female."

The zebra's trying to escape—it doesn't want to die. But the lion's too fast … She's caught the zebra! Say "die."
This is part of the food chain in Africa: the zebra eats grass, and the lion eats the zebra. Say "food chain."
What's that? It's a giraffe, and she's pregnant. Look how big and round her stomach is. Say "pregnant."
Now you can see a leopard under a tree, sleeping in the shade. It has a baby—it's tiny. It's just been born. It's so cute! Say "be born."
Think of a baby kangaroo—it can stay safe in its mother's pouch. Imagine how it feels to be in the pouch. Say "pouch."
Will you see a baby kangaroo here? Of course not! This is Africa, not Australia! What other animals can you see? What's that? Oh—an elephant's trunk. It came very close to you! Say "trunk."
And are those monkeys? Isn't it funny to watch how monkeys behave? What are they doing? Say "behavior."

TRACK 18
Unit 2, Vocabulary
E Listen and write. Then watch and say.
Welcome to our habitat

Welcome to our habitat.
It's where we're born and die.
A lot of lovely things to eat
Grass and flowers, but no flies.

You might find our behavior
A little strange, it's true.
Our feet are big and funny
So bouncing's what we do.

Got my baby in my pouch
But it isn't all carefree.
Got a dingo on my tail—
That's the food chain here, you see!

TRACK 19
Unit 2, Vocabulary
F Pronunciation. Listen and say. Copy the weak forms. Find other examples in the poem.
a lot of lovely things (×2)
grass and flowers (×2)

TRACK 20
Unit 2, Explore Language
A Listen and read. How many parts are there in the food chain Faris describes?
Carmen: Ooooh!
Faris: Wow!
Carmen: Isn't this field trip great?! I love birds … it's a pity the owls are asleep though.
Faris: Well, of course they are! Most owls are nocturnal so they hunt at night.
Carmen: Yeah, I know. Have you seen a baby owl yet? Jon's already seen three!
Faris: No, I haven't. And I haven't seen a hawk catch a mouse yet, but I really want to!
Carmen: Birds eat mice? Yuck!
Faris: Yes, some do. I've just read it on that infographic over there. It's all about the hawk food chain. First, there's the grass. Then an insect like a grasshopper eats the grass. Then a mouse eats the grasshopper, and when it's feeling full and happy—whoooompf!—out of nowhere the hawk swoops down and catches the mouse …
Carmen: Like that? Ha, ha, ha!
Faris: Hey! That hawk's just stolen my hat!

TRACK 21
Unit 2, Explore Language
D Listen and say.
1 Jon's already seen three.
2 It's just disappeared!
3 We haven't learned about that yet.
4 Have you read that book yet? Yes, I have.
5 They've already been on safari.

TRACK 22
Unit 2, Global Citizenship
A Listen to Iván and his dad talk about a problem in their garden. What solution do they decide on?
Iván: Ow! A mosquito just bit me. We really need to get rid of them!
Dad: There are a lot this year! Let's think about what we can do … Some people use pesticides, but I don't like using them. They're poison.
Iván: But mosquitoes are horrible, Dad! They bite us, they make people sick …
Dad: But if we use pesticides to kill them, that might harm other animals, too.
Iván: Oh—I've just seen baby frogs in the pond! I don't want them to be hurt.
Dad: Exactly. If we don't use pesticides, the mosquitoes will encourage more predators, like our frogs, to come into the garden searching for prey to eat.
Iván: Can predators kill all the mosquitoes everywhere?
Dad: No. We don't want to make mosquitoes extinct!
Iván: Why not? It's sad when you hear about endangered animals like tigers and black rhinos, but I don't care about mosquitoes.
Dad: Well, I don't like mosquitoes either. But if we kill them all, what will happen to the animals that eat mosquitoes? They won't have enough food. Then they'll become extinct and so on.
Iván: I didn't think of that. You're right, Dad. Natural predators are the answer. Hey, frogs, come and find your mosquito snacks here—they're delicious!

TRACK 23
Unit 2, Global Citizenship
B Look at the pictures and definition in A and write. Then listen and check.
1 pesticide
2 encourage
3 extinct
4 poison
5 harm
6 native
7 endangered
8 get rid of
9 prey
10 predator

TRACK B
Unit 2, Global Citizenship
Close your eyes. Listen, think, visualize, and say.
Some farmers use too many chemicals. Say "pesticides."
Others want to use more natural predators. Say "encourage."
Your mom doesn't want insects in the house. Say "Get rid of them."
Some snakes have this in their bodies. Say "poison."
What does poison do? Say "It harms you."
What animal is native to your country? Say "native."
Blue whales might soon die out. Say "endangered."
Dodos have died out. Say "They're extinct."
Lions eat zebras. Say "Zebras are their prey."
What are animals that eat insects? Say "predators."

TRACK 24
Unit 2, Global Citizenship
D Now listen to a science program. What do humans do that affects animal habitats?
Did you know that human behavior affects nature? We want to make our lives better—but this can make life more difficult for animals. For example, we cut down forests to grow food or build houses—but forests are where animals live! Then they lose their habitats. If they have nowhere to live, they can't survive. Today there are hundreds of endangered animals and plants. If we continue like this, many of them will become extinct. Imagine that: no more tigers or black rhinos.
And when was the last time you were in a car or on a plane? Did you think about the gasoline or airline fuel? No? Well, using fossil fuels causes changes to the temperature of our planet which make it hard for animals to find food. Did you know that at the North Pole the ice caps are melting? Animals like polar bears are finding it more and more difficult to find prey.
Do you go shopping on weekends? That affects the environment, too. Some companies that make the products that we buy put their trash into rivers. The trash poisons plants in the water, which poison the animals which feed on the plants, which poison the predators that feed on the animals … What might that mean for humans? We're part of the food chain, too.
So, ask yourselves, "Are humans really the only important creatures on the planet?" It's important to make sure we're healthy and safe. But let's not forget how our behavior affects all living creatures—people and animals.

TRACK 25
Unit 2, Explore Language
A Listen to Susie and Carmen and read. What effect have people had on these toads and frogs?
Susie: Did you know that all toads are frogs, but not all frogs are toads?
Carmen: No, I didn't. But did you know that in some places there are too many toads?
Susie: No, I didn't know that. Look, here's an article about toads and frogs!
Carmen: Great! Let's read it.
Susie: "Toads and Frogs at Home
How long have cane toads lived in Australia? Surprisingly, they've only been there since 1935, when an organization introduced around 100 of them, from Hawaii. Farmers wanted a predator to get rid of an insect that was eating their sugar cane crops. The cane toads didn't get rid of the insects and now there are millions, possibly billions, of cane toads, because no predators eat them. The government has tried to control them for many years, but there are just more and more. The toads can be dangerous to animals and humans. It hasn't been a good way to try to deal with the insect.
In contrast, scientists have only just discovered this little yellow-black rain frog in Ecuador and already it's endangered. It's lived in the forest for a long time, but because humans are cutting down the forests where they live, they're quickly losing their habitat."
Oh, that's sad. In both cases, it's us people who have caused these problems!
Carmen: Yes, we need to think more carefully about our actions.

TRACK 26
Unit 2, Explore Language
D Listen and say.
1 They've only been there since 1935.
2 How long have you known Jack? Since 2019.
3 I haven't seen you for a while.
4 Rhinos have been endangered for years.

Unit 3

TRACK 27
Unit 3, Vocabulary
A Listen. Who does Mrs. Karpov think stole the Zoomboard?
Boy: Wow! So this is the tech lab of Active Fun!
Girl: I want to see those shoes that make you run faster.
Boy: Me, too! But the best thing will be the Zoomboard! It's going to be amazing!
Girl: Yes—did you know that it …
Mrs. Karpov: You must find the Zoomboard, Detective! It's the only one we have!
Detective: Don't worry, Mrs. Karpov. We're interviewing everyone. We'll ask them lots of questions. We'll catch the thief who stole the Zoomboard. Now, where were you last night?
Mrs. Karpov: Me? Surely I'm not a suspect?! Talk to Greg, Greg White—I think he looks suspicious. I think he's hiding something …
Greg: Has anyone seen my earphones? I can't find them …
Officer: So, Mr. Barrow, you designed the Zoomboard?
Mr. Barrow (Mitch): Yes, I did. It's fantastic. People are going to love it—it's like flying! But it isn't ready yet. We've made one, but it's too expensive. We need to make it cheaper.
Officer: Do you have an alibi for last night? What were you doing between 8 and 11 p.m.?
Mr. Barrow: I was working in my office.
Officer: Alone?
Mr. Barrow: Um …
Susie: Good thing we're here, Paco!
Paco: I know! I was looking forward to being inside a tech lab, but now we get to figure out who committed a crime, too!
Susie: I just had an interesting chat with Mr. White, Mr. Greg White … I'm going to talk to Mrs. Karpov now.

TRACK 28
Unit 3, Vocabulary
B Find and number the words in A. Then listen and check.
1 commit a crime
2 thief
3 criminal
4 alibi
5 detective
6 interview
7 suspect (noun)
8 investigate
9 fingerprint
10 clue
11 suspicious

TRACK 29
Unit 3, Vocabulary
C Close your eyes. Listen, visualize, and say.
Imagine someone has committed a crime. A valuable necklace is missing! Picture the missing necklace. Say "commit a crime."
Somewhere out there is a criminal, or a group of criminals. Imagine them escaping. Say "criminal."
Ah, here comes the detective—she's going to find out who took the necklace. Say "detective."
Would you make a good detective? You need to investigate. Look around carefully—what do you notice? Say "investigate."
Oooh! You've found a clue! What is it? How can it help you figure out what happened? Say "clue."
There are three suspects. What do they look like? Are they tall or short? What color hair do they have? Say "suspect."
Now you want to interview everyone. What questions will you ask? Say "interview."
A man gives you his alibi. He tells you where he was at the time of the crime. Say "alibi."
Hmm, he doesn't look at you when he talks to you: that's very suspicious. Is he telling the truth? Say "suspicious."
You need to take his fingerprints. Feel the patterns at the end of your fingers. Say "fingerprint."
Aha! You've figured it out! The thief is Mr. Smith! Picture how he stole the necklace. Say "thief."

TRACK 30
Unit 3, Vocabulary
E Listen and write. Then watch and say.
Ace Detective

I'm an ace detective.
The first one here.
Try to find the criminal
Look far and near.
At last a fingerprint—one clue I see,
Don't think you can hide from me.
'Cause I'm an ace detective.

Need to investigate
Have to ask why.
Do a short interview
Don't be shy.
Did you really commit the crime?
Tell the truth—don't waste my time.
'Cause I'm an ace detective.

TRACK 31
Unit 3, Vocabulary
F Pronunciation. Listen and say. Copy the word stress. Find other examples in the rap.
detective (x2)
criminal (x2)

TRACK 32
Unit 3, Explore Language
A Listen and read. Who had coffee last night?
Susie: Mrs. Karpov, please check this out—Paco found a fingerprint with his special glasses!
Mrs. Karpov: Hmm, Paco said you were looking for clues. How smart he is!
Susie: Yes, and look—it's brown. The thief had coffee on their fingers.
Mrs. Karpov: Ah … interesting! When I said goodbye to Greg last night, he was holding a cup of coffee! I said he was the thief!
Susie: That's funny … I thought you were drinking coffee, Mrs. Karpov. Greg said that you spilled yours. He had to get a cloth from the kitchen and clean up the mess.
Mrs. Karpov: He said that? It isn't true. I don't even like coffee …
Susie: Hmm … Is Greg the thief? The detective said he didn't have an alibi. … There's something I can't figure out. The Zoomboard is big and the window's too small. So I guess the thief carried the Zoomboard out through the door? Why didn't anyone see that?
Mrs. Karpov: Aha! Why don't you ask Greg about the trash can?

TRACK 33
Unit 3, Explore Language
D Listen and say.
1 I said he was the thief.
2 They said there weren't any clues.
3 She said that she had an alibi.
4 You said the detective was interviewing the suspects.

TRACK 34
Unit 3, Global Citizenship
A Listen to Kim and Li Yong talk about a suspected crime. What happened to Kim's cell phone?
Kim: Oh! My cell phone! Someone's stolen it!
Li Yong: We should report this to the police. I'll call them. Hello, police please …
Kim: The police will want to interview witnesses. Um, excuse me, someone's stolen my cell phone. Did you see anything?
Customers: No, sorry.
Mom: Hello, kids. Ready to go?
Kim: Oh, Mom! My cell phone's been stolen!
Mom: Are you sure, Kim? Have you looked in your backpack?
Kim: Yes! It's not there!
Mom: OK. The phone's technology means we can track it and stop anyone using it. But first, let's retrace your steps to see if you left it anywhere.
Kim: Mom! I'm the victim of a crime!
Mom: Maybe you are, but let's just think about it.
Kim: OK, so we came in. Li Yong found us a table to sit at. I went to the counter to get our sodas.
Mom: And where was your cell phone then?
Kim: Oh, it was in my hand. There was a boy right behind me. He was in a hurry.
Mom: Well, before we accuse him or anyone else, let's go to the counter. Maybe the server can help. Hi, my daughter's lost her cell phone, have you seen it?
Server: Oh, yes! We put it behind the counter for safety. Here you are!
Kim: Oh, what a relief! Thank you so much! I guess I'm the guilty one this time! I immediately thought the worst.
Li Yong: Me, too. Oh, no! Here are the police! I'll have to tell them about our mistake …

TRACK 35
Unit 3, Global Citizenship
B Look at the pictures and definitions in A and write. Then listen and check.
1 witness
2 report
3 steal
4 track
5 risk
6 victim
7 prevent
8 solve
9 guilty
10 opportunity

TRACK C
Unit 3, Global Citizenship
Close your eyes. Listen, think, visualize, and say.
Criminals have stolen a famous painting. Imagine the space on the wall where the painting was. Say "steal."
Your brother's pencil case is missing. Is he the victim of a crime? Say "victim."
Are you a good witness? Can you remember what your teacher was wearing yesterday? Say "witness."

You have a backpack with a lot of pockets. Make sure they're all safely closed. Say "prevent."
Imagine you've lost your cell phone. Look on your computer and find it. Say "track."
The window of a store in town was left open last night. Thieves broke in and stole six computers. Say "opportunity."
The owner has talked to the police and told them what she knows. Say "report."
Imagine you're an ace detective. How quickly can you match the fingerprints to the criminal? Say "solve."
Never put yourself in dangerous situations. Don't take any risks. Say "risk."
Your baby sister has chocolate all over her face. She's eaten your chocolate bar! (laugh) Say "guilty."

TRACK 36

Unit 3, Global Citizenship

D Now listen to police officer Pat Jones talk about a crime prevention program. Has the program worked?

Interviewer: Officer Jones, thanks for talking to us. Tell us about the program.
Officer Jones: Sure. It's called Who I Am and it encourages young people to join after-school youth clubs, to learn new things, things that they want to learn. The clubs can be for sports, hip hop, acting, languages, computer programming … all kinds of stuff!
Interviewer: What made you want to help young people like this?
Officer Jones: Well, as a police officer a large part of my job is to make sure the town where I live is safe. Most evenings, I drive around and check on shops, homes, and parks. If people see me in my uniform, it might stop them from having a bad argument or from damaging someone's property.
Interviewer: True …
Officer Jones: A few years ago, I started to notice more and more young people on the streets and in the parks. Often, they were just hanging out, but I could see they were bored, and sometimes I'd find walls had been vandalized. Our town is small, and these groups of young people were beginning to make others uncomfortable—mothers with small children and older people didn't want to go to the park.
Interviewer: So, how did you get from that to Who I Am?
Officer Jones: I did some reading about why crimes happen. I came across some studies in Iceland by a team of researchers and psychologists. They found that being bored is a major factor. Young people don't always want to sit at home and they want to be part of a group, which can be positive or negative.
Interviewer: Do they have a youth program like yours in Iceland?
Officer Jones: Yes, they do, and in many other countries, too. We were inspired by their work. The reports on the programs in Iceland and elsewhere said that it's really helped improve the young people's self- confidence so that they started making plans for the future. We've noticed this, too.
Interviewer: How does the project prevent crime, exactly?
Officer Jones: Basically, everyone's too busy learning and having fun to have time to do anything criminal. In our program, teenagers work on art, music, dance, and other types of projects that they're interested in. We encourage the parents to get involved and show them how important it is to spend time with their teenage children. Everyone loves it.
Interviewer: I'm tempted to join a club too—it sounds great! Thanks for talking to us. That was Officer Pat Jones …

TRACK 37

Unit 3, Explore Language

A Listen and read. Who does Susie think stole the Zoomboard?

Susie: Paco and I have solved the crime!
Detective: Really?
Susie: Yes! Yesterday afternoon Mrs. Karpov spilled her coffee. She asked Greg to clean it up, so he went to the kitchen for a cloth. Later she said the trash can was full. She told Greg to take it outside. The Zoomboard was inside it.
All: (gasp)
Greg: But I didn't steal it!
Susie: No, you didn't! While you were in the kitchen, Mrs. Karpov had the opportunity to hide the Zoomboard in the trash can. That night, she got it out of the trash can and took it home for her son.
Mrs. Karpov: What? Nonsense!
Detective: It's the Zoomboard!
Susie: That's right. Mrs. Karpov doesn't know just how special the Zoomboard is. When Mitch pushes a switch in his office, the Zoomboard comes home! I told him not to use it until now. Detective, you'll find Mrs. Karpov's fingerprints all over the Zoomboard. I believe she's the thief!
Nr. Barrow (Mitch): Good job, Susie and Paco!

TRACK 38

Unit 3, Explore Language

D Listen and say.

1 She asked him to clean it up.
2 I told you not to do that.
3 He told us to find clues.
4 They told her not to be late.

Unit 4

TRACK 39

Unit 4, Vocabulary

A Listen. Which job do you think Gina likes best?

Gina: This is so cool, Aliya—we can ask all these people about their jobs. Look, here's a model of a theme park.
Architect: Hello! I'm an architect. I design rides for theme parks. Are either of you creative?
Gina: Yes, I'm Gina, and I'm good at drawing, and I have lots of ideas.
Architect: That's perfect. Architects are talented artists, too. You have to study hard to get a college degree. Then you could make something like this!
Aliya: Oh, look! A vet!
Psychologist: Actually, I'm a pet psychologist. I teach pet owners how to correct their animals' behavior.
Aliya: It looks really stressful … and difficult!
Psychologist: It's OK, kitty. Shh. Well, yes, it can be challenging. Sometimes it's difficult for people to change their habits with their pets, but it's also a rewarding job. It feels good to make pets and their owners happier.
Boy: So, what does it do?
Mitch: Well, this is a prototype, so it's not finished, but it takes photos from the sky.
All: (laugh)
Comedian: What kind of animal solves crimes? … An investi-gator!
All: (laugh)
Gina: (laughs) What qualifications do you need to be a comedian?
Aliya: I don't think you need a certificate or anything like that. But you have to be confident and good at speaking to crowds …
Gina: … and you have to be funny. That's definitely the job for me!
Aliya: (groans)

TRACK 40

Unit 4, Vocabulary

B Find and number the words in A. Then listen and check.

1 talented
2 qualifications
3 underwater photographer
4 party planner
5 degree
6 architect
7 creative
8 stressful
9 pet psychologist
10 challenging
11 comedian
12 rewarding

TRACK 41

Unit 4, Vocabulary

C Close your eyes. Listen, visualize, and say.

You visited the Jobs for You! Fair. There are so many interesting jobs. Which one's for you?
Imagine you're an underwater photographer. What does it look like when you're under the ocean? Get your camera ready; there's a shark coming! Say "underwater photographer."
Wow! Your pictures are really good. Smile. Say "talented."
Now you're a pet psychologist. What different animals do you help? Say "pet psychologist."
You're working with an unhappy parrot. What's it doing? Why is it unhappy? Say "challenging."
Now imagine you're an architect. You're in your office drawing a picture of a new theme-park ride. Say "architect."
You worked very hard to become an architect. You studied for a long time to get your qualifications. Say "qualifications."
Your ride is very special. How high is it? What does it do? Say "creative."
You hear children laughing and enjoying your ride. How does it feel? Say "rewarding."
Next you're a party planner. What do you need to organize? Are the guests at the party happy? Say "party planner."
Do you need any qualifications to be a comedian? Do you have a sense of humor? Can you tell jokes? Think of the funniest thing you can. Say "comedian."
Imagine preparing for a comedy show—you're not ready. How does it feel? Say "stressful."
Now think of your dream job. Do you need to study for a degree? What will it feel like to be a university student? Say "degree."

TRACK 42

Unit 4, Vocabulary

E Listen and write. Then watch and say.

That's the Job for Me

Let's talk about jobs
What do you want to do?
Something that's rewarding?
Challenging too?
Want the chance to travel?
Try something new?
Are you talented, and creative?
Imaginative too?

What do you want to do?
Want to get yourself a plan?
Then work really hard.
Be everything you can.
Be a pet psychologist with a university degree.
Be a party planner if you're really friendly.
But an underwater photographer just might be
The job for you—swim down and see!

TRACK 43
Unit 4, Vocabulary
F Pronunciation. Listen and say. Copy the intonation. Find two more questions like these in the poem.
Want the chance to travel? (×2)
Try something new? (×2)

TRACK 44
Unit 4, Explore Language
A Listen and read. What does a party planner do?
I've been a party planner for ten years and I love my job! Every day is different. And every party starts with a planning meeting. I ask the clients questions to find out what they want. I want to make every party special.
My job is to organize everything. I make a lot of lists! If it's a party to celebrate an 11th birthday, I might have to find a trampoline or crazy golf course. I order all the food and drinks. If the client wants live music, I'll find musicians. I buy the decorations and prizes.
On the day of the party, my team sets everything up. We have a detailed schedule to make sure everything happens on time. Sometimes things go wrong and then it can be stressful.
Party planning's a very rewarding job—it's wonderful to see everyone having a great time.

TRACK 45
Unit 4, Explore Language
D Listen and say.
1 I ask the clients questions to find out what they want.
2 Why are you here? To set up the tables.
3 She went to the store to get some bread.
4 He called to tell us the news.

TRACK 46
Unit 4, Global Citizenship
A Listen to Tyrone and Cody talk about starting a small business. What are they going to sell?
Tyrone: Hey, Cody! The other day I watched a documentary about a girl who has a business which makes phone cases. She started it on her own when she was our age, but now she has six people working for her!
Cody: Really? Wasn't it hard?
Tyrone: Well, yes. She said she had to learn a lot, but she sounded really enthusiastic. She inspired me! I think we should try to sell our frozen bananas. It'll be fun … and great experience for the future.
Cody: And I'm sure we can get our friends to help us.
Tyrone: No, let's be independent and do it on our own. We have lots of skills—you're good at math, I get along with people, and we're both resourceful. Remember how we made an umbrella out of banana leaves last summer?
Cody: Hmm, so—where can we sell our bananas? We want somewhere busy but not too busy.
Tyrone: How about the entrance to the park? People often get hot when they're playing games.
Cody: But I really think we should ask an adult to help us.
Tyrone: No! How hard can it be? My ambition is to be interviewed on TV about my amazingly successful business.
Cody: *Our* amazingly successful business, Tyrone!

TRACK 47
Unit 4, Global Citizenship
B Look at the pictures and definitions in A and write. Then listen and check.
1 ambition
2 observant
3 resourceful
4 experience
5 inspired
6 boss
7 independent
8 reliable
9 skills
10 business

TRACK D
Unit 4, Global Citizenship
Close your eyes. Listen, think, visualize, and say.
Think of a store you know: this is a business.
What does the store sell? Say "business."
Is the boss a man or a woman? How do you know this person is the boss? Do they give orders? Say "boss."
Now imagine the store clerk. He's new, and he's a bit nervous, but he's worked as a store clerk before. He knows what to do. Say "experience."
Why don't you work in the store, too? Go and ask for a job. How can you show the boss you are reliable? Say "reliable."
You're independent, too. What do you do in your life that shows it? Say "independent."
The boss needs someone who's resourceful. Think about a problem or difficulty you've been able to solve. Say "resourceful."
The boss needs someone who notices things. Look around. What can you see in the room that other people might not see? Say "observant."
Do you feel inspired to start your own business? Who makes you feel inspired? Say "inspired."
What skills are useful when you have your own business? Think about being a leader and working with people. Say "skills."
Think about yourself in 20 years. Where would you like to be? What's your ambition? Say "ambition."

TRACK 48
Unit 4, Global Citizenship
D Now listen to Nia Cole. What does she do?
My name's Nia Cole. I started designing cell phone cases when I was 13. I've always been imaginative, and I used to use old photographs for my designs. At first I just sold the cases to my friends, but then my uncle inspired me to think bigger. New Zealand is a great place to start your own business, and entrepreneurs are encouraged. I sat down with my parents and my uncle to make a detailed plan, and two years ago, MyOwnPhone was born. Soon I was selling to people all over the city. However, I quickly realized that I lacked some skills and experience. For example, I had a lot of ideas for designs, but I'd never created a website before. If I wanted my business to survive and grow, I needed help.
It's estimated that more than a third of small businesses all over the world close within five years, so it's important to have a strong team around you. I have a really great team. They're all resourceful and reliable, and often they're very different from me. For example, my finance director isn't very creative, but she makes sure we have enough money to buy the materials we need. We have team meetings before we make any big decisions. I've learned to listen to everyone's opinions. The team has helped me become a better boss. At the same time, I encourage everyone to work independently.
It hasn't all been easy! I agreed to employ a friend one summer, but she found the work too stressful. She didn't get orders to customers quickly enough, and that was bad for the business. But most of the time, I really love having my own business, and I'm always looking for new customers … So, do you need a new case for your cell phone!? (laughs)

TRACK 49
Unit 4, Explore Language
A Listen and read. Does Nancy-Yu have qualifications or skills as an underwater photographer?
Tareq: That's a cool camera! But you can't take pictures under water with it, can you?
Nancy-Yu: Yes, I can. It's a special underwater camera. I was just taking pictures of some sharks over there.
Tareq: Sharks? Eeek! That was dangerous, wasn't it?
Nancy-Yu: No, I was very careful.
Tareq: So, do you have a degree in photography?
Nancy-Yu: No, I studied biology in college.
Tareq: Oh! How did you learn about underwater photography?
Nancy-Yu: My aunt taught me when I was about your age.
Tareq: What other skills do you need to have? You need to be observant, don't you?
Nancy-Yu: Yes—to find the animals and fish you want to take pictures of. And you also need to be resourceful, to solve problems quickly. Oh, look! Another shark!
Tareq: Wait! You'll need your camera, won't you?

TRACK 50
Unit 4, Explore Language
D Listen and say.
1 You can't take pictures under water with it, can you?
2 They won't be late, will they?
3 She hasn't arrived yet, has she?
4 He went to take photos of sharks, didn't he?

Unit 5

TRACK 51
Unit 5, Vocabulary
A Listen. Is Tyler leading the team well?
Tyler: This expedition is fun, isn't it? Come on, everyone—I'm sure we're near the fourth checkpoint!
Hassan: Tyler's very enthusiastic, isn't he? He's so happy and excited about everything!
Emily: Yes …
Hassan: But why are you wearing your coat, Emily?
Emily: Because it always rains!
Hassan: Oh, Emily! That's a bit pessimistic, isn't it? It doesn't look like rain today!
Tyler: Where's the map? Oh, you have it, Atid! Great! Why are you looking so confused?
Atid: I can't see the ocean …
Tyler: Are you looking on the right part of the map? … OK, let's keep going anyway! Shout if you see a flag …

Hassan: Wait up, Tyler. Can we take a break?
Tyler: Oh, yes, Hassan, sure. Um, how are you all doing? … Oh, you look upset, Koji. What happened?
Koji: (crying)
Tyler: It's OK, don't cry! Um, Ella, can you help him? Oh! … What's wrong, Ella? You look furious!
Ella: (grunting and grumbling)
Tyler: Oh, I see, you've lost your boot. Oh, Billy! Your sandwich … I can see you're disappointed—I have some extra food in my backpack. We can share it. Um, you're having fun, right, Katie? Why do you look so worried?
Katie: The forest is full of dangerous spiders!
Tyler: No—of course there aren't dangerous spiders in the forest! Yukiko, you're going the wrong way?
Yukiko: No, I'm not!
Tyler: I think it might be better to … Oh, she's very determined!
Atid: Look! A flag!
Nancy-Yu: Atid, I'm delighted you've found your fourth flag! Excellent orienteering, everyone! Only four more!
All but Tyler: (grumble and groan)
Tyler: Aaaargh! I didn't see you there, Nancy-Yu!
All: (laugh)

TRACK 52

Unit 5, Vocabulary
B Find and number the words in A. Then listen and check.

1 determined
2 upset
3 furious
4 delighted
5 optimistic
6 pessimistic
7 disappointed
8 worried
9 enthusiastic
10 confused

TRACK 53

Unit 5, Vocabulary
C Close your eyes. Listen, visualize and say.

Imagine you're on an orienteering expedition in the woods. You love walking with your friends. You feel really happy. Say "enthusiastic."
It's warm. You feel optimistic because you think you'll win the prize easily. Say "optimistic."
Oh—what's that noise in the trees? Was it a wild animal?! You feel a little scared. Say "worried."
Oh, good—time to stop for lunch. Have a look in your bag. Oh! There's only a sandwich. Say "disappointed."
But what's this? Potato chips and chocolate. That's better! Say "delighted."
Time to start walking again. Climb over a fence—ow! Oh, no—your favorite jacket has caught on the gate and … there's a hole in it! Say "furious."
You're getting quite tired now. You need to look at the map. But where is it? You've lost it. Say "upset."
Which way do you go? You look around. Is it this path or that one? Say "confused."
Sit down under a tree. You don't think you'll ever find the way home. It's all a disaster! Say "pessimistic."
Then you realize you won't get home unless you try. So you stand up, pick up your backpack, and start walking again. Say "determined." Good job!

TRACK 54

Unit 5, Vocabulary
E Listen and write. Then watch and say.

Expedition Blues
I'm feeling pessimistic—I'm feeling quite confused.
I want to do my best but it's hard—who knew?
My compass broke, I lost my way,
Upset a raccoon stole my shoe.
Feeling down with those expedition blues.

I started off determined—don't know what happened then.
Some noises made me worried—I wondered what they meant.
Why are the woods so dark and scary?
Will I ever get home again?
Just can't beat those expedition blues.

Hello, Mom and Dad! Is it really time to go?
So much fun! I've had the best time ever even though
To start I wasn't optimistic,
Was down and didn't know
With my team I'd beat those expedition blues!

TRACK 55

Unit 5, Vocabulary
F Pronunciation. Listen and say. Copy the sentence stress. Find other sentences in the poem and notice the stress patterns.

I'm feeling quite confused. (x2)
Some noises made me worried. (x2)

TRACK 56

Unit 5, Explore Language
A Listen and read. What was making the scary noise in the forest?

Mason: GRRR!
Katie: What's that noise, Yukiko?
Yukiko: What noise, Katie?
Katie: That grrr, it's coming from the forest. It can't be a person, can it?
Yukiko: It could be a bear.
Katie: A bear! It must want our food. Help!
Yukiko: Don't panic, Katie! It might be a wild animal, but I'm sure it's not a bear.
Katie: Are you sure? Really sure?
Yukiko: Well, pretty sure … It may be a raccoon or something.
Mason: Hello!
Katie & Yukiko: (startled shriek / gasp)
Mason: Well—what do you think of my animal noises? I'm practicing for the school play!
Katie: Oh, Mason, you scared me! I thought you were a bear!
Mason: Did you? That's fantastic! Oh—sorry it wasn't a real bear. You must be disappointed!
Katie: Disappointed? No, I'm not—I was worried!

TRACK 57

Unit 5, Explore Language
D Listen and say.

1 It can't be a person.
2 He might need some food.
3 It could rain today.
4 You must be tired.
5 They may be lost!

TRACK 58

Unit 5, Global Citizenship
A Listen to an interview with Dr. Hernández, a child psychologist. What problem does he talk about?

Interviewer: Today, Dr. Rubén Hernández, a child psychologist, is with us to talk about how we can respond to challenges in a positive way. Dr. Hernández has worked with children and teenagers facing challenging situations for many years, from studying for difficult exams to training for the Olympic Games. Welcome, Dr. Hernández.
Dr. Hernández: Thank you. It's great to be here!
Interviewer: So tell us, how should we respond to challenging situations? What are we doing wrong?
Dr. Hernández: Well, people usually think that mistakes are bad news. They worry that if they make mistakes, their brain will learn the wrong thing. But that's not true. When you make a mistake and find out you were wrong, your brain pays special attention and learns better! So mistakes can actually help you improve!
Interviewer: That makes sense, but it can be embarrassing to realize you were wrong. And it's also frustrating when you've worked hard to get it right!
Dr. Hernández: Sure, but that negative experience might be helping your brain pay attention. It's important for children and adults to understand that mistakes are part of improving. Otherwise, they might feel insecure and not want to try harder.
Interviewer: Do you have any other advice for our listeners?
Dr. Hernández: Another thing that people often believe is that once you succeed at something, you have to continue to get better. And that's simply not true. We don't improve in a straight line. We have ups and downs. Sometimes we succeed and then something goes wrong and we fail before we can fix it and succeed again.
Interviewer: You heard the doctor, listeners. Be confident and know that that making mistakes doesn't mean you failed; it means you can learn and get better. Thank you so much, Dr. Hernández. It's been a pleasure …

TRACK 59

Unit 5, Global Citizenship
B Look at the pictures and definitions in A and write. Then listen and check.

1 succeed
2 fail
3 positive
4 make mistakes
5 frustrating
6 improve
7 insecure
8 negative
9 confident

TRACK E

Unit 5, Global Citizenship
Listen and say. What do you think of when you hear these words? Talk with your friend.

Succeed. Say "succeed."
Fail. Say "fail."
Positive. Say "positive."
Make mistakes. Say "make mistakes."
Frustrating. Say "frustrating."
Improve. Say "improve."
Insecure. Say "insecure."
Negative. Say "negative."
Confident. Say "confident."

TRACK 60

Unit 5, Global Citizenship
D Now listen to Erik. What disadvantage of living in Tromsø in Norway does he mention?

I'm Erik. I live in Tromsø in Norway. It's great here, but every winter, because we're near the North Pole, there are 60 days when the sun never rises. They're called Polar Nights. Can you imagine not seeing the sun for two months?

Everyone feels more negative in the winter, but living without daylight for 60 days actually makes some people sick with an illness called SAD. I've had it and it's horrible! You want to sleep all the time. You only want to eat unhealthy food—cakes, cookies, and candy! You feel insecure and worried, and you don't have any confidence. You don't even want to see your friends.
So it's really important to fight SAD! Here's what we do in my family:
One. We eat a healthy diet. And we have a spoonful of fish oil once a day. It's full of vitamins that keep us strong, including vitamin D, which we normally get from the sun. It's good for us—but it tastes disgusting! Yuck!
Two. We exercise! It always makes us feel better. We go skiing, snowboarding, and orienteering every week. Being out in the fresh air is great.
Three. We socialize. Meeting friends really improves your mood.
Four. And the best way to avoid SAD? Have a really positive attitude to winter! We have lots of festivals and parties, with special food, singing, and dancing. And we enjoy the northern lights, those beautiful displays of color that nature puts on in the sky!

TRACK 61
Unit 5, Explore Language
A Listen and read. How does Mason feel?
Jalen: Santiago looks so happy! How are you feeling, Mason?
Mason: Of course I'm delighted for him. He's really looking forward to moving back to Mexico.
Jalen: But you'll miss him, won't you?
Mason: No! What? I'm not insecure! I'll find a lot of other friends. I'll probably forget about him in a week …
Jalen: Are you sure? You've been friends for a long time.
Mason: Since we were five. Maybe I'll miss him a bit …
Jalen: Santiago's definitely going to miss you.
Mason: Really?
Jalen: Of course. He's very confident, but he's also scared about moving. And you're not going to be there to support him.
Mason: I didn't think of that. I'll email him every week. Perhaps we can do video chats, too.
Jalen: Great idea!
Santiago: Come on, Mason! I want to get a picture of everyone.
Jalen: Obviously you should be in the picture, too, Santiago. Let me take it for you, so you'll remember all your friends. OK, everyone—say CHEESE!

TRACK 62
Unit 5, Explore Language
D Listen and say.
1 I'll probably forget about him in a week.
2 Obviously it's broken.
3 Maybe he got it wrong.
4 Yes, perhaps he was confused.
5 We'll definitely be there at nine.

Unit 6

TRACK 63
Unit 6, Vocabulary
A Listen. What is HOP?
Hi, there! Welcome to HOP! My name's Santiago. It's great you all came by public transportation—that's very green! Now, let me show you where you're going to stay …
Weronika: Wow, that tree house is fantastic!
Santiago: And it's eco-friendly. All our electricity comes from the sun, and all our water comes from the river.
Shinji: The air's so clean—there's no pollution at all.
Weronika: We're going to take amazing pictures here!
Santiago: And you'll start this afternoon! My dad's going to take you to a Mayan temple.
All: (excited)
Santiago: Then tomorrow—well, Javier will tell you.
Javier: Hi, all. I'm going to be your guide when we visit the sea turtle sanctuary.
Shinji: I'm really looking forward to that!
Weronika: Are the sea turtles part of the Conservation Challenge, Santiago?
Santiago: Yes, they are! As you know, HOP is a tourism company which organizes vacations for people like you who want to go on vacation and help our planet. And the HOP Conservation Challenge gives you the opportunity to improve the environment. We ask each visitor to work on a project that will have a positive impact on the planet. You might plant trees, clear trash from beaches, help sea turtles or baby crocodiles—there's a lot to do! So, want to find out what project you're going to work on?
All: Yes, please!

TRACK 64
Unit 6, Vocabulary
B Find and number the words in A. Then listen and check.
1 tourism
2 conservation
3 eco-friendly
4 impact
5 carbon footprint
6 pollution
7 damage
8 waste
9 environment
10 public transportation (British English: public transport)

TRACK 65
Unit 6, Vocabulary
C Listen and say. What do you think of when you hear these words? Talk with your friend.
Tourism. Say "tourism."
Conservation. Say "conservation."
Eco-friendly. Say "eco-friendly."
Impact. Say "impact."
Carbon footprint. Say "carbon footprint."
Pollution. Say "pollution."
Damage. Say "damage."
Waste. Say "waste."
Environment. Say "environment."
Public transportation. Say "public transportation."

TRACK 66
Unit 6, Vocabulary
E Listen and write. Then watch and say.
A Green World

Pollution in the ocean,
Poison in the air.
We damage our environment
When we travel anywhere.

The explanation's clear—
Conservation is what we need.
Eco-friendly projects help
To keep our planet green.

So don't waste what we have.
Tourism needs a plan.
Keep your carbon footprint small.
Protect our precious land.

TRACK 67
Unit 6, Vocabulary
F Pronunciation. Listen and say. Copy the word stress. Think of other words with three or four syllables. Where's the stress?
pollution (x2)
environment (x2)
explanation (x2)
conservation (x2)

TRACK 68
Unit 6, Explore Language
A Listen and read. What activity is the group going to do?
Javier: Thousands of sea turtles start life on this beach, but tourism can have a negative impact on their habitat. Turtles may become extinct if we don't protect them.
Adele: Oh, no, that'll be terrible! But why is tourism a problem?
Javier: Well, sea turtles spend most of their lives in the ocean, but they lay their eggs in the sand on beaches like this one. When too many people stay in hotels near the beach, they can disturb the turtles' nests before the eggs hatch. Hotel lights are a problem, too. They shine on the beach at night and confuse the turtles when they're looking for places to nest. They can also confuse the baby turtles when they hatch and are looking for the water.
Adele: What can we do to help?
Javier: If we protect the turtles' nests, there might be more babies. We're going to look for a nest, and if we find one that isn't marked, we'll call the conservation experts. They'll move it to a safe place.
Adele: Sounds great! If we see some baby turtles, will I be able to take a photo?
Javier: Sure—but remember not to use the flash!

TRACK 69
Unit 6, Explore Language
D Listen and say.
1 Turtles may become extinct if we don't protect them.
2 If we don't change soon, it may be too late.
3 If we aren't careful, we won't be able to save the planet.
4 What might happen to the turtles?
5 If we protect them, they might survive.

TRACK 70
Unit 6, Global Citizenship
A Listen to Sandra and Ekaterina talk about being green. What two things does Ekaterina say she's going to do?

Ekaterina: The trash can's full again, Sandra—I can't get this bottle in!
Sandra: My grandparents say we need to stop throwing so much out. Guess how much trash they produced last year? ... One bag!
Ekaterina: Impossible! We have two bags of trash every week! How did they reduce it so much?
Sandra: They're completely self-sufficient—they grow all their own fruit and vegetables. Everything's organic—they never use pesticides. And they never use more than is necessary. In fact, their whole lifestyle is sustainable. That's very unusual in the 21st century.
Ekaterina: That's impressive! Do they keep animals?
Sandra: No, they don't eat fish or meat. And when they buy things from their local grocery store, they make sure they can recycle the packaging.
Ekaterina: I never know what you can recycle—I just put everything in the big trash can.
Sandra: That's not good! Here, look at your bottle. See this little green symbol? It means you can recycle it. But why don't you reuse it? Fill it with water for tomorrow.
Ekaterina: Yes—I'll do that! You know, I'm definitely getting greener! I know we're using up our natural resources too fast, so I'm going to stop taking showers.
Sandra: What?
Ekaterina: Think of all the water I'll save!
Sandra: Yuck—think of all the friends you'll lose!

TRACK 71
Unit 6, Global Citizenship
B Look at the pictures in A and write. Then listen and check.

1 sustainable
2 organic
3 local
4 symbol
5 global
6 reduce
7 recycle
8 self-sufficient
9 global warming
10 natural resources

TRACK F
Unit 6, Global Citizenship
Close your eyes. Listen, think, visualize, and say.

Think about how to be greener. It's important for people to look after the planet better. What are the effects of global warming? Say "global warming."
Imagine what you could do to live in a more sustainable way. Picture a tree being chopped down and imagine digging a hole to plant a new one. Say "sustainable."
Water is an important natural resource we shouldn't waste. Think of ways you could save water. Say "natural resources."
How you shop is important, too. You'll have a smaller carbon footprint if you walk instead of drive. Think of a local shop you could walk to. Say "local."
The shop sells lovely organic vegetables. Picture some big red peppers—no pesticides on these! Say "organic."
You want to waste less. Think of one thing you could do to reduce your carbon footprint. Say "reduce."
Now think of three things you use every day that you can recycle. Say "recycle."
Where are you going to put them? You need to find bins with the recycle symbol. Picture the symbol. Say "symbol."
Imagine growing your own food. What would it feel like to be self-sufficient? What would you grow? Say "self-sufficient."
You've thought of lots of things you can do to be greener. Now think of a global change that governments could make. Say "global."

TRACK 72
Unit 6, Global Citizenship
D Now listen to an interview with Lorena Rossi. What issue does she talk about?

Host: This week we've invited conservation expert Lorena Rossi on to the Green World show to tell us about palm oil. It's a global issue she cares deeply about. Why is it a global issue, Lorena?
Lorena: You may not know this, but there is palm oil in many of the things we eat and use every day, such as pizzas, cakes and cookies, soap, make-up, and shampoo, because it's cheaper and easier to produce than other oils, like olive oil. Some palm oil companies don't damage the environment, but many others cut down large areas of rain forest in tropical countries to make space for the palm trees which produce the oil. This has a huge impact on the local environment and causes climate change.
Host: Are you talking about global warming?
Lorena: Exactly. And global warming means more extreme weather all over the world—storms, floods, etc. Cutting down the rainforest also destroys the habitats of important animals and plants. We need to recognize that this kind of agriculture is just not sustainable.
Host: It's terrible! Is there anything we can do?
Lorena: Yes! Every time we buy something, we have a choice. Let's refuse to buy products made by companies which destroy the rain forests.
Host: But how do we know which products to buy?
Lorena: Products that contain palm oil which has been produced in a sustainable way have a palm leaf symbol on the packaging. It tells us the company which made that product has tried to protect the environment.
Host: Thanks, Lorena. That was really interesting. And I'll definitely look for the palm leaf symbol in future!

TRACK 73
Unit 6, Explore Language
A Listen and read. What kind of quiz is Adele doing with Lola?

Lola: Let's do this quiz on sustainable living. It's called "It's too hard to be eco-friendly. True or False?" Are you ready, Adele?
Adele: Yes, I am!
Lola: Number 1. The wind is always strong enough to make electricity. True or false?
Adele: Hmm. The wind can be a good source of clean energy, but it's not always very windy around here ... so, false!
Lola: Yes, you're right. Wind turbines make enough electricity to power entire buildings but only in places where it's windy. Next. Urban areas are too crowded to use clean energy.
Adele: That's false! All the apartment buildings in my neighborhood have solar panels which make electricity from the sun. They're on top of the buildings, so they don't take up much space.
Lola: Great! Last one. Most families can't grow enough food to be self-sufficient.
Adele: That's hard. Our garden isn't big enough for us to grow everything we need, but ...
Lola: You're right. Not everyone can grow everything they need, but the next page has some creative ways to grow food even in small spaces.

TRACK 74
Unit 6, Explore Language
D Listen and say

1 It's too hard to be eco-friendly.
2 I'm too tired to run for the bus.
3 We can't grow enough tomatoes to make a salad.
4 The sea is warm enough for us to swim.

Unit 7

TRACK 75
Unit 7, Vocabulary
A Listen. Which problem is real?

Girl 1: So, you have a burn on your hand?
Girl 2: Yes. I touched the stove—it was hot. I need some cream to disinfect it.
Girl 1: No! It's not dirty. You shouldn't put cream on burns or cover them with a Band-Aid. At least, not immediately.
Girl 2: What should I do?
Girl 1: You should keep the burn in cool water for twenty minutes. Here!

Boy 1: Oh! That's cold!
Boy 2: Yes, it's an ice pack. It needs to be cold to stop your leg swelling—when you fall or hit yourself, sometimes your leg can get really big. This will help.

Lola: When you're at the swimming pool, it's really important to follow the safety rules. Now Neerav, imagine that your sister, Amira, didn't. She had an accident. She was running and she fell. What should you check for?
Neerav: Bleeding and cuts!
Amira: My head ... I feel dizzy ...
Girl 3: Keep still! I can't put this bandage on.
Amira: I'm going to faint ...
Neerav: I won't catch you, Amira!
Amira: I'm just trying to make it realistic! Who am I? What happened? **Girl 3:** She must have a concussion. That can happen when you hit your head. She looks confused.
Neerav: Hey, Tanya—want to be my patient? Oh—are you all right?
Tanya: No—my lips feel very big. They're starting to swell!
Neerav: Yes, they are, and there's a rash on your arm. Have you been stung by a wasp? It looks like an allergic reaction. Can you breathe?
Amira: No, she can't! She can't breathe!
Neerav: Amira, don't panic. Go and find Lola—now. Tanya, sit down here. We're getting help.

TRACK 76

Unit 7, Vocabulary

B Find and number the words in A. Then listen and check.

1 injured
2 ice pack
3 swell
4 accident
5 faint
6 allergic reaction
7 rash
8 concussion
9 burn
10 cut
11 Band-Aid (British English: plaster)
12 disinfect

TRACK 77

Unit 7, Vocabulary

C Close your eyes. Listen, visualize, and say.

Imagine you're helping with first aid at a concert in the park. Everyone's having a good time—but then there's an accident: a boy has stood on some glass. Say "accident."
Look at the cut. How bad is it? Say "cut."
It's dirty. You need to clean it. Say "disinfect."
There isn't much blood, so you can use a Band-Aid. Say "Band-Aid."
Now someone else is hopping towards you—she looks injured. Say "injured."
Her foot is starting to swell. It's getting bigger! Say "swell."
Think quickly. What do you need? Say "ice pack."
A woman has a burn. How did she do it? Say "burn."
A tall man has hit his head. It isn't bleeding, but he has a concussion. Say "concussion."
Oh, no! There's a little girl who's too hot. She's going to faint. Quick, catch her! Say "faint."
And what happened to this boy? He has a rash. Say "rash."
Could it be an allergic reaction? Say "allergic reaction."
The concert's finished, and everyone's going home. What a lot of patients you've had!

TRACK 78

Unit 7, Vocabulary

E Listen and write. Then watch and say.

The First Aid Tent
If you're injured,
We'll check it out.
A cut or a burn
Just give us a shout.
At the First Aid, First Aid, First Aid Tent
We're here when there's an accident.
Hurt your ankle climbing a tree?
Need an ice pack
For your knee?
Want a Band-Aid?
Need a rest? Or just lie down
Till you feel your best?

TRACK 79

Unit 7, Vocabulary

F Pronunciation. Listen and say. Copy the linking. Think of other phrases like these.

you're injured (x2)
or a burn (x2)
your ankle (x2)

TRACK 80

Unit 7, Explore Language

A Listen and read. Are Neerav and Alex well prepared?

Neerav: So, as the lifeguards for my sister's pool party, it's our job to keep everyone safe.
Alex: Yes—if there's an accident, we'll be ready!
Neerav: Lola told me to make the rules very clear. No one's allowed in the water if we're not here. People who can't swim must wear waterwings. And to avoid cuts, drinking glasses aren't allowed around the pool. That rule and others about jumping, running, and pushing are shown on that poster. My dad made it!
Alex: What happens if anyone breaks the rules?
Neerav: They're told to leave the pool.
Alex: And if there is an accident? Where's the first aid kit kept?
Neerav: It's over there, under the umbrella.
Alex: And are Band-Aids kept in the first aid kit?
Neerav: Yes, they are. But the ice packs are in the fridge. And if anything serious happens, we need to get help. My parents are in the house.
Archie: Hey, Neerav! Alex! Watch me dive! … Whoah!
Neerav: Archie, be careful!
Archie: Aaaaaaaargh!

TRACK 81

Unit 7, Explore Language

D Listen and say.

1 No one's allowed in the water if we're not here.
2 Band-Aids aren't used for burns.
3 Where are ice packs sold?
4 Is first aid taught on Tuesdays? No, it isn't.

TRACK 82

Unit 7, Global Citizenship

A Listen to Mary and Isaac talk about volunteer roles. Why do you think the colored jackets are important?

Isaac: Hello, Mary. Why are you wearing that yellow jacket? I could see you from way over there!
Mary: I volunteered to be the new junior fire marshal for our class, and I've just been to a training session. The next time we have a fire drill and we all have to evacuate the building, I'll help guide people to the emergency exit—there's a map, you know, and I'll make sure everyone leaves the building quickly. And I have to make sure the windows are closed and that people don't panic and start running.
Isaac: I bet you'll be good at that—you're good at keeping calm, and you never seem too stressed. Do you have to sound the alarm, too?
Mary: Not necessarily—in a real fire, it should be done by the first person to see or smell a fire. But for the drill, which is just a practice, one of the teachers does it.
Isaac: That makes sense.
Mary: There's also a teacher who is the volunteer first-aider: he has a green jacket.
Isaac: Oh, yes, Mr. Murray, the P.E. teacher. I've seen him with his box.
Mary: Yes, he showed it to us and how he prepares it so it all fits in. He's the person we should call for help if someone gets injured during a drill or even in the yard at recess. And having the right stuff in the first aid kit is really important.
Isaac: Yes, I remember when Stefan fell during soccer practice, he told us that the most important thing before a first responder arrives is not to move the person. Ever!
Mary: Well, unless there's a fire …!
Isaac: Oh, yes!

TRACK 83

Unit 7, Global Citizenship

B Look at the pictures and definitions in A and write. Then listen and check.

1 emergency exit
2 sound the alarm (British English: raise the alarm)
3 first responder (British English: emergency services)
4 rescue
5 call for help
6 prepare
7 keep calm
8 panic
9 drill
10 evacuate

TRACK G

Unit 7, Global Citizenship

Listen and say. What do you think of when you hear these words? Talk with your friend.

Emergency exit. Say "emergency exit."
Sound the alarm. Say "sound the alarm."
First responder. Say "first responder."
Rescue. Say "rescue."
Call for help. Say "call for help."
Prepare. Say "prepare."
Keep calm. Say "keep calm."
Panic. Say "panic."
Drill. Say "drill."
Evacuate. Say "evacuate."

TRACK 84

Unit 7, Global Citizenship

D Now listen to a podcast about the origins of the first aid kit. What was the happy accident?

Host 1: Today's podcast is all about a chance meeting and how an idea changed the world.
Host 2: Imagine it's the year 1880 and a group of men are working hard building a railroad across the USA—it's noisy and dusty. Everyone's hot and tired. Suddenly, there's an accident! "Call the doctor!" shouts his friend. They wait. Eventually, the doctor arrives, but too much time has passed, and the man's injured hand is now in a very bad state. The patient won't work again. Now imagine it's a few years later, and a businessperson is traveling by train going on vacation. He starts talking to another passenger—a doctor. This isn't the plot of a movie; it's the true story of how the first aid kit came about.
Host 1: That's right. The businessperson turned out to be Mr. Robert Wood Johnson, the owner of a company making products for doctors and nurses, and the other passenger was in fact a top doctor working for the railroad company. Together they realized how they could help each other. After his vacation, Mr. Johnson got his chief scientist to create a box with sterile surgical products which the railroad workers could keep nearby. This meant they could provide immediate care after an accident often by disinfecting the injured area. The company talked to lots of doctors working on the railroads to decide what to put in the box. These little boxes became an essential part of the railroad equipment. Not long afterwards, Mr. Johnson's company also wrote a book of first aid instructions.
Host 2: Today, every school, home, office, railroad, and ship has its own first aid kit, just in case. In our schools, a first aid kit is used to treat cuts and scrapes, and sometimes we can help people with a headache, but when kids go on a school trip to another country, they take a different first aid kit with lots more things.

Not only that, but we also now know about being hygienic and washing our hands before treating a patient. Mr. Johnson and his conversation changed how we prepare for accidents and emergencies.
Host 1: That could be called a happy accident! Now I'm going to sign up for a first aid course so I know what to do with the things in the box.
Host 2: Me, too.

TRACK 85
Unit 7, Explore Language
A Listen and read. How has Archie helped his sister?
Aziz: Hi, Archie! We haven't seen you at the park for ages. Where have you been?
Archie: I've been with my sister. She's broken her leg and can't move around much. She hurt herself on a ski trip.
Paul: Oh, no! That must be really difficult—I can't imagine not being able to move!
Archie: It's not that bad, Paul! And it's only for a few weeks, while the bones heal.
Aziz: So, how did she do it?
Paul: Did she have to go to the hospital? Were there lots of doctors and nurses?
Aziz: Was there lots of blood?
Paul: Will she be able to ski again?
Archie: Stop, stop! I can't hear myself think! No, Aziz, there wasn't any blood, and yes, she did go to the hospital, and yes, she'll be skiing again very soon!
Aziz: So, what have you been doing?
Archie: I've been keeping her company. We've played some of our old games from when we were younger and recently, we've been teaching ourselves to play the guitar.
Paul: The guitar? Wow!
Archie: I know! You should try it yourself. It's so much fun! And the doctor says I've been doing an important job, helping my sister to heal mentally as well as physically.

TRACK 86
Unit 7, Explore Language
D Listen and say.
1 I can't hear myself think!
2 Don't hurt yourself.
3 Katrin cut herself on a knife.
4 Let's introduce ourselves.
5 Did they enjoy themselves? Yes, they did.

Unit 8

TRACK 87
Unit 8, Vocabulary
A Listen. How did the Ancient Chinese improve their lives?
Aziz: I love field trips! Did you know that the Ancient Egyptians had toothbrushes?!
Jasmin: Yes, I read that, too. Come on—let's look at this display about Ancient China. Oh!
Liu Wei: My name's Liu Wei. Welcome to Ancient China. Let me tell you about Ancient Chinese technology. They had phones and laptops? No, not that kind of technology! I mean other practical inventions that improved people's everyday lives. Do you have an umbrella? Do you use matches or fly kites? They all came from Ancient China.
Jasmin: Wow! This is interesting.
Liu Wei: We invented paper and printing using blocks of wood so we didn't have to write everything by hand.
Jasmin: I wouldn't want to write a whole book by hand!
Liu Wei: We were also famous for our engineering—we built the Great Wall of China. And to help us travel to countries far away to trade, we invented the compass. Some people say we invented pasta!
Aziz: I didn't know that.
Jasmin: Where now—shall we go to the Incas?
Aziz: Yes, let's go.
Jasmin: Look, Aziz—they used colored thread to record information. And they preserved potatoes by drying them outside in the cold—that's like having a really old freezer!
Aziz: Wow! Look at all of the people crossing that bridge! It must be very strong!

TRACK 88
Unit 8, Vocabulary
B Find and number the words in A. Then listen and check.
1 stone
2 record information
3 cross
4 solution
5 practical
6 printing
7 engineering
8 preserve
9 invent

TRACK 89
Unit 8, Vocabulary
C Close your eyes. Listen, visualize, and say.
You're in the history museum. You're looking at different ways to record information. Touch the pages of a book. Say "record information."
Look at the picture of food. How did people use to preserve it for the winter? Say "preserve."
Now you're standing in front of a map. Look closely. Is that a boat? Imagine it crossing the ocean. Say "cross."
Now you can have a go: take the block of wood and make a pattern on the material. Press down hard so the pattern stays. Say "printing."
Look at a picture of the Great Wall of China. How is it still standing after so many years, do you think? Say "engineering."
There's a stone like the ones used in the wall. Touch it. Is it smooth or rough? Say "stone."
Transporting the stones was a problem. Imagine the solution. Say "solution."
And this is a display of inventions. What's the most practical invention, do you think? Say "practical."
Can you invent something new to help improve everyday life? What is it? Say "invent."

TRACK 90
Unit 8, Vocabulary
E Listen and write. Then watch and say.
Famous Inventions

Ancient Chinese history
Is known for its technology.
We found practical solutions
To many of life's problems—
Just look around you and you'll see!

Famous for our inventions.
Kites and fireworks, did I mention?
Paper, silk, printing, too,
I bring them all to your attention—
Just look around you and you'll see!

Famous for our engineering.
The stones of our Great Wall
Have stood for over 2,000 years.
But we left it to the Romans
To invent concrete buildings …
Just don't stop looking and you'll see!

TRACK 91
Unit 8, Vocabulary
F Pronunciation. Listen and say. Copy the linking. Think of other phrases like these.
Just look around. (x2)
Great Wall (x2)
Just don't stop. (x2)

TRACK 92
Unit 8, Explore Language
A Listen and read. What does Jasmin want to do?
Jasmin: The Incas lived in the Andes in South America from the 12th century to the 16th century. Their empire grew big and powerful because they had very good engineers who built around 39,000 km. of roads. They also built amazing bridges.
Caleb: I didn't know the Incas were so good at engineering!
Jasmin: I know—it's fascinating, isn't it, Caleb?
Jasmin: Look! We can build a bridge like the Incas.
Caleb: Cool! So what did they have to do? I wonder how the Incas carried the stones for the bridges. I couldn't do that!
Jasmin: No! They didn't have to carry stones. They made the bridges out of rope.
Caleb: Rope? Were they safe?
Jasmin: Oh, yes. The bridges had to be strong enough for people and animals. The Incas didn't use vehicles with wheels.
Caleb: OK. But the bridges look dangerous! Did the people have to be careful?
Jasmin: Yes, they did—of course! They had to use the bridges in the mornings because it was often too windy later in the day.
Jasmin: Come on, Caleb. Let's get started.
Caleb: Yes! So first we have to tie the rope to the tree. Oooof!
Jasmin: What's wrong?
Caleb: This rope is so heavy!

TRACK 93
Unit 8, Explore Language
D Listen and say.
1 What did they have to do?
2 She had to preserve the food.
3 I didn't have to find a solution.
4 Did you have to cross the bridge? Yes, we did.

TRACK 94
Unit 8, Global Citizenship
A Listen to Umeko, and her dad talk about their yard. What solution do they find for their problem?
Dad: Umeko should we grow some vegetables?
Umeko: Um, where, Dad? Our yard's too small!
Dad: Well, I thought that, too. But last night I watched a documentary about ancient civilizations, and it gave me an idea. In the past, people found solutions to problems like ours all the time!
Umeko: Sounds interesting.
Dad: They said that a long time ago in Mexico, as the Aztec Empire grew, people needed to grow more food. The country had many lakes, so they developed a way of growing food in water—it was very successful!
Umeko: In water? How?
Dad: Well, their culture encouraged people to work hard, so they used their knowledge of plants to create "floating" gardens on the lakes.
Umeko: But we don't have a lake, Dad!

Dad: I know! I'm not saying we should copy the Aztecs exactly, but we can learn from them. First, we should assess what we have. Then we can figure out a technique for growing vegetables in small spaces.
Umeko: Hmm … we don't have space on the ground … but we have sunny walls, and those big pots! Could we grow plants on the wall or climbing up sticks in pots?
Dad: Great solution, Umeko! So—we need plants that grow tall.
Umeko: I know! Beans! And maybe tomatoes!

TRACK 95
Unit 8, Global Citizenship
B Look at the pictures and definitions in A and write. Then listen and check.
1 assess
2 discover
3 knowledge
4 create
5 technique
6 culture
7 develop
8 civilization

TRACK H
Unit 8, Global Citizenship
Close your eyes. Listen, think, visualize, and say.
Imagine you're living in the past in an ancient civilization. Which civilization is it? What are the people like? Say "civilization."
In this civilization, what do people know about growing food or building towns? Say "knowledge."
Think about how this civilization can change. What might be different in the future? Say "develop."
Look around. What do you have? What do you need? Say "assess."
Can you create something you need and don't have? Imagine. Say "create."
How are you going to do it? Experiment until you find a good way to do it. Say "technique."
You travel to explore the places around you. What new places and things do you discover? Say "discover."
What are the ideas and beliefs in this civilization? Are they the same as yours today? Say "culture."

TRACK 96
Unit 8, Global Citizenship
D Now listen to historian Dr. Abbas. Why do you think she's fascinated by the Ancient Romans?
This week on Amazing Civilizations, we're looking at Ancient Rome. Like the Aztecs, the Romans were brilliant at solving problems! We can still see some of their creative solutions in use today. So what sort of problems did they solve? Well, let's think first about the problem of getting water to big cities like Rome. There wasn't enough water in the River Tiber for everyone in the city, so they had to bring water from the countryside, often from a long way away. Water is heavy, so they couldn't transport it in buckets! The Romans didn't have any modern equipment, but they were very smart. They built aqueducts—huge bridges which carried water high above the ground. Aqueducts really improved the lives of people in the cities—for the first time they had a regular supply of water for drinking, cooking, and washing. And to continue with washing—the Romans also used their engineering skills to build public baths, where everyone could go to get clean. Baths were also places where people could meet their friends and relax!
I think we can learn a lot from the Ancient Romans. It's true that in the 21st century we don't need aqueducts because we've developed ways of transporting water under the ground. And most people have their own bathrooms, so we don't need public baths. But sharing resources in our communities, the way the Romans shared their public baths, is good. Which resources are shared in your community? Can you think of any others it would be good to share?

TRACK 97
Unit 8, Explore Language
A Listen and read. Why do people learn Latin now?
Caleb: What's that language? Who was it used by?
Juana: It's Latin. It was spoken by the Ancient Romans, but no one speaks it any more—it's a dead language. When I was in school, we were taught Latin to help us learn other languages.
Caleb: How does knowing an old language help you learn new ones?
Juana: Well, modern languages weren't created out of nowhere, you know. They were developed from earlier languages. French, Spanish, Italian, and Portuguese all came from Latin, and many English words do, too.
Caleb: So how does that make it easier to learn them?
Juana: Well, for example, you know the English word *audience*. That comes from the Latin *audio*, meaning *I hear*. So when I read the English word *audible* for the first time, I was able to figure out its meaning.
Caleb: Wow, that's pretty useful … but it's too bad you can't speak Latin with anyone.
Juana: Sure, I can—I can teach you!

TRACK 98
Unit 8, Explore Language
D Listen and say.
1 Who was it used by?
2 Their skills were admired by everyone.
3 Were you taught Latin in school? No, I wasn't.
4 The coins were discovered by a historian.

Unit 9

TRACK 99
Unit 9, Vocabulary
A Listen. Who did the princess turn into?
Juana: The plot of *The Snow Queen* isn't just exciting—it's thrilling! The story begins in a country far away. The narrator is an old woman. She introduces us to the main characters.
I knew her when she was a princess. She was very beautiful—but she was also cold to the people around her. When the king, her father, gave her a special mirror, she spent all her time looking at herself in it. She forgot to play. She stopped learning.
"This mirror is bad for you," her brother said, but when he tried to take it away from her, it flew out the window. The mirror broke into a thousand pieces. The princess gave her brother a cruel smile.
"You're now my enemy," she said.
"I'll fight against you to make this kingdom mine. I will be the Snow Queen!"
And she left the palace. The tiny pieces of glass from the mirror were blown by the wind. Some flew into people's eyes and hearts. Then they also became cold and everything in the world looked ugly to them.
Who could stop the princess once she became the Snow Queen? Perhaps the young hero Kay and the heroine Gerda, two friends who wondered why it was snowing, were brave enough to fight the Snow Queen.
Nadeen: What's going to happen? Tell us, Juana—don't keep us in suspense!

TRACK 100
Unit 9, Vocabulary
B Find and number the words in A. Then listen and check.
1 cruel
2 brave
3 suspense
4 enemy
5 cliffhanger
6 thrilling
7 narrator
8 plot
9 terrifying
10 characters
11 villain
12 hero
13 heroine

TRACK 101
Unit 9, Vocabulary
C Close your eyes. Listen, visualize, and say.
Now it's your turn to be the storyteller. Think about your story. How many characters are there? Say "characters."
Is there a hero? What's he like? Say "hero."
What's the heroine like? Is she brave? Say "heroine."
The villain is a bad man—why is he bad? Say "villain."
How old is the narrator? Say "narrator."
The villain does a cruel thing. What is it? Say "cruel."
The villain is the enemy of the hero and heroine. Why? Say "enemy."
Oh, no! The characters are in a terrifying place. Why is it so scary? Say "terrifying."
Oooh! The first part of the story ends on a cliffhanger. What will happen to the hero and heroine? Say "cliffhanger."
The story continues. They can't leave. We don't know what will happen next. Say "suspense."
They do something brave. What do they do? Say "brave."
Oh! How exciting! The ending is thrilling. Imagine the feeling. Say "thrilling."
What happens in the end? Picture the plot—the beginning, the middle, and the end of your story. Say "plot."

TRACK 102
Unit 9, Vocabulary
E Listen and write. Then watch and say.
Tell Us a Story, Storyteller

Can you tell us a story
With a really cool plot?
With a dragon and a hero
Who's rescued a lot
From a terrifying place
Even darker than space.
Tell us a story, Storyteller.

Can you tell us a story
With a cliffhanger now?
All the characters in trouble
We have to help them somehow!
The villain is coming!
What are they going to do?!
Tell us a story, Storyteller.

Let us follow you, Storyteller
Into those different worlds.
Please, tell us a story, Storyteller.

TRACK 103
Unit 9, Vocabulary
F Pronunciation. Listen and say. Copy the weak forms. Think of other phrases like these.
have to (x2)
going to (x2)
into (x2)

TRACK 104
Unit 9, Explore Language
A Listen and read. Do you think Gerda will find Kay?
Luca: That storytelling session sounds fantastic!
Nadeen: It was! Now, where was I? Ah, yes … a tiny piece of glass from the broken mirror went into Kay's eye. It made his heart cold, and he was cruel to his friend, Gerda. He just couldn't stop himself. The Snow Queen came to get him. "You're mine now," she said. "I'd forget about Gerda if I were you."
Luca: Oh, no!
Nadeen: Everyone except Gerda thought Kay was dead. She said, "If I were lost, Kay would look for me. I have to rescue him." And she went off to find him. The first person she met was a lonely old woman. Her house had a beautiful garden.
The old woman thought, "If Gerda were my daughter, she'd stay with me forever." She tried to make Gerda forget about Kay and stay with her. However, Gerda was very determined, and luckily, she was able to escape. But then she was attacked by some robbers! Oh, this is my stop!
Luca: You can't stop now! What happened next?
Nadeen: That's called a cliffhanger!

TRACK 105
Unit 9, Explore Language
D Listen and say.
1 I'd forget about Gerda if I were you.
2 If he were interested, he'd do some research.
3 If we had more time, we'd go skating.
4 They'd play better if they practiced more.

TRACK 106
Unit 9, Global Citizenship
A Listen to Harry talk to his grandpa about a local project. What stories does Harry's grandpa want to tell?
Harry: Grandpa, will you take part in the Memory Diaries project with me?
Grandpa: What do I have to do?
Harry: Just talk about your life. About what you did when you were young and how you came to live here. Then everyone will be able to share your stories.
Grandpa: I do have some funny anecdotes from when I was a construction worker.
Harry: That's great! What about?
Grandpa: Well, we always used to play tricks on new workers.
Harry: Why?
Grandpa: To welcome them to the team—it was just a bit of fun! My favorite trick was to send them off to buy rainbow paint.
Harry: Why is that a trick? … Oh, I get it!
Grandpa: And the tricks were passed on. When that worker had been with us for a while, he was ready to play tricks on the next new person!
Harry: Now I understand why you liked being a construction worker! I love stories like that. They really make you use your imagination. When I hear all the details, I can picture and feel what it was like to be you.
Grandpa: Yes, stories can help you empathize with other people. Like the story of how I got my nickname Spider.
Harry: They called you Spider! Why?
Grandpa: Ah—I'll tell you when they record my stories for the Memory Diaries.
Harry: Great! Thanks for bringing me fishing, Grandpa.
Grandpa: I love sharing these moments with you.

TRACK 107
Unit 9, Global Citizenship
B Look at the pictures and definitions in A and write. Then listen and check.
1 understand
2 imagination
3 empathize
4 fascinating
5 details
6 pass on
7 surprising
8 anecdote
9 moral
10 share

TRACK 1
Unit 9, Global Citizenship
Close your eyes. Listen, think, visualize, and say.
Think about the story of the Snow Queen. Why does Kay find the Snow Queen fascinating? Say "fascinating".
Can you understand why the princess was angry with her brother? Say "understand."
Imagine you're the heroine, Gerda. You're traveling through the snowy landscape. You catch a snowflake. Picture the details of the pattern. Say "details."
Now you're with the robber girl. She tells you an anecdote about her family. Is it funny? Is it scary? Say "anecdote."
Which of the characters do you empathize with most easily? Why is that? Say "empathize."
Build a picture of the Snow Queen's palace in your imagination. What's it like? Say "imagination."
Now imagine something surprising in one of the rooms. Say "surprising."
Who would you like to share the story of the Snow Queen with? Say "share."
Now think of a story you want to pass on to someone else. Say "pass on."
Does your story have a moral? What lesson can you learn? Say "moral."

TRACK 108
Unit 9, Global Citizenship
D Now listen to Zoë. What is the Memory Diaries project?
I set up the Memory Diaries project in our community for two reasons. I teach the trumpet, and I had the idea one day when the mother of a boy came to collect him after his class. Manu is a really good trumpet player, and he started to talk to his mother about how important music is to him. He asked his mother if anyone else in the family was musical. Her answer was surprising. When his great-grandma was young, she sang in a band in Mexico. She died years before Manu was born—before his parents came to live in this country—so he never knew her. But when his mother told him that story, Manu explained that he felt close to his great-grandma for the first time. It was very special to share that moment with him and his mom. I love stories. I always knew that reading stories was a great way to understand and empathize with people, and now I realize how powerful listening to people's stories can be, too. I wanted to help people make space in their lives to listen to each other. We're all so distracted by our smartphones and tablets, so busy studying and working, we forget that talking is such a special way to connect with people.
The other reason I started the Memory Diaries project is that we're losing so much information about life in the past. If a child asks his dad about the first house he lived in, his dad will start to describe the house—but very soon he'll go on to tell anecdotes about his sisters, his pets, his school, and how he came to live in this community. These stories are passed on and become part of the family's and the community's history. In the Memory Diaries project, I listen to people's stories, write them down, and then publish them on a community website so that everyone in the community gets to share them.

TRACK 109
Unit 9, Explore Language
A Listen and read. Who helped Gerda escape from the robbers?
Luca: They were robbers! Big scary robbers! Gerda was taken to their secret hiding place. She was very surprised when a little robber girl spoke to her. The girl was kind and decided to help Gerda. She told Gerda how to find the Snow Queen and said, "If I came with you, I wouldn't be much help." But she gave Gerda a reindeer so she could travel quickly.
Mostafa: Hurry, Gerda!
Luca: Gerda rode through the frozen fields. She was thankful for her strong, fast reindeer. If it weren't for him, she would be too late. At last she arrived at the Snow Queen's palace! Kay was there—but he didn't recognize Gerda.
Mostafa: I can't believe he's forgotten her!
Luca: Gerda was very worried. How could she save Kay? What would she do if he didn't remember her? Would he be OK if she looked after him?

TRACK 110
Unit 9, Explore Language
D Listen and say.
1 If I came with you, I wouldn't be much help.
2 Would you believe him if he gave you more details? Yes, I would.
3 What would happen if they didn't find the key?
4 The story would be fascinating if it weren't so long.

Unit 10

TRACK 111
Unit 10, Vocabulary
A Listen. Why does Mostafa think Dubai is a good place for the Design Club to visit?
Mostafa: This event is awesome! Have you seen the display of all the amazing places to visit in the city?
Tareq: Yes, it's incredible to see the work of so many talented and creative designers. The building which looks like the sail of a ship built on a man-made island …
Mostafa: And the skyscraper built to look like a desert flower! It's really beautiful, and it's super smart. The architects designed it so that the glass is protected from the sun and doesn't become a mirror.
Tareq: But energy from the sun is useful, too. Solar panels heat the water for the people in the building—the whole country uses a lot of solar power as well as energy made from recycling waste.
Mostafa: Just look at that design for a solar tower! I totally understand why our Design Club came to this city—I feel really inspired. I have so many ideas, I don't know where to begin!

Jasmin: Hey, Mostafa, Tareq! Come and look at the exhibition about how transportation is evolving in the city. I've just tried out an electric hoverbike—it was so much fun!
Mostafa: Wow, that's really original—I've never seen anything like it!
Jasmin: At the moment it's too heavy to carry easily, but the designers are working on making it lighter—then everyone will want a portable hoverbike!
Tareq: It makes my bike look pretty useless … Oh look! The Dancing Fountains have started … come on!
Mostafa: Is there time to watch them before they judge our designs?

TRACK 112
Unit 10, Vocabulary
B Find and number the words in A. Then listen and check.
1 evolve
2 original
3 useless
4 portable
5 useful
6 design
7 man-made
8 heavy
9 light

TRACK 113
Unit 10, Vocabulary
C Close your eyes. Listen, visualize, and say.
You're on vacation with your class. Have you got the right equipment with you? Are the items suitable for the vacation? Picture yourself using the items. How do they feel? What is it about the design that makes them feel like this?
A heavy backpack—oooof! Say "heavy."
A light sleeping bag—aaaaah! Say "light."
A useful phone with a camera—take a photo! Say "useful."
A useless flashlight—I can't see anything! Say "useless."
A portable chair—you can sit down wherever you want! Say "portable."
Some original sneakers—no one else has sneakers like these! Say "original."
A man-made souvenir—what is it? Say "man-made."
Camping and tents have changed a lot in the last 40 years. Imagine an old tent and a new one. Say "evolve."
You need a bigger bag to bring home your souvenirs. Draw a picture of it. Say "design."

TRACK 114
Unit 10, Vocabulary
E Listen and write. Then watch and say.
Design's My Line

If it doesn't look nice,
And it's heavy, too,
If you have something useless,
I know what to do.

I'll design you a bike
That's incredibly light
So portable and fast
You'll soon ride out of sight.

I'll design you a phone
So easy to use
With lots of useful apps
To keep you amused.

I'll design you a watch—
With original features
I can, yes, I can
I'm an inspired young designer!

TRACK 115
Unit 10, Vocabulary
F Pronunciation. Listen and say. Copy the linking. Find three more phrases like these in the rap.
you a bike (x2)
so easy (x2)

TRACK 116
Unit 10, Explore Language
A Listen and read. What does Archie's watch do at the end?
Miguel: Nice watch, Archie!
Archie: But it's not just a watch! It's an ActiveTime. That talk on watches yesterday inspired me to buy one!
Miguel: I missed that talk. What was it about?
Archie: A designer at the museum was talking about watch design. It was really interesting. First he asked how many of us wore a watch. Then he described how watch design has changed over the centuries. Watches used to be big and heavy. People carried them in their pockets.
Miguel: Like me! I don't wear a watch. My cell phone is my watch!
Archie: But people wanted something more portable and easier to use, so watches were designed to go on our wrists, not in our pockets. And of course, today watches can do much more than tell the time—they connect to the internet, they help you if you get lost, they help you keep fit … like my ActiveTime! This morning it asked me if I needed to do some exercise.
Miguel: Wow—cool! How did it do that?
Archie: Sorry—got to go! My ActiveTime told me not to be lazy!
Miguel: But I asked you how it did that? I really want to …

TRACK 117
Unit 10, Explore Language
D Listen and say.
1 He asked how many of us wore a watch.
2 I wanted to know whether he liked the design.
3 We asked him if it still worked.
4 She wondered if the trip was useful.
5 They asked her whether it was portable.

TRACK 118
Unit 10, Global Citizenship
A Listen to Inès talk to Rafael. Why is Rafael's backpack special?
Inès: Wow! I love your backpack, Rafael!
Rafael: Thanks, Inès.
Inès: Where did you get it? I'm looking for a new one.
Rafael: Well, you won't find one like this anywhere!
Inès: Why not? Did you buy it when you were on vacation?
Rafael: No—I designed it myself.
Inès: No way! How did you do that?
Rafael: First, I looked carefully at the design of ordinary backpacks. Then, I assessed my needs and customized this design for myself.
Inès: So this backpack is exactly what you need?
Rafael: That's right. I play a lot of sports and my bag gets dirty, so I chose a material that would be easy to clean. Look inside. There's a special place for my keys—I was always losing them! My lunch fits in here. And at last I have enough space for my books!
Inès: What are the buttons for?
Rafael: That's the best part! They're to play music from my phone so I don't have to take it out of my backpack while I'm walking.
Inès: Wow! Your design is very effective. Was it difficult?
Rafael: There was a bit of trial and error. Some things didn't work at first, so I had to do them again.
Inès: Could you make different backpacks?
Rafael: Yes! This design is flexible—you can change it in lots of ways.
Inès: Could you adapt the backpack for a BMX helmet?
Rafael: Um, yeah—I could do that!
Inès: Oooh—could you make one for me?
Rafael: I'd love to!

TRACK 119
Unit 10, Global Citizenship
B Look at the pictures and definitions in A and write. Then listen and check.
1 adapt
2 feedback
3 material
4 effective
5 flexible
6 trial and error
7 user-friendly
8 customize

TRACK J
Unit 10, Global Citizenship
Close your eyes. Listen, think, visualize, and say.
You have the opportunity to design a new product. Think about the material you need to use for it. Feel it—is it strong or soft? Say "material."
The design is good—but it's not quite right. What feedback does your teacher give you to make it better? Say "feedback."
You make a mistake. Never mind—try again! Say "trial and error."
You want to make it special for you. How do you customize it? Say "customize."
Your design is effective—how does it meet the needs of potential customers? Say "effective."
Will people know how to use it, or do you need to give instructions? Say "user-friendly."
Is it a design you can adapt for other people? How? Say "adapt."
Can you change your design for different people's needs? Will you be flexible and let other people give their ideas? Say "flexible."

TRACK 120
Unit 10, Global Citizenship
D Now listen to Sadie and Misha being interviewed. What is their project?
Host: I'm talking today to two students at Carlton High School who are involved in an exciting community project. Sadie, what's the project?
Sadie: Well, we have a really great design teacher at our school—Mr. Khan. At the beginning of last semester, he told us about a class of design students from Lynbrook High School in New York who had solved real problems for real patients in a children's hospital. Mr. Khan asked us if we wanted to do something useful like this in our town. Of course we said yes! We spoke to the organizers of a weekend activity center for young children with learning difficulties, and we were able to visit them and talk to the parents and children. We found out that it can be difficult for them to use everyday things, so our project was to find some solutions.
Host: That's great! Misha, can you tell us about some of the things you've designed?

Misha: Well, we've customized things like spoons and forks to make them easier for the children to use. And we've made plastic toys to help them improve their knowledge of shapes and how things fit together.
Sadie: We've also made some new games for them—they really love the one with dinosaurs.
Host: That's great! So, who makes the products for you?
Sadie: We do! We draw the designs for our products, and then we use the computer to make them into 3-D models.
Misha: Of course we show all our designs to Mr. Khan and get his feedback before we make them on the 3-D printer.
Host: Wow! You're really talented.
Sadie: We all love designing—it's great to design and adapt things that make life better for people. And it's very rewarding to work with the children.

TRACK 121
Unit 10, Explore Language
A Listen and read. Which two designs do Susie and Archie talk about?
Susie: This trip has been great, hasn't it?
Archie: Yes, it has. And the suspense is nearly over. Only a few minutes before we know who the Young Designer of the Year is.
Susie: Yes! Have you seen some of these other amazing designs? I love this door that opens out to make a table tennis table!
Archie: That's awesome—I'd like one of those at home!
Susie: Me, too! And what about this skateboard parking unit?
Archie: It's too bad I don't have a skateboard at the moment.
Susie: Neither do I, but I want to get a new one soon.
Archie: So do I. I've been saving up, so I might be able to get one next month.
Susie: Three more minutes! The designs for the competition have been very creative this year, haven't they? I really don't know which one is going to win.
Archie: I don't either. All the ideas are fantastic.

TRACK 122
Unit 10. Explore Language
D Listen and say.
1 I'd like one of those at home. Me, too!
2 Sid's design is great. So is Sara's.
3 He didn't do his homework. She didn't either.
4 We're going to Art School. So is John.

Literacy Book

Literacy Review

TRACK 1
Literacy Review, Fiction, *A Shaky Start*
Narrator: Suddenly, Barry and Bella heard a loud crack and then a rumble from inside the volcano. The ground started shaking. Barry panicked. He turned back to the eggs, just in time to see one of them rolling down the side of the volcano. Barry chased after it as it rolled faster and faster down the dangerous path, to the sea below.
Bella: Hurry! You have to save it!
Narrator: shouted Bella, flapping her wings wildly over the nest. Barry flew even faster. The volcano rumbled again. More black sand and rocks fell around him.
Barry: *Our nest wasn't in a safe place! The egg won't survive in the cold water,*
Narrator: he thought as he flapped his wings. Then the egg rolled off the side of the volcano and into the sea. Barry flew up high and then dived straight down into the water.

TRACK 2
Literacy Review, Nonfiction, *Welcome to the Galápagos Islands*
Off the coast of Ecuador in South America are the Galápagos Islands. These volcanic islands are a UNESCO World Heritage Site. They are home to some wonderful animals. Many of these animals do not live anywhere else on earth!
Marine Iguana
These are the only sea lizards in the world. When they arrived on the islands millions of years ago, there wasn't enough food on land so they learned to swim and started eating seaweed from the salty seawater!
Galápagos Penguin
Most penguins live in Antarctica, but Galápagos penguins live at the Equator. They survive there because cold water from Antarctica flows north past the islands. They spend the day in the sea hunting for fish and return to the land at night.
Blue-Footed Booby
This funny-looking bird has bright blue feet and its name comes from the Spanish word *bobo*, meaning fool. It can dive from up to 100 meters in the air into the sea to catch fish.

TRACK 3
Literacy Review, Nonfiction, Spelling Pattern, Final *–ed*
Listen and write. Complete the table.
grabbed
moved
decided
learned
slipped
hugged
pointed
recognized
waited

Unit 1

TRACK 4
Unit 1, Fiction, *You're Out!*
Luis: Hello, and welcome to the students-versus-teachers dodgeball game. I'm Luis.
Victoria: And I'm Victoria. We're your hosts for this exciting game today. The referee is our principal and the whole school is here, waiting for the game to begin.
Last year, the teachers won easily, but it's going to be a much tougher game today. The students trained a lot!
Luis: These are not beginners, Victoria, and there's a big reward for the students if they win: a pizza and movie party.
Victoria: The students' team has a new captain, Sara Lopez. Sara is a dodgeball hotshot. Bay Elementary has never seen a player catch so well, or throw so fast.
Luis: Sara's the player to watch today.
Victoria: Everyone looks ready to step up to the plate!
Luis: Everyone dashes towards the balls.
Victoria: Oh! The librarian, Ms. Ruiz, gets the first out.
Max: Aw, man.
Luis: Max did NOT see that coming.
Victoria: Out! Mr. Martin, the math teacher, is gone.
Luis: What's this? Camilo hits Mr. Nuñez!
Victoria: Mr. King tags Erica!
Luis: Camilo takes out two teachers with one ball. Two teachers …
Victoria: … and two students left. It's neck and neck.
Luis: Ms. Ruiz launches the ball …
Victoria: … it barely misses Camilo …
Sara: Ow!
Luis: … and Sara, the students' team, captain is out!
Sara: You've got this, Camilo!
Victoria: It's two against one.
Principal: Mr. King, you're out of bounds. You're out!
Mr. King: Nooooo!
Luis: It's just Ms. Ruiz and Camilo now! There hasn't been a game this close since first grade.
Victoria: It's heading straight for him.
Luis: … and he catches it! Ms. Ruiz is out! Wait, is he saying no?
Camilo: I didn't catch the ball in the air. It bounced first.
Principal: Oh, Ms. Ruiz is NOT out!
Luis: What great sportsmanship from Camilo! He looks tired. Can he go the distance?
Victoria: Ms. Ruiz throws the ball …
Luis: … and he's caught the ball! This time Ms. Ruiz really is out!
Luis and Victoria: The students win!
Principal: Both teams played with great energy and sportsmanship. You looked like you were really enjoying yourselves!
Victoria: It's pizza and movies for everybody!
Luis: What an unexpected performance from Camilo! Wow, what a game! I'm Luis …
Victoria: And I'm Victoria. Thanks for watching, and see you next year!

TRACK 5
Unit 1, *You're Out!*, Words in Context
Find these words in the reading. What do you think they mean?
hosts
tougher
strikes
shakes
sportsmanship

TRACK 6

Unit 1, Nonfiction, *The Ultimate Game*

The History of Frisbee

It all started with a pie tin.

Many years ago, a group of students in the USA discovered that the empty tins from the Frisbie Pie Company flew really well when thrown. They shouted "Frisbie!" while they were throwing the pie tins, and a sport was born.

Today, people around the world play with Frisbees for fun, but there are Frisbee sports, too. One of the most popular is ultimate Frisbee.

Ultimate for Beginners

You Need:

A Frisbee

Two teams of at least seven players each

A field about the same size as a soccer field—100 meters long, and 37 meters wide

Two end zones.

How to Play:

1 One team stands in one end zone and defends it, keeping the other team from scoring points. The other team stands in the other end zone and defends it. The teams face each other.

2 To start, the teams flip a coin to see which team throws the Frisbee first. This throw is called the pull.

3 The team with the Frisbee is the team on offense. The players try to pass the Frisbee up the field from one player to another. To score a goal, they must catch the Frisbee in the other team's end zone.

4 The team on defense has to try to stop the other team from scoring.

5 The winning team is the first to score 15 goals. Another way to play is with a time limit. The team with the most goals at the end of the time wins.

Basic Rules:

Don't run with the Frisbee.

Don't hold the Frisbee for more than 10 seconds.

Don't make contact with other players.

Don't grab or knock the Frisbee from another player's hands.

If two players catch the Frisbee at the same time, it goes to the team trying to score a goal.

The Frisbee goes to the other team if:

the Frisbee hits the ground;

a player throws the Frisbee out of bounds;

a player on the defending team catches the Frisbee.

When a team scores, its players stay in that end zone and start the game again with a pull. Now they have to defend. This means that after every goal, the scoring team plays in a different direction.

A player can be substituted, or replaced, after a goal or if a player is hurt.

Playing Fairly

In many sports, the referee, or umpire, controls the game. They decide when goals are scored or if there has been a foul. In ultimate, there is usually no referee. The players organize the game. If there is a problem or a foul, they talk about it calmly and decide what to do.

Sportsmanship is a key part of ultimate. Teams do their best to win, but fair play is as important as winning.

So, grab a Frisbee and take part in the ultimate game.

TRACK 7

Unit 1, *The Ultimate Game*, Words in Context

Find these words in the reading. What do you think they mean?

defends

flip a coin (British English: toss a coin)

on offense (British English: attacking)

substituted

referee

foul

Unit 2

TRACK 8

Unit 2, Fiction, *Arthur's Adventures*

Dad: Arthur,

Narrator: Dad said,

Dad: you've lived in this tide pool since you were born. You're old enough for your first shell now.

Mom: You need a strong shell to protect you,

Narrator: Mom added.

Mom: You need to be safe! The open sea can be dangerous.

Deka: Can I have a shell too, Mom?

Narrator: Arthur's little sister, Deka, asked.

Mom: Not yet,

Narrator: Mom answered.

Mom: Soon.

Dad: Good strong shells are hard to find, so choose well,

Narrator: said Dad.

Sales Crab: Looking for a shell?

Narrator: the sales crab asked.

Sales Crab: All cool hermit crabs have these.

Arthur: Oh, wow! They're so shiny. I'll be cool if I have this one, Dad!

Narrator: said Arthur. Dad checked the shell.

Dad: Hmm … It looks weak to me, but you have to decide for yourself. It's your shell.

Narrator: said Dad.

Arthur: I'll take it!

Narrator: said Arthur.

Arthur: *I'm looking good!*

Narrator: Arthur thought, walking deeper into the sea. But Arthur didn't see the fishing boat. When the fisherman saw him, he threw Arthur back.

Arthur: (screams)

Conrad: Are you OK?

Narrator: a voice asked.
Arthur was scared. He turned around. It was another hermit crab! Before Arthur could answer, the other crab said,

Conrad: Oh, you need a new shell. Don't worry. Come with me. I know where we can go!

Arthur: Thanks. I'm Arthur. It's scary out here,

Narrator: Arthur said.

Conrad: Well, it *is* the open sea!

Narrator: the other crab replied.

Conrad: There are predators everywhere, but like my dad says, a good shell will protect you. We can go together, if you want to. By the way, my name's Conrad.

Conrad: I'll wait and trade for that bigger shell. Then, you can have mine. It'll fit you perfectly,

Narrator: Conrad explained.
But Conrad's shell was too plain for Arthur. What he really wanted was something shiny and striped. Disappointed, he went to change into Conrad's old shell.

Stranger Crab: Psst! Over here!

Narrator: a stranger crab whispered.

Arthur: Yes?

Narrator: Arthur asked.

Stranger Crab: What a plain shell! You know, I could trade you mine. It's super shiny!

Arthur: Really? OK!

Narrator: Arthur said, happily.

Arthur: *I don't believe it. I traded a really good shell for a fancy one with a hole in it,*

Narrator: Arthur thought.

Arthur: I always feel like someone's watching me,

Narrator: Arthur told Conrad.

Conrad: You ARE very easy to see, but if we stick together, we'll be safe,

Narrator: Conrad replied.

Arthur: *Conrad is calm and happy in his strong, ordinary shell,*

Narrator: Arthur thought.

Arthur: *Maybe I need a stronger shell, but I also want to look good. I need to find the right shell for me.* I'm going to find something else to wear!

Narrator: Arthur decided.

Conrad: Wait for me!

Narrator: Conrad went after him.

Arthur: *This shell is perfect!*

Narrator: Arthur thought.

Arthur: *And if I put these beautiful sea anemones on it, they'll protect me and look good.*

Narrator: Arthur saw the seaweed shake behind him.

Arthur: Hello? Hello?! Is someone there?

Narrator: Arthur asked.

Conrad: What is it?

Narrator: shouted Conrad.

Arthur: It's my sister, Deka!

Narrator: Arthur answered.

Deka: Hi, Arthur!

Narrator: Deka called.

Arthur: What are you doing here?

Deka: I missed you! When I got my first shell, I came to look for you!

Arthur: I can't believe you found me!

Narrator: said Arthur.

Arthur: And we decorated our shells the same way. These sea anemones are so—

Deka: Cool!

Narrator: said Deka. Arthur, Deka, and Conrad started their journey back to the tide pool. It took them a long time to find their way home.

Mom: Deka! Arthur! You're back!

Narrator: Mom cried happily.

Mom: My, you've both grown a lot since we last saw you,

Dad: Welcome home!

Narrator: Dad said.

Dad: How's that shell, son?

All: (laugh)

TRACK 9

Unit 2, *Arthur's Adventures*, Words in Context

Find these words in the reading. What do you think they mean?

shell

protect

shiny

ordinary

sea anemone

TRACK 10

Unit 2, Nonfiction, *Fire Ecology*

Forest fires happen in summer when it hasn't rained for a long time and everything is very dry. For many years, people have thought of forest fires as natural disasters that harm the forest, but they are also an important part of the life cycle of a forest. The science of fire ecology studies the connection between fire, plants, and animals in forest fires. With every fire, the forest is born again.

Forest Fires and Plants
Forest fires often start when lightning strikes a tree, but people can also cause forest fires. Sometimes they don't know what they did, and it happens by accident, but other times it's done on purpose.
Once a fire starts, it burns away the dry leaves and branches of the canopy, but it doesn't completely destroy the trees. The fire also gets rid of overgrown plants, fallen leaves, and bacteria in the soil that cause diseases. Plants on the forest floor need space and sunlight to grow. They have short life cycles, so they can grow and make seeds quickly. By the time the forest canopy has grown back, these plants have already completed their life cycles.
The Life Cycle of a Forest
1 Lightning strikes a tree.
2 A fire begins to burn the understory. Then, the fire spreads up and burns the canopy.
3 Heat and smoke cause seed pods to open.
4 Sunlight can reach the forest floor because the canopy isn't there.
5 The burned plants feed the soil.
6 New plants start to grow from the seeds.
7 The canopy grows back and the forest floor is in the shade again. It takes many years for the trees to grow fully.
Forest Fires and Animals
When a fire starts in a forest, every creature tries to escape.
Birds fly away and mammals usually run away. Larger animals, such as elk, sometimes stand in streams or lakes for safety. Small creatures (such as chipmunks, frogs, mice, and insects) hide underground, in logs, or under rocks.
Some of the weaker animals die, but many survive. This is called survival of the fittest, because the animals that don't die in the fire are the strongest and healthiest.
Animals have learned to live with fire and some even benefit from it. Fires give predators the chance to hunt insects and small animals that have to leave their hiding places to escape. Some birds of prey, such as falcons, even drop burning twigs to start fires deliberately!
After a fire, scavengers that may not be native to the forest come to feed on the bodies of dead animals. Woodpeckers and other birds follow fires to eat the dead insects from under the bark of trees. There are lots of things for animals to eat in a burned forest.
Animals soon go back to their homes in the forest and plants start growing again. The life cycle of the forest starts all over.
Hundreds of species of plants and animals live together in forests. Fire ecology helps us to understand the complicated interaction between their life cycles. It's possible for people to see forest fires more as natural wonders than natural disasters.

TRACK 11

Unit 2, *Fire Ecology*, Words in Context
Find these words in the reading. What do you think they mean?
accident
natural disasters
canopy
benefit
deliberately
scavengers
species

Unit 3

TRACK 12

Unit 3, Nonfiction, *Solving Crime with Science*
When someone commits a crime, detectives have to investigate the crime scene very carefully. Every crime is like a puzzle which the police have to solve by putting together the pieces. They use scientific methods called forensic science to help them.
Forensics uses the idea that criminals usually leave clues at a crime scene, or take clues from the crime scene away with them. The police use many different methods to find these clues.
Collecting Fingerprints
Every time we touch something, our fingers leave behind small amounts of oil, sweat, or skin in our fingerprints. No two people leave exactly the same fingerprints; everyone's fingerprints are unique. There are often fingerprints at a crime scene. Detectives have used fingerprints to solve crimes for more than a hundred years.
Studying fingerprints is a good way to identify who the criminal is and solve crimes. Fingerprints can show if a suspect has committed more than one crime. They can also show if more than one person committed a crime.
Loop, whorl, and arch are the three main fingerprint shapes. The loop fingerprint looks like a bean, the whorl looks like a circle, and the arch looks like a wave.
Tracks
Like fingerprints, footprints (the marks feet or shoes make) can also be valuable clues. Detectives study footprints to find out what type of shoe left tracks at a crime scene. Perhaps the suspect's shoes match the tracks. They can do the same with tire tracks. This information can help the police find the criminals faster.
Digital Tracks
We leave tracks in the digital world as well as in the real world. Detectives can follow an electronic trail to find evidence. When a crime happens, they can sometimes find information on electronic devices such as phones, tablets, or computers. These devices might give clues from search histories, emails, text messages, maps, or GPS information.
DNA Evidence
DNA is in the cells of all living things. It carries our genetic information, the building blocks of our bodies. Each person's DNA is a mix of genetic information from both parents, and it decides their characteristics, such as eye color and height.
Criminals often leave behind some of their DNA at a crime scene. It might come from their sweat, hair, or skin cells. If the criminal had a drink of water, there might be DNA left on the glass. Because everyone's DNA is unique, it is possible to use it to identify a specific person.
Recording the Evidence
At a crime scene, it is important to record all the evidence to solve the crime. The police take photos of the crime scene and of all the evidence to show exactly what they found and where. They interview people, ask lots of questions, and take notes about everything. They also check where people were and who they were with. Then the police decide if the people are suspects or not. Together this information helps detectives find out what really happened. The police use many forensic tools to solve crimes.

TRACK 13

Unit 3, *Solving Crime with Science*, Words in Context
Find these words in the reading. What do you think they mean?
puzzle
forensics
amounts
unique
identify
genetic

TRACK 14

Unit 3, Fiction, *The Red-Headed League*
Narrator: Sherlock Holmes and Dr. Watson are listening to a very interesting case.
Jabez Wilson: You see, my little shop in the city hasn't been very busy.
I've been very worried about money for a long time.
Two months ago, my new assistant showed me a newspaper advertisement.
He told me to apply and try to get the job.
Assistant: Your hair's very red, Mr. Wilson, and you need the money.
Jabez Wilson: An excellent idea, Smith.
My assistant took me to the interview. Every red-headed man in London was there, but my assistant pushed me to the front of the line.
Crowd 1: Why is this line taking so long?
Crowd 2: Sir, you cannot just go to the front of the line!
Crowd 3: Hey, what's he doing?
Crowd 1: Sir, you must wait like everyone else!
Duncan Ross: Excellent, Mr. Wilson! You're perfect for the job. Come to this office every day and write all the words in the dictionary in this notebook.
Jabez Wilson: It seemed a strange job, but I needed the money. So, every day for eight weeks I worked at that office by myself. I never saw anyone else.
My assistant said he would look after the shop. But this morning, the Red-Headed League was shut when I arrived. A note said, "Permanently Closed."
What's happening, Mr. Holmes? It's all very strange.
Sherlock Holmes: We must investigate, Watson.
Narrator: Sherlock Holmes and Dr. Watson are visiting Mr. Wilson's shop.
Sherlock Holmes: Interesting.
Narrator: Holmes stops on the street. He taps his cane on the sidewalk outside Wilson's shop. Then he walks down the street tapping the sidewalk.
Assistant: Can I help you?
Sherlock Holmes: My friend and I are lost. Which way is the Strand?
Watson: But you know the way to the Strand …
Sherlock Holmes: Yes, but I wanted to look at Mr. Wilson's assistant.
Watson: What did you see?
Sherlock Holmes: I'll tell you later.
Narrator: Sherlock Holmes is playing his violin while he thinks. Suddenly, he stops.
Sherlock Holmes: Meet me outside Mr. Wilson's shop at 10 o'clock tonight, Watson. We must stop a serious crime!
Narrator: That night, Sherlock Holmes, Dr. Watson, a police officer, and the manager of the bank are outside Mr. Wilson's shop.
Sherlock Holmes: Please open your bank, and take us down to the vault in the basement!

Narrator: The bank manager unlocks the door. He takes them down some dark stairs. They hide where they can see the vault.
In the dark, they see a stone in the floor move. There's a light under it! A hand pushes the stone to one side.
Assistant: All clear!
Sherlock Holmes: Not so fast, Mr. Smith.
Watson: How did you know about the robbery?
Sherlock Holmes: Do you remember our first visit to Mr. Wilson's shop? The clues were all there: I noticed it was near the bank. I tapped the sidewalk and listened. In some places it sounded empty near the bank. And I saw the dirt on the assistant's knees.
Why was the assistant dirty? From digging a tunnel into the bank. The Red-Headed League was simply a trick to get Mr. Wilson out of his shop every day so they could dig the tunnel.
I knew they were planning the robbery for tonight because the company closed down this morning!
Jabez Wilson: Well done, Mr. Holmes!

TRACK 15
Unit 3, *The Red-Headed League*, Words in Context
Find these words in the reading. What do you think they mean?
apply
dictionary
serious
vault
trick

Unit 4

TRACK 16
Unit 4, Nonfiction, *The Hero of Lime Rock*
Narrator: When Ida Lewis was growing up in the 19th century, it was very unusual for a woman to row a boat at sea. But Lewis had excellent rowing skills. She was once called "the bravest woman in America" because she saved so many people's lives.
Born on February 25, 1842, in Rhode Island, USA, Lewis was the oldest of four children. Even as a young girl she loved the ocean and used to accompany her father when he went to work at the lighthouse. He told her stories of storms, shipwrecks, and drownings, but also of many rescues. Most important of all, he taught her how to row a boat.
When Lewis was 15, her father became the keeper of Lime Rock Light, a lighthouse in Rhode Island. Her family moved to Lime Rock, the island where the lighthouse was. Her life was busy. She rowed her brother and sisters to the mainland, where they all went to school. In the evening, she helped with chores. She loved working in the lighthouse. She filled the lamp with oil and polished the lens on the light so that it shone brightly out to sea.
Sadly, her father got sick soon after the family moved to Lime Rock. Lewis and her mother had to do all the work in the lighthouse. Lewis lit the lamp at night and spent many hours looking out to the ocean. If she saw a boat in trouble, she wasn't afraid to row out to rescue people who were in danger.
Lewis' most famous rescue took place one stormy morning in March 1869. Her mother noticed a small boat rocking wildly in the rough waves. Lewis was in such a hurry to rescue the boat that she forgot to put on her coat and shoes when she ran out to her rowboat. In the distance, she saw strong waves capsize the small boat, flipping it and throwing two soldiers and a boy into the icy water.
Boy: Help!
Man: Help!
Narrator: Lewis used all her strength to row out to the boat with her younger brother. Together, they rescued the soldiers, but the boy was never found. The newspaper reported the rescue and Ida Lewis was awarded the Gold Lifesaving Medal for saving them. She was the first woman to receive this medal.
Official records, kept by the local government, say that Lewis saved 18 lives, but some people say it was many more, and it wasn't only humans! Once, a sheep fell out of a boat. Three men on the boat tried to save the animal, but the weather was terrible, and their boat capsized. Lewis rescued the men and brought them to safety. Then she rowed out again and came back with the sheep!
Lewis became very famous for her rescues. Hundreds of people came to visit her, including the President of the United States of America. Then, in 1879 after her parents died, Lewis became the first female lighthouse keeper at Lime Rock.
Ida Lewis was 69 when she died of natural causes on October 24, 1911. In 1924, Lime Rock became Ida Lewis Rock. She was a hero who risked her own life in order to save the lives of others.

TRACK 17
Unit 4, *The Hero of Lime Rock*, Words in Context
Find these words in the reading. What do you think they mean?
row
rescues
took place
capsize
official

TRACK 18
Unit 4, Fiction, *Delivery Dan*
Ella: Hey, Dan, you look like the unhappiest guy in the world!
Narrator: said Ella, as they volunteered as ushers at the theater.
Dan: Yeah,
Narrator: Dan replied, trying to smile.
Dan: Remember that audition you helped me practice for last week? Well, I didn't get the part.
Ella: Oh, Dan, I've told you a million times. Keep practicing! You'll be on the other side of the curtain one day,
Narrator: said Ella.
Dan: (singing)
Narrator: Dan kept practicing. He sang day and night. He sang everywhere he went! He wanted to be an opera singer more than anything in the world. Dan loved singing the beautiful old songs. He volunteered at the theater on Saturdays, but he needed to start earning money to pay for singing and Italian lessons.
One day on the way back from the theater, he saw an ad in a store window.
Dan: *That's me!*
Narrator: he thought … and three days later he was a bicycle delivery man!
Dan received orders by text and he rode his bike many kilometers delivering food to customers all over the city. One evening, he had to deliver pizzas to hundreds of hungry kids at a birthday party.
Kids: Wow! Thanks!
Narrator: cheered the kids when he arrived.
Man: Come in and share our pizzas!
Narrator: said the dad.
Dan: Thanks!
Narrator: said Dan.
Dan: I'm starving!
Narrator: Dan thought it was very rewarding making hungry people happy, but he had a problem. He wasn't getting enough time to practice singing. Then one day he had a great idea.
Dan arrived at 96 52nd Street.
Dan: I have your burgers and your fries,
Narrator: he sang.
Dan: I have your soda and your le-mon-ade …
Narrator: The customers were very surprised! When he finished, they clapped and gave him a nice big tip.
One night, there was an order for lobster soup to go to a beautiful, big house on the river. Dan rang the bell, took a deep breath and sang:
Dan: I have your lovely lobster soup. It smells delicious, to me-e-e …
Narrator: He sang one verse, then another, and another.
The door opened slowly and a well-dressed woman appeared. She took the soup, then closed the door.
Dan: *What? No tip? That was a bit mean,*
Narrator: he thought as he biked home.
Dan: *I sang really well, didn't I?*
Narrator: A few days later, Dan received a text, but this time it wasn't a food order.
Dan: Look at this text from my boss,
Narrator: he said to Ella.
Ella: You might get to see a performance, Dan! You should go,
Narrator: she said. The next Monday at the Opera House, a woman greeted Dan.
Dan: Oh! I delivered lobster soup to you last week, didn't I?
Narrator: he said, surprised.
Antonia: Yes, you did!
Narrator: she said.
Antonia: I'm Antonia Allegro, the director here.
Dan: Thanks for inviting me,
Narrator: said Dan.
Dan: When's the show?
Antonia: There isn't a show today,
Narrator: she said.
Antonia: This is your first rehearsal for our next opera. You'll practice with the cast today. You already passed your audition.
Dan: I did?
Antonia: Yes, at my house last week. You have one of the most beautiful voices in the world. You're so talented! Congratulations. Welcome to the show!
Narrator: Dan's first opera performance was in front of thousands of people, and he didn't sing about burgers or fries or lemonade!

TRACK 19
Unit 4, *Delivery Dan*, Words in Context
Find these words in the reading. What do you think they mean?
ushers
audition
opera
starving
tip

Unit 5

TRACK 20

Unit 5, Nonfiction, *Using Your Emotional Toolbox*

What do we do when we feel delighted, worried, or upset? That depends on what is in our emotional toolboxes.

First, let's think about emotions. They're a big part of our everyday lives.

Emotions range from fear, anger, and sadness, to surprise, love, and happiness. All of them are completely normal, natural, and happen to all of us.

Sometimes emotions hit us when we don't expect them. When we don't know they are coming, they can be very hard to deal with.

Everyone feels difficult emotions sometimes, but we can learn to deal with them better. There are healthy ways to deal with strong emotions.

Get to Know Your Emotions

In order to deal with our emotions in a healthy way, we can follow these three simple steps.

1 Name the feeling. This will help you identify it every time you feel it.
2 Find the cause. This will help you understand why you feel the way you do.
3 Think about the last time you felt this way and how you handled it then. This will help you figure out the best strategy, or plan, to handle how you feel.

Encourage Positive Emotions

Research has shown that encouraging positive emotions makes us healthier and happier. It can also help our learning and our friendships. The more strategies we have in our emotional toolboxes, the better. Here are some ideas about how to handle difficult feelings and increase how often we are feeling calm and well.

Breathe Deeply

Maybe you're feeling scared or nervous, confused or disappointed. First, remember to take a moment to notice what emotion you're feeling. After you identify the feeling, take in a long, deep breath. Feel your chest fill with air. Then breathe out slowly. Do this five or six times.

Count to 10

Are your emotions so strong that you feel out of control? Count slowly from one to ten. When you reach ten, you will probably feel better.

Smile!

They say that smiles are contagious and spread quickly. If you're in a positive mood, share the joy! A friendly smile can help improve someone else's day.

Take a Break

When you have a difficult emotion, it's OK to feel it, but it's OK to take a break from it, too. Sit with your sadness or disappointment for a little while and see what the feeling may have to tell you.

Express Yourself

If taking a break isn't what you need, maybe try expressing yourself. Talk to a friend. It could help you work through the difficult feelings.

Do Something Kind

Give someone a helping hand or write them a friendly message.

Practice Yoga

Yoga is not only good exercise, it also encourages good breathing. Try some "bee breaths." Sit up straight, smile, and gently put a finger in each ear. Take a deep breath. Then slowly let your breath out—and while you do, make a buzzing noise like a bee. *Sports*

Exercise can also help. Throw a ball. Go for a run. Do some jumping jacks. Exercise stops us from thinking about our worries too much. It also changes the chemicals in our brains to make us feel better!

Whichever strategy you choose to use from your emotional toolbox, remember that emotions are normal. Everyone has them. The next time you feel angry or sad or frustrated, try using one of the strategies you just learned.

TRACK 21

Unit 5, *Using Your Emotional Toolbox*, Words in Context

Find these words in the reading. What do you think they mean?

expect
deal with
strategies
contagious
mood

TRACK 22

Unit 5, Fiction, *How I Feel*

Escape to the Park

Boy: Sometimes, when I'm down and feeling blue,
A dark, gray cloud blocks my view,
Drops of cold rain fall on me. What should I do?
Never mind,
says my sister with her usual sunny smile.
Escape to the park! Let's ride our bikes for a while.
So we grab the bikes and race down through the neighborhood,
She's right, as always, this does feel good!

Hammerhead Shark

Girl: Among its prey, a hunter searches in the deep, dark water.
Feeling its way through the shadows of the sea:
Razor-sharp teeth, hard eyes like stones,
And its huge head like a giant hammer.
Impossible to put my legs in the water!
Do you dare, or are you too scared?

Scary Movie

Boy: Somewhere in the dark, there's a creature with sharp claws.
Crunching its scary red jaws.
Afraid of something I can't see, I know it's hiding there,
Ready to attack and grab my hair.
Escaping through the air, then it swoops down low …
Do you think I should watch this scary show?

I Was Not Out!

Boy: Am not! I am NOT out! My foot was on the base first!
No way. You never tagged me. You weren't even close.
Go on then, tell the umpire. Tell the whole town. See if I care!
Really, no one saw that?
You want to let me try again?

Joy

Girl: Joking around with my best friend
Outside or inside, we play pretend
You're the best part of my weekend!

Party

Boy: Something wonderful, amazing—
Unexpectedly, Mom called me.
Running in from the yard I wondered why.
Pushed open the door
Right there in my living room, but
It was dark inside. How strange.
Something told me to look behind the couch and then
Everyone shouted, "Surprise!"

Family Vacation

Girl: Love, to me, means my whole family
Out on the beach, we swim, splash, and play.
Vacation starts today. Salt water, sandcastles, and sailboats.
Everyone together under the sun. This is family fun.

My Favorite Things

Girl: Hanging out with friends on a trip to the zoo,
A fresh pizza from the oven, cheesy melted goo.
Painting a picture, my best by far,
Purple room, purple flowers, and a purple toy car.
Investigating the sound inside a seashell,
New books, especially the way they smell.
Entering a theater, warm popcorn—a treat.
Sitting in the sunshine, enjoying the heat.
Socks, straight from the dryer and onto my feet!

TRACK 23

Unit 5, *How I Feel*, Words in Context

Find these words in the reading. What do you think they mean?

never mind
dare
attack
swoops
hanging out

Unit 6

TRACK 24

Unit 6, Nonfiction, *Not-So-Fantastic Plastic*

How much plastic is in your life? You're probably touching some right now: your water bottle, your pen, even your clothes. It's in our phones, our computers, and our cars. Food and drinks often come in plastic containers. Plastic is everywhere!

It can be soft or hard, colorful or transparent.

It can be made into any shape or size. Plastic is fantastic … or is it?

Plastic is not a natural product. It's made from oil, like gasoline. It's not biodegradable; most of the plastic ever made still exists today. For more than sixty years, plastic has caused many problems for animals in all of the world's ecosystems.

It has damaged habitats where animals live and spread dangerous chemicals in water and soil. Our overuse of this material is causing an environmental disaster. We need to stop using so much plastic.

There's pollution on beaches around the world because of plastic. This makes the beaches dangerous for humans and animals. Billions of kilograms of plastic float in the world's oceans.

Using evidence found around the world, scientists estimate that every year one million sea birds and 100,000 sea creatures die from eating plastic because they think it's prey. In some parts of the world, some grocery stores have stopped using plastic bags, and others ask customers to pay for them. All supermarkets should ban plastic bags.

There are two large garbage patches on opposite sides of the Pacific Ocean. Near the coasts, these two collections of plastic trash are hundreds of kilometers wide. From the water, they look a lot like plastic soup with bottles, bags, toys, toothbrushes, and other plastic items floating on the surface and trapped in the water below.

Scientific reports have shown that plastic waste in the oceans is entering the food chain. It breaks down into smaller and smaller pieces, but it never completely disappears. Fish then eat the tiny particles, so if we eat fish, we might be eating tiny amounts of plastic, too.

Recycling helps to solve the problem, and many people believe that most plastic is being recycled. Unfortunately, this is not true. Almost half of all plastic goes into landfills, where it won't break down for hundreds or even thousands of years. Only a very small amount is recycled, but all the rest is trash.

Many people also believe that they can't make a difference on their own, but they're wrong. We should avoid using plastic products like sandwich bags, takeout containers, straws, and juice boxes. We should recycle and reuse as much as possible in our homes, offices, and schools. If we all make changes, we can help the environment.

Some businesses are trying to reduce their plastic waste. They ask customers to bring their own bags and cups. This saves the businesses money and helps the environment. Some stores and cafés even give money back to say thank you to their customers for contributing.

It is clear that pollution is a global problem and it is too serious to ignore. We must all play our part in reducing our use of plastic. Everybody can help to protect our oceans, if we stop using disposable plastic today. If we don't take action now, our planet will be in great danger in the very near future.

TRACK 25

Unit 6, *Not-So-Fantastic Plastic*, Words in Context

Find these words in the reading. What do you think they mean?

biodegradable
overuse
disaster
estimate (verb)
ban
garbage patches
ignore

TRACK 26

Unit 6, Fiction, *A Greener Life*

Dad: Tired of the city, it was time for something new,
Surrounded by concrete, in search of a different view.
"Let's move to the country," I told my kids and wife.
"If we care about this planet, we should live a greener life."
We sold all our possessions—all we had except the car,
And bought a small cottage in a village not too far.
At first the kids were miserable—they didn't want to move.
They couldn't understand how our lives might improve.
First, we dug a stream, deep in the ground,
Then built a water wheel with wood that I found.
The wheel turns and generates enough power
To run the refrigerator each and every hour.
Then I built a wind turbine as tall as a tree.
With arms that turn and make wind energy.
That power is turned into electricity
So at night or without wind, we can still see.
We bought ourselves some chickens, sheep, and goats.
We love the eggs and the milk—the sheep give us our coats.
We started bee-keeping—the suits are so funny.
We never buy sugar—we always have honey!
We collect enough rain to cook, wash, and drink.
When we're done cooking, we wash dishes in the sink.
There's plenty of water but we don't use a lot,
Solar panels on the roof make the water nice and hot.
We grow organic vegetables, fruit, and berries,
We've learned to make jam with strawberries and cherries.
We share with our neighbors, our food's all home-grown.
We're out of the city but we're never alone.
We've become self-sufficient, with everything we need.
Without the latest gadgets we have more time to read.
The stresses of the world all fade away
We live a simple life here; it's nature's way.
Everything was calm and simple, no cause for alarm.
There must be others who would love our simple farm.
We decided we had more to give
And invited the city to share the way we live.
Now kids come in groups of up to thirty
To visit us and get their hands and faces dirty!
They travel here in buses from cities far and wide.
Some haven't ever been to the countryside.
Where does honey come from? Some didn't know.
Others helped dig to find out how potatoes grow.
Sometimes we teach how milk becomes cheese
And they get to eat apples they picked from trees!
We ask the kids to think about the kinds of food they ate,
And about how it gets from the farm to their plate.
We teach them how to grow good food for themselves,
So they won't always rush to the supermarket shelves.
The visitors help us—they like working on the land,
They plant carrots, lettuce, and peppers by hand
They collect eggs and feed the tiny baby sheep
They milk the goats and watch the animals sleep.
We left the city and didn't look back
We have all that we need, there's nothing we lack
On our little farm there's so much to do
We're living the green life and so can you!

TRACK 27

Unit 6, *A Greener Life*, Words in Context

Find these words in the reading. What do you think they mean?

surrounded
possessions
miserable
generates
wind turbine
solar panels

Unit 7

TRACK 28

Unit 7, Fiction, *The Chopper*

Narrator: Sophia pushed play and the music started.

Papa: Sophia, you know I can't dance.

Narrator: Papa laughed, but he got off the sofa and started to follow the dance moves on the TV screen. Sophia laughed, too.
Then, in the middle of the song, Papa started breathing hard. Suddenly, he stopped dancing.

Sophia: Don't stop! You're doing great.

Narrator: said Sophia. Papa fell onto the couch.

Papa: I … don't feel … so good,

Narrator: he said, trying to catch his breath. Sophia watched Papa as he coughed and wheezed.

Sophia: Are you having an asthma attack?

Narrator: she asked. Papa nodded.

Papa: I can't breathe. I need my inhaler.

Narrator: Sophia looked everywhere. She searched the whole house, but she couldn't find Papa's inhaler. Papa's wheezing was getting louder and faster. She rushed to his side. Her mind raced. She had to calm herself down.

Sophia: *First Aid. Scouts. Last week. What did they say to do in an emergency?*

Narrator: Then she remembered.

Sophia: I'm calling an ambulance!

Narrator: she said.

Natalia: You did exactly the right thing,

Narrator: said Natalia the paramedic. Papa lay on a stretcher in the ambulance.

Natalia: And you did it just in time.

Sophia: Will he be OK?

Narrator: Sophia worried.

Natalia: Now that he's gotten the medicine, it's not too serious. Of course, he'll be OK, said Natalia. The ambulance driver put down his radio.

Ambulance Driver: We've missed the last boat off the island. I've called for the air rescue team. You'll both get to ride in the chopper.

Papa: Cool,

Narrator: Papa said, with a weak smile.

Papa: I've always wanted to ride in a helicopter.

Narrator: Sophia stood next to her father. She felt worried and hugged herself. The night breeze made her shiver. Just a little while ago, she and Papa were in the living room dancing.
The helicopter landed on the high school soccer field. It was like a giant, flying monster. Its blades cut through the air, and its lights blinked like red eyes.
Two paramedics wearing helmets jumped out. They ran to the back of the helicopter and opened the doors.
Natalia and the ambulance driver took Papa to the helicopter. Sophia followed behind them. Natalia swung up into the helicopter and helped Sophia into the cabin.

Natalia: We'll take care of you both, Sophia,

Narrator: Natalia shouted over the noise of the blades.

Natalia: Your papa is in safe hands. Don't worry,

Narrator: she added as the helicopter blades spun faster.
The helicopter cabin rattled. Natalia handed Sophia a set of headphones. She pulled them over her ears and then held onto her seat.
Then the chopper took off, and lifted straight up into the night sky. Papa lay on the stretcher, staring out of the window.

Sophia watched nervously as they went higher and higher. The lights of the houses below were a long way down now. The chopper swayed a little in the wind like a kite. Then it raced across the island, and flew out over the sea.

Natalia: Try not to worry.

Narrator: said Natalia. Her voice sounded loud in Sophia's headphones.
Sophia could see the city lights ahead. They were so close to the hospital now.

Nurse: Did you call the ambulance?

Narrator: asked the nurse. Sophia nodded.

Nurse: Nice job.

Narrator: he said.

Nurse: What do you want to do when you grow up?

Narrator: Sophia didn't know.

Nurse: Well, maybe you should join us. We need people like you who can think on their feet.

Papa: My rescuer,

Narrator: Papa smiled. He took Sophia's hand and squeezed it.
Sophia squeezed his hand back. She felt herself beginning to relax. Everything would be fine.

TRACK 29

Unit 7, *The Chopper*, Words in Context

Find these words in the reading. What do you think they mean?

wheezed
paramedic
stretcher
shiver
blades

TRACK 30

Unit 7, Nonfiction, *First Aid for Beginners*

When an emergency happens, it's important to act fast. It's also important to keep calm and get an adult's help.

Before an emergency happens, everyone should learn basic first aid skills. Every home, school, office, and car should have a first aid kit.

Let's look at some emergencies and how we can deal with them.

Cuts and Scrapes

These are injuries to the skin.

The first aider should:

wash their hands and put on gloves.

disinfect the injury, using clean water, or a saline solution.

cover the wound with a sterile, or clean and germ-free, gauze pad.

press gently on the wound, or, if there is a lot of blood, press down harder.

elevate, or raise, the injured area if the bleeding doesn't stop.

take off the gauze and cover with a sterile dressing or Band-Aid when the bleeding has stopped.

Sprains, Bruises, and Strains

Sprains, bruises, and strains are soft tissue injuries. They can happen in muscles, ligaments, tendons, or the places around joints. A soft tissue injury might cause pain, swelling, and probably a bruise.

To remember what to do, spell RICE:

Rest: have the patient lie back or sit down.

Ice: wrap an ice pack in a cloth and put it on the injury for ten to twenty minutes.

Compression: wrap an elastic bandage around the injury. It should press on the injury without cutting off the blood supply.

Elevation: raise the injured area.

Broken Bones

It's sometimes difficult to know if a bone is broken. A bone may be broken if there is swelling, or part of the body looks bigger than normal; the skin around the injury has changed color; the person can't use that part of their body; or there is a lot of pain. While you wait for help, have the patient rest, stop the injured part from moving, and support the injury with blankets or clothes.

Stings and Allergic Reactions

When a bee, wasp, or other insect stings someone, it injects a venom, or poisonous liquid, into the skin through a needle-like stinger. Sometimes a stinger is left in the skin.

Brush or scrape the stinger away, but avoid squeezing it because more venom may come out.

Put a wrapped ice pack on the sting right away.

If possible, elevate the area.

Be Aware!

Stings can be dangerous and can cause allergic reactions in some people. Signs of an allergic reaction are:

an itchy, red rash on the skin

a tight feeling in the throat and/or chest

difficulty breathing

swelling around the face, lips, tongue, throat, or eyelids

Call a doctor immediately!

Hypothermia

Hypothermia can happen when someone has been cold for a long time. They look pale and their body temperature drops below normal. They shiver and might be confused. Hypothermia can be serious.

Start warming them immediately.

Get them to a warm place and make sure they're wearing warm, dry clothes.

Wrap a rescue blanket around them and cover their head.

Give them a warm drink, and a high-energy food, like a cereal bar, to eat.

Now you know a little bit more about basic first aid. Remember the first thing to do is to get a grown-up. Then try to use what you know to help.

TRACK 31

Unit 7, *First Aid for Beginners*, Words in Context

Find these words in the reading. What do you think they mean?

gauze
bleeding
soft tissue
inject
venom

Unit 8

TRACK 32

Unit 8, Fiction, *The Great Race*

Narrator: Long ago in ancient China, the Emperor needed guards for his palace. He invited his favorite animals to race across the river to his palace.

Emperor: The first twelve animals will be my guards,

Narrator: he said.

Cat: Wake me up early before the race,

Narrator: Cat asked her friend Rat, but on the day of the race, Rat was so excited he forgot to wake Cat, and ran to the river alone.
Rat didn't like swimming, but he had an idea. When he met Ox at the river, Rat asked Ox for a ride. Rat said he would pay for the trip with a song. Ox agreed and Rat jumped onto his back. Ox listened to Rat sing as he swam easily across the fast river.
Before Ox got to the palace, Rat jumped down and ran to the Emperor. The Emperor admired how Rat cleverly crossed the river and gave him first place. Ox was pleased to be second.
Now, Tiger was in the water. The river's current was very strong. She fought against it with her muscular legs. It took all of her effort, and when she crawled onto the river bank, she was exhausted. She ran to the Emperor and was awarded third place for her strength.
Rabbit saw Tiger struggling and knew he couldn't swim well enough. Instead, he hopped from stone to stone and then onto a floating log. When he reached the log, his quick feet slipped. From high in the sky, Dragon saw Rabbit holding onto the log. Dragon flew down to Rabbit and blew smoke to push the log across the river. Rabbit's quickness put him in fourth place.
Suddenly, Dragon swooped down from the sky. He explained his lateness to the Emperor; instead of worrying about his place in the race, he helped Rabbit. For his kindness he was given fifth place.
Next, Horse crossed the river and was galloping quickly towards the palace when she noticed Snake was wrapped around her hoof! Frightened, Horse stood up on her back legs. Snake dropped down to the ground and slithered quickly towards the palace. Snake beat Horse to the Emperor.

Emperor: Ha, ha! You're sneaky, Snake!

Narrator: said the Emperor,

Emperor: You're sixth!

Narrator: But Horse didn't let her fear stop her. Soon, she was running again.

Emperor: Well done, Horse,

Narrator: said the Emperor.

Emperor: You're seventh for your bravery.

Narrator: Then Monkey and Rooster crossed the river on a raft. Goat swam across the river and pushed the raft with his nose. Monkey paddled and Rooster steered, holding his wings out wide. All three worked together in order to get across. For their teamwork, the Emperor placed Goat eighth, Monkey ninth, and Rooster tenth.
Meanwhile, Dog emerged from the river, with his coat dripping wet.

Emperor: Did you have fun playing in the water?

Narrator: asked the Emperor. Dog wagged his tail happily and was given eleventh place.
Now, there was only one place left. Slowly, Boar appeared out of the river and waddled towards the Emperor.

Emperor: You worked very hard and didn't give up, diligent Boar,

Narrator: said the Emperor.

Emperor: You're twelfth!

Narrator: Boar was pleased, but he was tired. He lay down for a nap.
Poor Cat was too late. She wasn't happy with Rat. Since then, cats and rats haven't been friends.

Emperor: Congratulations!

Narrator: said the Emperor to the winners.

Emperor: You had to use your skills and talents to cross the river. Now, you are all my guards.

TRACK 33

Unit 8, *The Great Race*, Words in Context

Find these words in the reading. What do you think they mean?

current
sneaky
effort
slithered
diligent

TRACK 34

Unit 8, Nonfiction, *Mysterious Malta*

Ancient Remains

The island of Malta has six prehistoric temples, which are among the oldest standing stone buildings in the world—older than Stonehenge in the UK or the Pyramids in Egypt. Hal Tarxien has three of the six temples and is one of the most famous archaeological sites in Malta.

The temples were built between 3100 and 2500 BCE, but the civilization that constructed them disappeared around 2500 BCE. No one knows why or what happened to the people who lived there at that time. As a result, the history of ancient Malta is still a mystery.

Today Hal Tarxien and the other temples are recognized as a UNESCO World Heritage Site known as "The Megalithic Temples of Malta." This means they are seen as a very important part of Malta's, and the world's, history. They will be preserved for people to visit and study for many years to come.

Amazing Architecture

Hal Tarxien was discovered by local farmers in 1913. The buildings have many interesting features that are similar to those in the other temples on the island. They usually faced south or southeast and had an oval space in front of the entrance. The site has several semi-circular rooms which are connected by doorways.

The main entrance was constructed of three huge stones. Two stand vertically and one lies horizontally across the top.

Walls of Stone

The temple walls were made of enormous stones that were transported to Tarxien from other parts of the island. The small spaces between the large stones were filled with smaller stones and dirt, perhaps to stop cold air from getting into the buildings. Very hard stone was used for outside walls, but the stone used inside was soft and, therefore, easier to carve. Scientists investigating Hal Tarxien hypothesize that the people there had very good building skills because they created such detailed carvings and blocks with square corners. But the researchers don't know for sure.

Decorations

Many carvings and paintings of plants, animals, or people were found inside the rooms as well as objects such as metal bowls, pottery, and statues.

Stone Floors

Floors were made of enormous flat stones, each a meter deep. Small round stones were discovered under these stones. The people may have used them to roll the floor stones into position.

Stones with Holes

Stones with two holes were found in front of temples. Perhaps they were used to tie up horses or other animals. Similar stones were found inside the buildings. Perhaps they were used to hold doors open.

Water

There was a large stone reservoir in the area in front of the temples at Tarxien which held enormous amounts of water for the community. The water came from an underground spring, but at other temples on the island, the reservoirs collected rainwater. This clay pot was possibly used to collect rainwater.

Mysterious Tracks

All over Malta, there are mysterious lines carved into the stone on the ground. These ancient lines are called "cart ruts" because the pairs of parallel tracks look as if they were made for pulling carts along. Some lines disappear into the sea, which shows how the land has changed because the sea is higher now than it was thousands of years ago. Many people believe the ruts were used to transport stone for the buildings. However, none of the ruts goes straight to them. Some experts hypothesize that the ruts carried rainwater, but that doesn't explain why they are in pairs. They also say that carts didn't make ruts because the people didn't know about wheels. Nobody really knows why the lines are there. They are another of Malta's mysteries!

TRACK 35

Unit 8, *Mysterious Malta*, Words in Context

Find these words in the reading. What do you think they mean?

archaeological
constructed
architecture
researchers
hypothesize
ruts

Unit 9

TRACK 36

Unit 9, Nonfiction, *Storytelling Around the World*

The art of telling stories probably goes back to prehistoric times. People told each other stories long before writing was invented. Prehistoric people probably sat around the fires in their caves and listened to stories—there were no televisions or tablets in those days! The stories helped them understand and remember their past and gave them useful information. Storytelling has been with us ever since.

Across the globe, there are many different ways to tell stories and many different kinds of storytellers.

In the West African tradition, a *griot* is more than just a storyteller. Griots give advice, and help people solve their problems. They are also talented musicians who sing songs to praise and remember people and places. They keep the stories of their local communities alive. They preserve their history.

Griots often perform at important ceremonies such as marriages or funerals. They sing, tell stories, and play the kora, an instrument made out of a hollow gourd which has 21 strings.

In ancient India, storytellers traveled the country, visiting villages, and entertaining crowds. To make their stories more interesting, they added hand movements and gestures. This became *Kathak*—a dance that tells stories.

Instead of words, Kathak dancers use actions. Bells are tied to the dancers' ankles. As they dance, the sounds of their feet match the beat of the drums. Kathak dancers also use hand movements, and the many different expressions on their faces are very important. They make lots of movements with their eyes. The dancers make the myths and ancient stories of India real in the same way that actors do in a play on stage.

In North Africa and the Middle East, traditional storytellers are known as *Hakawati*. Before modern technology and entertainment, their tales were very popular. People gathered under the stars to listen to tales of heroes brought to life by the storyteller's voice.

A typical Hakawati tale has strong characters, and a plot full of drama to grab the audience's attention. The story often tells how good beats evil, and gives moral messages about life. Famous stories like the ones in *One Thousand and One Nights* come from this tradition.

Today, while storytellers in the Middle East and North Africa aren't as common as they used to be, there are still some performers who keep the oral tradition alive.

Shadow theater is another a type of storytelling with a rich history. It comes from Turkey and Greece, and reaches all the way to Southeast Asia. In Java, shadow theater is known as *Wayang Kulit*, and is still very popular today.

The puppets used in shadow theater are made of leather attached to sticks. The arms of the puppets have hinges on them to make them more lifelike and easier for the puppeteer to move.

As night falls, people gather in the open air. Hidden behind a cloth screen, the puppeteer uses light and shadow to show stories to the audience. The characters are either heroes or villains. The audience can easily tell the difference. There are so many ways to tell a story!

TRACK 37

Unit 9, *Storytelling Around the World*, Words in Context

Find these words in the reading. What do you think they mean?

ceremonies
gourd
gestures
expressions
myths
puppeteer

TRACK 38

Unit 9, Fiction, *The Weaver*

Narrator: Princess Mariam was annoyed.
Mariam: I don't want to weave,
Narrator: she complained.
Mariam: Can't I just have my normal lessons like math, writing, and music?
Ayeisha: Weaving's an important skill for a princess,
Narrator: said Queen Ayeisha.
Jahmal: Your mother's right
Narrator: said King Jahmal.
Jahmal: Tomorrow, your tutor will teach you weaving.
Mariam: If I had a choice, I would have my head in a book or play my oud,
Narrator: said Mariam.
That night Mariam had an idea. She sat down at her desk and started writing a story.
Farida, the kind tutor, arrived the next day ready to teach Mariam. She was carrying books, a loom, and a basket of wool.
Farida: Math and writing first,
Narrator: said Farida.
Mariam finished her normal work very fast.
Farida: Now, it's time for weaving,
Narrator: said Farida.
Mariam: Before we start,
Narrator: Mariam said,
Mariam: I want to tell you a story.
Farida: A story?

Narrator: asked Farida.
Mariam: It's really amazing! If I were you, I would want to listen!
Narrator: Mariam said.
Mariam started reading her tale of heroes and villains.
Mariam: Once upon a time, brave Harun left home to rescue his father, who was taken in the middle of the night by a cruel kidnapper …
Narrator: Mariam's story about Harun's adventures went on until it was the end of the lesson. There was no time for weaving!
Farida: We'll start tomorrow,
Narrator: said Farida. That night, Mariam wrote for hours. The plot became more complicated and more exciting.
The next day, after their normal lessons, Farida announced,
Farida: Today, we must weave.
Mariam: But perhaps more of the story first?
Narrator: said Mariam.
Farida: As you wish, but please keep it short,
Narrator: said Farida.
Mariam continued her tale.
Mariam: Harun reached the villain's cave high in the mountains. There were fierce gray wolves with terrifyingly sharp teeth all around it. "You don't frighten me," Harun shouted.
Narrator: Mariam's voice was as loud as a lion's roar! Again, the time passed in the blink of an eye.
Farida: "You tell an extremely thrilling tale,"
Narrator: Farida said excitedly.
The next day came, and with it more of Mariam's story.
Mariam: Harun and the kidnapper both drew their swords.
"I have you now," said Harun.
"Never!" shouted the villain. With loud cries and a clash of metal, they began to fight.
Narrator: Again Mariam's lesson passed in a flash.
The same thing happened the next day, and the next, and the next. A month went by, and no wool touched Mariam's hands.
Mariam: In the end, Harun beat the kidnapper. With the villain tied up, Harun and his father headed home. And they lived happily ever after …
Narrator: Farida clapped her hands.
Farida: What a wonderful story! And it has a fine moral. You're a really great storyteller.
Narrator: Just then, the King and Queen appeared out of the shadows.
Mariam: Mother! Father!
Narrator: gasped Mariam.
Jahmal: So this is your weaving, daughter?
Narrator: said the King.
Jahmal: Not a rug, but a story?
Narrator: Mariam blushed and her cheeks warmed.
Mariam: Yes, Father, I use words instead of wool.
Narrator: The King smiled.
Jahmal: Well, I think your story is wonderful!
Ayeisha: And very exciting,
Narrator: agreed the Queen, clapping her hands.
Jahmal: If I were you, I would be extremely proud,
Narrator: said the King.
Ayeisha: And if I wrote a story like that, I would want to put it in a book!
Narrator: said the Queen.
Mariam agreed.
Mariam: Now that is a good idea!

TRACK 39
Unit 9, *The Weaver*, Words in Context
Find these words in the reading. What do you think they mean?
tutor
kidnapper
fierce
announced
blushed

Unit 10

TRACK 40
Unit 10, Nonfiction, *Designing Drones*
Drones can be lots of fun for everyone. They are very popular, and are affordable and accessible all around the world. People build and race them. There are many local, national, and international competitions. Because many students are interested in this hobby, some schools have drone clubs.
Other Uses for Drones
Farming
Farmers need to check the health of their crops frequently, because disease or drought can destroy them. Traditionally, farmers had to walk many kilometers through their fields to check the health of their crops. That took a lot of time and energy, so designers decided to adapt drones to do the work. They made drones more aerodynamic so they moved through the air faster. They made the wings slightly flexible, added special cameras with different sensors, and included GPS technology.
A drone can fly over large areas of land very quickly, taking photos of the crops in the fields. Special software gathers information and allows farmers to review and analyze data about plant growth, soil health, and irrigation needs.
The results are very encouraging. Farmers have reported that their harvests are larger because of the information from the drones. Drones are cheaper and more accurate than human beings!
There are many benefits for the environment. When farmers understand the health of their plants better, they can use fewer chemicals and control irrigation more efficiently. Soon, more famers will be using this technology.
Saving Lives
In an emergency, every second counts. If people can be located quickly, it's more likely that they can be saved. However, after a disaster, finding them can be very difficult. Roads may not be usable and buildings may be dangerous. It can take a long time for rescue workers to find the people who need help.
Designers have adapted drones to help rescue workers locate people and provide help. They have put drones on the roofs of emergency vehicles, such as ambulances. They can be launched and controlled from the vehicle. The drones have GPS technology and cameras which scan the disaster area looking for people who need help. Then they report the location to rescue workers. The data shows that this is much faster and safer than rescuers searching on their own.
Another type of drone, The POUNCER™, is designed to deliver food, water, and medicines to hard-to-reach places when there is a drought or famine (when there's not enough food).
These drones are faster and cheaper than planes. They are designed to be used only one time. They can be launched from a plane up to 35 kilometers away from the disaster area so rescue workers are not in danger. The food in one POUNCER™ Drone can feed up to 40 people. Made from biodegradable material, after the drone has landed, its parts can be used for shelter or as fuel for cooking food.
Transporting People
Human beings have always dreamed of flying. Today, in our world of traffic jams and crowded buses, the idea of taking to the sky fascinates us. Scientists recognized the potential in drone design and adjusted it to be functional for transportation.
The AAV (Autonomous Aerial Vehicle) is big enough to carry one person. First the passenger chooses an address on a touchscreen. The drone then uses GPS to decide the quickest and safest route. It flies above roads at speeds of up to 100 km. per hour for a maximum of 30 minutes. Its inventors say it is the smartest, most eco-friendly vehicle for short journeys.
New drone technology will be evolving and transforming well into the future.

TRACK 41
Unit 10, *Designing Drones*, Words in Context
Find these words in the reading. What do you think they mean?
aerodynamic
data
famine
fuel
touchscreen

TRACK 42
Unit 10, Fiction, *The Restore Key*
Sky: Things were difficult for Dad and me for a long time after Mom passed away. One day, when I was 12, Dad told me we were moving back to the city.
I don't want to go!
I went outside to sit by myself and think.
Dad: Sky, are you OK?
Sky: I don't know anyone there.
Dad: I know, but you'll make new friends and Meteor will come, too. You'll see. It'll be better for us there.
Sky: Later, we started packing up the garage.
Dad, is that me?
Dad: Yeah, you were just eight months old and so cute! Your mom had me take this of the two of you.
Sky: Meteor, look what I found!
Meteor: That tablet belonged to your mother.
Sky: I tried different passwords: Mom's birthday, Dad's birthday … then mine.
What is that?
Meteor: That is the plan for a space elevator designed in 2043.
Sky: Is this real?
Meteor: The Space Elevator Project was never completed.
Sky: Why not? This is so cool!
Meteor: This is the site for the Space Elevator Project.
Sky: That looks like our town, but something's different …
That's our house and backyard. Why's it on Mom's tablet?
Dad: You were too young to remember. They tried to build the elevator. Your mom led a team with an ambitious dream to transform space travel. They needed an open space for the energy to connect with the space station. That's why we came to live here. They worked so hard and your mom was excited about the test, but something went wrong. It was completely destroyed and your mom didn't survive.

Sky: Why didn't you tell me?
Dad: I didn't know how to. You were just a baby and then it had been so long, more than ten years.
Sky: Dad, was the elevator behind the house?
Dad: Yeah, why do you ask?
Sky: Maybe we can rebuild the elevator …
Dad: We tried before but we can try together. How can I help?
Sky: Well, this design shows the elevator base and where they built it.
Dad: OK. First, we need to clear the dust and dirt to prepare the area.
Sky: We were cleaning the site when I had a strange feeling. Suddenly, I remembered something and ran back into the house.
Sky: Look, Dad! I found this playing here once when I was little. Is it important?
Dad: I think it is! Let's install it in the tablet and see what it does.
Sky: OK, I can do that!
Dad: We need to take it to the control room.
Sky: Let's go!
Computer Voice: Access granted. Connect object generator.
Sky: OK, here we go.
Dad: Look, Sky …
Computer Voice: Pairing.
Sky: It's moving!
Dad: That doesn't look right.
Sky: I think … something is wrong with the code. The design isn't using enough energy. I can update the code and it should fix the problem. Here goes.
Suddenly, there was a bright light reaching up through the clouds and into space. It was beautiful! The computer told me that the elevator connected with the space station in orbit above us. Then, inside the elevator beam, a pod appeared. It started moving towards us.
Dad: That's strange. Why is it doing that?
Sky: What's happening? I didn't touch anything.
Dad: Something is operating the elevator!
Sky: How is that possible? We've only just rebuilt it.
Dad: Ca … Cassia?
Sky: Mom!
Mom hugged me until I could barely breathe. We went back to the house and she told us about the day she disappeared.
Mom: Since, I was responsible for the project, I wanted to be the first to test it.
I stepped into the pod and my team gave the order to send it to the space station. But then … everything went dark.
We designed an automatic backup for everything to be saved on a restore key.
Dad: The team looked for the key but couldn't find it. They said it was destroyed in the accident.
Sky: I'm so sorry, Mom. I had the key all this time.
Mom: I'm so pleased you found it, Sky! I'm thrilled that you brought me back home. We get to be a family again.

TRACK 43

Unit 10, *The Restore Key*, Words in Context
Find these words in the reading. What do you think they mean?
elevator (British English: lift)
ambitious
code
beam
backup

Video Scripts

Language Book

The video scripts for the spoken word poems and chants in the **Language Book** are exactly the same as for the audio scripts and the text on the page. Please refer to the relevant unit in the Audio Scripts on TB pp. 215–238.

Unit 1

CONVERSATION

Get Involved

Gene: Wow!
Lloyd: What are you up to, Gene?
Gene: Hi, Lloyd. I'm watching this amazing man BMX racing! Do you want to watch it with me?
Lloyd: Oh, BMX racing ...?
Gene: Don't you like it?
Lloyd: I used to love it. I trained twice a week when I was younger.
Gene: So, why did you give it up?
Lloyd: Well, one day I fell off and hurt my arm. I didn't really enjoy it after that.
Gene: Were you any good?
Lloyd: Yes, I was pretty good. I won a race once. Races were really fun.
Gene: I've never done BMX racing, but I'd really like to try it! Oh, look! Isn't he fantastic?
Lloyd: I used to be able to do that! Sometimes I wish I still did BMX racing.
Gene: So, why don't you?
Lloyd: I'm not fit anymore. And it's hard once you haven't trained for a long time.
Gene: But think about how much you loved it.
Lloyd: I like the idea ... But, I might fall off again.
Gene: Not if you're careful. You've just lost your self-confidence. Once you get that back, you'll be even better! Give it a try.
Lloyd: I'm not sure.
Gene: How about showing *me* how to do it?
Lloyd: You really want to try BMX racing?
Gene: Yes. I bet you're a great teacher.
Lloyd: Well, maybe I could show you ...
Gene: I'd really like that. Let's start tomorrow after school.
Lloyd: That would be great. Thanks, Gene!

Unit 2

PRESENTATION

You Can Help

Linda: Our presentation is called "The Disappearing Bees." It's about bees and their role in the human food chain. We're going to talk about how human behavior is affecting them.
Maria: Why do we need bees? Well, bees are very hardworking insects. Honeybees make delicious honey, but all bees help plants grow. If we don't have bees, fewer plants will grow, which means we'll have less food to eat.
Linda: There are fewer bees than there used to be. What has caused this? There are two main reasons: first, pesticides harm bees by making them forget how to find their way home. And second, too many houses mean that there are fewer habitats for bees.
Maria: So, what can we do to stop bees disappearing? Well, we could write to food producers to ask them to stop using pesticides.
Linda: And there are lots of things we can do to make our yards at home more bee-friendly. Planting flowers that bees like is a great idea. You can also encourage bees with water or sugar syrup. Like us, they get tired and thirsty!
Maria: You could even become a beekeeper and collect your own honey! We hope that you have enjoyed our presentation and that you'll help us save the bees. Thank you.

Unit 3

CONVERSATION

Know Your Neighbors

Wade: Hi, Maria. What're you doing?
Maria: Hi, Wade. I'm delivering invitations to all our neighbors—we're having a barbecue at my house on Saturday.
Wade: Wow! How exciting! Are you celebrating something?
Maria: No, I'm not. I just want to get to know my neighbors better. A police officer came to our school the other day and said that in communities where people knew each other, less crime was committed.
Wade: Really? That's interesting! Why is that?
Maria: Well, when people know their neighbors better, it's easier to notice if something is out of place. If I know my neighbor's on vacation and I notice that their window is open, I can call the police to go check and close it for them. If I don't know them at all, I won't notice that their window is open when it shouldn't be. Knowing your neighbors makes it easier to look out for each other.
Wade: Huh! True. So, are you just going to have a party, then?
Maria: No, I'm going to do lots of things. Why don't you help me make a SLOW sign for our street?
Wade: A SLOW sign?
Maria: Yes, we can put it up to tell drivers to slow down, which will make our road safer.
Wade: Huh! That makes sense. So, do you know *all* your neighbors' names?
Maria: Um, no, not yet ... but I soon will!

Unit 4

CONVERSATION

Do You Have What It Takes?

Veronica: Wade, can you tell us why you're interested in being a reporter on the school magazine?
Wade: Well, I'd like to be a part of the team that investigates the news.
Veronica: And what experience do you have?
Wade: Well, I've read the magazine for two years, and I've written stories all my life. Um ... let me think ... I won the spelling bee last year, so I'm good at spelling!
Gene: And you enjoy sports, don't you? Tell us more about that.
Wade: Can you repeat the question, please?
Gene: Yes, I think you enjoy sports.
Wade: Yes, I love playing and watching sports. Sometimes I go along to support my friends, and afterwards, we talk about the game. I often think people would like to read fun reports from me about the games.
Veronica: That sounds great!
Gene: Do you have any other useful skills, Wade?
Wade: I'm sorry. I'm not sure what you mean.
Veronica: Well, how good are your computer skills?
Wade: Oh, I think they're fine. I can use all the main software packages.
Veronica: Good. One more thing—do you have a good sense of humor? We want to include more jokes and cartoons in the magazine. Can you write jokes?
Wade: Um, no, I can't. But I'm passionate about my writing, and people like talking to me, so I can interview people and write about them.
Veronica: That's excellent. Now, do you have any questions for us?
Wade: Well, if I get the job, what will I be writing about?
Gene: New reporters usually start on our regular features—interviews, funny stories, jokes. How does that sound?
Wade: Good! Very interesting!
Veronica: Thanks very much for coming, Wade. We'll let you know our decision tomorrow.
Wade: OK. Thank you. It was great meeting you.

Unit 5

PRESENTATION

My Advice

Linda: Today my presentation is about giving presentations! Most people are nervous about giving presentations. And I used to be nervous! But now that I've given a few presentations, I feel more confident, and I promise you'll be fine, too! So don't worry.
The first thing to remember is that many of the people in your audience have given presentations, so they know what it feels like. They want you to do well.
Before I gave my first presentation, I had three worrries: my voice, boring my audience, and making mistakes.
First, the voice. When I'm nervous, my voice sounds funny, and I worried that everyone knew I was scared. *But my dad told me to practice again and again in different voices.* I had to whisper, shout, and pretend to be Australian—it was funny! Then I had to use my normal voice, and suddenly I felt more confident.
Next, the bored audience problem. The important thing to remember is that if you're really enthusiastic, your audience will be, too.

And now those mistakes. Well, we all make mistakes sometimes—it's not the end of the world!
And lastly, if you still feel nervous, you can use the trash can. Yes, the trash can! Let me explain—a friend of mine used to walk up and down a lot when he was giving presentations, so no one could hear what he was saying! Then his teacher made him stand in a trash can to give his presentation! He keeps still now!
So, for your next presentation, practice a lot, but remember, everyone is on your side. Tell yourself you're going to be great, and you will be! Go for it!

Unit 6

PRESENTATION

Together Is Better

Maria: Hi. I'm Maria.
Wade: And I'm Wade.
Maria: We're here today to ask for your help. This school has a problem.
Wade: The problem is—us! Look at this picture. Yes, this is our schoolyard. Maria.
Maria: There's trash everywhere. And the trash cans are too full to fit it all in. We're all throwing out too much stuff!
Wade: We started to wonder how much waste we produce. So we did some research.
Maria: The results are surprising. This cartoon shows that each student in this school produces 45 kilos of waste every year!
Wade: That's a lot of trash, right? And that doesn't include the trash we throw out at home—it's only what we produce in school!
Maria: As you can see, the waste is mainly paper and card, and cans.
Wade: We can recycle most of that, which will be better for the environment—and for our schoolyard!
Maria: We've identified two problems—trash in the schoolyard and too much waste—and we've made a plan, and here we've shown how we can solve them.
Wade: But Maria and I can't do this on our own. We're looking for people to be a part of our project.
Maria: And if we have enough volunteers, it might not take too long.
Wade: With your support, we can really make a difference. Please do come and join us!

Unit 7

PRESENTATION

The Story of My Scar

Summer: Our school winning the snowboarding competition is awesome, isn't it? But that reminds me of how my early ambition to be a champion snowboarder got me into trouble … Did I ever tell you about how I got this scar on my head?
My hair completely covers it now, but it's the result of an accident I had when I was only five. All my family are good at winter sports, and I learned to ski almost as soon as I could walk. My older brother was a real snowboarding expert, and from as early as I can remember, I wanted to be like him. My parents had promised me a snowboard for my sixth birthday. It was only a week away, but that was when I decided I couldn't wait.
Even now, I'm not normally allowed into my brother's room, but that morning he was busy, so I took my chance.
I went in quietly and took his snowboard. I set it at the top of the four stairs that go down to my parents' bedroom.
You won't believe this, but I thought snowboarding would be just the same as skiing. I stood on the board and held onto the sides of the stairs to prepare myself. It was then that my mother saw me. She shouted my name and made me jump. I let go, and all of a sudden the board slipped from under me …
What do you think happened next?
I didn't fall far, but my head hit the board, and there was blood everywhere. I wasn't hurt apart from my cut head, but I had to go to the hospital. My cut was stitched and it soon got better. But I decided I didn't want a snowboard for my birthday after all!

Unit 8

PRESENTATION

Looking Back

Veronica: My presentation is about life in the USA 25 years ago.
I'm going to cover three areas: firstly, how people lived, after that we'll look at architecture and inventions, and finally, I'll talk about what we can learn from those times.
I'll begin with how people lived. At that time it was common for people from many different countries and cultures to live side by side in American cities. Lots of different languages were spoken, and lots of different types of food were eaten, too. People were busy: they worked and studied hard. In their free time they watched TV, played video games, or hung out with their friends, often on social media.
The other thing that people then loved to do was travel all over the world, not just in the USA.
Now I'll move on to architecture and gadgets. In cities there were large apartment buildings where lots of families lived together, although they didn't always know each other. Almost everyone had a car, and it was normal to drive everywhere. And everyone had a cell phone, which helped them communicate with each other easily.
Let's look now at what we can learn from those times. Living together with people from other countries helped everyone learn about different cultures, which was great. But using cell phones and social media meant that they sometimes forgot to talk to each other face-to-face, which was not so great. And all the traveling that people did caused a lot of damage to the environment.
I'd like to recap the points I've made: I talked about how people lived 25 years ago. Then we looked at architecture and inventions of the time. And finally I discussed things we can learn from those times. Thank you.

Unit 9

CONVERSATION

What a Plot!

Gene: Wow! That was such a good movie, wasn't it?
Lloyd: Um, I'm not sure. It was OK …
Gene: But don't you think the animation was amazing?
Lloyd: Oh, absolutely! It was so realistic.
Gene: I know! The jungle and all the animals when they're all running from the tiger. Awesome!
Lloyd: Yeah—that was great.
Gene: So what didn't you like?
Lloyd: Well, I don't think the hero in the movie reacted well in the face of danger. In real life, people aren't that silly.
Gene: I don't agree. Some people can be brave and stay calm.
Lloyd: But why didn't the boy go find other people sooner? If the film were more realistic, he would know that he has to find other people to live with.
Gene: How could he? He grew up with the animals. How would he know where to go?
Lloyd: Hmm, I see what you mean. But surely he could see that he looked different from them?
Gene: Well, even if he did, I think he had some good friends in the animals who took care of him.
Lloyd: Oh, I think so, too. Come on, let's go! I didn't like the part where the snake almost eats him!
Gene: Neither did I! That was scary. But she was just one of the villains of the story.
Lloyd: And what about when the tiger and bear fight? A tiger's so much faster; it would easily beat a bear!
Gene: Bears are huge. If they're not running, I'm sure bears are as strong and as fierce as tigers.
Lloyd: That's a good point … and the ending was surprising! After all that suspense and action …!
Gene: So, do you want to go the movies again next week?
Lloyd: Sure! I really enjoyed myself this afternoon!

Unit 10

CONVERSATION

What Do You Think?

Lloyd: OK, OK, what's our favorite design? We really need to choose! We have to announce the winner this afternoon.
Veronica: Yes, let's look at this camera again. So, it's used to take pictures of big groups …
Lloyd: You can do that with any smartphone. I already said I didn't think that was very special.
Veronica: … But you can be in the picture, too. It's voice activated, so you just say, "Take it!"
Linda: That is quite smart. But what about this pen? You can point it at something, it copies the color, and then it writes in that color.
Lloyd: It's fun—but it's really just a toy, isn't it?
Linda: Well, you choose something, then! All you've done so far is say our choices are wrong!
Veronica: Perhaps we should think about what the designs are supposed to do.
Linda: Good idea … OK, so we're looking for the most effective design.
Veronica: Would it be better to find one that solves a problem?
Lloyd: Exactly!
Veronica: Why don't we look at those glasses again?
Linda: Well, they're designed for people who are color-blind. They help them see colors in the same way that most people do, which must be good.
Veronica: Yes, that is good. It must be so dangerous if you can't see colors properly. I know some people can't tell the difference between red and green. That's a huge problem especially if you drive a car! If it were up to me, I'd go with the glasses.
Lloyd: So, do we agree? We're choosing …
All: The glasses!